Tourism: An Introduction

Adrian Franklin

SAGE Publications
London • Thousand Oaks • New Delhi

First published 2003

 SAGE Publications Ltd
6 Bonhill Street
London EC2A 4PU

SAGE Publications Inc
2455 Teller Road
Thousand Oaks, California 91320

SAGE Publications India Pvt Ltd
32, M-Block Market
Greater Kailash – I
New Delhi 110 048

British Library Cataloguing in Publication data

A catalogue record for this book is available
from the British Library

ISBN 0 7619 7232 3
ISBN 0 7619 7233 1 (pbk)

Library of Congress Control Number available

Typeset by Mayhew Typesetting, Rhayader, Powys
Printed in Great Britain by TJ International Ltd, Padstow,
Cornwall

For Daisy Franklin
1898–

Contents

List of figures

Introduction

Not surprisingly, then, tourism in Boston does not stand far apart from the city's other commercial, cultural and recreational activities; to a great extent then it is absorbed into the daily life of the city.

Ehrlich and Dreier (1999: 157)

I may have noticed a few birds careering through the air in matinal excitement, but my awareness of them was weakened by a number of other, incongruous and unrelated elements, among these, a sore throat that I had developed during the flight, a worry at not having informed a colleague that I would be away, a pressure across both temples and a rising need to visit the bathroom. A momentous but until then overlooked fact was making its first appearance: that I had inadvertently brought myself with me to the island.

De Botton (2002: 17–20)

No changing of place at a hundred miles an hour will make us one whit stronger, happier or wiser.

John Ruskin, quoted in De Botton (2002: 222)

SUMMARY

- Tourism: Key questions for the twenty-first century
- Tourism as an ordering of globalisation
- Sensing tourism
- Tourism and everyday life
- Tourism and rituals of transformation
- Tourism and 'fast time'
- Structure of the book

Tourism: Key questions for the twenty-first century

This book is an up to date guide to understanding the theory, practice, development and effects of tourism. It considers general theories of tourism to be inadequate on their own and goes on to develop a new approach that recognises tourism as a complex set of social and cultural phenomena. This approach requires a variety of theoretical perspectives, a theoretical pluralism, that can make sense of its various connections and engagements within the constantly changing social and cultural milieux of modernity. Unlike some approaches this book does not view tourism as merely based on the pleasurability of the unusual and the different. Instead, tourism is viewed also as a serious individual engagement with the changing (and fluid) conditions of modernity with implications for nation formation and citizenship, the rise of consumerism, cosmopolitanism, the natural world and globalisation. The book argues that tourism is therefore a central component of modern social identity formation and engagement, rather than something shallow and insignificant that takes place on the social margin. It identifies the transformative and redemptive components of tourism and in so doing places more emphasis on its ritual, performative and embodied dimensions. Here tourism can be understood as spaces and times of self-making – rather special types of space and time that allow latitudes, freedoms and experimentation. As such it opposes more standardised accounts based on the tourist gaze and the central significance of authenticity where both the tourist and the objects of their gaze stand apart. My approach emphasises the interaction and effects of people and these objects. It is argued that tourism cannot be separated from the cultural, political and economic conditions in which it has developed and changed, and critically, the book argues that tourism is no longer something that happens away from the everday lifeworld. Rather tourism is *infused* into the everyday and has become one of the ways in which our lives are ordered and one of the ways in which consumers orientate themselves, or take a stance to a globalised world.

This book is a guide to understanding tourism, particularly as different writers have tried to understand it and to keep track of it as a changing cultural and commercial form in modern life. But tourism is now far too blended into everyday life and the global flows of people and things to be treated as a detachable phenomenon. So, unlike many other tourism texts, this book will also identify how tourism configures with everyday social relations and cultures. I will tackle two broad questions. First, how can we understand tourism in social and cultural terms; what precisely are people doing and how do they come to be doing it? Students and some scholars too tend to view tourism as rather self-evident, so obvious that it requires little in the way of explanation. But it does not take much to make the same people see it as a puzzle. Why, for example, do so many people find *old* objects so fascinating? A modern toilet block could not be sold as a tourist attraction; it needs to acquire the patina of time, but why? A communal Roman latrine, on the other hand, is a fascinating object to behold and will sell postcards by the thousand. In fact, sometimes what is offered to tourists does not 'work'. I once went to the Big Pit Mining Museum in South Wales, a mining heritage site in which the high point appeared to be switching our lights off some 300 feet underground to experience total darkness. Some of the young, affluent French students in the tour party, ostensibly in the UK to learn English, were seriously unable to come to terms with what was happening to them. They were not seeing the point of it; and I was struggling too. Equally, tourism is often something of a paradox. Tourism is commonly portrayed as an escape from work and essentially about *pleasure* but so many forms and experiences of tourism seem to involve, on the face of it, the opposite. Why is it that some people will spend their two precious weeks of summer enduring such difficult and uncomfortable conditions as 'camping' or 'back packing', for example? For those fourteen days they are prepared to sleep on hard floors, in cramped conditions, living on sub-basic foods, at the mercy of biting insects, tropical diseases and other risks; working very hard, and covering long distances, carrying heavy loads through unpredictable weather conditions. One sees those holiday cyclists, heavily loaded down on steep inclines, toiling through torrential rain and traffic; it is possible to ask oneself what on earth they are doing and why? But even at the most luxurious end of the market, for those travelling by air to faraway luxury resort hotels, the amount of stress and work involved can be quite staggering. Getting to, through and between airports is one of life's greater challenges; not in any way enjoyable but fraught with all manner of hazards and worries. Aircraft conditions are perilous as the excellent book *Jetlag: How to Beat It* (David O'Connell, 1997) makes perfectly plain. Economy class cabins have little humidity and very little oxygen and can expose passengers to quite profound mixtures of germs gathered from every corner of the earth. Low oxygen and low humidity combine to make people tetchy and bad tempered. Low humidity and inactivity has been associated recently with the new travel anxiety, *deep vein thrombosis* (Brown et al., 2001: 18). As Zygmunt Bauman sums it up, '[t]here are many hardships one needs to suffer for the sake of tourist's freedoms: the impossibility of slowing down, uncertainty wrapping every choice, risks attached to every decision . . .' (Bauman, 1998b: 98). Why tourism continues to grow despite all of this is a secondary aspect of this first question. The answers to these simple questions are surprisingly complex, and in order to gain an adequate understanding we will have to embark on a major exploration of the culture of travel and tourism as well as a consideration of attempts to answer them. What we certainly cannot do is to imagine that a definition of tourism will get this question out of the way, smoothing the path for the more routine description of the workings of the tourist industry. There are many existing books that do precisely this and their strategy does not need to be reproduced again. This point was made even stronger in a recent essay I wrote with Mike Crang, where we outlined what we took to be 'the trouble with tourism and travel theory' and we made it the launching pad and rationale for our new tourism journal, *Tourist Studies*:

> . . . tourist studies has been dominated by policy-led and industry-sponsored work so the analysis tends to internalise industry-led priorities and perspectives, leaving the research subject to the imperatives of policy, in the sense that one expects the researcher to assume as his own an objective of social control that will allow the tourist product to be more finely tuned to the demands of the international market. (Franklin and Crang, 2001: 5)

That essay and now this book make a break with this trend and offer a way of understanding tourism as a cultural activity, and not merely a commercial exercise.

The second question to be addressed in this book concerns the place of tourism in contemporary life. It seems to me that we cannot continue to think of tourism *merely* as an industry, separable from all other industries and separable from our everyday lives. As Franklin and Crang argue:

> Tourism is no longer a specialist consumer product or mode of consumption: tourism has broken away from its beginnings as a relatively minor and ephemeral ritual of modern national life to become a significant modality through which transnational modern life is organised. Recent books on leisure by Chris Rojek (1995) and the holiday by Fred Inglis (2000) both place tourism as a central part of understanding social (dis-)organisation but also show how it can no longer be bounded off as a discrete activity, contained tidily at specific locations and occurring during set aside periods. As we see it, tourism is now such a significant dimension to global social life that it can no longer be conceived of as merely what happens at self-styled tourist sites and encounters involving tourists away from home. The new agenda for tourism studies needs therefore to reflect this growing significance. Nor should 'tourist researchers feel a need to legitimate their seemingly frivolous topic by pointing out its economic and social importance' but instead we might 'view vacationing as a cultural laboratory where people have been able to experiment with new aspects of identities, their social relations or their interactions with nature and also to use the important cultural skills of daydreaming and mind-travelling. Here is an arena in which fantasy has become an important social practice' (Löfgren, 1999: 6–7).

It is easy to understand why so many tourism texts make this error since in the popular imagination tourism is *by definition* what takes place away from the everyday. Surely tourism is separated from normal life by the long distances people often travel in order to be tourists. Surely tourist places themselves are separated from workaday places not only by their remoteness but also in their possession of those special 'touristic' qualities that everyday places lack. However, it turns out that most places are more like Boston, the subject of the quotation at the beginning of this chapter, and in Boston, tourism is 'to a great extent . . . absorbed into the daily life of the city'. What does this mean?

In the case of Boston, as in a great many other places globally, the everyday world is increasingly *indistinguishable* from the touristic world. Most places are now on some tourist trail or another, or at least, not far from one. In addition, most of the things we like to do in our usual leisure time double up as touristic activities and are shared spaces. This is as much true for hanging out in fashionable cafés as it is for local art exhibitions and museums or local theme parks, shopping malls, food halls, beaches, sporting activities and local nature features. In fact, many leisure investments made ostensibly for tourists and tourism rely on the fact that local people will visit them too, and as the global population becomes increasingly settled in larger cities, so the metropolitan populations around each investment become ever more significant. Another way of looking at this is that an increasing number of 'things to do' in each of our localities began life with a view to attract and entertain visitors. The major cities and resort areas of the world are now in competition with each other for tourists, the convention and conference trade, and even to attract other companies to invest or relocate in their city. As a consequence much of our everyday lives are spent doing what tourists do, alongside tourists, and in what we might call a touristic manner.

This last point brings me to another: that increasingly, the manner of the tourist has become a metaphor for the way we lead our everyday lives in a consumer society. So rather than being an exceptional or occasional state of being in modern societies, or even as some have said, an escape from it, the manner of the tourist has come to determine a generalised *stance* to the world around us. In a globalised world, our stance as consumers of it is modelled and predicated on the tourist.

> To begin with, this tourism of everyday life might be seen rather like the expansion of flanerie (Tester, 1994): no longer confined to the cosmopolitan sensibilities of the emergent modern capital cities, most people are now alerted to, and routinely excited by, the flows of global cultural materials all around them in a range of locations and settings. We casually take in these flows, never fully in possession of their extent or their temporality, never expecting them to be complete or finalised as a knowable cultural landscape around us. The repertoires for this appreciation and taste are drawn from travel and tourism, but, owing perhaps to the greater speed and extent of the circulation of peoples, cultures and artefacts, we find the distinction between the everyday and holiday entirely blurred. The relationship between transnational culture and tourism of the everyday is a dimension of tourist studies that will surely prove to be significant. (Franklin and Crang, 2001: 8)

Tourism as an ordering of globalisation

If we cast our minds back in time, we would be able to find, at various times and places, examples of people whose lives were more or less locked into the singular affairs of their village, small town, or even district, neighbourhood or suburb. Everything there was stamped by the familiar, the known and the personally interconnected. People and things from elsewhere were outsiders, *foreign*, derogatory terms that conjure up the opposites of belonging: fear, loathing, misunderstanding or even hatred. Although we must be careful not to cast such places as stationary and fixed, because very often their inhabitants were involved in a degree of travel (see Clifford (1992) for an excellent essay on the mobility of cultures typically modelled as sedentary by anthropology), nonetheless, we can say that there were times when travel beyond the safe confines of a known locality (or range(s)) and culture(s) was certainly not romantic and longed for, but, if anything, feared as Other; it was the unknown and the dangerous, and boundaries were observed separating the home world from that of the traveller. Although there was certainly curiosity about the world beyond the everyday, it was not a generalised interest about the world, a routine thirst for things new, exotic and startling. That thirst developed slowly in modernising nation states, and one of its vehicles for development was tourism. Tourism, provided a pleasurable introduction to a world beyond the locality, and the basis of that relevance was the beginnings of a globalising world, starting first with nation formation and the establishment of universal discourses that began to link localities rather than separate them, and then the routinisation of international trade that did very much the same on a wider scale. Increasingly, the relevance of these wider scales of social transaction – and especially the success of western overarching and universal themes – meant that travel, and the knowledge and experience that come from travel, became an important source of cultural capital. As this speed of transaction and innovation increased, it produced the dizzy pace of change and novelty associated with modernity, and maintaining an interest and curiosity for the new became passionate and addictive; defining what it is to live in a consumer society. In short, tourism required less and less effort to travel in order to obtain the same degree of sensation and difference that formerly only travel could provide. Instead the world moved in reverse, back to the homelands of western tourists in the form of commodities, cultures, musics, foods, styles, and peoples. In a city like London, much bigger and older than Boston, we can say that this process has reached its most advanced stage. In a way, the entire world flows into London at a remarkable rate, transforming it and changing it as it goes. Virginia Woolf was entranced by these flows in the 1920s, and she saw them as natural with an enchanting and bewildering beauty and poetics – much in the manner of a tourist. Baudelaire saw them too and used the word *flanerie*, a touristic word, to describe the pleasure of strolling around in a large city, or sitting in cafés, taking in all the excitement and change. Today London is no different except that the flows are greater, the piles of commodities are higher and come from an even wider catchment and, critically, a larger proportion of the population can afford them. From London, any capital of Europe is within easy reach and return flights are currently as little as fifty pounds, the price of a few rounds of drinks in a pub, or the price of five taxi rides between Padding-ton and Victoria railway stations. But the domain of superlatives belongs, properly, to journalists, and in this matter I defer to one of the world's most travelled men, John Simpson, the BBC's World Affairs Editor. Although he does not say it in precisely these terms, in his book *A Mad World, My Masters* (Simpson, 2001), he makes it clear that the distinction between tourism and everyday life has collapsed, that the world is now distinguishably *touristic*:

> The feeling is growing, especially in the United States, that there is no need to travel abroad, since abroad is travelling to you. In Washington DC I have been driven by a taxi driver who had been the leader of an Afghan mujaheddin group, and in Paris by another who had been an Iranian air force general. In Denver I once found a taxi was driven by a North Korean who spoke not a single recognisable word of English, and in New York City a taxi driver from, I think, Equatorial Guinea who had no idea where or what Wall Street was. (Simpson, 2001: xxiv)

But again, the point is that this new touristic world of flows, migrations and what Urry (2000) calls *travellings* of peoples and objects is not confined to the USA. In a great many places rendered touristic, objects of tourism such as foods and tastes and ethnicities flow backwards into the origins of western tourism, profoundly changing them through fusions, multi-culturalisms, and often quite spectacular cultural collisions. Here is John Simpson again:

> In London there are colonies tens of thousands strong of Columbians, Thais and Ethiopians – people without the remotest colonial connection to Britain. There are Japanese restaurants in Kinshasa, Beijing and Geneva, and Italian restaurants in Amman, Minsk and Pretoria. You find the best Thai food in Australia, the best Balti in northern England, and the best Persian *fesanjun* in Los Angeles. Tandoori has become the quintessential British dish, while curry has supplanted fish and chips as the most popular takeaway food. Hamburgers are more popular among the thirteen to eighteen age group in France than *steak-frites* or *maigret de canard*. (Simpson, 2001: xxv)

Some readers might object to the spin I am putting on these strange new cultural configurations; surely this is covered adequately by the term *globalisation*? However while we might sense 'globalisation', and there are those who have identified some of its dimensions and scales, its economics, its politics and its postmodern qualities, in itself it does not capture or specify the newly emerging cultural *consequences* of its own presence in the world. Bauman (1998b: 1) likens globalisation to other vogueish words, which 'tend to share a similar fate: the more experiences they pretend to make transparent, the more they themselves become opaque. Such human practices as the concept tried originally to grasp recede from view, and it is now 'the facts of the matter', the quality of the 'world out there' that the term seems to 'get straight' and which it invokes to claim its own immunity to questioning'. But we are still as he says, 'unpacking the social roots and social consequences of the globalisation process' and my argument is that tourism has been one of the more important but neglected cultural processes of globalisation, but also, that it has produced a globalised world in its own image. This is why I argue that the world has become touristic, or at the very least, that tourism has become a metaphor for the consumerist society most of us live in, which is inextricably connected to a world of flows of peoples and objects.

Of course, by these means the world of touristic *difference* has shrunk. But we can go even further than that. According to Bauman, 'distance does not matter that much. Space stopped being an obstacle – one needs just a split second to conquer it' (Bauman, 1998b: 77). Of course, he is referring to the difference that the Internet and other global communications have made. But for my purposes here, it has become possible to go places by sitting at home in your living room, study or bedroom. We surf the net routinely whizzing about the world at fantastic speeds, and this does indeed cancel distance, but the point I want to make here is that we surf *like* tourists and the web is set up in a touristic way. Take the language of the web for a start. We 'visit' web 'sites'. We wander around sites as the mood takes us, leisurely or erratically; sites provide us with 'maps' and when we arrive anywhere we are given 'itineraries', 'menus', 'gateways', 'access'. It is a language of movement, 'back', 'forward', 'go', 'stop' and so on. There is also something touristic about the way sites are constructed, they aim to attract us, make us linger, entertain us and of course sell us something. The web is our virtual world and it is just as we like it: constantly changing. We are now *like* tourists all the time, we are restless, addicted to motion, itching to set off. We seem to inhabit many places simultaneously. But this travel can be just as meaningful and eventful. For example, we can go overseas to do some shopping and buy things not available locally. In Australia this is very handy as a recent survey of internet use makes clear: in the twelve months before May 2000, 43 per cent of internet users in Australia purchased or ordered something from overseas, and 12 per cent of them bought holidays (Australian Bureau of Statistics, 2000: 13).

Sensing tourism

In the 1990s, tourism research was particularly inspired by the visual dimension of tourism and indeed in Urry's *The Tourist Gaze*, tourism behaviour was explained as the pleasurability of seeing or gazing upon the different and unusual, as a contrast to the familiarity of everyday life. In addition, tourism was conducted in precisely constructed and decoded semiotic fields: tourists were held to be collectors of views and gazes on objects and landscapes that reference or symbolise something else, an essence. The Eiffel Tower referenced Frenchness; thatched cottages referenced Englishness and so on. The visual technologies of the 1990s, that enabled replication, simulation, distortion and mixing to be possible on a new and unprecedented scale, also detached the signs from the things they referenced and these became objects of pleasurability in their own right. A television soap opera is not real life, but for many living in the television age its reality is irrelevant, it exists and is compelling. Television becomes 'the clearest embodiment of the replacement of reality with representation' (Rojek, 1993: 130). In this way, as we have seen above, a postmodern world of virtual reality became possible and was increasingly a normative expectation of playfulness. The so-called 'post-tourist' no longer needed authentic objects to confirm their gaze but enjoyed the fakery, the games of simulation and the virtual imaginary that the thematised tourism 'worlds' of the 1990s provided. The web, we can say, extends and normal-ises that virtual world of tourism and plants it very conveniently at home, and for an increasing number, at work.

These new visual technologies combine with the ubiquitous presence of the camera as the defining, if not enabling, technology in all decades of modernity, to give the impression that tourism is indeed carried out essentially in the medium of vision. In this world, intrepid travellers are positioned at a distance from the objects under their gaze; they are safely remote and detached from the world before them. And since the work involved in tourist consumption was largely cognitive, making essentially *mental* connections between the concrete signs and their abstract referents, we can say that it was largely a disembodied exercise. John Urry and Chris Rojek are notable innovators and synthesisers of what we might call visual theories of tourism, but in recent years more emphasis is being given to embodied perspectives on tourism. This is a reaction to concerns that important aspects of the body were being ignored or sidelined, and also that despite the new virtual world (and perhaps also because of it), a new tourism of the body was emerging which eschewed the limitations of the tourist gaze. As Saldanha (2002:43) argues 'Don't tourists swim, climb, stroll, ski, relax, become bored perhaps, or ill; don't they go other places to taste, smell, listen, dance, get drunk, have sex?' We can perhaps say that as the 1990s faded into the 2000s more people wanted to get their hands on the world, to taste it, feel it, smell it and importantly, *do things with it* and not just look at it. Inspired by Veijola and Jokinen's (1994) paper 'The Body in Tourism' we are starting to see a new tourism of the body, from Saldanha's paper on music tourism in Goa, to Hall et al.'s (2000) book on wine tourism to Crouch's (1999) edited collection. This book will explore the new embodied tourism in a variety of ways, but particularly through an examination of the *ritual* and performative nature of tourism (in which the body becomes the focus of transition) as well as chapters on the body and tourism and sex and tourism. However it is important to stress that these new directions in tourism research continue to work with and build on the tourist gaze and the semiotics of tourism. As Franklin and Crang (2001) argued:

Indeed, the parallels of tourism and semiotics were spelled out in a path-breaking article by Jonathon Culler (1981) some 20 years ago. There he outlined the way tourism as language acts to mark out, signify and categorise the world. If we take this seriously we see a version of semiosis where 'display not only shows and speaks, it *does*' (Kirshenblatt-Gimblett, 1998: 6). Tourism is a productive system that fuses discourse, materiality and practice. There are now developing avenues of thinking trying to move beyond a study of representation towards seeing tourism as a system of presencing and perform-ance. Thus some accounts focus on the nature of so much tourism as per-formances, from folk dance to performing dolphins, and we might take up Cantwell's characterisation of 'ethnomimesis' where performances always pick up previously circulating representations, and work them through in a poetics, stringing together images, visitors, performers and the history of their relations. (Cantwell, 1993: 284; 1992) (Franklin and Crang, 2001: 17)

Tourism and everyday life

This book is a different guide to tourism because tourism has left the confines of resorts and other spaces of tourist *destinations* (where most tourism texts hang out) and as tourism has covered more and more spaces and activities, coming closer and closer to home, it has changed the sort of world we live in and how we live in it. Tourism is therefore more signi-ficant than most people would believe, and its founders and innovators such as Thomas Cook should be properly acknowledged alongside other authors of modernity such as Henry Ford and Karl Marx (to my knowledge, only Lash and Urry (1994) come close to doing this). In fact there is a long history of holding tourism in contempt as a derisory, shallow and vulgar sort of activity, but these sorts of comment tend to be made by social elites who find that more and more of the world that was once accessible exclusively to them is now available to all, or almost all. Tourists, who by definition are inferior sorts, get in the hair of these elites by over-running the exclusive resorts they used to escape to and by swarming around their homes in the pleasant English countryside or charming cathedral cities or the commercial centres of New York or Frankfurt. So tourism is also a metaphor of everyday life because it is about freedom and democracy, accessibility and choice.

But just as tourism has become a way of life for a global world, it is, not surprisingly, becoming increasingly difficult to travel anywhere new or different that is in any way free from hazards: '[t]here are only a handful of places left on earth where you can escape all this [global sameness]; as I write there is no McDonald's in Cuba, no Coca Cola in Libya, and no television in Afghanistan. But in order to find real difference you have to travel well outside the political pale' (Simpson, 2001: xxvi). Most people do not travel outside the political pale and so they find themselves increas-ingly travelling inside the realm of the familiar. Every city throughout the world for example, seems to be selling the same things. As Simpson argues, 'large parts of the entire world's population, from Kuwait to Sydney, and from Galway to Dalian, buy their clothes at Gap . . .' Global sameness reduces cultural difference:

> 'I recognised him because he was dressed like a foreigner,' says a character in a pre-war Graham Greene novel, and as late as the 1970s you could still recognise Frenchmen from the cuts of their jackets, Englishmen by their checks and brogues, Italians by the narrowness of their trousers, Americans by the shortness of theirs and the thickness of the welts on their shoes. (Simpson, 2001: xxv)

Tourism and rituals of transformation

As the difference between here and there, home and away, working life and leisure life becomes blurred or collapses, it does not therefore hail the end of tourism because what has been reproduced everywhere is the entertaining, and fast moving world of novelty consumerism, fitness, beauty and individual redemption that was once only available after the travails of travel. Tourism is not synonymous with travel; it is a modern stance to the world, an interest and curiosity in the world beyond our own immediate lives and circles. As Franklin and Crang argue, 'The routinisation of touristic sensibilities in everyday life is . . . created by enhanced spatial flows of people – a shift from cultural tourism to touristic culture (Franklin and Crang, 2001: 10; Picard, 1996). But this modern quality of tourism is not all there is. The wisest accounts of tourism also note aspects of continuity-in-discontinuity: tourism and its antecedent forms of behaviour such as pilgrimage and carnival involve the individual in what I am going to call here *rituals of transformation*. It is clear from many writers that even the most contemporary forms of tourism are ritualistic, most closely resembling rituals of passage where the individual is delivered from one state or condition of the life course into the next. Clearly, tourism is not part and parcel of contemporary rituals of passage but it is clear that the ritual forms of tourism are similar to those of rituals of passage, particularly because some change, effect or transition is routinely intended or anticipated.

It will be made clear that the effects and transitions that tourists looked for varied at different moments of modernity. Many have commented on the similarities between early forms of tourism and pilgrimage and they both overlap in their association with health and personal renewal. Health has remained a continuous theme but at other times and places, other effects were looked for or anticipated. In the twentieth century, for example, tourism became associated with the consumption of luxury and the novel but for many people, especially ordinary working people whose incomes were only just beginning to run to an annual holiday, and whose material worlds were extremely limited, their holiday to places such as

Blackpool or Brighton, offered the prospect of transition into the consumer world. These places were magical and compelling precisely because they initiated them into the bright and dizzy world of emerging consumerist modernity. As Bennett's analysis of Blackpool very clearly shows, it is the latest technologies and the advanced edges of modernisation that were most evident and emphasised – and attractive. At one level Blackpool offered pleasure, pure and simple, but underlying that rather extreme form of excitation and fever that observers recorded, was the feeling of being transported to the future. Here was a future world, not only of technologies and the transformations they will bring to everyday life, but a consumer world unfolding. In the summer of 1938, one of the first destinations holidaymakers made for after arriving by train in Blackpool was 'The Biggest Woolworth's in the World', one of the first superstores ever conceived. Its range of goods far exceeded anything they could see in normal life, but at the same time it also held the transformative promise of the future: *progress*

> From its earliest days as a seaside resort the by-word of Blackpool, recurring again and again in its publicity brochures, has been *Progress*. . . . If Manchester could claim that what it thought today, London did the next day and the world heard about it the day after, then Blackpool's claim was to be even one step ahead of Manchester. Nor was the claim an idle one. Blackpool has an impressive number of 'firsts' to its credit – the first town in Britain with electric street lighting (1879) and the first town in the world to have a permanent electric street tramway (1885). (Bennett, 1983: 146)

Even though Blackpool was in these ways quite exceptional, its character as embodying progress was the stamp of seasides everywhere to a greater or lesser extent. As we will see, there was a lot going on at seasides but although this took place in distracted and frenzied excitement, capping the entire experience was exposure to, and perhaps also initiation into, the pleasure world of modernity.

Recent research and writing on modern consumption and our relationship with 'things' emphasises not their association with the mundane as one might expect but with their more magical and transformative place in our lives (Campbell, 1995; Warde, 2001). Campbell argues, persuasively I think, that consumerism has important links to Romanticism, particularly the way in which objects of the world were (literally) 'conjured' up through acts of imagination, longing and anticipation. Romanticism established an ability to mantle objects with an imaginative magic, first for objects of the natural world but then also other objects of desire. He argues that consumerism involves the same restlessness and spirituality. Things are most intensely enjoyed in the imagination, in their anticipation whereas the act of possession is often swiftly followed by anti-climax, and the search for something else. This is surely why shopping is so intensely enjoyable – and such a central tourist activity.

Figure 1.1   *Fairground 'Frisbee'*. Source: Ian Britton

Tourism and 'fast time'

Even while contemporary tourists shop as never before, constantly using consumerism as a channel of personal transformation, renewal and change, towards the end of the twentieth century we can identify the beginnings of yet another ritualisation of tourist experiences. At a time when it became increasingly difficult to get away and find difference, a time when distance seemed to have been cancelled and a time when we have all become tourists most of the time, it was also true that we became subject to what some have called 'fast time'. The tyranny of the present is not boredom or the lack of difference and colour or excitement in our lives but the opposite: we are over-excited, bombarded by stimulation, information, possibilities, connections and access. It is claimed that our lives are too busy; we are trying to do too much too often; electronic communications speed up our ability to do things and the pace and extent of our transactions. We are bereft of time to commit to things we consider important like long-term relationships, our children, careful planning and leisure (Hylland Eriksen, 2001). The phrase 'stressed out' belongs to this period but not to periods before. It will be claimed that many of the new forms of tourism we are beginning to see and research owe their origins to these conditions of fast time, and can be considered rituals of slow time, activities designed to slow down the body and to maximise not the next moment, but the present. We can begin to make certain links between

Figure 1.2 *Bush walking in the wilderness.* Source: Michelle Whitmore

these rituals of slow time with more embodied forms of tourism, particularly to a range of body techniques that establish links with aspects of the natural world. Chapter 8 is dedicated to exploring these links with examples ranging from surfing, climbing, walking and retreat tourism to cabins, shacks and naturism.

   If it is essential in these sorts of activities to understand tourism as embodied experience, it is also important to be symmetrical and use the experience of tourists to inform our knowledge of tourism everywhere. In many tourism texts, what tourists actually do and what they think and feel about what they are doing is conspicuous by its absence. Similarly, one criticism of tourism theory to date is that it has relied for too long on general theories of tourist behaviour and motivation and has failed to use its extensive generation of empirical studies to refine and fine tune (see

Rojek and Urry, 1997: Franklin and Crang, 2001). Theory very rarely seems to derive from empirical studies. However, we are also beginning to see more phenomenological approaches being used to cast light on tourism, and this has been particularly evident in the politically contentious case of heritage tourism. This sort of research views tourism as the outcome of the interaction between the intentions and designs of the providers of tourist sites and their interpretations of the objects on display and the background and biography of the visitors themselves. In these accounts there is no universal tourist and what is of interest is the range of effects that are produced at heritage sites. Here the outcome of tourism is not the rather simplistic collections of signs and experiences but often a more passionate and personal set of experiences, transitions, understandings and additions to the way people construct a sense of self. At one level, as Rojek (1993) argued, there is an important educational component to tourism, and detractors of heritage tourism who see it as 'bogus history' seem to miss this point completely. History is always contested and socially relative. The work by Mike Crang on heritage reinforces a general point made in this book, that the relevance of 'tourism' is not confined to tourist sites alone: it is also what tourists bring with them (their identity, their past, their diversity, their neuroses etc.) and what they take back with them (their new knowledge, the ways in which they were inspired, interpellated or assimilated etc.) and beyond that its additive quality, how one experience builds on another and the effects of their combined outcomes on the community at large. Again, we can say with some justification that the effects (or impacts) of tourism have been generally studied at the immediate site of visitation and interaction and so these wider effects have been lost. However, we have only to think of food and the globally shifting nature of taste that derives from tourism to appreciate the wider impact and relevance of tourism.

In sum this book explains what tourism is as a cultural activity, not through recourse to general theory but to theoretical accounts that can adequately explain tourism in its multiple and varied spaces, times and cultures. This book does concentrate mostly on how tourism emerged and developed within western cultures, but one of its central claims is that it has ceased to be a minor and relatively unique form of leisure activity and has expanded to comprise one of the main ways in which contemporary life and experience is ordered. In this respect, tourism can be identified as one of the social orderings of a globalised world, and in this way the book is of far wider interest. I will now explain briefly how the book is structured and what you can expect in each of the chapters.

Structure of the book

The book is divided into three parts, and although it makes a lot of sense to read each in sequence they are designed to be self-standing and can be dipped into, as can each chapter. The first part offers a critical evaluation of tourism as it has been conceived by others and offers a modified perspective based on this reinterpretation as well as an analysis of tourism in the 2000s. As I have already indicated, attention will be paid not only to what we mean by tourism but how tourism can be understood as an integral and important part of social and cultural life in modernity. Part of this understanding requires us to see tourism changing quite profoundly in relation to the development and change of modern societies. Part of the problem with other tourism books is that the history and development of tourism are often treated rather like tourism itself, as a self-standing and separate domain of modern life. In such a developmental history it is as if present forms of tourism slowly evolved from previous manifestations, rather like motorcars developed from previous archaic forms of transport. This is OK as far as it goes, but if new forms and developments owe their origins to general and specific changes in modern life *away from the resort*, as I will argue they did, then this rendering of history is very limited and partial. Chapter 1 sets the scene through an initial examination of the nature of tourism, and Chapter 2 establishes what I want to call the foundations of modern tourism, particularly through a look at its relationship to the nation state. This I feel has been a much-neglected area and my hope is that scholars and students anywhere will be able to use this perspective in their research and writing wherever they live. The role of the state as an ordering vehicle for modernity and the cultural processes of nation formation are critical to understanding how modern tourism came about. In a variety of ways nation states also provided the conduit for the emergence of forms of governance and ordering strategies through the domains of sport, leisure and tourism. In this way, tourism is not unrelated to attempts to establish social order in modern societies, and although tourism is perceived as a domain of escape and freedom, we have always to understand that this takes place against a background of legislations, controls, subsidies, policies, nationalisms and controls and manipulations of public spectacle, ceremony and building. With tourism there is always a tension, therefore, between the attempts to order and influence civil society and the essentially individual pursuit of freedom and redemption. The final chapter of Part One is called 'Elaborations of Tourism' and denotes the variety of ways in which tourism evolved both in new tourist practices but also as a presence in modern social life. In other words I argue that tourism leaves important traces and consequences.

Part Two 'Objects and Rituals' consists of two chapters that develop ideas raised in Part One. In Part Two I explore a central idea in the book that tourism does not reduce simply to the achievement of pleasure through the sighting and visitation of unusual, new or authentic objects of the world, though of course such activities do take place. Rather, my emphasis will be on what seems to me to be a quality common to most forms of tourism: the search for individual forms of transition, change and redemption. Of course the sorts of transition hoped for or anticipated have changed over time and vary within any one period, but they all seem to have one thing in common: the quest for personal transition, no matter how modest, always seems to follow ritualised formats, and these ritual forms and the objects of tourism that are a critical part of them make up the main content of Part Two. Chapter 5 explores the presence of tourist objects in tourism as well as the notion of rituals of tourism. It takes readers on a detailed exploration of forms of ritual activity that preceded and relate to modern tourism: carnival and pilgrimage. These ideas carry through into Chapter 7, which examines the object-rich, ritualised world of heritage tourism. This is a major domain of tourism and Chapter 7 will outline key perspectives on heritage and analyse the principal arguments. Since heritage is by its very nature concerned with social identity, agency and history it is a politically charged and contested terrain. In the hands of contemporary nationalistic discourses, heritage can be assimilating, hailing all and binding everyone into a common project. In the hands of local groups, specific cities, classes, regions, ethnic groups and so forth, it can be a means whereby they address the world, making statements about their culture, background and project; literally a means of writing themselves into history. In this chapter we will see how objects as well as discourses produce heritage effects, but in order to do that we have to be in the thick of things, seeing how visitors' biographies encounter the interpreter's discourse.

Part Three also carries forward themes developed earlier but concentrates on two important domains of tourism in which what we might call 'the tourist body' has become the object of greater attention. Rather than the essentially disembodied viewing tourist, concentrating on objects of the tourist gaze, these forms of tourism have returned in many ways to themes that dominated pilgrimage: health and illness, individual redemption, spirituality and a concern with sacred objects. But rather than the sacred shrines of martyrs and saints, the contemporary tourist visits nature, the ocean, mountains, forests, wildlife. Rather than employ the technologies of prayer, devotion, chants and meditation, the contemporary pilgrim to nature achieves ecstatic moments through a range of technologies that blur the difference between the self and nature. Nature is inscribed on the tourist body by the 'hard work' and technique involved with walking, climbing, and trekking. Some techniques require such concentration and physical skill that practitioners lose themselves in natural surfaces: the surfer, the paraglider, the skier, the skydiver and the snowboarder for example. Ecstatic moments occur when the degree of skill and concentration required focus all attention on the moment, and where temporary fusions between nature and the body are experienced: some have called this 'flow'. There is no doubting the growth of these nature-based and high adrenalin tourisms, and they mark out stages in the trend towards a more active and performative tourism. These sorts of activity have been related to changing conditions in contemporary culture, particularly in reaction to the experience of fast time and the feeling that the body is bombarded by a dissonant series of stimulations in everyday life and where concentration, attention and contemplation have become sacrificed. Whereas Chapter 8 concentrates on this relationship between the body and contemporary culture and homes in on a series of case studies from eco-tourism to surfing, climbing, naturism and taste, Chapter 9 examines the related topic of sex and tourism. Sex is universally associated with the heightened states of excitation produced by ritual occasions, and a heightened state of sexuality has accompanied most forms of tourism. However, the nature and degree of sexuality in tourism has varied considerably over time. Chapter 8 attempts to put some perspective on this variation and enables the reader to compare the place of sex in the seaside holidays of the mid-twentieth century with later periods. Tourism options have been specified by a more and more explicit reference to opportunities to experience sex. Chapter 9 concludes with an extensive discussion of tourisms that are focused around experiencing sex. In this we draw on similar themes, notably the more reflexive sensibilities of late modernity that have not only made the body a fitting and appropriate focus of attention but developed the means for people to do so in an unlimited and unfettered manner. Chapter 10 concludes the book, providing a summary of the key arguments and themes of the book. It makes a clear case for considering tourism to be one of the most important activities of the globalised modern world.

Further Reading

Bauman, Z. (1998b) *Globalisation – The Human Consequences*. Oxford: Polity.

Franklin, A.S. and Crang, M. (2001) 'The trouble with tourism and travel theory?', *Tourist Studies* 1(1): 5–22.

Hannigan, J. (1998) *Fantasy City*. London: Routledge.

Inglis, F. (2000) *The Delicious History of the Holiday*. London: Routledge.

Löfgren, O. (1999) *On Holiday: A History of Vacationing*. Berkeley: University of California Press.

Rojek, C. (1995) *Decentring Leisure: Rethinking Leisure Theory*. London: Sage.

Urry, J. (2000) *Sociology Beyond Societies – Mobilities for the Twenty-first Century*. London: Routledge.

Part 1

Questions and Scope

2

What is tourism?

Nowadays we are all on the move. Many of us change places – moving homes or travelling to and from places that are not our homes. Some of us do not need to go out to travel: we can dash or scurry or flit through the Web, netting and mixing on the computer screen messages born in opposite corners of the globe. But most of us are on the move even if physically, bodily we stay put . . . jumping in and out of foreign spaces with a speed much beyond the capacity of supersonic jets and cosmic rockets, but nowhere staying long enough to be more than visitors, to feel *chez soi*.

Zygmunt Bauman (1998b: 77)

Tourism is everything and everything is tourism.

Ian Munt (1994: 104)

People are much of the time 'tourists' whether they like it or not.

John Urry (1990: 82)

More Canadian package tours go to the West Edmonton Mall than to Niagara Falls.

Ritzer and Liska (1997: 103)

Seaside towns and inland spas have, under local Acts, extensively developed municipal services [sports and other leisure facilities]. The object has been, of course, to make staying in these resorts pleasant for visitors. Is it not reasonable to suggest that the same efforts should *everywhere* be directed towards making a place attractive to its inhabitants?

Henry Durant (1938: 255)

SUMMARY

- Tourism: Accessing the modern world
- The nation state and the birth of mass tourism
- Characteristics of modern tourism
- Attempted definitions of tourism
- Tourism as Romanticism?

This a new and different type of introductory text for tourist studies. In the first place it is new in the sense that it seeks to introduce students to the very latest developments, ideas and concepts emerging in tourism research and theory. In the second place this book will argue for a new perspective on tourism at the beginning of the twenty-first century. It will be argued that tourism is no longer a temporary and unusual state of existence in a world otherwise organised by life at home and life at work. More than that, for many people and in many places tourism has become more dominant in the *organisation* of everyday life. In many ways we can also say that the appeal and logic of tourism has expanded into more forms of social life, more spaces of contemporary cultures (especially in the west) and more time in our daily, weekly and annual calendar. For Thomas Cook, the founder of modern tourism, this would certainly have been a wish come true. For him, accessibility to the world, its natures, histories, peoples and cultures was an urgently needed resource for modern individuals and nations; tourism was a route to enlightenment in a globalising world. For Cook extending the numbers and sorts of people who had access to travel and a world beyond their home was seen as a positive, democratising project that could produce a more evenly educated civil society with more equal life chances and a society more tolerant of others; a civil society that could more easily take part in national life and a more peaceful cooperative world. As we know, he pursued this dream with considerable zeal, indeed, viewing it as part of his religious commitment.

Tourism: Accessing the modern world

Later in the book we will see how his considerable innovations in information technology, finance and credit, flexible consumerism, bureaucratic interfacing, freedom of movement, education and gender equalisation make Cook very clearly one of the great innovators and creators of modern societies. The point to stress is that Cook had more in mind for tourism than simply travel and pleasure. It was a serious business with important social and political implications. More importantly it was to be a central part of being a modern person. As markets were opened up beyond regions and nations; as politicians and diplomats tried to engineer peaceful relations and governance between very different nations, peoples and cultures; as manufacturing became ever more dependent upon informed and educated workers and as ideas and innovation were dependent upon freedom of movement and exchange of information, extending access to the world and the production of confident skilful tourists was an essential task. Cook anticipated an emerging globalisation and he saw tourism as a cultural expression of it. I have emphasised these serious underlying implications of tourism because I want to make it quite clear that this book will depart from many tourism texts that have so far trivialised the social and cultural significance of tourism as a phenomenon. One of the themes of this book is that existing tourism theory and textbooks have made a fundamental error, usually right at the beginning of their account. Tourists, they argue, are searching for something. In some cases it is something better than what they have got in their everyday lives; in other accounts they are searching 'for the real thing', the more authentic world beyond that of their own (inauthentic) lives. Modern people have frequently pondered the effects of living in the ever-changing conditions of modernity. Such rapid social, technological and environmental changes seem to pull humanity further and further away from things that are vaguely conceptualised as our 'roots', our origins, our true state of nature and culture. Whereas these roots can be considered to be an organic accommodation between culture and nature that has endured through much of our past, the conditions of modern life at any one time are frequently considered to be synthetic, inorganic, and ephemeral. Modernity has generated a sense of being somehow *false*.

For other writers such as Urry (1990; 2002), tourists are looking for difference and the unusual, a relatively simple search for the pleasure of the new and surprising. This account is not a reaction against modern-isation but perhaps a celebration of it, because modernity is all about novelty. Against all of these I will argue that these views fundamentally mistake the nature of the modern world in which most people live. The view of the modern world that most theories conjure is a dull, unchanging, grey, repetitive and uneventful world, as typified by the conditions and relations of mid-twentieth century factory *work* or perhaps the more frenzied life of almost all careers in the twenty-first century. In a style typical of social science this view also casts modern living as somehow meaningless, shallow, artificial and depressing. It is normally so bad that we all need a holiday or break from it from time to time. We need to bathe in the revitalising light of the new and fresh and ponder the true meaning of life by surrounding ourselves with more authentic objects, cultures and peoples – elsewhere. We also need stimulation and fun. Although this may sound plausible, and variants of this thesis have been circulating for over 25 years now, it is flawed and needs revision.

In this book I will argue for a directly opposite account. In this account modernity and modern life is by its very definition a very rapidly changing cultural formation. It has brought us new things in a dazzling array of forms and technologies. It has kept up this procession of the new for a very long time: the first steam passenger trains (considered a wonder at the time) began running in the 1840s. Most importantly, the swirling and dizzying nature of all this change has remained exciting, perhaps too exciting (or shocking) for some, but with modernity there is never a dull moment. There are, for example, always new fashions, films, books, and technologies – even during wars and economic depressions. And there are always new discoveries. The critical point is that the ordinary person in the street is not insulated from all of this, far from it, they are always in the thick of things, in the swirling times not outside them. Baudelaire wrote about this in the Paris of 1840–1860 and for him the central figure of the Paris streets was the *flâneur*, literally the stroller, the watcher, imbibing the changing shops, the crowds, the lights, the wonderful life of the *modern* city. As John Jervis writes: 'For Baudelaire and other writers of his time, what was new was the sense of novelty itself, and the difficulty of pinning it down. Novelty is repetitive, but each time the content changes; as Berman put it, "The fact that you can't step into the same modernity twice makes modern life hard to grasp"' (Jervis, 1998: 66). Hard to grasp perhaps but addictive too. Virginia Woolf was also impressed if not intoxicated by London in the 1920s for similar reasons although she likened the city to a natural phenomenon, 'notably in the all pervasive metaphor of street life as river-like, conveying a sense of dynamism and creative flow that is essentially organic' (Jervis, 1998: 70). These are the great flows of modernity, the flows of people and the flows of things and the new waterways, tramlines, roads, rail, canals. So in a sense it is a false opposition to see modernity as inorganic, heading away from nature. If nature is essentially evolutionary, then so too is modernity. Baudelaire and Woolf were privileged and middle class and did not spend their entire days in unpleasant factories and mines or stuck in contemporary commuter traffic jams. But the point really is that they were among the first to sense this modernity and even before the 1930s, ordinary working people had begun to sense it too. The engines of modernity brought the new to the heart of every city in terms of flows and pulses. With it came news of the origins of things, the cultures elsewhere, the great seas and the great ports, overseas dominions and travellers' stories. Modernity created novelties and the demand for them. And just as the engines of modernity could bring the new to the city, they could also take the city back out along the same routes; it was the love and thrill of modernity and the modern city that created tourism, not the opposite – an escape from it. This is why it is so difficult (and pointless) to define tourism in spatial terms: it simply is not behaviour that only takes place away from home. Tourism is certainly a particular type of extension of modern life, but it is a celebration of it rather than an escape. Rojek (1993) described it as a heightened experience of ordinary life. That is far more like it. But we should follow the clue left by Berman: modernity is constantly shifting and therefore our theoretical understanding of tourism needs to be mobile and nimble too. Tourism is likely to be influenced not as a (negative) reaction to what happens in cities and modern cultures but as a positive response to them. Up until now, because tourism was cast as a fundamentally different other world to the modern – often conjuring up notions of liminality and ritual – it is often described as a special pleasure zone. It isn't, it is the quintessential expression and performance of modern life.

The nation state and the birth of mass tourism

In this book new ways will be employed to introduce and understand tourism. To begin with, I will be arguing that nation states and nationalism were responsible for the application and articulation of modernist ideas to the construction and the performance of tourism. Tourism is often a phenomenon without a very clear sense of authorship or agency. Whose idea was it anyway? Who directs developments and sets new things up? It seems we are usually left with three sorts of ideas: visionary figures like Thomas Cook, poetic inspirational artists like Wordsworth or Turner and entrepreneurs like Freddie Laker in the 1970s and Richard Branson in the 80s and 90s. But there seems to be little in the way of an organising historical framework within which we can situate tourism, or at least how it emerged in the form that it did. Of course, I am arguing that it was primarily and intricately involved in the establishment of modernity, but its specific forms do, it seems to me, require a more thorough-going theoretical framework.

So in addition to other known influences on the emergence of modern tourism, I will, for the first time, be arguing that the nation state was an important primary agent and constructor of tourism. This is no surprise since nation states were also the principal organisers and articulators of modernity. These days when everyone seems to be announcing the arrival of globalisation and the death of the nation, we seem to have forgotten just how important nations were. But I am also going to suggest that in matters of consumption like tourism, they still are. Nation states have explicitly employed tourism as a means of creating a sense of citizenship and social solidarity in a modern world where such things are prone to disintegration – and they still do. Nation states have created many spaces of special *national* significance, and these have become shrines of nation-hood and the focus for secular forms of pilgrimage – and they still are. Nation states have produced policies that are directly formative of tourism practices – and they continue to do so (Franklin, 2002a). Nation states have used tourism as a part of their international policy and international relations – and this continues. Nation states have used tourism as a major means of income generation – and this is still important. By focusing some of my analysis around nations and nationalisms I hope that students anywhere in the world will be able to relate to the arguments developed here and more importantly, to be able to use them in order to reflect on the nature of tourism in their own country. By such reflection we might be able to decentre tourism theory and understand its contingent qualities and variable forms.

Characteristics of modern tourism

Let us have a look at all this in slightly higher magnification. We will start by looking at the definitions of tourism that other studies have used and identify problems associated with them. I will work towards an analysis of tourism that identifies the following as formative of what we might mean by tourism:

- Tourism derives from the condition of life in modernity and the experience of modernity not an escape from it.
- Modernity is about the permanence of novelty not an escape to it.
- Tourism is more than travel; tourism is more about the accessibility of novelty and the modern world generally. A stream of new communicative technologies of modernity permit that access under what might be called a general escalation of mobility. Things and people can move and as they do so tourism extends its spatial range from the home to outer space.
- Tourism *is* consumerism in a globalising modernity.
- The specialised intellectual faculty for touristic consumerism and also its opposite, an elitist distain for tourists and tourism, was first created by Romanticism.
- A framework for the development of touristic practices and an economy and geography of tourism were powerfully influenced by nationalism and nation states and later by cities and regions.
- Tourism is an embodied experience not simply a visual experience. Consumption, identity, belonging and social order work on and through the body, as do their opposites, freedom, transgression and disorder. As consumption is an expressive activity in modernity, tourism tends to be always expressive or performative. In these ways, tourism as leisure is never *simply* rest, relaxation and pleasure. It always operates inside a political and moral context. A lot of scientific work, political speeches, public debates and legal cases took place before people could routinely lie semi-naked on a beach.
- Tourism is not only a way of accessing the world, it is increasingly an important means of locating ourselves in it. In a migrant modernity most people are living away from home viewing their home after the manner of tourists; equally among those people and places 'left behind' in less migratory flows, tourism often steps in to provide work and a future. As it does so it sifts through people's pasts and, often for the first time, seeks to stamp a cultural identity on the landscape, offering a history to those whom official history chose to forget.

Attempted definitions of tourism

According to the procedures of scientific method adopted by some formalistic methods in the social sciences and particularly in geographical and economic analysis, theory is dependent upon measurement and in order to properly measure any one thing one must ascertain its phenomenal distinction from all other things. Definition must precede measurement, evidently. However, what are actually very complex historical and cultural phenomena, related to relationships and ideas, can become in this way reduced to formal characteristics, often a list of items. Definitions can be contested and debates clouded. In trying to understand whether tourism constitutes a single industry, and tourists and tourist companies a singular economic activity, economists, geographers and government analysts and planners have persuaded themselves that there is sufficient coherency and universal meaning for a definition to be useful. Even though it is hard to find any text that does not point up the dangers, pitfalls and contradictions of defining tourism, few allow it to stop them. They fear the question; well what exactly do you mean by tourism? Define your term!

Hence for example, Mathieson and Wall (1982: 1) define tourism as: 'the temporary movement of people to destinations outside their normal places of work and residence, the activities undertaken during their stay in those destinations and the facilities created to care to their need'. Similarly, for Buckart and Medlik (1974) '[t]ourism denotes the temporary short-term movement of people to destinations outside the places where they normally live (Buckart and Medlik, 1974: v). This is almost a routine assumption about tourism: O'Reilly (2000: 43), for example, argues that many theorists, including Graburn (1989), Smith (1989) and Voase (1995), define tourism 'more by what it is not than by what it is – it is *not* home and it is *not* work; it is a change of scenery and lifestyle, an inversion of the normal'. Typically, such definitions bring together groups and activities that seem at best unrelated and at worst opposites. They bunch together, perhaps on the same aircraft travelling from a capital city such as Sydney to a major tourist city such as Brisbane, those going on holiday and those going to work or on business or perhaps to a specialist hospital for treatment. For this reason, formalist procedures typically invoke sub-definitions to cover these extreme variations. Hence we obtain the 'non-business tourist' ('a person who undertakes one or more recreational activities in leisure time, at a location temporarily away from the normal place of residence and at locations at which such recreational activities are normally undertaken') as distinct from the 'business tourist' (a person who undertakes work related activities at a location temporarily away from their normal place of residence and work') (Carroll et al., 1991). It is not clear how this definition distinguishes tourism from, say, travel. The geographers Shaw and Williams (1994: 5) and urban sociologists Judd and Fainstein (1999) adopt the formal definition preferred by international organisations such as the World Tourism Office, that 'tourism includes all travel that involves a stay of at least one night, but less than one year, away from home'. This, therefore, includes travel for such purposes as visiting friends or relatives, or to undertake business. Such a definition places the travel–accommodation connection and its associated industry at the heart of tourism, signalling at the same time that it is the provision and purchase of these commodities rather than tourism behaviour and culture that is central to our interest.

These formal definitions, driven by the desire to quantify tourism and to measure the performance of the tourism economy, not only denude tourism of some of its more interesting and important characteristics, they tend to reduce tourism to acts of leisure and recreation at the end of acts of travel. This takes formalist theorists into the quicksands of defining leisure and recreation (notoriously difficult, see Rojek, 1985; 1995) and away from the more fruitful and firmer practice of locating tourism as a *mode* of relating to the world in postmodern cultures. It undermines the consumptive, playful, ironic, intellectual, mental, passive, romantic, aesthetic, reflexive, performative and spiritual content of tourism whilst over-emphasising mobile, physical, active and muscular dimensions. Because tourism cannot properly be reduced to the acts of travel and the leisure and recreation activities at the end of discrete bouts of travel, some authors have gone for the opposite of narrow abstraction in favour of mindless incorporation and extension. Tourism becomes absolutely everything associable with acts of tourism, or put into its proper tautological form, 'tourism is tourism' or 'tourism is what tourists do'. An example of this style of incorporation comes from Weaver and Opperman:

> Tourism is the sum of the phenomena and relationships arising from the interaction among tourists, business suppliers, host governments, host communities, origin governments, universities, community colleges and non-governmental organisations, in the process of attracting, transporting, hosting and managing these tourists and other visitors. (2000: 3)

With some exceptions, the tendency has been to regard tourism as simply a part of the entertainment industry – a separate and not altogether respectable or admirable industry. Clearly a lot of tourism is structured around entertainment and pleasure but as with the sociology of sport or food, the sociological importance and meaning of soccer, cricket or eating out is not simply about entertainment and pleasure. Reducing tourism to an industry that delivers a service (pleasure, entertainment) tends to obscure its wider sociological significance. Significantly, such a perspective places all the action and agency in the hands of the tourism industry, its companies, designers and organisations. It is as if they produce the tourist product and deliver it to a passive, consumer-tourist. Moreover focusing tourist studies only on those industries, places and exchanges ignores the cumulative effects that tourism has on individuals, cultural groups, nations and global society. We can immediately obtain a sense of what is often wrong with tourism studies by looking at how tourism is defined and how tourism is explained as a kind of behaviour within the more sociological accounts. These tend, perhaps inadvertently, to reproduce some of the problems noted above.

As we will see, tourism is defined in an odd and contradictory manner by non-sociologists and sociologists alike. Almost all definitions of tourism identify one or two things that *distinguish* it from other activities: first it involves travel away from an individual's home environment; second, it consists of the exposure of individuals to activities and places that are different and unusual (critical here is a necessary contrast between the familiar and the unfamiliar). We will see how a variety of *explanations* of tourism use this contrast. These vary in interesting ways: some employ the escape metaphor to highlight the essentially problematic conditions of everyday life in modern capitalist societies. For many the realm of work, whether at home or in the labour market, involves a series of pressured, alienating and stressful conditions that require the occasional timeout. A change being as good as a rest? Probably not. And are holidays truly restful or do they demand energy, hard work and endurance? Mine frequently do.

Owing to an in-built bias in the social sciences in favour of production, particularly technology, science and manufacturing, tourism and other leisure and consumption activities were not taken very seriously from the 1950s to 1970s, indeed they were treated rather like superfluous or decorous activities of little consequence. Considering the sheer scale of the expansion of mass tourism in the 1950s and 1960s it produced very little by way of response or comment from sociology, geography or the other business disciplines that now champion tourism. MacCannell's *The Tourist* (1976) has to be judged in this context. Viewed from the position of American sociological theory at the time it was not surprising that it problematised and tried to explain tourism almost as a *deviant* activity, a somewhat disturbing behaviour resulting from the alienation and cultural disturbance of modernisation and modern social relations. Tourism was treated somewhat clinically as a necessary period of recovery from the intolerable conditions of modern life. Some of the classical anxieties of 1960s sociology were wrapped up in this book: alienated workers, dysfunctional family life, a world of synthetic unreality, a highly differentiated and fragmented world ruled by rationalised and bureaucratised procedures. In comparison with premodern cultures where the individual was locked into a stable and secure social framework, the modern individual was at sea, literally, looking for meaningfulness and finding it the categorical opposites of modernity: the past, the exotic other, pristine nature. In short, MacCannell declared the modern world to be inauthentic and troubling and tourism was the somewhat pathetic and pointless search for the authentic and an antidote of some short-lived kind. While plausible in itself it left tourism very much in the same place it was found: a marginal, somewhat spurious escape attempt from the true reality, whether unsavoury or not. It is all the more surprising then how this thesis and the authentic–inauthentic dualism continues to be drawn upon as a way of explaining tourism behaviour or at least the taxonomy of tourist objects. It is indicative of the stagnant or withering state of tourist studies at the present time (see Franklin and Crang, 2001). In the absence of many other general theories of tourism researchers are more or less obliged to refer to it. Of course the better studies refused to see tourists as cultural dupes, preferring to acknowledge a commonplace sense of ironic self-deception among tourists (Cohen and Taylor, 1976; Feifer, 1986; Urry, 1990). Conceptualising tourism and tourists as intellectually challenged and culturally vacuous is extremely common but also revealing of something important. We will come to this a bit later.

Accounts influenced by the philosopher Friedrich Nietzsche argue that capitalist societies of the West have trapped people inside the disciplines of work and education and buried them inside a bureaucratic and stifling culture of control. These accounts underlie the manner by which a so-called true human nature has been stifled and constrained and needs to be released for more creative, physically demanding and less inhibited activities. Tourism in particular is identified as a principal escape valve of this sort. This is nowhere better demonstrated than in Cartmill's analysis of the dominant hunting and outdoor leisures in the USA, and the development of the national park areas and policy debates that even drew in Presidents (see Cartmill, 1993). After all, does not tourism take place outside normal everyday disciplines and beyond the gaze of everyday surveillance? Is not tourism characterised by a greater tolerance for sexual freedom, gambling, fooling around, adventure, drug-taking and drinking and looser controls over the purse strings? Other accounts, while not emphasising this liberational rationale, nonetheless take as axiomatic that tourism provides a compelling series of pleasures that derive from the simple relief from the monotony of everyday life. So, in Urry's account tourism is explained in terms of the pleasurability of the different and the unusual. How else are we to explain the somewhat bizarre objects that tourists will pay money to see? For Urry, the ultimate goal of tourists is to feast their eyes on different and unusual objects, landscapes and townscapes. It is as if these visions are a reward in themselves, visions that can be captured by visual technologies and stored and kept rather like any other commodity. Urry's *The Tourist Gaze* is the other landmark in theoretical developments in tourism of this period although it is a very different sort of thesis. Urry does not offer a particularly clear link between tourism and the *conditions* of modern life, and certainly tourism is not explained as a *response* to the conditions of modern life. Rather, tourism is located very clearly as an emerging cultural activity in modernity and a positive outcome of modernity, clearly linked to the extension of leisure and holidays to workers, the democratisation of travel (and security in travel), an extension of the Victorian notion of improvement and approved leisures; and globalisation. Writing in the late 1980s Urry linked tourism theoretically to patterns of social change in the last quarter of the twentieth century. As we have already seen, Urry does not provide a particularly clear explanation for touristic behaviour per se and this is a weakness. Vague references to the pleasurability of 'the different' and 'the unusual' or the non-everyday only *assert* some form of pleasurability from these abstract things, they do not account for it. Missing is an account of the aesthetic sensibilities of tourism, especially in the new tourisms of recent decades. At best Urry's account draws on an historical momentum in which the educated middle classes acted as the initial travellers and tourists establishing a pattern of touristic consumption that the working class and mass markets simply emulate and copy through critical innovations such as Thomas Cook's package tours. Here though, the emphasis is on notions of personal improvement through education, experience, exposure to different places and people, and the pursuit of health and fitness – all established values of Victorian modernism. However, the implicit aesthetic content of this diffusion model is based upon the older notion of high and low culture: tourism offered those born to low culture the opportunity of glimpsing and being improved by icons and displays of high culture. Urry accounts for more recent forms of tourism consumption in terms of the social and economic restructuring implicit in the notion of post-Fordism.

The fragmentation of mass tourism of the mid-twentieth century resort holiday into a series of different and niched markets by the 1980s is explained by Urry in terms of the collapse of Fordist – or mass forms of production and consumption. Fordist styles of production were based on the extension of mass produced markets through innovations in production line and assembly plants. Fordism describes the extension of former luxuries such as cars to all workers and indeed the growth of capital generally. Fordist styles of consumption were standardised and monotonous. Henry Ford himself was quoted as saying that consumers could have any colour Model T Ford they liked so long as it was black. Post-Fordist forms of production, which grew rapidly from the late 1970s, favoured smaller, leaner and more flexible forms of production that could respond better to fluctuations in the shaky aftermath of the post-war boom economy and the growing power of consumers in the credit-rich affluent markets of the western world. Under conditions of greater choice, greater credit and the breakdown of mass popular culture, individuals tended to identify less with older repositories of identity such as social class, political alignment, gender, region and workplace and more in terms of lifestyle groups with their emphasis on consumption, leisure and style. In a way teenagers of the 1960s began this style, establishing youth sub-cultures, ways of life separable from their parents and grandparents. The idea took off and expanded, creating fresh rounds of separation or de-differentiation (where former distinctions become blurred and confused). Tourism industries responded to the emergence and proliferation of lifestyle groups by providing a range of specialist niche markets, greater flexibility, choice and self-direction. The tourism market became segmented into a series of consumer groups catering quite specifically for different tastes and styles. Again, early examples were based on the desire of young people to spend their holidays together. Age, income, class, occupation continued to frame broad patterns of taste, but other dimensions such as generation, sexual orientation, sub-culture, style, family cycle stage, leisure and enthusiasms provided templates for quite specific forms of consumption (for example, it seems that Goth style can be summed up by the maxim: buy or wear anything providing it is black). Even though such a general characterisation as this is widely agreed upon, it sits awkwardly with Urry's emphasis on the necessary pleasurability of difference and the unusual at the heart of the tourism experience. To a major extent then, tourism is *increasingly not* offering an essentially different or unusual set of experiences for tourists but tailoring their experiences in line with their chosen forms of *everyday* culture: their style, their preferences, their fellow travellers, their fantasies, taste and so on. This can be seen perhaps through corporate executive trends in tourism and the standardisation of the international five-star hotel. If you have been in one you have been in them all.

In all of these accounts the tourist is a passive consumer of services (museums, lookouts, art galleries, historical monuments, nature reserves etc.) that are crafted and commodified by a knowledgeable industry that knows what it is they seek or need. Even these lifestyle groups are presented as the innovation of a clever marketing and advertising industry. The degree of passivity varies of course. Some people put a lot of effort into researching and planning their tourism. At the other extreme are the fully guided tour bus consumers who simply pay and watch.

So what is wrong with these accounts? Surely people need to move out of their everyday spaces and to do that they need to travel? Surely they are looking for pleasure and difference? Surely people do lead humdrum lives and need relief from the monotony? It is not that these accounts are completely wrong so much as confused and incomplete. Because they see the tourist as an essentially passive subject driven by forces external to and greater than them, this emphasis on escape, search and the pleasurability of a world beyond their own is completely compelling. For these accounts, travel away from the everyday and the *rupture* that this is held to produce is central to their theoretical understanding of tourism. I disagree with most of this.

Certainly, these claims are largely asserted with barely any empirical justification or follow-up. This is not a serious objection to theoretical claims per se, but I mention it in passing. I would also mention that these accounts echo many of the anxieties of sociology as a discipline. It has never been entirely comfortable with capitalist consumer society (see for example Miles' 1998 book *Consumerism as a Way of Life*) and has always tended to shroud it in negative, pathological and more recently, in unsustainable terms. Sociology has always believed that capitalist relations undermine a true human potential or its development. In this way tourism is portrayed as a kind of displacement activity: a slightly sad perversity, a less than satisfactory or fruitless search for compensation. But sociology is only a subset of intellectual opinion, and the broader intellectual opinion on tourism has been largely negative: tourism is mindless, moronic and futile (see Rojek, 1993: 174–5 for more on this). Crick (1989: 308) specifically mentions the activity of a collective social science representation of tourism and asked 'whether we yet have a respectable scholarly analysis of tourism, or whether the social science literature on the subject substantially blends with the emotionally-charged cultural image relating to travel and tourists.' Commenting on the failure of social scientists to take mass tourism and tourists seriously, O'Reilly (2000: 19) argues that 'more recent researchers in the fields of geography, social policy and sociology have only been able to approach the topic since it became defined in terms of the elderly, retirement, tourism and the environment, or in terms of migration and poverty; in other words they were able to approach it only as something serious as opposed to the frivolous and trivial.' I mention all this merely to reinforce the point that there is a long tradition of thinking about tourism in this way.

Activity 2.1

If we pause to consider what we mean by tourism, we must surely agree with Alain de Botton (2002), who argues that tourism is an attitude to the world or a way of seeing the world, not necessarily what we find only at the end of a long and arduous journey. Indeed, de Botton reminds us that the age of Romanticism threw up the character of Xavier De Maistre who published two volumes of rather unusual travel in 1790: *Journey Around my Bedroom* and *Nocturnal Expedition Around my Bedroom*. In these, De Maistre demonstrates a fundamental truth: that while we are prepared to look very carefully at almost everything we see in new and exotic places on our travels, we barely take any notice of the equally interesting and often exotic nature of our own immediate surroundings. De Botton decided to try out this form of tourism for himself, and in *The Art of Travel* (2002: 247–54) we are treated to his own journey around his bedroom and his journey around his own neighbourhood in Hammersmith, London. As an exercise, it is useful to read the outcome of these journeys, and also to conduct similar expeditions of your own. It is worth bearing in mind that this is precisely what the tourism industry does itself when deciding to try to market new destinations. Most destinations or sites are transformed from places of the humdrum and ordinary to places where their extraordinary and exotic dimensions are pointed out and annotated. So the point of this activity is to discover and highlight the touristic potential of ordinary everyday spaces in your immediate surroundings.

Tourism as Romanticism?

Romanticism is not easy to fit into an analysis of tourism, despite the fact that introductions to tourism that include a brief history of tourism place it as a foundational idea and movement, one of the principal models for the mass tourism industry that followed. Urry even sees it as 'part of the mechanism by which contemporary tourism has been globalised' (Urry, 1999: 83). Certainly, if we follow Elias's thesis that social elites establish norms of civil behaviour that are later copied and emulated by their status inferiors, then this makes some sense. In this way we can see the highly ordered and rule-bound leisure life in early nineteenth century resorts such as Bath Spa as some kind of model that was eventually passed down to the mass seaside holidays of the English working classes. There is also room to make parallels using Veblen's thesis of conspicuous consumption: the conspicuous (if more tasteful and refined) splendour of Bath and Brighton in their hey day with the similarly spectacular later working class version at Morecambe and Margate. We might even make a comparison between the spiritual focus of nineteenth century forays to the wild margins of Britain, Europe and America as undertaken by the educated upper classes and the mass tourism to national parks and natural areas from the 1950s onwards. Certainly, those of a Romantic disposition were behind many moves to create *national parks* and create the idea of a national heritage.

However, we must be careful here. There are certainly links but we must be aware of important differences also.

The most important difference concerns the notion of consumption, particularly, how these places were to be visited and what dispositions were required in order to visit them *properly*. The Romantics upheld the view that certain old buildings, sites and cultures were important to visit and study because for them classical antiquity became the model of human perfection. They were not looking at 'the other' but trying to emulate, learn and model what they considered to be their cultural inheritance. For Romantic sensibilities, Greek and Roman civilisations were the high points of humanity's development, a period when philosophy and the arts flourished, when great strides were made in mathematics and architecture and when a stable and healthy lifestyle was created around notions of citizenship, education, fitness, rights and law. Notably, this was a time when humanity and nature were more fluid categories of thought prior to the dualism wrought by Cartesian innovations. Romantic aesthetic sensibilities embraced the Greek and Roman pastoral ideal and, indeed, extended them to other more simple cultures such as the many indigenous cultures that were being seen by Europeans for the first time. And by extension too, the world of unspoilt natures and of natural forces themselves became compelling to the Romantics. They perceived such places to be the pinnacles of perfection and beauty but their appreciation required the prepared mind. Indeed preparation, anticipation and imagination were key intellectual properties of the Romantic mind. It was a mind capable of understanding and constructing in poetic and spiritual terms the relationship between the individual and nature. Nature was not some objective reality, what we might call a realist category, but always a mediated thing conjured up by the human imagination. For all of these reasons, the manner in which one visited ancient civilisation or nature was critical to this proper appropriation. The Romantic traveller was an exclusive figure: not only from the educated upper classes with the time and resources to travel and ponder the world but also exclusive in the sense of excluding others. Essentially the Romantic traveller was a lone figure, needing to be alone in nature or in the silent appreciation of historical sites – or even alone, on the road. This is perfectly illustrated by the painting by Caspar David Friedrich *The Wanderer above the Mists* (1818) or from the title of the book *Figures in a Landscape: a History of the National Trust* by John Gaze (1988). Both illustrations underline the individual student or 'figure' in the landscape as opposed to the group or the crowd. Romantic writers were famously opposed to their routes and special places being copied or visited by the wrong sorts, typically the ill-educated workers on a day trip from the factories. Wordsworth was among many who set up an antipathy to tourism as the wrong sort of approach to these sacred sites and communions with nature. Further, one can trace that antipathy and opposition to tourism through to the present day where the traveller is opposed to the tourist and the authentic is opposed to the inauthentic. So in this sense we can say that Romantic travel and commercial tourism were and still are in tension with one another. Educators and churchmen like Thomas Cook may have wanted ordinary people to share in these culturally and spiritually uplifting experiences but their very presence ruined what the educated elites were looking for. It is for this sort of reason that academics tended to share the Romantic disapproval of tourism seeing it, on balance, as a destructive force.

It is ironic then that some have argued that Romanticism was directly responsible for the very cultural foundations of the consumerism that modern tourism embodies (Campbell, 1995). Jervis puts it well:

> For the Romantics, wedded to the creative role of the imagination in the exploration of beauty, the exercise of the imagination was inherently pleasurable, and this could be intensified through strong emotion. While the Romantics were strongly anti-utilitarian, and contemptuous of bourgeois ideals of comfort, this non-materialist ethos nevertheless entailed what Gouldner [1975] suggests was an attempt to endow 'the ordinary, everyday world with the pathos of the extraordinary', since 'the insignificance of things was born of a failure of imagination'. Indeed, they were not only interested in nature, but in books, paintings, clothes, china – the sort of 'expressive' goods that had led the surge in consumerism in the preceding period. (Jervis, 1998: 105)

In this way objects and things performed a new role in modern life: 'Just as the external world required "representation" by and for a self now clearly seen as separate from it, so the self, too, as a mysterious inner entity, could only be manifested through externals: language, clothes, objects, can become "our way of manifesting through expression what we are, and our place within things"; we become "expressive beings"' (Jervis, 1998: 106 quoting Taylor, 1992: 198). Hence contemporary touristic practices, such as car boot sales (currently the most popular weekend leisure activity according to Gregson and Crewe) were born a long time ago to a social elite who had no idea what they were unleashing on the world.

This is an important point: all tourists, rather like all consumers, use their imaginations, longings, dreams and fantasies in thinking about what a holiday will be like, and this imaginary activity is pleasurable. Jervis again: 'where daydreaming intervenes, *anticipation* is possible, and anticipation *itself* becomes pleasurable. One might almost say that the wanting rather than the having become central to pleasure; we refer to pleasure seeking, after all' (Jervis, 1998: 106). As Bauman puts it: 'desire desires desire', not satisfaction. So the paradox is that Romanticism spawned the *desire* and the capability to imagine the pleasurability of consuming things, a capability that was formative of mass popular culture, consumerism and mass tourism, as well as a cultural disdain for mass consumption, modernism and *especially* crowds of tourists among the social elite. It seems quite clear that this cultural bifurcation and the tension it breeds have been maintained. It is certainly far from clear that the Romantic gaze, as Urry calls this elite form, has become 'considerably more significant and the mechanism by which tourism has been globalised' (Urry, 2002: 75).

But in disagreeing with this tradition of loathing tourists I want to come back to our hero, Thomas Cook.

Thomas Cook knew about the really bad times in the history of capitalism. He was approaching middle age when he produced the very first excursions for ordinary people in 1841. He had lived through and seen the grimmest moments of capitalist development in England. He knew very well the limitations of a life spent merely in a locality around a workplace. He could speak expertly on parochialism, the intolerance of strangers, the boredom of an unchanging life in poverty, the intellectual limitations of ordinary village or small town life. The celebration of the simple life of peasants, mercifully saved from the main currents of capitalism, that was so characteristic of later twentieth century thinking would have been lost on him. With zealous energy Cook wanted to undo the complacent and vulnerable world of the unchanging village. He wanted to open everyone's eyes and minds to the entire world, to a world that was changing in new and exciting ways, to new landscapes and cultures, to a world of infinite possibility. It was heady stuff. For Cook, then, tourism was not about escaping modernity BUT JOINING IT. And this is the lesson, and another reason why the anti-modernist social elite loathed it. Tourism should be thought of in this more positive and progressive manner. Instead of an emphasis on rupture, escape, seeking a more authentic world that can only exist away from everyday life in modernity, tourism is one of the main ways most people can connect with it, access it, take a part in its universalising and mobile character. Tourism then is one of the necessary building blocks of modernity not the escape route out of it. What does this entail? Baudelaire's figure of the *flâneur*, the stroller, the imbiber of the spectacle of the nineteenth century modern city was in some ways a role model for something which became more extensive and permeated into contemporary cultures: the revolutionary *touristic* experience of hanging out in the modern city, but there is more. Take for example the nation and the birth of nationalism everywhere. In the next chapter I will try to build connections between tourism and nationalism that take us away from the need to view tourism as a reaction to the negative experience of modernity but instead to link it to the most positive and exciting experience of modernism. Nation-building was a major project of modernity and nationalism – possibly one of the most pervasive and exhilarating experiences of it. As we will see, nation formation and nationalism not only gave rise to the conditions necessary for an interest in the world wider than our own locality, but created most of the original touristic shrines and the incentives to visit them, rather like pilgrims occupied in devotions before religious icons.

In the next chapter the relationship between nation, nationalism and tourism will be explored in more detail.

Further Reading

Campbell, C. (1995) *The Romantic Ethic and the Spirit of Consumerism*. Oxford: Basil Blackwell.

MacCannell, D. (1976) *The Tourist: A New Theory of the Leisure Class*. New York: Schocken.

Rojek, C. (1993) *Ways of Escape*. London: Routledge.

Urry, J. (1990) *The Tourist Gaze*. London: Sage.

Withey, L. (1997) *Grand Tours and Cook's Tours: A History of Leisure Travel, 1750 to 1915*. Berkeley, CA: University of California Press.

3

The foundations and traces of modern tourism

Summary

- Tourism and nation
- The traces of tourism
- Communitas
- Places of significance and return
- Commodification and cultural reproduction
- Natural attachments

In this chapter we turn away from explanations of tourism behaviour and consider further the origins and traces of tourism. It will be argued that tourism is not a decorative and superficial activity or even a compensatory activity for the ills of capitalism or modernism. Instead it relates centrally to modernity in a number of dimensions: politically, morally, technologically, and economically. However, as we will see in considering its intimate relationship to nation formation and nationalism, tourism can be considered one of the new cultural expressions and performances of nation formation. Prior to nation formation most people's lives were tied up in their immediate locality, with their land or trade, with their kinsmen and neighbours. Certainly there was travel, a great deal of it for various reasons, but for most of the time the spaces of relevance were essentially local. With nation formation a world beyond the locality was opened up and made relevant and compelling.

Just as tourism is socially and culturally central to modern life and not an escape from it, so too are its consequences or traces as I call them here.

There are a large number of traces that tourism leaves but in this chapter I want to consider tourism's effects on multiculturalism, ethnic interrelations and more generally the relationships between strangers that it disturbs. Next I want to consider what I call places of significance and return because contrary to the impression one obtains from many tourism texts, a large proportion of travel is not to new and different places, but the regular return to a place of familiarity. This sets up a different sort of relationship between tourists and the places they visit: not here today, gone tomorrow, but a more layered, enduring and meaningful sort of relationship – of various sorts. Again this observation speaks to those theories that see tourism as *essentially* travel from and stays away from home: this form of tourism establishes a home from home, a very different thing, requiring a different kind of explanation. The third example of touristic tracing concerns tourist objects, namely those that are made for tourists by locals. We will briefly see that these are nothing like the ephemeral and superficial objects often attributed to tourists' souvenirs. We will see that they have an important social life of their own, with some surprisingly important effects for the people who make them. Finally, I will consider the traces that remain from the very significant touristic pilgrimage to nature. Is it all destructive, unsustainable and disturbing as the pessimists have it or are there more positive traces? I will argue that nature is in many ways only made available and significant to us by spending time with it and getting to know it. Paradoxically then, it may be very important for conservational organisations to make sure that sufficient numbers do establish a relationship with nature and will defend it politically against spurious and damaging forms of development. My point here is that tourists are the potential saviours of nature, not, inevitably its enemy.

Tourism and nation

Modernity and modernisation entailed first of all the emergence of a world of nation states. These came together during the life of Thomas Cook, mainly in the nineteenth century. According to Gellner (1983), James (1996) and others, the nation states were not based upon primordial or ancient social ties but upon entirely new ones, organised by new institutions of learning and culture and made possible by transformations in transport and communications. The institutions and personnel who maintained high culture (universities, monasteries and so on) in agrarian states were authoritative, holding some influence over, or supporting the centralised state, but they were autonomous and separate, and remained 'mysterious' and 'inaccessible'. At this stage, high culture espoused literacy, over-arching philosophical, scientific and moral concerns and spatially extended forms of communication. These contrasted with the parochial nature of many spatially scattered, sedentary, and illiterate 'low' cultures associated with village and region. However, with industrialisation this separation was to disappear, opening up the possibility of the spread and homogenisation of high culture. The massive task of maintaining and providing this institutional homogenisation – through national educational and communication systems – could now only be achieved through collaboration with 'political support and underpinning' and 'its only effective keeper and protector' could be the state. In this way large areas of formerly separated people became bound together by a commonality of culture and order. But the idea of creating a nation in this way preceded its emergence: 'It is nationalism that engenders nations and not the other way round' (Gellner, 1983: 55).

According to Gellner then, the necessary collaboration between the institutions of high culture and state produced a territorially and culturally defined discourse of nation. National interests and discourses framed the work of scholars, teachers, writers and artists, and they, in turn, tend to produce nationalised knowledges. These might include *for the first time* (national) natural histories, histories of a nation's 'people' (especially the notion of folklore as an authentic cultural expression of national legitimacy), cultural and scientific traditions such as music, theatre, architecture, engineering and industry. Nation formation or nationalism produced great enthusiasms for nationalism among the newly unified peoples as we know, but these enthusiasms drew people away from their home and village and towards the objects that these new discourses of nation named, the new spectacles of nation such as the new great capital cities; and the nineteenth century Exhibitions designed to showcase national industry and art; new national parks to showcase national natures and geographies; the new national monuments to symbolise their national achievements (the Eiffel Tower, the Statue of Liberty, Nelson's Column); new museums to house a nation's historical objects and/or its imperial collections and showcase its international power and influence. In a powerful way then, nations and nationalisms determined in so many ways what was relevant, what was interesting, what was exciting in the modern age. Through nationalism its special places and objects spoke directly to those who visited them and in this sense they were powerful sacred objects. Further, such experiences of selfhood as nationhood could be reproduced many times and indeed mobilised for other social corporations – real and imagined – based on region, ethnicity, city or sports teams.

The railways were what made nations possible and the railways opened up a life beyond the home and village for almost everyone in modern national states. Here you see tourism created in the same moment as modernity, not as a later compensation for it. This is a critical point. Even before the dawn of the twentieth century most villages in Europe were not far from a railway line and railway lines connected most European nation states with regular steam ship connections across bodies of water. The spirit of nationalism entailed a feeling of belonging to a bigger unity than

Figure 3.1 *Nelson's Column*, Trafalgar Square, London. Source: Ian Britton

the locality and although localities would continue to be important in most people's lives, modernisation and nation formation began to under- mine their significance and character very early on. And it is in the context of the creation of this greater sense of belonging that we have to situate tourism – always.

Nationalism and modernism undermined the contrast between the world of the everyday and a world beyond. To begin with, nation building and modernisation entailed standardisation. It took quite a while to standardise railway gauges between companies and regions initially but it was an inevitable next step. National education programmes standardised what people knew; national markets standardised what people wore, ate, traded and shopped for. Second, information about the world beyond became available though new medias, especially municipal libraries, newspapers and by 1920, radio. National radio stations have had a particularly long and successful history and even in the face of so much media competition, national radio audiences are still robust. Increasingly then, it became possible to know about places in advance of travelling to them. Third, people began to travel more, not just in formal tourist modes but also at weekends and national holidays, for work and to migrate. Again, what was their world now? Where did it begin and end? It was the extent of world markets, the network of global societies and cultures; it was all the way to the end of the line. So tourism was not 'getting away from it all', at all; it was getting to it all, and that was what made it exciting. The origins of camping are interesting in this context. Have you ever asked yourself where *camping* came from?

The early twentieth century established various orientations to the consumption of 'nature'. Romanticism launched nature tourism in new national parks, in wilderness areas, and in activities like alpinism and walking. Other influences, however, include the allures and adventures of colonial living, often perceived to be a cheek-by-jowl existence with exotic, dangerous or at least primitive natures and primordial cultures. The adventurer, explorer, pioneer, prospector etc. dominated occupations in the colonies, in the popular imagination, and colonial histories were punctuated with gold rushes, land subdivisions, discoveries and conquests. Such activities generated a dramatic new demand for a new technology for living in temporary and ephemeral locations, and it gave rise to the somewhat paradoxical leisure aesthetic that came to be called 'camping' (Ward and Hardy, 1986: 1–7). Ward and Hardy show how popular nineteenth century magazines idealised and lavishly illustrated the outdoor living of the colonial adventurer, and these heroic 'types' were keenly received by a British readership. The new camping technologies were ultimately offered, very tentatively at first, to small bands of brave holidaymakers who forsook the comfort of the coastal hotel for a field in a damp corner of Wales. Ward and Hardy identified the first business to offer a commercial, touristic camping experience, and somewhat improbably, it became a fashionable and popular diversion. Although a cow pasture on some windy coastal hinterland was hardly the veldt, outback or steaming jungle, the new technologies placed the campers on the same rustic, basic footing, and these primitive conditions seemed also to call forth a primitive mentality and communitas. Initially, camping involved much organised collective 'camp' activity, sports, fireside singing, joint meal preparation, learning craft skills. It also gave rise to a form of improving youth leisures, that could be justified as training in the sorts of skills and experiences appropriate to colonial/military nations: Scouting and Guiding, Brownies, Cubs and Woodcraft folk. While the Romantics established a thoroughgoing antimodernist discourse among educated circles, the acceptance of modernity, of progress, technological advance, new synthetic materials, products and medicines was widespread. States of pathology caused by modernity, for example, cooped-up bodies (that were genetically predisposed for a ranging, hunting and gathering existence) in metropolitan offices, schools and factories, were acknowledged but dealt with through regular immersions in nature:

> the camps are the principal events of the [Woodcraft folk] movement . . . for camp life combines the general romance of the movement with the material delight of sleeping in tents, of making fires, bathing in sun and water, tramping over the hills, and singing around the fire. The leisure-time group becomes for a little while, the full-time tribe with its own laws, practices and traditions. (Paul, 1938: 15)

So the argument I am making here is that tourism and travel were always tied into modernity, and that modern cultures were necessarily mobile and inquisitive cultures. They were either poking around the planet, seeking to pull the world into the modern orbit or in the case of camping, parodying it in a 'useful' manner. It is a nonsense to imagine tourism as an escape from modern ways of life when it is *par excellence* the way of modern life. For a very long time now the day-to-day life of most individuals has been integrally tied up with national and international life. Even if we want to construct other people's lives as dreary and hard it is scarcely possible for anyone to participate in modern cultures without knowing and participating in events and processes that go on elsewhere. Take soccer if you like. In the last World Cup and European Cup events the TV audience was among the largest ever recorded. These days, soccer interest embraces both home national leagues and the domestic leagues of other nations as well as international competitions themselves. It involves much international travel to see games. I am writing these lines in Oslo, Norway. Every Thursday, local travel companies dispatch hundreds of Oslovians to England to watch their favourite Premier League club play in England. This sizeable phenomenon occupies a large proportion of international flights out of Oslo on Thursdays in the English soccer season. The TV soccer events such as *Euro '98* were annotated with segments showing in a touristic manner, the significance of the city and region in which different games are played. Events to do with warfare, market activity, union politics, labour market changes, commodity prices and so forth all provide the stimuli to take a specific interest in the lives and affairs of others. War zones now provide a new source of interest for travellers, and a specialised tourism now places tourists within earshot and sight of battlefields.

Nationalism made an entire world beyond the village relevant to individuals and provided the means of understanding what it was, where it was and how to get to it. Not surprisingly then, nation states and dominant companies within them encouraged travel and tourism; it was part of a package of approved leisures. Of course, the capitalist world relied on mobility, movement, and change. Paid holidays and national holidays became a part of national modern life. In short, tourism must be seen as participating in modern life not escaping from it. In visiting the shrines and foundational places of modern nation states the modern tourist performs an affirmation of national identity and citizenship. These types of site tended to proliferate as nation states became more complex and layered social formations, forever reinventing themselves through wars, exhibitions, anniversaries and other celebrations, heroes and champions, achievements, sporting victories and so on. Indeed some of the first and most enduring holidays were *national* holidays, gifts to the citizens and a celebration of who they (now) were. The attacks on New York and Washington of September 2001 currently fill the TV screens and radio. It is all very sad, the entire world watches in horror and disbelief. However much we need to understand these events in their global contexts, it is also undeniably a moment of *national* importance in the USA. One saw young men wearing the star and stripes as head scarves, small flags spontaneously came on sale in the streets of New York and elsewhere; people took to wearing small flags on their backs. *Ground Zero*, the space occupied by the Twin Towers of the World Trade Center, will become a national monument visited by millions. Its website already has.

National natures as enshrined in national parks become literally *national* treasures, of national importance. To be concerned about national natures is to be concerned about the nation; and membership of organisations such as the UK National Trust, that combine this concern with the preservation of buildings of national significance, defines what it is to be a proper citizen. I am not convinced by the globalisation thesis that nation states are withering away. At least, one should have no doubts about their meaningfulness to civil societies. Nationalism is also very obviously a central component of international tourism. Not only does one's own sense of national identity presuppose the existence of and interest in others, but also the language of nationalism enables tourists to navigate in other places and find significance. Modernist universal values have always valued internationalism, finding common ground, modes of communication that straddle national, cultural, ethnic and linguistic differences. This is a profoundly important component of international tourism. It is quite explicit in the international business and conference trade of course, but it is implicitly a part of international tourism culture. It is quite obvious when one thinks about the manifestly *national* imagery projected to tourists. Although travel *savants* will scoff and roll their eyes, I think the projection of nation in the airport retail boutiques and souvenir shops, and in the general content of activities and sights offered to tourists conforms to the logic of inter-nationalism: one literally buys into a different national culture by learning and visiting what it takes to be the important historical, natural and cultural icons of a nation. A great bulk of this material is actually bought by or for young people, or perhaps for those who have not travelled widely. I suspect that the travel *savants* passed through such shops in the distant past with just as much glee and in fact trade amongst themselves in what they take to be a more sophisticated and refined knowledge – knowledge of a national wine list perhaps, a national cuisine or art, but it amounts to a very similar thing. However, as Lury (1997: 86) points out, tourist objects *and* non-tourist objects are increasingly marketed using national imagery; she quotes Papadopoulos and Heslop (1993) who argue that 'thousands of companies use country identifiers as part of their marketing strategy and hundreds of researchers have studied the ways in which these identifiers influence behaviour. As markets become more international, the more prominently the origin of products will figure in sellers' and buyers' decisions.'

Think also about the international organisations that facilitate so much international tourism. Think about the international liaison and exchanges between schools and universities. Think about the international sporting organisations and the international sporting competitions. Think about the international twinning schemes that link specific towns in an open-ended relationship of exchange visits. Think about the links between religious organisations that span continents if not the globe. Common to most if not all of these and others is an emphasis on communication, bridging differences; taking an interest in and forming an understanding of the lives and cultures of others. Thus to isolate the different and the unusual as the basis for an abstract pleasurability in tourism is not to miss the point completely but it is to miss an important and serious basis and consequence. Tourism is a product of modernism and nationalism and it is part of the creation of over-arching, linking and communicating themes. Learning a language ahead of travel to where it is used or even learning a smattering for basic transactions is to seek translation and equivalence, not simply the thrill of difference.

In this way tourism leaves a thick trail of significance and consequence behind it. However, most theoretical accounts of tourism tend to view it as a fleeting, restless experience; collecting significances and moving on quickly to yet more thrilling difference and oddity. However, the foundations upon which tourism is built consist of more solid traces and establish a wide range of relationships between people, between people and places, cultures and natures. As part of taking tourism more *seriously*, we might now investigate some of these foundational traces.

The traces of tourism

A cigarette that bears a lipstick's traces, An airline ticket to romantic places, And still my heart has wings –
These foolish things remind me of you

According to many accounts of tourism its rather shallow course leaves very few traces of great consequence or moment. According to Urry the tourist 'gaze' is the central moment of tourism and that is a characteristically fleeting event in what is generally described as a restless activity. Moments of intense anticipation and excitement prior to the gaze melt away to boredom and an anxiety to be away. Tourists do, of course, collect and value souvenirs and they enter into a domestic economy of no small significance. According to my perspective, however, tourism leaves profound and important traces on the world and these should provide the basis for a more robust, expanded study of tourism. To date, however, accounts of their longer-term impact have been one-sided. Many books in recent years have been concerned about the *damage* tourism causes to the spaces it passes over but few have reflected on its wider value and social consequences. We often see studies of the negative consequences of tourism for the people who live in and around touristic places. The essay by Peck and Lepie (1989) reminds us that tourism has consequences on land and property prices; and where competition for those resources is among wealthy overseas businesses their activity can place land and dwellings beyond the pocket of local people. In addition, tourism industries that enter a hitherto depressed or undeveloped economy can rapidly become politically powerful as it gradually becomes the principal source of income and wealth. Reiko (1991) shows how the political interests of overseas-owned companies can be placed before the political agendas of local people. Tourism has also been cast as a blight on the moral and physical well being of a community. Seabrooke (1996) has argued that the history of tourism in South-east Asia has encouraged the development of a variety of sex-related tourisms that lead to a variety of ills: child prostitution; child slavery; the spread of Aids and other diseases; the importation and use of dangerous drugs; the disruption of family and community life. It has also been argued that tourism undermines local cultures by introducing a different entertainment-orientated economy in which local religion, economic activity, sexuality, local social relations and art are trivialised by front staged displays, by the 'trinketisation' of material artefacture and by the selective use of cultural forms acceptable to foreign visitors (see Ewins, 1999; 2002 for a good discussion of this). Tourism can also disrupt local economies and create problems for local agriculturalists such as the shortage of labour for planting and harvests, or some activities can even be deemed 'unsightly' and be removed from areas where they were an integral part of local community life. Wilson, in his description of the building of the Blue Ridge Parkway in the USA during the 1930s and 40s, gives a good example of this. The grand design of these touristic routes that opened up vast forest areas to tourist visitors, but also outdoor recreation and camping, was to produce an edifying visual spectacle. Roads were designed so as to maximise the visual impact of mountain and forest views and panoramas. Bends were carefully placed to provide sudden and dramatic changes in landscape. Trees and shrubs were rendered uniform (indigenous only) and landscaped around the roads and parking areas. There was a certain purity and simplicity in the design that met with one principal snag: relatively poor, ragged and scruffy hillbilly farmers throughout the area produced a discordant 'other'. Their tumbledown farms with rusty outbuildings and piles of broken farm equipment; their unpicturesque fields of mixed animals and their general poverty and antipathy to strangers was not tolerated and they were removed. Of course, in typical fashion the selective use of local culture by the tourist industry replaced them in the landscape in a controlled and sanitised mode: bands of hillbilly musicians and dancers entertained tourists at regional tourist centres and cleaned up rustic farm produce was sold in gingham-frilled 'olde stores' (see Wilson, 1992: 36–7).

Of course one of the principal accusations in recent years has been that tourism has become an environmental hazard. Uncontrolled access by tourists to areas of natural importance has been identified in many studies as undesirable. Tourists disturb environments and therefore disrupt natural breeding, migration and feeding patterns among threatened species. Further, large numbers of tourists bring into fragile environments many forms of pollution and environmental degradation: tourists generate the needs for chemical sanitation agents; they can create sewerage dispersal problems; vehicle use brings noise, pollution and traffic hazards to wildlife. The so-called environmentally friendly form of nature tourism, eco-tourism, has been accused of being unsustainable as even walkers and trekkers leave long-term and damaging traces of their travel. Along the famous Overland Track in the wilds of Tasmania the large numbers of walkers bring erosion, faecal and other pollutions, as well as a major disturbance factor. In addition their presence has contaminated local water supplies creating sickness for themselves as well as other wildlife. Other fragile eco-systems attractive to tourists are prone to other less visible forms of damage: some grasses are highly sensitive to walking; some beach nesting birds' breeding sites have been effectively destroyed by regular walking tracks; beachcombing itself disturbs the valuable foods and shelter that some species rely upon.

The tension between an allegedly declining natural world and the desire to see and experience it has resulted in the figure of the tourist being framed as an environmental danger. New ways of controlling access, behaviour and impacts have been at the forefront of much recent research, but recently evaluations of eco-tourism cast question marks over its claims for 'sustainability'. These fears have been exacerbated by pressures from governments to secure clean green industries through tourist development in natural areas. As a result, tourism continues to be considered an environmental bad. New roads and developments to open up forests for tourism are as likely to attract protest and the mobilisation of direct action against them as they are tourism development. Since there is now a considerable literature on many of these concerns I will not reproduce all of their arguments but refer you to key specialist texts such as France (1997); Mowforth and Munt (1998); Hall and Lew (1998); Wall (1999).

While many or all of the above examples make a case for the problematic nature of tourism they should not be seen in isolation from many other examples that indicate the longer-term benefits of tourism, and they are many, potentially. We will now turn to some of the more positive traces of tourism: tourism produces a unique form of social bond between fellow travellers called communitas; equally, many tourists have stable and long-term relationships with particular places and are less easy to cast as indifferent outsiders; tourism has also had beneficial *unintended consequences*, on indigenous cultures and even 'nature'. We will look at each of these in turn.

Communitas

The word communitas is widely used to describe a unique social bond between strangers who happen to have in common the fact that they are in some way travelling or 'on holiday' together. The term communitas comes from the anthropological analysis of ritual activities and many have argued that tourism contains a similarly *ritual* component of behaviour. Typically human rituals are *like* a journey in that they have a beginning a middle and an end and take place away from the spaces of the everyday, usually at sacred sites of one kind or another. During rituals of passage (weddings, funerals, puberty rituals, initiations etc.) one or a number of individuals travel the path from one life-stage and status to another but they usually have with them a congregation of 'fellow travellers', those invited or required to attend this important transition. Human rituals of passage typically take place over several days and mark out a considerable period away from everyday life. It's a sort of in-between or liminal time zone and space and the congregation are cut off from their own personal circles and stranded, as it were, with their ritual travellers. Such rituals are also marked by their performative characteristics, there is a lot of song, dance, drug-taking, heavy drinking and sexual licence associated with them, and a generalised state of excitement and anticipation exists between the assembly. These performative characteristics bring participants into close and intense interactions and, as a result, they are temporarily but very significantly bonded. Turner and Turner (1978) extended this analysis to Christian pilgrimage in Europe, and they argue that communitas is a generalised state of friendliness and closeness experienced by those travelling the road together, as often as not forming into temporary groups. Chaucer's *The Canterbury Tales* begins as a dialogue between one such group that had already formed up on the southern outskirts of London in readiness for their pilgrimage together to the sacred site of Thomas Becket's shrine at Canterbury. *The Canterbury Tales* is the result of their agreeing to a competition among themselves to entertain each other with lively and pithy accounts of their lives, an opening up to strangers that would not normally occur so easily or spontaneously. However, it is quite easy to analyse more modern forms of travel and tourism in this way. Take for example the ritual life of a cruise ship.

One may make friends very easily on board cruise ships, indeed one is expected to. One may be predisposed to want to meet fellow passengers, or indeed one may feel obliged to be sociable and affable with everyone. Various cultural forms engender communitas: to stay with the cruise ship example, there is the culture of communal dining as opposed to dining at private tables as one would normally do in a restaurant. To this is added the special treat of dining at the captain's table. In addition there are activities that encourage generalised sociability. Ship's sporting competitions, dances, receptions and parties aim in part to bond a ship's company in multiplex ways. Then there are specific sub-rituals within the overall ritual of 'the cruise': famously of course the initiation/baptism into the cult of Neptune upon crossing the equator. Touristic communitas has been identified at all levels of tourism, however. Take for example the seaside holidays of the 1950s, when workers from industrial and commercial centres flocked to crowded beaches all around the western world. Relations of communitas were documented in great detail by the Mass Observation exercise conducted at the seaside at Blackpool. Further south, in Graham Greene's novel *Brighton Rock* the opening scene shows how freely and easily strangers in the pubs and cafés intermingled. It was a scene that Greene, a seafront resident of Brighton knew only too well.

Similarly, among contemporary backpackers there is a code of friendliness and cooperation on the road, there are backpacker hostels where groups can form and splinter and from which groups can set out, rather like Chaucer's pilgrims at the Tabard Inn, on an adventure into the unknown.

Obviously, the benefit of this openness can be measured against the relatively closed manner of interaction in normal everyday life. Think, for example, about being on public transport, say the London underground or the New York subway. Here one conforms very easily to the norm of social avoidance. So, tourism permits a looser and friendlier bond of friendship to exist between individuals, and for precisely this reason, holidays are notoriously associated with making friends and romantic experiences. While these are of inestimable value in themselves, they may be considered less significant than the role tourism plays in reducing the fears and distrust that exist between people from different cultures, between the tourist and the host culture.

Again, many studies to date have shown the problems and barriers that tourism creates between visitors and local people. In Smith (1989), for example, Arctic tourism is shown to have been disruptive and antagonistic to the local Inuit people of Nome. Western tourists made unwelcome comments and asked impertinent questions of local women attempting to butcher seals for example. On the other hand, in some other parts of the world tourists themselves become victims to predatory locals. As a result of handbag snatching in Rome and Barcelona or assaults on backpackers in Australia, tourists have also found ways to place barriers between themselves and locals. Some resorts are now firmly secure from local people and even discourage their guests from wandering off campus. MacCannell's study of ethnotourism shows how the pressure from tourism also creates the opposite of communitas, the erection of barriers to prevent tourists penetrating the everyday spaces of local cultures. Instead they erect stages or front stages with which to perform their cultures at times and places convenient to them. The stage creates a distance and separation at the same time. But again we must ask how generalisable this is. At one level, of course, one can point to this sort of phenomenon all around the world, from Fiji to the Costa del Sol. However, to leave it there is to miss a fundamental point, that these displays are not the only place where tourists meet local people. Indeed, these places may be the easiest place to study the interaction rather than being the typical spaces of interaction. There are various levels of interaction that have potential long-term significance. The first might be simple observation of other ways of life. Other cultures may be scary, hard to understand, aesthetically confusing or distasteful and we may all have been subject to a great deal of racial and cultural vilification or unsympathetic stereotypes. However, tourism puts such claims to very stringent tests. Tourists see very easily how similar other cultures are to their own; indeed the similarities may prove to be the most eye-catching and noteworthy. For example, to see the way every culture values its children is genuinely reassuring. More often than not local people will help tourists who appear lost, in distress or in trouble. If I cast my mind back I can think of many such occasions and one of their characteristics is a generosity of spirit for no apparent gain, other than the rewards that hospitality has always brought. Once I was hitchhiking or backpacking around Turkey with my girlfriend in the late 1970s before Turkey had developed much of a tourist resort industry. Everywhere we went we were taken care of by local people, very concerned that we had no local protection. At various places we were given shelter, a safe haven for camping, food, a party and drinks. When I was travelling in the Sudan once, I was robbed of all my money and my passport at a rooftop bar. A local prostitute took pity on me and helped me to find the police and the British High Commission; she paid my taxi fares and bought me food and drink. She was wasting her own valuable time and there was simply no financial reward possible since I had none to give. I think she was embarrassed about what had happened to me in her country and wanted to show me a better side to their humanity. She did. At another time in the USA, jetlagged from my flight from Australia, I had failed to change my watch as I travelled from LA to Chicago. As a result, in Chicago I missed the last flight out to my destination. O'Hare quickly became deserted and there were suddenly few counters available to assist. However, one person saw I had a problem and stopped to help me; I told her my story. She was black and I was white. She was on her way home and clearly in a hurry but since she worked for the airline I travelled with she saw a way of helping me. She reopened her desk and issued me with an overnight ticket at the Chicago Hilton with a taxi fare and a breakfast voucher. She admitted that passengers do not always know to change their watches and aircrew do not always remind them enough, but basically I had got myself in a jam and she was just being nice. When I checked in again the following morning I realised she had put her neck on the line and got herself in trouble. I immediately wrote a letter thanking the airline for their superb customer service, promising to let my company, friends and family know of their singular standards of care. Hers was an act of kindness that I suspect takes place routinely everywhere between local people and tourists, but they are acts that have a cumulative effect, building trust that didn't exist before and undoing the negative work of prejudice and wilful racism. However, my own anecdotes cannot count for much and more research is needed to investigate the relationship between tourism and racism and other forms of ethnic prejudices and xenophobia – and their opposite. However, there are some indications that tourism does favour a realistic assessment of other cultures. The first indicator, albeit crude, is the emergence of cosmopolitanism in the travelling West. We may say that cosmopolitanism tends to oppose nationalism in many ways, first in that it expresses an open interestedness in other cultures and second in that it favours trans-national relations, organisations, and exchanges. Cosmopolitan development can be indexed to a number of transnational activities such as the proportional increase of international communications, the internationalisation of labour markets and sexual partnering but in a recent paper, Beck (2000) sees international travel and tourism as significant too. In addition, the routinisation of tourism in key world tourist centres has produced relatively peaceful international havens for tourists; spaces where the presence of 'others' is normative. By and large the streets of London, Singapore, Bangkok and Amsterdam are full of a great mix of ethnic and national groups but the benign presence of the tourist coupled with their economic worth tends to produce a relatively peaceful interchange. As ever the boundary between work, domicile and travel is entirely blurred in the multicultural cities. If there is such a thing as the metropolitan mentality and life world, it is one where singular national and ethnic identification and networks do not dominate, but on the contrary it is where they are necessarily hybrid and heterogeneous. Tourism is actively reproducing such a mentality by suggesting that one should take an absorbed interest in the life and cultures of others and that one's life will be the richer for it. Metropolitanism itself is the subject of much introspection and navel gazing; it is associated with voyeurism, subjecting others to a spectatorial gaze, of flitting between places and having no commitment or owning no attachments to place or people. Much of this must be conceded but equally we must be careful to weigh up the positive side of the metropolitan lifestyle. This is predicated primarily on the free and easy possibility of travel and access to the world, but it is not at the same time wishing to conduct this travel in an ethnically sanitised tourist bubble because the metropolitan mentality relishes exposure to otherness. While practitioners of metropolitanism cannot commit to community and local participation they are more open to relationships outside their own ethnic identity. We need to understand the subtle but extensive effects of tourism on the relationships between strangers, if only because, as Bauman (1998b) argues, cities are becoming once again spaces of strangers.

Activity 3.1

It is worthwhile pausing to consider your own experience of communitas while on holiday or travelling.

- Did any of you experience any form of communitas with fellow travellers or with locals? Try to describe these relationships.
- What impression of each other did you take away?
- Have you ever made friends while on holiday? What sort of friendships?
- Have you ever helped or assisted a traveller or tourist in difficulty? What motivated you to provide such help?
- In your own mind does tourism achieve a positive or a negative overall effect on relations between different people and cultures?

Places of significance and return

The tourism literature tends to place great emphasis on tourism as a restless, fleeting and spectacular experience. As we have seen, the most influential theories that became general theories of tourism both tend towards this view. MacCannell's (1976) view is that tourists seek authentic experiences since the normative aspects of their lives are felt to be superficial, artificial or contrived. This takes them away from their life world and sets them on a course of visiting the true and authentic coordinates of humanity. In Urry's view the sights of tourists are set much lower and can be set simply on the unusual and the different. Both sorts of account tend to emphasise critical high points of touristic experience as the culmination of the travel. For MacCannell it is sitting and experiencing the performances of authentic cultures. These are typically displays or performances and are not lasting or enduring episodes, because for most of the time the authentic others need to protect themselves from the tourist gaze. For Urry it is reaching and gazing upon a specific tourist site, an object, view or spectacle, and once seen, the act of consumption is quickly over. As Urry suggests, such episodes are fleeting and produce a restless urge to proceed to the next one on the itinerary. Indeed, the site's attractiveness is based upon its difference and its unusual qualities and tourism becomes a kind of collecting behaviour. Although these theories suggest that tourists place great significance and importance on the objects of their travel, they do not suggest that they place much value in returning to see them again, indeed one tends to assume that such repetitive actions were almost the opposite of tourism, by their accounts of them. And yet, there is substantial evidence to show that repetition is a well-established phenomenon and that what many tourists seem to enjoy is the return to the familiar. In other words, tourism can produce such powerful aesthetic responses to certain places that a return outweighs the excitement of a new voyage. Indeed, there is some considerable evidence to show some tourists entertain the dream of return to a place to live for some or all of their time, and that some places become a mix of new tourists, return tourists, temporary long stay visitors, season visitors and expatriate migrants. Reviewing a new biography of Penelope Lively, Claudia FitzHerbert (2001) reminds us that 'there is nothing new in the English countryside being populated by metropolitan holidaymakers returning to put down roots'. More recently the combined effect of forty years of cheap overseas holidaymaking has turned some places in Europe into little Englands. Such a place is the Costa del Sol, on the southern coast of Spain. O'Reilly (2000) shows how the Costa del Sol has been transformed by British tourism to the region since the 1950s. Spain captured the imagination of the post-war British upper classes, writers, artists, authors, retired diplomats and officials and some of the earliest visitors settled there more or less permanently. Spain and the Mediterranean region generally were very powerful icons of British modernism, despite the illusion that what people found attractive there was the peasant lifestyle, diet and habitus. These and later visitors did not see the Spanish peasant life as attractive for them or as an attractive alternative to modernity. Rather, the idea of a warm, dry, climate, new and varied diets, a brightly lit landscape and the aesthetic of modern Spanish art and architecture were seen as additive to and a relief from the rather dismal drizzle soaked post-war modernity of Britain. Spain could literally brighten the austere grimness of Britain, transform it and inspire it. This was not simply an observation made by the privileged few. The Mediterranean aesthetic became somewhat ironically the icon of British modernism. Of course the architectural influence arrived earlier as a result of the popularity of the Mediterranean in the early part of the twentieth century. A good example of this is the widespread building of public swimming pools:

> A feature of many of the new European parks of the 1920s and 1930s was the lido – the open-air swimming pool. The word 'lido' was borrowed from the Italian word for coastline, but made famous by the reputation of the Venice Lido, and so the lido became the city's beach. (Worpole, 2000: 113)

After World War II this aesthetic became widely and routinely drawn into modernising fashions and interiors. So for example, 1950s and early 1960s wallpapers, curtain fabrics, dinner sets and furniture represented this Mediterranean other. One thinks of 1950s salad sets and salad trays

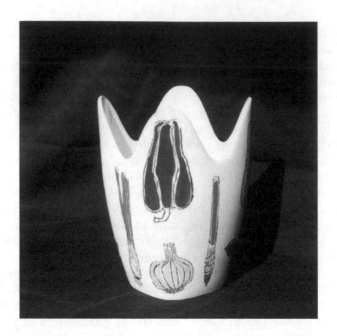

Figure 3.2 *Salad Ware* by Terence Conran (c.1956) for Midwinter Pottery. Source: Adrian Franklin

featuring the exotic vegetables and fruits of the region: garlic, peppers, gourds, artichokes, capers and chillis. One thinks of the dinnerwares of the period with their bright colours and romantic coastal village landscapes. Sir Hugh Casson, for example, designed a picturesque series of tablewares for Midwinter pottery entitled 'Riviera'; the young Terence Conran designed a saladware series, also for Midwinter, called *Salad Ware*.

In these ways the Mediterranean was used to brighten up and add colour to the post-war British home. During the 1960s it became possible for ordinary Britons to take holidays in Spain for the first time. Increased real incomes and leisure time combined with innovations in the packaging and selling of overseas holidays and the challenge to monopolists' airfare prices by companies such as Laker Airways produced a mass market for package holidays to Spain. Worldwide foreign holidays grew from 25 million in 1950 to 330 million in 1989 (O'Reilly, 2000: 31). In just five years British tour operation 'developed into a competent mass industry that was able to offer entire holidays for less than the cost of a scheduled flight'. As a week's holiday in Spain became affordable for almost every Briton, Mediterranean lifestyle became an added possibility for European modernism, and not just a household decorative dream. As O'Reilly (2000: 32) argues, 'during this period a holiday abroad joined consumer society's demand for the good life, along with the car and the television'.

Spain and other places like it had an additive quality; it became a part of what modern life could be; it was added to the growing scope of

Figure 3.3   *Riviera* by Sir Hugh Casson for Midwinter Pottery (1950s). Source: Adrian Franklin

consumerism. The Mediterranean and other places could be thought of as playgrounds, leisure zones that might be the chosen setting for leisure time. The structure of the industry and the nature of demand created an uneven geography of European consumption of the new leisure spaces. Through its specific mix of package holiday companies, Britain dominated certain stretches of coast and certain towns and village clusters, while Germany and France and Scandinavia favoured others. It meant that the experience of Spain was also in a sense a non-colonial extension of Britain, and indeed, it was not long before some Britons established their own businesses, hotels, bars or holiday homes. This ancillary ring of British businesses and presence created the conditions for a labour market for British workers and gradually a British community developed consisting of a range of migratory types, from extended stays and seasonal workers and residents to the long term business investors and retirees. O'Reilly's analysis of the town of Fuengirola on the Costa del Sol shows that approximately two-thirds of the British community had become full residents while a fifth were returning residents and a further fifteen percent were peripatetic and seasonal visitors.

These sorts of relationships and communities are not restricted to Britain or to Spain. In an earlier era many Londoners typically took their holidays in Kent (and working class London families enjoyed working holidays in the Kentish hop fields, returning each year to their own host farm), and in the post-war period large numbers of bungalows were built by retiring Londoners, so that they could live out the rest of their lives in those remembered spaces of their romances, their childhoods or the happy days of their family weeks away. The middle classes of the home counties of Britain have long dominated the Devonshire cottage industry while Lancashire developed a similar relationship with north Wales. Peck and Lepie (1989) document a similar relationship between the big cities of the East coast of the USA and coastal towns of North Carolina.

However, it is not always clear that the relationship between these paired places is one of colonisation by the affluent metropolitans. Parisians form a dominant group who regularly visit the Cantal, but it would be a mistake to assume that there was an asymmetric relationship between the two areas. As Abram (1997: 32) has found, this relationship is often more complex: 'although tourism is often seen as a meeting of them and us, as a replaying of the colonial encounter, such a simplistic stereotype breaks down upon closer inspection of the intra-national or intra-European tourism'.

> Hence the majority of visitors to the Cantal are French people, many of whom have an ancestral link (and often an associated ownership of property) to the region, and this has coloured the way tourism has developed according to particular themes. Many of the visitors to the Cantal are still either migrants from the region or their descendants. (Abram, 1997: 32)

Such was the demographic disruption of the nineteenth and twentieth centuries that one must imagine that many more such pairings owe their origins to returning natives. Even where the precise migratory bonds may have been forgotten, it is likely that such return visits develop their own aesthetic following in particular places. The sociology of these paired places is very interesting but also of interest is the establishment of networks of individuals and families – children as much as adults – that build up around shared leisure time and spaces. We know very little about these informal and fleeting arrangements but they are clearly highly valued. What is certain is that they play off familiarity and belonging and entail a sedentary, slow form of tourism in comparison with the form most often analysed in tourist studies.

In other parts of the world we can note similar, if not exact, replications of these types of vacation arrangement. In Scandinavia, for example, there has been a longstanding biannual migration – not between paired sets of human spaces but between human settlements and the wilderness and mountain areas of the interior and West coast. During the summer and again during the winter season, the 50 per cent of the population who have access to wooden cabins spend a considerable amount of time in these primitive living arrangements and natural conditions (Hylland

Eriksen, 2001: 157–158). These visits can become familial concentrations or decentralisations but their regularity ensures that they produce semi-permanent local communities at different times of the year, and as we shall see in a section below, they also leave important traces in terms of ties to natural areas, wildlife and forest.

In Australia and New Zealand a similar migration takes place to, respectively, shacks and bothies. These are something of a cross between the British pattern and the Norwegian. Like the Norwegian *hytta*, *shacks* (Australia) and *bothies* (New Zealand), are typically built up along non-settled coastlines or in the mountains. In Tasmania they can be found all along the East coast and in the highlands and as with Norway, they are very well used on those occasions when a family or an individual can get away. Like the British examples, however, they have also become permanent settlements in some places or places of permanent or semi-retirement. Like British coastal retirement communities, such an influx changes the nature of the area, both sociologically and politically. In such areas, for example, the new residents may oppose traditional farming and rural sports in favour of modern leisure activities such as walking, bird watching and the like. In sum, places of significance and return seem to confound most theories of tourism since they seem to establish a home from home, rather than the excitement of being *away* from the familiar. It is the familiar that forms the attraction, either because these have social ties created by migration or because such places conjure places of sentimentality and memory or because, in the case of returns to remote cabins, familiarity with natural areas provides a better experience of them ('knowing where things are', complex ski or walking routes, good fishing and hunting, berry and mushroom spots and so forth) and a better 'back to nature' experience than flitting from one natural area to another. As the global population becomes ever more concentrated in large cities, we might expect places of significance and return to become more prominent than they already are. In Norway and Sweden, for example, many of the existing huts are in areas where their current owners' descendants had a special relationship, often with a local landholding. In England, the southern villages have lost much of their labour markets to mechanised farming and increasingly their cottages are becoming weekenders or retirement homes for city dwellers. If Hylland Eriksen (2001) is right, the appeal of such places of significance and return relates to the need to find places of 'slow time'. Whereas the more typical holiday may be just as fast paced and hectic as everyday life, where 'the tyranny of the moment' is just as dominated by the speeding up of time and the filling of every moment with more activity and connection, the cabin in the mountain or on the coast provides a disconnection from 'fast time', a chance to slow down, to take one's time, to take the watch off. I will return to this theme in Chapter 8; however, for now we might say that Hylland Eriksen's thesis provides an interesting new angle on tourism theory because what he appears to be arguing is that ordinary everyday life has become too exciting, too full, too relentless; that people are fragmented by their very accessibility and their own access to a wider world. This instantaneous world of accessibility could be considered the ultimate cultural expression of a touristic world, a world where, as Bauman (1998b) argues, 'distance does not seem to matter much'. Perhaps, what we are seeing in this new search for 'slow time' is the need to find a refuge from a touristic world?

Activity 3.2

As an exercise it might be worth considering this issue as a research or project question. It would be useful to investigate whether people do return to their summer cottages, cabins, *hytta* or rented apartments for the reasons considered above. To what extent do these sorts of places facilitate bathing in the luxuriously rare 'slow time'? And to what extent do these summer migrants make social and natural roots in these places? Some of you may be able to investigate the historical dimensions, how specific places and people get twinned with places of significance and return.

Commodification and cultural reproduction

Some anthropological studies (see Greenwood, 1989; Crain, 1996) join the sociological refrain that there is something culturally damaging or reductive about modern tourism. In these views the shallowness and ephemerality of tourism are made to contrast with the historical strength and depth of local cultures. When tourism arrives, so the account goes, rich and complex cultures are reduced to simplistic, easy-to-consume-in-a-hurry forms. This is evidenced by the so-called front stage performances of dance and music, specially prepared and performed out of context for the convenience and entertainment of tourists (as opposed to performing a real and useful function for the local community). It is also evident in the tawdry reduction of local material artefacture and crafts to the tourist souvenir shop wares – shops that literally sell 'culture by the pound' (see Greenwood, 1989). Such tourist wares are often specially contrived to be small and convenient for the tourist. Ewins (1999) describes how *tapa* or bark cloth that was traditionally the clothing material for Fijians has been reduced to small light pieces that airborne tourists can take home. Further, many souvenir cultural artefacts are actually mass manufactured overseas by companies that 'make' for thousands of different local cultures. Again, the implication of all this is that tourism is reducing the world to a set of plastic signifiers that have no social life beyond the decorative exotica and the impact of tourism on the cultures it intrudes on is largely negative or diminishing. All this can be summarised as a process of commodification and the disappearance of authenticity – that mysterious quality that tourists allegedly crave.

However, it is not at all clear that things are this simple. Again it appears as though the traces of tourism are more elaborate, lasting and positive than this account allows for. In the first place, Boissevain argues that the commodification of material cultures for touristic consumption also performs a useful local purpose. Citing a paper by Cohen (1988) he writes 'that by marketing their culture, people (re)discover their own history and traditions and begin to realise their own worth' (Boissevain, 1996: 13).

> The same occurs with heritage parks, festivals and food and handicraft markets. Black's (1996) study shows that in spite of dire predictions and the massive influx of tourists, the inhabitants of Mellieha have retained their integrity. Abram sums up the case for thinking with greater care about cultural commoditisation: 'commoditisation is part of a very positive process by which people are beginning to re-evaluate their history and shake off the shame of peasantry. (Boissevain, 1996: 13)

Similar conclusions seem to have been made by Teague (1997: 185) in respect of Nepalese art, Short (1991: 221–2) in respect of Australian aboriginal art and Howell (1995: 165) in respect of the usefulness of the concept 'authenticity'. Meethan argues that these studies demonstrate that tourism has initiated new cultural forms, not bad cultural forms and their hybrid nature often offers new forms of understanding and negotiation and not simply cultural negation (Meethan, 2001: 109–10). As Thomas (1991: 208) argues, 'the outcomes of liaisons with artefacts cannot be predicted, there is no sense in which both positive ramifications and political damage can always run beyond initial expectations; it is perhaps this instability, historicity, and lack of historical containment that epitomises the entanglement we all have with objects'. Ewins' (1999) work on the production of bark cloth or *tapa* for tourists in Fiji is interesting in this respect. He argues that while all manner of westernisation took place including the substitution of western textiles for bark cloth the fact that *tapa* became a valuable trading commodity with tourists ensured that its production and artwork remained a local skill. As a result, during a period of great threat to indigenous Fijians' sense of identity, *tapa* was on hand to enable what he calls 'an efflorescence of Fijian ritual and exchange'. In short, *tapa* had three social lives: as a pre-contact exchange item, as a tourist souvenir and in postcolonial cultural revival and nationalism.

So, we need to see tourism in its ethnographic presence, in the thick of things (see Pickering, 2000; 2001) constantly being worked into and used by the cultures it comes into contact with and see it as a form of cultural exchange rather than an erosive agent let loose on an otherwise authentic, proper and fragile world. Tourism leaves interesting and important traces on the world that can be liberating, reviving, demythologising and hybridising.

Natural attachments

In this final example of the traces of tourism it will be suggested that tourism contributes to environmentalism and nature conservation by building strong bonds between (typically urban) visitors and natural spaces, and that that occurs as a result of repeat visits to favourite places. As with favourite leisure spaces such as Spain (for the English working class) and Devon (for the English middle classes of the south), natural areas tend to build up a following who return on a consistent basis. This is built into the structure of individual and family ownership of huts and shacks in those countries where they are common, but I will argue that this occurs even in areas that are more lightly visited, as part of a walking holiday, trips to national parks, wildlife tourism or perhaps a few days camping or fishing.

Around most British towns and cities there are natural areas that form favourite picnic areas, courting areas and dog walking circuits. These are quite intensively used and it is for this reason that the major motorway building plans of the 1990s ran into so much local opposition. Often it was local opposition that proved more determined and difficult to deal with than the environmentalists who roamed from one protest to another. These sorts of spaces are the first sort of touristic attachment that one can point to that has political implications for the environment. It was precisely this sort of strong bond that the organisation Common Ground sought to exploit and 'to explore the subjective, imaginative, emotional and spiritual links between people and their local environments' (Macnaghten and Urry, 1998: 56).

> It has sought to counterbalance the scientific with the personal, the rare with the everyday, the spectacular with the ordinary, the global with the local, abstract space with particular places, the general public with people who have complex, ambivalent identities and histories. (Macnaghten and Urry, 1998: 56–7)

Other tourist spaces are further afield and the object of specific weekends or sojourns away from home. Again, Britain and the USA have many such areas that attract repeat visits from their devotees. Some are coastal such as the many areas of coastal footpaths, others are based around the moors and highlands, some are centred on forests such as the Forest of Dean or the New Forest, others favour certain rural counties such as Dorset or the Weald of Kent. The principal manner of visiting these places is on foot. Walking has become a firmly entrenched, slow form of tourism pursued by a growing following (see Shoard,1987; Edensor, 2001; Michael, 2001; and Macnaghten and Urry, 2001). Return visits to the same spaces make sense in terms of the benefits of familiarity as we saw above: one knows where to look, one learns new things from each visit, one watches the nature of the place change and grow, one's appreciation of place is cumulative. Returns make sense as one builds up a knowledge of places over the course of the seasons and different types of seasons, drought years, floods, snow, spectacular wild flower seasons and so on. Repeat visits intensify the experience in these and other ways. Mike Michael (2000: 45–6), for example, describes three repeat visits to the Samaria Gorge in Crete, a place that for him fulfils his desire for the natural sublime. 'It is one of the supposed features of sublime nature that the strength and depth of the sublime experience grows with repeated visits' (Nye, 1994). Walking has given rise to a range of other activities that consolidate the bonds to and appreciation of nature: bird watching is a major one, but also photography, sketching, mushrooming and berry picking, fishing and more muscular activities (climbing, potholing, surfing, canoeing, and so forth). Borrowing from de Certeau's (1984) writing on walking, Macnaghten and Urry discuss the way in which walking (and other activities presumably) is actually constitutive of particular places. De Certeau was referring to the ways in which walking was constitutive of the city in the same way speech acts are of language (Macnaghten and Urry, 1998: 204). In this way we might say that nature is only properly knowable and therefore revealed through various forms of constitutive performances: birds only become properly revealed by observation and regular repeat visits to observe them throughout the changing calendar. The same might be said of rural or wilderness spaces by walkers or climbers, or of rivers and lakes by anglers. These places hardly exist to be defended without their active presence, and in a sense we can extend this presencing to what Ingold has called *dwelling*. In the modern world some places are dwelt in predominantly by consumers as opposed to the more typical presence of producers such as peasants and farmers. Tourism research should ideally be investigating this promising line of inquiry, rather than making the assumption that the goal is to keep humanity as separate and as distant from nature as possible. It may well be, for example, that one of the traces that tourism leaves behind it is a series of knowledges, familiarities and attachments of variable degree and intensity, which *matter* politically. So, for example, in Tasmania during the 1980s, the enormous furore over a proposed dam on the Franklin River became a national and international incident. As a result of a major and intense mobilisation of people the Prime Minister cancelled the project. At the time the success of this mobilisation was couched in terms of environmentalist logics, that the dam was an irrational and an unnecessary diminution of natural diversity and fragile ecosystems. These claims seemed reasonable enough but we must ask how it was that so many people (both from the scientific community and ordinary people) came to express them, why so many people cared that much that they literally placed their bodies on the line, before the plant machinery and in acts of civil disobedience (the British botany celebrity David Bellamy was imprisoned during the episode). We must entertain the idea that at least some if not all of them did so because they had had a personal experience of this area and that their visit left a lasting impression in their imagination; somehow some of this experience detached itself from the place and became embedded in their lives. Could it be that visitors' experience of a place like the Tasmanian Rainforest is more likely to result in stronger feelings about its protection than those of conservationists/ environmentalists who consider it in the abstract, as an example of a rainforest or natural area? Similarly, we might ask whether wildlife visitors come to form attachments to animals they encounter that in any way measure up to those strong bonds made with animals in other contexts? These remain important empirical questions because, depending on what the answers are, policy makers for natural areas must decide whether tourists have a role to play as public supporters.

Tourism is often marked down for its erosion and disturbance of nature but one must also look at the more positive and enduring benefits. Since tourist studies typically view tourists as here today (doing damage) and gone tomorrow, such benefits have not been investigated, but their value may be profound.

Further Reading

Boissevain, J. (ed.) (1996) *Coping with Tourists*. Providence R.I.: Berghahn Books.

Hylland Eriksen, T. (2001) *Tyranny of the Moment*. London: Pluto.

James, P. (1996) *Nation Formation*. London: Sage.

Macnaghten, P. and Urry, J. (1998) *Contested Natures*. London: Sage.

O'Reilly, K. (2000) *The British on the Costa Del Sol: Transnational Identities and Local Communities*. London: Routledge.

Ward, M. and Hardy, D. (1986) *Goodnight Campers! The History of the British Holiday Camp*. London: Mansell.

4

Elaborations of tourism

Residents of the first world live in *time*, space does not matter for them, since spanning every distance is instantaneous.

Zygmunt Bauman (1998b: 88)

'If we can control the environment completely, location won't matter any more,' argues Halperin. 'Some people will, perhaps want the real thing in terms of travel. But I'm not sure I know why; once you can interface with someone as if you're having a conversation in the same room, or once you can explore a place as if you're there. What's the difference?'

James Halperin 1997, cited in Jonathon Margolis (2001: 226–7)

'Air travel has lost its glamour,' observes Professor Ffowcs Williams of Cambridge. 'There are few exotic places any more – cheap travel is ruining all that – and the communications revolution now makes it practical and nicer working from home. So I can imagine aircraft being used less in the future. At the moment, capacity is still rising, but in twenty years, it will be falling unless the airlines can get us about faster or make it more fun, like the early 747s, which had a piano bar on the upper deck.'

Ffowcs Williams in Jonathon Margolis (2001: 227)

SUMMARY

- Nationalism and low cultures
- Tourism and low culture
- Mobility of people and objects
    - Mobilities I
    - Mobilities II
- Sensual tourisms
- Feel the moment; make it last: the body in contemporary tourism

---

In the previous chapter I argued that tourism can only be understood in the light of its birth under the social conditions of modernity, and I have given special emphasis to nation formation and nationalism, as well as currents of change arising from intellectual movements such as Romanticism and new modes of governmentality (through new emphases on leisure and the body, for example). Nation formation encouraged the practice of tourism as part of its wider concern with universal values or over-arching values and interests. These might include acquiring a knowledge of science and technology, an interest in art and design or an understanding of national histories (natural as well as social). I argue that tourist space is frequently characterised by this universal or over-arching interest, a content with more than simply *local* relevance. In characterising tourism in this way we can avoid the unsatisfactory and unconvincing thesis that tourists are turned on or pleasured, somewhat abstractly, by the 'unusual' and the 'different'. To say that is to say very little. We have to be able to say why it is that the different and the unusual can be appealing, so universal to so many people in the world. When we appreciate how deeply imbued most people are with modernist values such as nationalism and universalism we can begin to see tourism as a participation in the spirit of modernity. So what is tourism? How do we explain what tourists do? According to my argument here much tourism is a focused (and in many ways necessary) interest and curiosity for a fast changing world around us. We are locked into it by logics of nationalism, by the logics and orderings of modernity and by its very seductive powers of novelty and change. It is an artefact of modernity in that for most people, a familiar, local and largely finite world ceased to exist (this is part of the liquefaction of the 'solid' premodern world that Marx and then Bauman speak of) and instead new and greater worlds of relevance opened up before them, worlds that they belonged to like nations or federations or great companies, or unions and other worlds that they were nonetheless connected to. Tourism describes the nomadic manner in which we all attempt to make sense of modernity (and enjoy it) from the varied and multiple positions we hold. As Bauman (1998b: 78) puts it '[w]e became nomads – who are always in touch'. Tourism does not require us to travel very far in order to find objects, peoples and places that stimulate that curiosity or feed that desire to know about this wider world, and the knowledge we glean from tourism becomes cultural capital, tangible knowledge with real use values. Consumer markets (and consumers themselves) are driven by the need to provide and consume new things, the unusual and the different, and in this way they become after the manner of tourism; touristic, we can say.

> For consumers in the society of consumers, being on the move – searching, looking for, not-finding-it or more exactly not-finding-it-yet – is not a malaise, but the promises of bliss, perhaps it is bliss itself. Theirs is a kind of travelling hopefully which makes arriving into a curse. (Bauman, 1998b: 83)

Bauman quotes Taylor and Saarinen's (n.d.: 11) most succinct expression of this condition of postmodern times: 'desire does not desire satisfaction. To the contrary, desire desires desire'.

In order to placate our unquenchable appetite for new things we might travel, but, we do not need to travel at all, because sufficient things, peoples and places flow to us – more or less wherever we are, but especially in the one sort of place where most of us will end up: the metropolis. But even to take an extreme example, in faraway Belize, they do not produce what they consume or consume what they produce (Wilk, 1991). But to return to a previous point, what do I mean by 'places flowing to us'? Yes, the sheer extent of our curiosities and the relevance of exercising that curiosity create a market for virtual travels of many kinds and various channels of information and products now bring other places to our homes and home cities. I know a lot about LA because I have visited it in books, films, travel and articles and it visits me on TV often without me knowing or being invited. I am genuinely curious about the biggest city in the world and a lot less curious about Denver, Colorado. But then I am far more connected to LA than to Colorado. For others this will not be the case I am sure. The literatures we read and the film and television we watch become attached to their places of origin in such a way that the fictional TV series *Dallas*, for example, provides most of us with our knowledge and understanding of what Dallas is, and in turn, the TV series will be used to market and showcase Dallas itself (Rojek, 1997). This is generally true but it has also spawned a new form of tourism where visitors visit the fictional landscapes of Dickens' Kent, Hardy's Wessex or Catherine Cookson's South Tyneside (see Rojek, 1993: 152–60). In this case though, these literary landscapes came first to the reader and only subsequently did the reader visit the landscape.

As for definitions of a tourist that hinge on at least one night spent away from home (and this includes the World Tourism Organisation's definition), this suggests not so much a tourist but a hotel client. To understand the tourist in a more rigorous manner we need to understand how this essentially modern behaviour elaborated in relation to changing conditions of modernity. We can say that once born modern tourism began to develop a social life of its own. Once the modern icons of tourist devotion had been constructed around national themes (national memorials, capital cities, historic sites, national parks etc.) the habits of a tourist culture and market could evolve along many lines of elaboration. We will turn to some of these in this chapter, focusing on the emergence of a touristic interest in the everyday; the effects of increasing mobilities of people and objects and new ways of sensing a touristic world.

Nationalism and low cultures

The account I have developed so far is structured around the new modern cities that were in place by the mid-nineteenth century, the great nations that had gobbled up the world by the early years of the twentieth century and the great high cultures of the world's nations that predated nations but came to dominate and define them. High cultures – indeed high culture itself – identified the important values, arts, crafts, and skills of the modern nation state and were in stark contrast to the folk traditions of low cultures (crafts, dances, musics, stories etc.). Initially tourism was in no small measure the celebration of high culture and the pilgrimage to its sites. Nationalism in part was the recommendation of the former to the latter, and often the suppression of the latter. A good example of this is the suppression of regional languages: aboriginal languages, Sami languages, Welsh, Gaelic, and Basque etc. Nationalism created a tourism that made centres and shrines of high cultures and demolished and modernised the centres and former shrines of low culture. In Chapter 5, we will see, for example, how regional Christian pilgrimages were banished from sixteenth century Protestant Britain and how in the early nineteenth century, new and powerful industrial cities undermined or banned the older local and regional fairs and revels. So how did we ever get to a position where tourists wanted to see *low* cultures, its material lives, its folk traditions, its foods, its musics, and its pasts? How precisely were low cultures rescued from oblivion and rendered interesting and relevant?

The answer to this question is complex because while nations did indeed suppress ties to local and regional cultural identity in favour of citizenship and nationalism they faced a major problem: nations had no existence prior to their formation, this was pure political and cultural innovation. In other words they had no prehistory and with no prehistory they had no objects, landmarks, monuments with which their citizens could *imagine* their solidarity, their identity. According to Gellner this is why all nations put together a fictitious past using the cultural shreds and patches of folk cultures from within. 'Society no longer worships itself through religious symbols; a modern streamlined, on-wheels high culture celebrates itself in song and dance, which it believes (stylising it in the process) from folk culture, which it fondly believes itself to be perpetuating, defending and reaffirming' (Gellner, 1983: 52). So when we look at the young nations of Europe around the beginning of the twentieth century, we find an enormous interest in folklore, which involved academic and semi-academic voyages of discovery into the interiors and margins to find the nation's stories, myths, musics and, importantly, dress.

There is nothing quite like clothing to establish identity and belonging to a social corporation. So at this time, just as these nations were becoming industrial and fully modern around their great cities, the countryside was yielding up a suitable sartorial version of their common past. In some places a 'national costume' emerged out of the much greater variety that preceded it. In others such as Sweden and Norway, local and regional markers were kept within a newly enhanced national style; the basic format was national, the impetus to define and refine the costumes was national, the days on which they were worn were national but they varied only in detail according to locality. In Germany at this time the centres of high culture were extremely busy inventing a Germanic past as if the nation had always had a destiny within a recognisable common people, as if the nation was a natural category. As Hegel said, 'Nations may have had a long history before they finally reached their destination – that of forming themselves into states' (Gellner, 1983: 48). This is the curious reality of nations: they were properly forward looking social formations and they alone were able to advance modernity through its industrialising periods of the nineteenth and twentieth centuries. In this way their true symbols were their vibrant and exciting cities and networks of technologies, new innovations and design-work. However, in order to make them cohere, in order to work the trick of social solidarity, they had to invent and maintain as important some version of their common historical past. One of the reasons this was critical is that former ethnic and regional rivalries could at any time segment new nations. As an artefact of the need for a common past modern societies needed museums, school curricula, archaeologists, historians and, most important, *sites*. The sacred sites and shrines of modern nations.

Added to this, modern nations and their high cultural institutions have always tended to identify cultures which they admired, emulated and longed to visit – whether they were still in existence or long dead. So for example, the English of the eighteenth century (who were quite early on in the business of nation formation) admired classical antiquity enormously. In addition, and in a related fashion they greatly admired Italy, which had been so prominent in the Renaissance and the development of modernity. The Grand Tour was explicitly a journey whose high point and objective was an immersion in classical antiquity and the later achievements in the arts, architecture and literature. Although ostensibly concerned with these quintessential high cultures, it seemed everything, including the simple lives of peasants could be interesting and attractive. Indeed, the Grand Tour often involved extended periods of time immersed in local cultures, learning languages and cultural mores. As we have already seen above, the Romantic movement grew out of these trips and for the cultural elite of modernising and industrialising England, these simple peasant lifestyles, the remote landscape of the alps through which they travelled and the wild margins of England that they championed as refuges became models for the imagination of yet more pathos and beauty. That imagination was propelled considerably by the cultural and economic events that occurred towards the end of the twentieth century.

Tourism and low culture

In the last quarter of the twentieth century we have seen a proliferation of touristic curiosities that are neither organised by or through the nation state. The model of tourism developed by nationalism and national commercial organisations is not of course bound by them and we have begun to see cities and towns and villages clamour for the tourist dollar. Typically these sorts of enterprises and places do not make nationalistic appeals (although that is one option available to them) for the attention of the tourist, but appeal to something else. Somehow the lives of ordinary people – what we might call tourism of the everyday – became mantled with aesthetic appeal. How did that happen?

Urban tourism tends to be accounted for as the product and creativity of an expanding tourist industry, a series of disparate activities with disparate histories and origins amalgamated and placed in a taxonomy of tourism businesses. In this case the dominant type of explanation is that the tourism industry is forever and necessarily expanding, applying its logic to new and emerging materials and places and themes. It has to do this because markets are quickly satiated and consumers easily bored and also because tourism companies must find new products to invest their profits in. Such an argument reduces this tourism to a logic of capitalist expansion and marketing. In this case the balance of investment expanded or shifted from mid-century investment portfolios comprised of resorts around the coast, holiday camps, theme parks and sun holidays to sites and activities in the city, especially those designed to feed major new investments in the hotel and convention trade (Holcomb, 1999). The idea of expanding into the great cities required identifying a form of tourism specific to the city. Was this the manner in which industrial archaeology became a theme for tourism? Was this why city cultures were sponsored for displays and spectacles? Was this why the ordinary lives of city people living in the less salubrious past became 'interesting'? Was this why we now pay to see how New Yorkers once crowded into slum tenement blocks? In part, yes. But there is more.

An expansive capitalist tourism industry is only one sort of explanation. It has also been explained in terms of urban economic restructuring, that in order to make up for jobs lost through deindustrialisation and mobile capital, local political organisations such as city governments look to exploit tourism possibilities (Fainstein and Judd, 1999: 2). In effect they create them by interpreting, performing and displaying local city cultures and heritages. This is the opposite sort of argument: that to keep local political organisations and the communities they serve afloat and to prevent widespread migration of capital and taxpayers, public sector-led initiatives that are predicated on essentially *immobile* local resources (such as tourism sites) are explored. Provided that a sequence of local resources can be interpreted as interesting, meaningful, aesthetically pleasing or amusing, a local tourism industry can in theory be developed anywhere. However that theory, which is implicit in Judd and Fainstein's book on urban tourism, tends to involve a somewhat naive model of tourism aesthetics, namely that tourists 'desire [. . .] the extraordinary and the unusual. Tourist spaces are designed to produce liminal moments that lift the tourist above ordinary everyday experience' (Fainstein and Judd, 1999:

9–10). This simplistic reduction also lies at the heart of Urry's general theory of tourism: tourists obtain 'intense pleasure' from gazing at places 'on a different scale or involving different senses from those customarily encountered' (Urry, 1990: 3). More specifically:

> the tourist gaze is directed to features of landscape and townscape that separate them off from everyday experience. *Such aspects are viewed because they are taken to be in some sense out of the ordinary.* The viewing of such tourist sights often involves different forms of social patterning, with a much greater sensitivity to visual elements of landscape or townscape than is normally found in everyday life. (Urry, 1990: 3)

But this leaves out as much as it explains. Why should difference and the unusual produce pleasurability? Why not fear and loathing? Are all differences and unusual things equally appealing and pleasurable or might some actually be grotesque, revolting and appalling? The theory relies on plausibility and normative practices among readers rather more than *explanation*. What this theory lacks is a theorisation of aesthetic sensibilities among tourists. However, before we take a look at this important dimension we should backtrack to a more sensible and modest explanation offered by Judd and Fainstein: city tourism owes much to the restructuring of private and public business organisation. *Decentralised* large companies and groups of companies operating at a national and *global* level increasingly involved the need for centralised meetings, conventions, and conferences. Although airports are increasingly gaining a hold on this market, it was the larger nodal cities that had the most to gain from this. As these cities expanded this trade, new tourism services from prostitution to heritage trails exploited their presence – and what a presence: people who were affluent, away from home and (often) at a loose end. City governments have been in competition for this trade for many years, offering favourable conditions for companies to build tourist infrastructure and markets as well as to be tourists themselves. As mediators between the tourist and the tourist industry, they have had to build both ends of the market: they have to give tourists things to do and they have to have tourists to visit them.

But this is only one thread to the story we need to tell. We also need to work out how tourists came to be easily and variably entertained by, well, almost anything!

We have seen how nationalism provides an aesthetic appreciation of the epic and heroic city sites, national galleries and so on, but how do we set about explaining our apparent curiosity for old brass tools, old bread ovens or an industrial chimney in Accrington, Lancashire? At least four questions need to be addressed:

1 Why should people find some things pleasurable?
2 From where does this aesthetic sensibility emerge?

3   How do these sensibilities vary across cultures and social groups?
4   How and why do they shift and change?

In thinking through these questions one is reminded of the recently developed concept of aestheticisation, a process linked to postmodernity in which more and more ordinary objects of the world become mantled in aesthetic beauty and more and more people can lay a claim to an aesthetic appreciation where taste is always relative, never absolute (Welsch, 1997). Welsch argues that as the old distinction between high and low culture collapsed (i.e. the older view that beauty had a specific and formal content that had to be learned through attentive training in the highest colleges of art and could be distinguished from popular or low traditions of crafts and ornamentation) all manifestations of human cultural creativity were left with equal claims to aesthetic content. The entire world of objects – from major works of art and architecture through decorative arts such as jewellery, to more everyday objects such as tools and containers and vernacular architecture – suddenly acquired an aura of their own. These objects 'speak' of their manufacturers and traditions of art and craft, but also to deeper structures of social and cultural formations/contexts, histories, conflicts, poverties, diseases, warfares and so on. As this 'aestheticisation process' emerged in the 1970s, it was linked to a variety of institutional and cultural practices. One can list a number of these as examples: the extension of museums of the everyday; the extension of objects and buildings that could be valued as heritage; the dramatic growth in gentrification or the restoration of former working class homes by more affluent groups (Butler, 1997; Smith, 1996); the surging interest in collecting twentieth century objects of the everyday (e.g. matchboxes, thimbles, egg cups) (Pearce, 1995); the recycling of former fashions and even the wearing of recycled clothes from the past; the dramatic growth in car boot and garage sales (Gregson and Crewe, 1997c); the discovery and recovery of industrial art and design (Franklin, 2002b); the growth in the readership of the historical novel. So we might say that high culture gave us nationalistic tourisms while the collapse of the distinction between high and low culture paved the way for a massive expansion of objects that might be said to have an aesthetic appeal. Of course, prior to this period of aesthetisication, these objects had been ignored, stored or simply thrown away. The excitement that this form of tourism generated was all about revealing past and present everyday worlds, it was about revelation, interpretation, restoring, conserving, reusing and re-loving.

Sensitivity to the aestheticisation process enables us to acknowledge the role that *ordinary* people play in the development of new tourist sensibilities rather more than some other theories do. One can begin to appreciate this when one considers many of the scathing views expressed in relation to proposed tourist developments in former British and American industrial and manufacturing towns (Buckley and Witt, 1985, 1989). Put simply, people on the ground at the time simply did not believe that such pitiful remainders could constitute a tourist attraction. And even Urry (1990: 105) describes Bradford and other northern former industrial towns as 'unlikely places' for 'the development of heritage-based tourist development'. If it were merely difference and the unusual behind touristic pleasure why would Urry describe the somewhat unique Bradford as unlikely? In sum, many in the industry and the localities themselves did not believe tourists would find such places attractive enough to pay entrance monies. However, the extent to which aesthetic sensibility had grown to value and cherish such objects *was* surprising. As Urry himself acknowledged, the steady growth in memberships of heritage organisations such as the National Trust (according to Paxman (1999) one in seven Britons are members) was preceded not so much by middle class gentrification but 'plebeian' movements – 'for example railway preservation, industrial archaeology, steam traction rallies and the like' (Urry, 1990: 110). If aestheticisation relies on the development and growth of aesthetic sensibilities, then we can also ask what sort of necessary preconditions have come into being such that tourism can expand into more areas of everyday life? Why would a decrepit worker's cottage be worth demolishing in 1960 but be worth preserving for posterity in 1980? We are dealing with a very powerful transformation here, not least what we might call the development of tourist experiences and skills in mass culture. If we can point to the aestheticisation process emerging from the 1970s in general terms, how specifically can we theorise its transmission into popular mass culture? Urry's railway preservers and steam rally enthusiasts and all the hoards of weekend garage salers provide the clue: it is transmitted through practice and performance. Tourists take something other than souvenirs and memories away from tourist sites: in performing the interested, open and fascinated observer of popular history role, and in learning to glean information from guides, dioramas and displays, tourists develop what might be called a generalised receptivity and predisposition to objects of the everyday.

First and rather obviously (too obviously perhaps), we may conclude that tourism is something of a skill or set of skills that can be learned, mainly through trial and error – on holiday. Obvious yes, but think how many other accounts render the tourist as essentially passive, even stupid, and tourism generally a kind of loathsome, mindless distraction relative to the more respectable *traveller*. Rojek dedicates a substantial section of *Ways of Escape* to the various ways tourists and tourism have been vilified, from the lamentations of the great French anthropologist Lévi-Strauss to the tabloid rage of London's *Evening Standard* (Rojek, 1993: 174–5). However, Rojek is not convinced by the snobbery and elitism of the educated travellers who complain that tourists are too uneducated to appreciate the finer points of travel 'without the capacity to sublimate, to release himself to the unknown' as one critic put it (Rojek, 1993: 174). By contrast Rojek finds the objects of their curiosity perfectly consistent with a desire to learn and extend their knowledge. Tourists, for example, can and do learn to appreciate a whole range of things that they might otherwise not at home. For example, many people have been profoundly moved by Florentine art and have developed an interest in art more generally as a result. The same might be true of wines, architecture, nature, gardens, historical periods, popular culture and events, foods and fashion. Others have argued that by making historical interpretations relevant to their specific audiences, tourist sites often fold ordinary people into an ownership of their own history as opposed to a feeling of existing outside it.

A generalised local interest in art might be the necessary condition for successfully mounting or hosting an art exhibition in any given city, say Bradford, but the knowledge, confidence and interest that builds up in any one locality may depend on the introduction to, and experience of, art elsewhere, most often while on holiday or travelling.

Tourism also builds up what might be called 'repertoires of curiosity'. Not just a curiosity about other people, places and cultures but, more significantly, the ability to break through the more obvious difficulties of understanding and interpretation. Critically, building on earlier nineteenth century tourisms, twentieth century patterns of tourism elaborated a wide repertoire of curiosity in cultures and natures. Although it could not be described as an academic anthropology, tourism developed a more popular anthropological interest in social and cultural life. From an initial concentration on classical antiquity, tourism quickly spread, rather like anthropology itself, to peasant and tribal cultures, from the tropical islands of Polynesia to the arctic and desert interiors. As with professional anthropologists, tourists were interested in obtaining material artefacture and homes became display cabinets for their collections. And in the closing decades of the twentieth century, the heritage tourism industry became possible through the extension of this popular anthropology into the material and social cultures of an earlier modernity. In short, these industrial and urban heritage tourisms were predicated on repertoires of curiosity, tourism performance, skills and abilities that preceded them in combination with a new aestheticisation process that rendered them relevant, desirable and pleasurable.

Of course the very process of aestheticisation (a proliferating, expanding and self-generating process) is critical here, as more and more surfaces and textures of everyday life could assume the mantle of aesthetic beauty and attraction. In these ways of course, the ability and the desire to consume touristic objects coincided with a more acute awareness and appreciation of the ordinary and the everyday and also a (modern) world that was disappearing. Retro cultures or the re-consumption of objects and popular culture in a more rarefied manner (i.e. as tourism) thus circulated faster and faster as the century drew to a close. By the 1990s the 1980s were beginning to be re-consumed in terms of both music and fashion, whereas the 1950s had not been influential again until the 1970s. However, if we can begin to talk of touristic abilities and predispositions as necessary conditions for the expansion of tourism into everyday life (and remembering all along that some urban tourisms were experiments that were not thought at the time to be viable), another important precondition was the relative and absolute increase in the *mobility* of people and objects.

Activity 4.1

We are currently in the process of transforming 1950s–1970s junk into appreciated, even revered objects. In their second time round as consumed objects 'retro' has the special glow of history, of opening up a world of glamour and decadence from the past. The retro look in fashion, film, domestic interiors, cars and motorbikes, toys and even architecture is in such demand that manufacturers have turned to re-releasing some of their older designs. Since this process is still under way it is worthwhile considering why, in a period of unprecedented technological sophistication, we find retro objects so compelling and attractive? Both the Museum of American History in Washington and the Power House Museum in Sydney currently display 'retro' objects in the opening museum spaces. Upmarket and exclusive hotels have started to add retro flourishes to their interiors. These objects are neither new nor particularly old. Do all things become touristic after a while or does retro possess something special? If so, what might it be? Do you like Robbie Williams' retro Sinatra sound? If so, why? Ditto Oasis's recycling of the Beatles or the general revival of jazz?

Mobility of people and objects

This inevitably implies another sense of 'home', of being in the world. It means to conceive of dwelling as a mobile habitat, as a mode of inhabiting time and space not as though they were fixed and closed structures, but as providing the critical provocation of an opening whose questioning presence reverberates in the movement of languages that constitute our sense of identity, place and belonging. There is no one place, language or tradition that can claim this role. For although the journey from the centre into the periphery seeking the unexpected, the bizarre and the wonder of it all, may still dominate this literature . . . such stories ultimately represent a weak echo in the volume of travel, migration and dislocation that so many people coming from elsewhere faced and continue to experience. So, *I* finally come to experience the violence of alterity, of other worlds, languages and identities, and there finally discover my dwelling to be sustained across encounters, dialogues and clashes with other histories, other places, other people. For the return of the native not only signals the dramatic necessity 'to abrogate the boundaries between Western and non-Western history', but also returns to the centre the violence that initially marked the encounters out in the periphery that laid the foundation of *my* world. (Chambers, 1994: 4–5)

Dramatic increases in mobility and communication were defining features of western modernity and the emergence, as we have seen, of nationalism and indeed, as Chambers (above) reminds us, of colonialism/imperialism. In its social and cultural effects, however, this increase was not linear and progressive and we can perhaps identify at least two periodisations of mobility that have had a profound effect on tourism. For simplicity I will call these periods Mobilities I and Mobilities II. Mobilities I is roughly the period from the establishment of dense networks of railways to the beginnings of mass car ownership and the establishment of commercial airlines in the 1950s, a period of approximately 150 years in many places in the west. Mobilities II is what came after that, a period in which cheap air transport arrived, when multi-car families became commonplace, when superhighways began to take over from rail. However, there is far more to these periods and their mobilities than changes in transport technologies.

Mobilities I

Mobilities I describes a modernity that was relatively sedentary compared with Mobilities II. Both capital and labour were comparatively immobile and this produced the powerful image of modern life as organised around industrial communities, industrial towns and industrial regions. During this period the life of a company and a factory and workforce was relatively long. A working career was often a cradle-to-grave experience and a number of companies employed many generations of local families. It was a common experience for industrial centres to grow; to expand and build a lifestyle for their residents based more or less on locally provided facilities and resources. In this way localities and regions were self-sufficient and much like each other in terms of leisure and consumption. Neighbourhood communities were relatively stabilised around regular work. The basis of these communities was dense local networks of families and friendships. The neighbourhood communities were moral entities, where individual behaviour and character were monitored, discussed and policed. Individuals lived among a community who would remain the most important people in their lives and rivalries between such communities were common. It was because life was so often like that that we sometimes hear of old people saying they have never left the town they were born in. Certainly, apart from periods of disruption such as economic depressions and wars, these communities did very little routine or even spasmodic travelling. Economic depressions in Europe and America saw massive migrations to the USA and especially to the big metropolitan cities, and indeed migration also took place between the peasant south of Europe and the industrial north. Tourism at the time was characterised by an annual holiday week and a few public holidays. Often these holiday weeks would be to the nearest seaside, and often, as with the Lancashire mill towns, entire factory towns took off together to their regular seaside town (see

Chapter 6). Even tourism in Mobilities I was organised around work. Even early sporting leagues were essentially local leagues. It is not surprising that throughout Mobilities I personal transport was dominated by the bicycle: on almost all occasions the bicycle could take most people anywhere they wanted or needed to go.

During this period we also see the consolidation of a broad middle class, who are distinguished by their relative mobility. Increasingly they would acquire motor cars, take expensive holidays on steam liners, travel more routinely for trade and business purposes (associated with expanding capitalism) and develop a summertime holiday culture around rented cottages or second homes in the country (for example, the setting for Enid Blyton's *Famous Five* adventures; Agatha Christie's *Miss Marples'* 'whodunits', Mary Wesley's novel *The Camomile Lawn*). By and large it was dominated by national mobility afforded by the motorcar and it opened up local cultures and natures to the outside view for perhaps the first time in any systematic way. The spaces they explored on their outings were the hinterlands and villages and ordinary spaces that were overlooked by Thomas Cook who searched out the spectacular and the sensational.

Mobilities I also describes a relatively localised circulation of material cultures. Although world trade had globalised by this period, it was a trade on global primary commodities and raw materials such as rubber, tea, iron ore and timber. The material cultures of the communities described above stayed with them, and developed within them. Prior to industrialisation and even the development of rail links, the localisation and sedentary nature of culture gave rise to a massive diversity of types of things. It seemed every place did things slightly differently, adding shape and distinction to them. Take for example, cheese. Because cheese was a perishable commodity and did not travel well before refrigeration, it was consumed in the same place it was produced. Pastures and cows varied a great deal from one place to another, as did cheese-making techniques and even the strains of mould used to make them and the means of storage. Although rail transport made it possible to move cheeses between the regions, the relatively sedentary nature of consumer cultures tended to homogenise taste cultures and rendered them uninterested in strange foods from distant places. For these reasons it was still possible for Bourdieu to generalise about French taste in the 1960s, at the end of the period of Mobilities I. National taste structures were interesting because at stake here were not just food items, flavours, beverages, and their distribution between gender and social class but also the structure of taste in particular meals, styles of cookery, cuisine, brewing and the assemblage and structure of social meals (see Mary Douglas, 1975 for an example of the English meal). During Mobilities I national taste structures were relatively homogeneous; food varied along national or perhaps regional lines but tended not to cross national boundaries very much.

Contributing to this of course was the relatively restricted nature of trade between countries and also relatively long periods of isolation through wars. Wars between France and England had been periodic for a long time and cultural exchange was also limited by the two world wars in the twentieth century. Wars and international antipathies reduced the mobility of people across borders – indeed border guarding and trade taxes and tariffs were an endemic feature almost throughout Mobilities I.

Mobilities II

Mobilities II can also be thought of as globalisation, although it is helpful to see not only how places were joined up but also how people and cultures were changed. To begin with, all forms of transport became considerably cheaper so that a wave of private car-dominated travel preceded a further wave of air travel, packaged holidays and fly-drive deals. Travel became ever more adventurous and by the 1980s there were few places that people could not and did not travel to. Cars and trains underwent dramatic improvements, shortening travel times and shrinking geography. London to New York was now only a matter of hours, the M4 motorway west from London all the way to Cardiff in Wales became a new economic region, the M4 corridor; increasing numbers of British towns were linked by roads travelling at 70 miles per hour (plus), travel time between London Heathrow and central London was reduced to 15 minutes by fast rail.

Beginning with technological developments is in a way misleading, it suggests that change was travel technology-led and this was only partly true. Indeed new travel *needs* were as much the prime mover of technological development. These needs derived primarily from a more mobile capitalism. The so-called Fordist nature of production in Mobilities I was related to the development of stable post-war mass markets. Products and product lines had a long production life and homogeneous national taste was consistent with the standardised nature of the consumption–production nexus under Fordism. That accord broke down as a result of a series of economic crises in the 1970s and the fragmentation of those stable taste structures and patterns of consumption. Fordism tended towards an austere and standardised format and consumption itself was restricted through controls on credit, luxury taxes and duties on imports. New lifestyle groups emerged and created new configurations of taste, often as a result of their experiences abroad and contact with other taste cultures. Young cultures broke away from national taste uniformity. A period of experimentation in consumption and lifestyle gave way to unpredictable and fickle markets. As a result, many of the older industries struggled and collapsed or restructured. Newer more flexible forms of production came into being in new areas of manufacturing and services. The geography of production changed dramatically and with it those sedentary communities were gradually broken up. Deindustrialisation was very rapid in the 1980s and the thriving areas of manufacturing became seriously depressed areas of unemployment. Local economies spiralled downwards. Local communities and industrial towns bifurcated into the rundown council estates of the unemployed and the new suburban developments of the employed service classes. People also moved to the new centres, such as the M4 corridor. Many of the local service industries and retailers that were reproduced up and down the country in Mobilities I, became consolidated into smaller numbers of national companies. Centralised national banking, insurance and retailing groups operated internal labour markets and during the retail boom of the 1980s and 1990s these companies moved their personnel around the country in their tight schedules of new openings and expansions. Congestion in the bigger cities and stiff competition for professional workers encouraged many head-quarters to move from London and other capital cities out to a new rank of fashionable smaller towns.

In some ways mobile corporate life replaced the former sedentary life around Fordist manufacturing. Corporate life was not simply mobile it was also about change, managing, implementing and then rethinking change. This was partly because of a highly competitive and consumer dominated market and partly because of fast changing technologies in working environments. Change was also taking place at the individual level: people no longer trained when young for skills and jobs that would take them through to retirement. Through expanded university and training sectors, individuals were able to remake and remodel themselves many times over.

The extent to which almost all occupational groups have become mobile in terms of their search for work, the organisation of that work and as a *component* of that work has grown very dramatically indeed. Take for example the in-work conference and training industry. Conferences and training are now an essential means by which public and private industries attempt to reshape and restructure organisations and human resources. Taking people away from their immediate work environment and reward-ing them with a trip away from home that combines important business with some pleasure is widely believed to be a productive and profitable activity, a part of modern work practices. Such activities are used to build, bolster or mend production teams, to introduce new technologies or work practices, to plan and brainstorm for new phases of work or as simple rewards for excellent work. In addition, the national and international nature of large companies means that for much of their business (meet-ings, exhibitions, sales, promotions etc.) at least some of their personnel must be on the road, or in the air.

Conference and training markets have tended to favour the big capital cities especially New York, Washington, Seattle, Chicago, London, Paris etc. and these provide enormous income to such centres. When Washing-ton's National Airport was closed after the events of September 11 2001, the local hotel trade lost $10 million per day. When it reopened amidst fears of anthrax, its losses were estimated at $5 million per day. Hotel occupancy around the end of October was down by 50 per cent even though prices were down by 40 per cent. Nationally, one third of the nation's unionised hotel workers, some 265,000, were laid off.

In addition to these in-work Mobilities, it is a fact that nowadays labour has become as mobile as capital. At one level the economic imbalance between western developed and thriving economies and their depressed, peripheral and poorly developed neighbours results in massive movements, often illegal, of unskilled labour into the service sectors of major metropolitan areas. They move into those social vacuums of labour shortage and while they enter grey areas of social acceptability their presence is unofficially tolerated. It is a fact that many of these migrants move in from precisely those areas that western tourists have turned into a pleasure periphery – Mexico, Spain, Greece, Morocco. Many of these workers carry out tasks that the ethnic majority will no longer do but in time many invest in businesses that recreate the pleasure periphery inside the metropolis. Typically these businesses are cafés, restaurants, wholesalers, manufactures and take-aways but they have also extended into bakeries, ethnic general stores, decorative arts importers, travel specialists, and certain crafts. These are typically concentrated in particular areas and these can become 'little Italies', after the famous Manhattan model earlier in the twentieth century.

As the economic geography was rewritten in the second half of the twentieth century, so we have also seen major shifts in population within western nation states. In Britain this can be described as a generalised shift to the affluent south and east of the country, while in the north, Manchester, Glasgow and Edinburgh have grown at the expense of other towns. The growth of key cities generally is another feature of Mobilities II, however it is not the uniform, even and homogeneous growth of the Fordist industrial city. Cities that are in the stakes to attract capital now realise that a critical factor in their success is to become attractive to the key professional, scientific and creative workers competed for by the corporations and thriving businesses. Cities such as Bristol and Glasgow are good examples. Rather than creating a functional city, these cities have made major efforts to become aesthetically pleasing cities. Both Bristol and Glasgow have entered the European City of Culture league for example. Today, arts centres, theatres, cafés, restaurant districts and a mix of gentrified and modern architectures must create a sense of lifestyle possibilities for these discerning workers. These cities are aiming to create a sense of touristic pleasure. Waterfronts and water developments seem to be a necessary feature, so also does a critical mass of ethnic and social diversity. A city must have depth in terms of eating, drinking and entertainments, it must be beautiful, and it must have an aura. It must also have excitement, and this is generated through a calendar of special events, of the sort that Richard 'Beau' Nash created for the first tourist town of Bath in the eighteenth century. In 1704 he became master of ceremonies at Bath, where he conducted the public balls with splendour never before witnessed. His reforms in manners, his influence in improving the streets and buildings, and his leadership in fashion helped to transform Bath into a fashionable touristic spectacle of a sort that the upper classes and royalty could feel comfortable in. He realised that to produce such effects there had to be a policy governing the 'look' and development of a place. Typical among contemporary spectacles that only cities in this league can provide are regular firework displays, food festivals, arts, theatre, cinema and comedy festivals, major art exhibitions (there are now 17 biennale cities in the world), major sporting events (especially an annual event such as a Formula One race, the Sydney-Hobart yacht race or major soccer or athletics competitions). Again, I want to underline the point that these showcase places model themselves on tourist resorts and generate a kind of holiday atmosphere all year round. What is more, the residents of cities such as these are increasingly visiting similar cities elsewhere. Urban tourism, especially in the winter, offers cultural depth, fine shopping, good wine and food, sophisticated arts and entertainments and pleasing spaces in which to relax and hang out.

However, as these places become more complex, expensive and subject to greater mobilities new companies have recently emerged that specialise in relocation services for individuals and families. According to Middleton, 'The past ten years have seen a steady growth in demand for UK residents who can not only explain Britain to foreigners, but also steer them around all the cultural and practical obstacles that present themselves to new arrivals' (Middleton, 2001: 6). Karen Deane Relocations in London, for example, assists with housing, schooling and health matters but also offers a relocating family up to ten hours talk time. Whenever a teething problem presents itself to the relocatees, away from all sources of informal help formerly provided by kin, friends and neighbours in Mobilities I, this company provides an expert ear and advice, even direct assistance. Such a company is called into being by Mobilities II and is joined by other companies and services: professional baby sitting and nannying, dog walkers and pet sitters for the many homes left temporarily unoccupied, house sitters, security companies, foreign language schools, orientation programmes.

As these sorts of places come to dominate the life worlds of the west in the twenty-first century we can see how Mobilities II has radically transformed the world. They are drawing the entire world into them through migration, refugee movements (they tend to be racially, ethnically and religiously tolerant places), economic restructuring and corporatisation. At the same time the entire world is opening up to them in terms of their access to cheap travel and the proliferation of destinations. Taste in tourism changed from occasional trips to familiar places consistent with national taste configurations, in favour of multiple trips to the unfamiliar consistent with the desire for diversity in cosmopolitan taste configurations.

With Mobilities II, the distinction between the world of work, home life and the world of tourism became blurred. Both the spaces and times of work, home and holiday bleed into one another. Work might offer an overseas trip, home life might involve a day at an international sporting event and holidays with the children may seem like very hard work for parents. However, the point to really grasp here is that although we are talking about changes at the level of production, economy, work, domestic and community life, consumption and leisure, much of contemporary life is organised in a touristic manner: its fluidity, mobility, spectacle and leisure orientation have created a life far more like tourism and travel than the sedentary industrial villages and towns that preceded them. However, it is a lifeworld where the distinction between tourist and non-tourist, host and guest is increasingly difficult to identify. The extent of mobilities and migrancy is such that the cosmopolitan world we live in is too big for any of us to master in the way we did in Mobilities I. We are all tourists or at least touristic now, for most of the time.

Chambers (1994) helps to establish this point:

> In the oblique gaze of the migrant that cuts across the territory of the Western metropolis there exists the hint of a metaphor. In the extensive and multiple worlds of the modern city we, too, become nomads, migrating across a system that is too vast to be our own, but in which we are fully involved – translating and transforming what we find and absorb into local instances of sense. It is above all here that we are inducted into a hybrid state and composite culture in which the simple dualism of First and Third Worlds collapses and there emerges what Homi Bhabha calls a 'differential communality', and what Felix Guattari refers to as the 'process of *heterogenesis*'. The boundaries of the liberal consensus and its centred sense of language, being, position and politics, are breached and scattered as all our histories come to be rewritten in the contentious languages of what has tended to become the privileged *topos* of the modern world: the contemporary metropolis. (Chambers, 1994: 14)

It is not just the vastness of the modern metropolis that confounds our ability to be familiar with its cultures; it is also the speed, scale and continuity of in-migration that prevents previous patterns of co-existence. As Bauman puts it:

> Strangers come in such numbers that one can hardly assign them to marginal places and functions; their presence is much too fresh to allow for any degree of habituation and ritualisation; in an increasingly deregulated world, one cannot hope to confine them to any particular places and tasks, or hold them at a distance; one cannot even force them to obey local custom, since – unlike the ethnic or cultural strangers of the past – they are proud of their own traditions and customs and do not genuflect to the habits and fads and prejudices of their hosts as unambiguously superior to their own. (Bauman, 2001: 88–89)

Chambers and Bauman point therefore to a new feature of Mobilities II: the rendering of the familiar as unfamiliar. This breaks down a fundamental attribute of tourism in established theories of tourism, namely, that tourists seek a breach with the humdrum familiar everyday. Increasingly in

Mobilities II, then, distance is not critical to the perception of difference, it is all around us and will not stay still enough for habituation to occur.

It is implicit in the foregoing that it is not only people but also objects that flow more freely and further in Mobilities II. One type of object that has moved quite impressively through the media of tourism is food. The experience of eating the foods and cuisines of others in modern cities is an area of contemporary life that has been re-organised and re-spatialised by tourism. Modern food halls offer a changing fare of world foods. New tastes that were established first of all by tourism (or migrants) become routinised and then entrenched in modern taste formations. For example, in the UK, garlic was first experienced by white British people as an exotic and not altogether welcome feature of overseas travel and tourism. Today we are garlic eaters, chilli eaters, soy sauce eaters, olive oil eaters, Sushi eaters, pizza eaters, or at least, if we are not then we are still surrounded by these foods in local restaurants, supermarkets and homes. Now we demand only the very best coffees, wines, balsamic vinegars and so on. A similar argument can be made for one of the most important activities of contemporary life: shopping. We no longer shop merely for a set of known and familiar commodities. An important part of shopping has become looking for the new and exotic products from the globalised markets. We are as likely to find goods offered for sale from our own country in those destinations we fly to as 'proper' tourists as we are to find products from these holiday destinations on sale at home. I am writing these words in Oslo, Norway. Not far from my desk I can choose between several English pubs all selling English beers and of course the English pub experience. In the supermarket just up the road I spotted Spitfire Ale yesterday, a beer made by Shepherd Neame near to my hometown in Canterbury, England. However a trip down my High Street in Canterbury offers an Australian styled pub selling beers made in my adopted home in Hobart, Tasmania. In both the Australian pub in England and the English pub in Norway (to say nothing of the Scottish and Irish pubs) we orientate ourselves as consumers in a tourist manner: trying out the exotic products, rituals of consumption (English pints of beer are in stark contrast to the local small glasses) and the ethnic spaces (we all have to stand in the Australian bar in Canterbury). Not only is this a globalising world it is a world in which what used to be ordinary folk cultures (and they do not come much more ordinary than the English pub), and what used to be referred to as 'low' cultures are now highly sought after.

Iain Chambers sums up the combined effects of Mobilities II that includes, of course, our intellectual response to it.

> To live 'elsewhere' means to continually find yourselves involved in a conversation in which different identities are recognised, exchanged and mixed but do not vanish. Here differences function not necessarily as barriers but rather as signals of complexity. To be a stranger in a strange land, to be lost (in Italian *spaesato* – 'without a country'), is perhaps a condition typical of contemporary life. To the forcibly induced migrations of slaves, peasants, the poor and the

ex-colonial world that make up so many hidden histories of modernity, we can also add the increasing nomadism of modern thought. Now that the old house of criticism, historiography and intellectual certitude is in ruins, we all find ourselves on the road. Faced with a loss of roots, and the subsequent weakening in the grammar of 'authenticity', we move into a vaster landscape. Our sense of belonging, our language and the myths we carry in us remain, but no longer as 'origins' or signs of 'authenticity' capable of guaranteeing the sense of our lives. They now linger on as traces, voices, memories and murmurs that are mixed in with other histories, episodes, encounters. (Chambers, 1994: 18)

In Mobilities II, it is possible to say that a touristic stance to the world is now part of everyday life and not the episodic escape from everyday life that holidays in Mobilities I once constituted. Equally, middle class western cultures can no longer consider themselves the only travellers let loose in the world. As Bauman argues, nowadays 'we are all on the move' and 'tourism is the only acceptable, human form of restlessness' (Bauman, 1998b: 78; 94). For Bauman, however, not everyone can be a tourist. Those designated to be flawed consumers and tied to poor neighbourhoods or those living in dangerous locations anxious to move away tend to be regarded as vagabonds when and if they move: 'for the inhabitants of the second world, the walls built of immigration controls, of residence laws and of 'clean streets' and zero tolerance policies, grow taller; the moats separating them from the sites of their desires and of dreamed of redemption grow deeper, while all the bridges, at the first attempt to cross them, prove to be draw bridges' (Bauman 1998b: 89). Despite this Bauman's *vagabonds* are 'the alter ego of the tourist', sharing much in common with them, and together constituting a universal touristic world:

> The tourist and the vagabond are both consumers, and late-modern or postmodern consumers are sensation seekers and collectors of experiences; their relationship to the world is primarily *aesthetic*; they perceive the world as a food for sensibility – a matrix of possible experiences; . . . and they map it according to the experiences occasioned. Both are touched – attracted or repelled – by the promised sensations. They both savour the world, as seasoned museum-goers savour their *tête-à-tête* with the world of art. This attitude-to-the-world unites them, makes them like each other. (Bauman, 1998b: 94)

Savouring the world as a tourist has also undergone elaborations of a multiple sensual kind. We will consider this in some detail in Chapter 8 but I will provide an outline in the next section.

Sensual tourisms

Two of the examples we have looked at earlier (drinking beer and eating exotic foods) point to the significance to tourism of sensuality. Mostly we consume tourism through our senses: vision, touch, smell and taste. Of course we can consume tourism mentally or cognitively, especially when we conjure up the intense pleasure of anticipation. However, that would be difficult to do if it were not related ultimately to an embodied experience and it seems to me that we cannot ignore this dimension of tourism, or, as I will suggest others have done, restrict it mainly to the *visual* sense.

To date most scholars have singled out the visual sense as the dominant sense in tourism (Adler, 1989; Urry, 1990; Macnaghten and Urry, 1998; Rojek, 1995; Crawshaw and Urry, 1997). By this they mean that tourism is not only consumed as an essentially visual phenomenon and commodity (this view, that landscape, this building, that famous painting and so on) and tourism as an essentially visual practice, but that it is also organised in visual terms as a set of signs and mediated by a set of visual technologies. This argument draws on yet another key theme in the development of modernity: the rise to dominance of visualism or the visual appropriation of the world.

Macnaghten and Urry write about the impact of the enlightenment, scientific procedure, new technologies, modern leisures and the technologies of social control and power as having had a profound effect upon the *hierarchy* of the senses and the sensing of the natural world in particular. Whereas in traditional societies great emphasis was given to multi-sensed experience; to oral accounts of the world, story-telling and auricular skills; the aesthetics of touch, proximity and social intimacy and a less inhibited and restricted olfactory sensibility, they argue that in modern societies the visual has become dominant and sidelined other senses.

Although Macnaghten and Urry wish to produce a fully embodied sociology of contemporary society and nature, they are persuaded, particularly by Lefebvre, 1991; Rorty, 1980; Bermingham, 1994; Fabian, 1992; Heidegger, 1977; Jay, 1992; Foucault, 1970 and others that the visual, or what Fabian calls 'Visualism', has dominated the sensing of nature in the west, and should properly be included in a list of globalising trends. For this reason sixteen pages of their chapter called 'Sensing Nature' is given over to vision while just over six are given to the other senses, of which barely over one page is given to the auditory.

First they argue that the visual was a bias inherited from philosophical traditions dating back at least as far as Aristotle. Visuality was developed during the medieval period through the architecture of stained glass windows, the growth of heraldry as a complex visual code, through fifteenth century innovations in linear perspectivism, the science of optics, the fascination with mirrors, an emphasis on the spectacular rituals of public life and the invention of the printing press (Macnaghten and Urry, 1998: 109).

Visualism as an apprehension of nature became entrenched in the scientific practice of disciplined *observation*; a development that undermined any scientific claims based on the mere experience of travel and its written or oral account. Observation sanitises experience of nature by removing other senses and feelings, as if truth itself is merely what can be seen. This was fixed in such orderings as the Linnaean classification that was based solely upon observable structures. Race was another concept of nature that was 'read' visually and directly (and tragically) from the mere 'surface' of nature.

Travel itself was influenced by its former connections to science and discovery. Adler shows how travellers were less encouraged to give emotional accounts of their experience than eyewitness statements and accurate descriptions of visual aesthetics, '[E]xperiences of beauty and the sublime, sought through the sense of sight' (Adler, 1989: 22, cited in Macnaghten and Urry, 1998: 112). According to Urry (1995) this generated what he calls a comparative connoisseurship of nature among the upper class few who were in a position to travel and, literally, collect experiences of nature. The visual consumption of nature was consolidated by further developments. The package tours of Thomas Cook (from 1841 onwards) innovated guidebooks, the identification of scenic sites and the railway carriage as a platform from which nature could be taken in continuous panoramic vision. New technologies such as photography, postcards, maps, piers and promenade walkways focused attention on vision, even to the point of establishing a vision rich mode of 'leisurely walking'. The romantic vision of nature was focused around the visual even though it gave rise to other emotional embodied responses such as fear and awe. It also defined a subset of appropriate natures, opening up areas of mountain, moorland and rugged coast as well as arousing interest in nature leisures, caving, alpinism, and backpacking.

This spectacularism of the romantic gaze popularised the marginal wildernesses and uplands, but they could also be brought home and domesticated through art and souvenirs and by creating simulations through landscape gardening among the rich and bequeathed to others in municipal parklands. According to some gardening analysts (for example, Pugh, 1988) 'gardens were intended for visual consumption' (Macnaghten and Urry, 1998: 113). However, with the technologies of mass tourism and with the proliferation of photography as *the* legitimate representation of nature in place, the natures of the romantic gaze became the focus for holidays and trips for an increasingly wide spectrum of society. From early in the twentieth century when the first national parks were built to the New Deal developments of parkways into specially designed areas of natural beauty in the USA, it became clear that such large numbers of tourists needed to be organised. With few exceptions it was the ordering of their visual senses and visual itinerary that became the principle of management in natural areas. The Blue Ridge Parkway described by Wilson (1992) is a 470-mile long tourist route linking five mountain ranges in Virginia and North Carolina, built in the depths of the depression in the 1930s.

The Blue Ridge Parkway pioneered many of the techniques of landscape management taken up by the tourist industry in the 1950s and after. One of these techniques is signage: like railroads, the Parkway is periodically marked by mileposts, their purpose being to orient motorists *vis-à-vis* their itineraries and to aid road maintenance and administration. [. . .] Other road signage, especially at the entrances is standardised to underline the special qualities of this specially created environment. Gouged wood signs point out road eleva-tions, local history, and the names of distant features of the landscape. Other diversions organise the motor tour: parking over-looks, short hiking trails, local museums, campgrounds, and parks spaced every thirty miles. In this way the planners designed tourist movements into the land itself. (Wilson, 1992: 35)

Macnaghten and Urry note that visitors to natural areas are themselves the objects of surveillance and control by rules of conduct and routing, but more importantly perhaps we can see how tourists and visitors are con-fined to a visual experience, often to visual sites/experiences that have been selected, framed and interpreted (while others may be obscured, bracketed off or 'protected'). Tourists are so used to collecting sites in a fleeting and restless manner that one can understand how this has become a significant way of interacting with the natural world. Even those who prefer making their own routes are to some extent managed visually by the maps they use, the selection of features deemed relevant and the path ways deemed legitimate.

The reduction of nature to visual representations and an increasingly ocular mode of sensing it directly in countryside leisures describe perfectly the manner by which many people in the west experience it as *tourists*. Visualism, the dominance of the visual, partially disembodies relations with the natural world. The pressures of tourism combined with manage-ment strategies to minimise environmental damage further renders any-thing more than the gaze problematic: picking wild flowers, making off-track forays, disturbing rocks or forest or foreshore litter, touching old stonework or fragile tapestries and so forth minimise the acceptance of touch and taste. The continuous flow of tourists into prescribed routes and places enables birds and animals to keep their distance and so renders such places virtually soundless. The scope to gather, taste and smell nature are so reduced that tourism effectively inhibits their activation in anything other than the simulations and hands-on features of visitor centres.

Visualism is consistent with Urry's definition and objectives of tourism: the 'different' and the 'unusual' belong quite clearly to a lexicon of the visual. Detecting difference and placing different objects and phenomena in classifications and taxonomies has tended to be based on surface, visual characteristics. One thinks of the dominant Linnaean system of classifying natural species largely according to differences in visual and surface feature; one thinks of racial classifications; classifications of archaeological finds; classifications of buildings and so on. Similarly the unusual has visual overtones in objects, species and individuals that are anomalous to standard classificatory schemes or entirely new to existing classificatory schemes. In this way, the first marsupials to reach Europe had the power of spectacle and as anomalous creatures they had crowd-drawing potential (Ritvo, 1997). For much the same reason, a rather grim museum of anomalous anatomy (two-headed individuals, extra large organs, Siamese twins etc.) has always drawn crowds at the working class seaside resort of Blackpool, UK.

However against Urry, I want to argue that in many ways the visual has been significantly displaced as the primary sensual modality of tourism, although it is not clear when this may have occurred. One is tempted to think that excitement was always the main thrill in places such as Brighton, UK or Bangkok. Visualism is still very much a part of the tourist experience, how could it not be, but I want to argue that the essentially passive nature of visual consumption in tourism, Urry's *Tourist Gaze* of 1990 and for that matter most of the twentieth century, is now in decline, and more fully embodied modes of tourism are increasingly sought after. It is consistent with this view that tourism is now a way of life, an everyday experience. It is characterised by activity. An indicative list might include: performance, tactility, taste and smell, excitement, acquiring new things, especially through shopping (though not necessarily *new* things), dance, drugs, sex and music. Whereas the visual mode of consumption places distance between the object and the viewer, such that it is the greatest distances that offer the best views, contemporary tastes may still value a view but make greater demands to touch, taste, feel and explore. One senses this is correct when one touches base with developments among one of the most visually orientated sub-group of tourists, the international Japanese tourist. In recent years Japanese tourism taste has changed quite dramatically. Famed for their fleeting photo-opportunity-and-run dashes through tourist spaces, their legendary habits of carting all of their food requirements around with them (from Japan, of course), and their love of photo-technology, the Japanese tourist has made an about turn. According to research of Japan's tourist brochures (Moeran, 1983) the most important concept used in defining the properly touristic is *jibun no hada ni snaka suru* or to 'participate with their own skins'

> They want to experience not sights but action, to 'participate with their own skins' (*jibun no hada ni snaka suru*). [. . .] It is suggested [by holiday brochures] that [tourists] can be party to the smells, to the laughter, to the fun of an evening in Taipei, Barcelona or Los Angeles. He can 'melt' [*toke-komu*] into his surroundings, not 'just as passing traveller, but in touch with the lives of local people. As the Japan Travel Bureau's catchphrase goes: 'Travel is contact' [*tabi wa fureai*]. 'Contact' is the vital word. (Moeran, 1983: 96)

We will analyse this sensual elaboration in the next section.

Feel the moment; make it last: the body in contemporary tourism

'Excitement' and 'relaxation' are central terms in the lexicon of contemporary tourism that reference changes in the significance of the body, whereas the search for the 'different' and the 'unusual' conjures up a more outmoded and possibly cheesy mid-twentieth century sort of experience – very much associated with reducing people, cultures and objects to visual spectacles, objects of desire or amusement and the aesthetic and moral judgement of others. Other 'body' words are associated with excitement and relaxation: challenge, demand, energetic, thrilling, sensational. All of them testify to the tourist focused on their active bodies and their senses as opposed to the largely passive viewing tourist. Identifying the different and the unusual as *visually* relevant belongs also to the language of western imperialism, pornography, romantic idealism and the fleeting world of the free and privileged traveller, prospector, voyeur or flâneur. I want to argue that excitement and relaxation are related to a more recent emphasis on sensual, embodied experiences. It might be the adrenalin rush from risk taking and danger – gambling; flirting; bungee jumping and so on; it might be the experience of 'flow' from surfing or diving; it might be an E or whiz rush or the experience of trance music or a 'big' red wine and its sensory length on the palate; it might be the thrill of climbing, horse-riding, fly fishing or white water canoeing; it might be the excitement of shopping for bargains or hunting for treasures in flea markets. In particular I want to argue that these embodied tourisms are related, even if not exclusively, to a range of technologies of the body that have grown considerably within the tourism industry (see Bell and Lyall, 2001 for a history of growth in 'excitement' tourism or what they call the 'accelerated sublime'). Excitement and relaxation here also relate to a generalised growth in our interest and concern with our bodies, the terms excitement and relaxation deriving from sensory effects that we can learn to stimulate, control and enjoy. These new techniques or technologies of the body have appeared in greater numbers in recent years and have begun to appear regularly in tourism brochures. One thinks here of yoga, meditation, Tantric sex, body building, weight loss, workouts of every kind, diving, skiing, hand gliding, fly fishing. All of these have utilised the format of tourism to extend their markets, notably in the short residential course, the weekend retreat and specialised alternative resorts, lodges and camps. But we are not merely concerned to be healthy, that after all was also the object of eighteenth and nineteenth century spa resorts. We are also trying to *rediscover* the potential of our bodies.

Some sociologists argue that in the period following the Enlightenment we have tended to favour (and also develop) cognitive skills, mental capabilities and intellectual ambitions while at the same time neglecting or sidelining our other sensory capabilities and our bodies more generally. Here we can note that the visual was most clearly and centrally related to cognition and intellectual activity. Some have argued that the body became an awkward, if necessary, appendage to the rational, calculating and scientific objectivity of the mind (and the mind's eye). As modernity progressed, so the story goes, older more highly tuned technologies of the body such as the repertoires of smell acquired by hunter gatherers were lost (Porteus, 1985; 1990; Rodaway, 1994). Our ability to 'read' natural signs using more developed sensory abilities and techniques was lost as science and scientific expertise displaced them and as they were no longer practised by the newly urbanised workers now attuned to working with the machines and instruments of modern manufacturing. Rodaway (1994: 80) for example, argues that the rich smells and odours of an Arab souk contrast powerfully with the sanitised and odour-free western city centres where packaging blocks, sanitising odours and engine fumes mask the 'olfactory potential' of the modern world. This fairly typical claim seems to be quite selective. Car fumes are still a smell as are the deodorising agents used to perfume city spaces in certain ways (indeed perfuming spaces is now a major growth industry). The perfume industry that has achieved this new application would argue that they have been influential in educating the western nose in recent years as both men's and women's perfume sales have rocketed. They would also argue that perfuming a space is not hiding smell but introducing smell. The smells of the city are different perhaps but no less distinct. Certain towns have industries that odorise in distinctive ways. Many British towns such as Bristol and Blandford Forum still have centrally located breweries that generate powerful intensities of malts and hops. As one alights from the train in Warrington, Lancashire one is immediately informed of the local washing powder factories. Equally in New York and other big metropolitan cities the smells of foods and flowers and other products are a defining feature. Anyone who has been in a New York delicatessen will know the smellscapes of individual shops. London's Soho fruit and flower markets announce their proximity despite the fumes of double-decker buses and Sydney streets are a blend of coffee, beer soaked pub floorboards and the semi-tropical scent of recent rain.

Sound is also an important dimension of tourism, typically buried by emphases on vision. If tourism texts were written by people in their teenage years and their twenties I think sound would feature a great deal more. A quick glance through the magazines and journals they read produces masses of instances of the extent to which they travel to hear music. There are at least three sorts of trip made. The first is a trip, usually packaged into weekends, to see a major band. Mostly these are to concerts at least one flight away, in major venues in or near major cities. Second, there are the summer festivals of music, now hugely diversified, which run over upwards of one week. These attract people from very wide circumferences and include, typically, many who drive. Finally we are beginning to see a music/dance scene develop around certain more distant areas that might be part of longer long-haul travel plans. Saldanha (2002), for example, has researched a form of music tourism that has emerged in Goa, India.

So why is it that we should now be more concerned to realise the potential of our bodies through touristic activities as we commence the twenty first century? After all we have become even more machinic, more tied into new technologies, more dependent on expert systems.

One answer is that we have become *generally* disaffected with machines, or at least reliant on the technical systems and the body of experts that used to handle our everyday infrastructures (for example, drinking water quality, food standards; trains and planes; power generation and so on). According to some we live in a risk society where technologies can no longer be viewed as useful additions to our life but contain hidden and unforeseeable risks to our well-being. There is a reaction against science and machines and a generalised wish to recapture and retune our own bodies to our surroundings. It is a generalised search to privilege and restore an involvement in natural processes, including a re-familiarisation with our own bodies (Franklin, 2002a). A pertinent example here is scientific medicine. Just at a time when there have been huge advances in medical technologies and research, western consumers have become highly sceptical of their value. In the *Sunday Times* of 17 September 2001 it was reported that one in ten people admitted to British hospitals become infected with a serious illness. The incidence of dying as a result of mistakes made by doctors (the term is iatrogenic death) is very high, one of the most significant causes of death in recent times. Private medicine has been shown to increase the incidence of surgical interventions and hospital stays, leaving consumers in no doubt as to whose interests it serves. All of this has fuelled a massive recourse to alternative, natural medicines and medical techniques, some of which place more control and responsibility in the hands of the consumer and require them to master new techniques and awareness of their body. One thinks here of the home birth and the breast-feeding movement; the Alexander technique as a therapy for backaches and meditation as an intervention in depressive illnesses. However, scientific medicine is also quite explicitly orientated towards the treatment of illness, not its routine prevention. While at the beginning of the twentieth century scientific medicine made huge advances in curing diseases such as Tuberculosis, Polio and Tetanus – diseases that killed a large proportion of the population – at the end of the century such advances were difficult to sustain. Moreover, the majority of medical problems are now of a different order: depressive and mental disorders; backaches and other chronic but not life-threatening conditions; persistent headaches, allergies, obesity and bad diets. The educated, web-assisted reflexive consumer of the past decade or so was perfectly situated to take over the management of their own preventative medicine, and a range of media advice and therapists entered the market in order to inform and train them. The *Futures* magazine of 2000 predicted that by the year 2025 individuals themselves would address most health problems using simple preventive measures such as fitness and dietary techniques, a trend that is already in train. The tourist body is undoubtedly influenced by these developments. Whereas modern medicine was critically involved in the development of tourism, particularly via the water cures at spa towns and seaside, the embodied experience of this was very passive (relative to the activity of the doctors, nurses, assistants etc.) and involved much lying about (under the healing powers of water or sun) and waiting (for such slow cures to take effect or for the body to convalesce). More recent forms are characterised by their activity, self-direction, the learning and practising of techniques and their reflexivity. Aside from the general aim of fitness is an emphasis on control of the body, and mastery of techniques of the body. Unlike the sun tanned body of mass tourism the contemporary tourist body must be in constant training and development. This has dramatically altered the aesthetics of bodies. The wasted thinness of the 1960s and 1970s may still prowl the catwalks of high fashion but the anorexic look has been mostly replaced by the fit body on tourist trails. But it has also meant that tourism is no longer a period of unqualified indulgence and excess. For these reasons the fit body is no longer exclusively the young body, as depicted by mid-twentieth century holiday postcards. At a rough count on my last three trips to the beach (that just happened to be in Australia, the UK and Norway respectively) almost everyone around me oscillated between relaxation (either sitting reading or sunbathing) cooling down in the sea (swimming and playing) and fitness orientated activities (strenuous games, jogging, running or fitness walking). However, there were also instances of massage, tai-chi, surfing, windsurfing, kite flying, fishing, diving, and horse riding. One intuitively thinks of the classic beach scene as largely inactive, but the eccentric range of active body technologies that once defined the Californian beach are now ubiquitous.

The BSE and Foot and Mouth disease scares of recent years alongside genetic modification of foods and animals have added further doubts and scepticism about the essential beneficence and value of science and technology. Such a view has inevitably enhanced the arguments of those who promote natural alternatives to synthetic and scientific interventions. This has not only resulted in the search for natural healing and natural diets but, arguably, a new aesthetic of the natural world. Whereas areas of pristine natural beauty have appealed to tourists since the early nineteenth century one can identify certain changes in the appeal in recent years. In the nineteenth century the main appeal of nature was essentially aesthetic conjuring up for the properly prepared Romantic sensibility a mystical-visual experience of the Romantic sublime. The archetypal aesthetic experience was derived from the appreciation of the awesome scale and power of nature, and in order to maximise this the tourist had to view nature somewhat at a distance – from the vantage point of mountains, cliffs, gorges and so on where the very widest angle of view could be obtained. The pleasure was in the contemplation, a poetic and intellectual preoccupation and to a lesser extent in capturing that feeling of sublime using verse, sketches or photography. Today the emphasis is arguably the opposite. While people still want to climb hills and mountains for their view, and many still own cameras, there is now a more hands on, embodied desire for contact with the natural world. This is evident from the relatively different types of nature that people wish to experience. The woodlands and forests that were once the preserve of the affluent have become more attractive at the turn of the century and here where the view of landscapes is minimised the detailed textures, smells, and tastes are maximised. As Macnaghten and Urry have found in their research on modern British people and trees 'the experience of trees and woods appear to have intimate bodily significance for many people – as providing contact with nature, as a source of tranquillity, and as a distinct social space where people feel at one with themselves and their family or friends (Macnaghten and Urry, 2001: 179). Moreover they found 'a plea for greater bodily involvement in woods and forests. This appeared to transcend the conventional distinctions between "recreation", "environment" and "education". This was because what many people appeared to be articulating was a desire for a deeper, more continuously *engaged* connection with the life and continuities of woodlands in their areas' (Macnaghten and Urry, 2001: 180). Trees that once obscured the view for the Romantic tourist have become something of a cult object (Rival, 1998). Why this is so is interesting and the answers that emerge from the work of Rival, Macnaghten and Urry and others gather together several postmodern themes. They seem to embody a slower, longer time frame (not the frenetic pace and shortness of the present); they embody a rootedness in place (as opposed to the hypermobility of contemporary life); they are tied into a primordial ecology (not the manufactured natures of the genetic engineer); and they are tied into us culturally through ancient tree cults and pagan ritual. Moreover they stand in the path of progress, new motorways, new towns and retail complexes and have become associated with environmental politics. Getting closer to the forest floor in the proliferation of forest walks is mirrored by new technologies for getting closer to the forest canopy. Canopy walks are now a major new innovation in national parks and even commercial forestry areas. Although we might be hugely concerned about all manner of environmental dangers, not least the destruction of the major forests, our trips to those that remain are reassuring. Reassuring that they are being looked after and that deforestation can be halted. Reassuring also that our visits to them, as tourists, will guarantee their commercial viability. Rojek (1993: 205) also talks of the reoccurrence of reassurance in the tourisms of late modernity. He writes: 'Many popular leisure and tourist attractions are based upon idealised roles and stereotypical situations which are calculated to deliver the feeling of reassurance. [. . .] Our lives seem fraught with complex and ambivalent implications. Against this the nostalgia industry offers a gallery of coherent stories and satisfying resolutions'.

Equally distinct from the Romantic natural gaze are those activities often organised in touristic packages that put the individual back into some meaningful engagement with the natural world. Survival courses in which individuals have to pit themselves against testing situations, obtain local foods and shelter and so on are a major business area, both in terms of books and advice, television and video as well as training courses themselves. All across America in almost every state there are several schools catering to this market (over 2000 in all), notably wilderness schools and primitive skills training courses (see Box 4.1).

Box 4.1   Welcome to Two Coyotes Wilderness School!

At Two Coyotes our goal is to provide a fun environment where participants develop an understanding of the natural world and a feeling of comfort in the woods. We mentor youngsters in survival and awareness skills practised for thousands of years by native cultures around the globe. Our participants actively engage in making and using many survival tools from materials they gather in a traditional way. We augment these skills through storytelling, games, and crafts. As these skills grow our students begin to see their relationship to the animals and plants around them. These skills are found in all our ancestry. Wherever we trace our roots to, not too long ago our forebears lived very close to the land, they knew how to live in harmony with the land. It is our hope that by reconnecting with these ancient teachings we can learn to live in balance with the natural world once again.

www.twocoyotes.org/

The *UK Survival School* offers a large range of individual, group and corporate survival courses (around 35 annually) from its base in the mountains of Wales as well as in tropical locations, arctic conditions and the Australian bush. Clearly some people have a professional need to understand survival in the Welsh or other mountains, but the numbers do not seem to justify such an elaborate operation. Although corporate team building is also a significant part of its business, as their own home page suggests, their key client groups are those wishing to take up the challenge of adventure tourism (see Box 4.2).

However, survival, wilderness and primitive skills courses are not the only tourism that specifically places the human body into a non-simulated engagement with the natural world. Other good examples are hunting and fishing, diving, sailing and so on. All of these have been central to vacation experiences all across the western world for a long time and have shown dramatic growth in recent years (see Löfgren, 1999; Gill, 2001; Franklin, 1999), although they are conspicuous by their absence in the tourism literature.

Box 4.2

Nature is neutral and by learning to live with the environment and climates we hold the key to survival, the most fundamental human instinct. At the UK Survival School we aim to be innovative in the delivery of our courses. The first objective is to create a wider under-standing of nature and to provide essential knowledge and skills to sustain and save life. The second objective is to have fun learning these skills.

The body and mind have a unique ability to cope with challenging and arduous conditions and it is to this end that the UK Survival School has developed courses structured to provide not only the knowledge and skills to overcome such conditions, but also to give confidence to those people for whom the world of adventure is yet to be discovered. There are infinite opportunities and exciting experi-ences to be found in the world's remote regions, from the mountains to the deserts and the jungles to the Poles – the UK Survival School can provide the key to open that door.

www.uksurvivalschool.co.uk/about-us.htm

On the basic survival weekend you will learn how to prepare for and react to a survival situation, to acquire water and food, how to make fire and cook with it, to find and build a shelter, how to cross rivers, despatch a distress signal, and to navigate by nature and a compass.

www.uksurvivalschool.co.uk/basic-survival.htm

One of the ways in which contemporary Japanese tourists attempt to achieve 'close touch' is through food and drink. Gone are the days when tourists took home-produced foods with them or only ate domestic foods when away from home. From at least the mid-1970s eating local foods has become normative, and indeed one of the most prominent ways of establishing place identity and establishing touristic anticipation in tourist marketing. In this way western 'taste' has expanded considerably and food has become the basis upon which to structure tourism, as opposed to being merely a pleasurable by-product. Hence there is now a considerable market for wine tourism all around the vine-growing world. Cheeses, beers, mushrooms, whisky, ports and sherry for example, all now generate tourist trails. Meanwhile western supermarkets attempt to keep up with tourist-led taste by making sure foods enjoyed on holiday become available at home. Indeed one of the by-products of the tourism industries is the market they create for export industries. Hence Spanish agriculture has made fabulous economic gains on the back of tourism from northern countries such as Britain, Germany, and Scandinavia, particularly during the slacker winter period. Thus, the exotic foods that represented modernity on the curtains and tableware of the 1950s have now become part of our routine diets, via an extended period of *sensual* tourism.

Further Reading

Chambers, I. (1994) *Migrancy, Culture, Identity*. London: Routledge.

Crawshaw, C. and Urry, J. (1997) 'Tourism and the photographic eye' in C. Rojek and J. Urry (eds), *Touring Cultures*. London: Routledge.

Fullagar, S. (2000) 'Desiring nature: Identity and becoming in narratives of travel' *Cultural Values* 4 (1) 58–76.

Saldanha, A. (2002) 'Music tourism and factions of bodies in Goa' *Tourist Studies* 2 (1): 43–63.

Wilson, A. (1992) *The Culture of Nature*. Oxford: Blackwell.

Part 2

Objects and Rituals

5

Tourist objects, tourist rituals

SUMMARY

- Social constructivist or humanist tourism theory
- The social life of souvenirs
- Objects of travel
- Ritual and tourism: heritage, carnival and pilgrimage objects
- Antecedents to rituals of tourism
- Carnival
- Pilgrimage
- Nationalist heritage and the interpellative nature of national objects

Here is a paradox. Tourism abounds with things, tourist things, and tourists are tied up in a world of tourist things for a considerable period of their time. And yet, if you read all the past and current text books on tourism, and make a list of all the really important explanations of tourism, the key concepts and theoretical developments, you will discover that these things are not held to be very significant. At least, not in themselves, that is. This needs immediate qualification. In tourism theory tourist things are both omnipresent and impotent (or inert, passive). Tourist things tend to be significant only in what they represent; as a meaningful set of signs and metaphors (of *social* things, mainly ideas, values, discourses etc.). In *The Tourist Gaze* this is particularly evident when Urry talks of the *fleeting* nature of the gaze upon tourist objects: whatever the significance of an object, and its relationship to the specific social discourses that authorise the gaze upon it, we can say that it is purely semiotic. Elaborating this we can say that through discourse, tourist objects are purposefully mantled with *socially* relevant sign values (see also Hitchcock, Teague and Graburn, 2000 for the relevance of souvenirs for memory and meaning).

So, in *themselves* they are secondary, passive, arbitrary, inactive, inert; their meaning and significance are measured in other terms. As Law (1994: 23) argues, 'often it seems to me that it is *only* human agents and their knowledge, certain kinds of social interactions, and texts that are taken seriously'. This paradox (tourism abounds with objects, which in the literature refer mainly to, or reflect, the non-object human world) and its solution provide the main framework for this chapter. The solution to this paradox is remarkably simple: tourism teems with tourist things because they are absolutely essential for its very existence; because tourism is comprised of necessary and important *links* and *relationships* between humans, machines, animals and plants and an enormous universe and variety of objects, and because their interrelationship produces *effects* that ought to interest us. As with any form of organised, ordered activity, tourism can really only be thought about in terms of these assemblages because to think about only say, the human dimension, is to artificially reduce the complexity and the number of relationships (and assemblages of relationships that have consequences), at our disposal; tools and props needed to understand how and why particular tourist things happen. What I will be suggesting then is that things (as well as humans) play an enabling role in tourism, they enable it to happen and they enable those processes that are central to tourism to unfold.

It might appear difficult to grasp at this stage but I am saying that tourist things are active agents in the production of tourism. This is difficult because we are used to thinking about the world as if everything in it is arranged into classes of things, each class having specific and defining features of its own. In this way we are used to according agency mainly to humans (depending on who you are, degrees of agency are also attributed to some animals of course) and we tend to find the idea of an object (such as a stick of seaside rock or a postcard) as having agency absurd. However, this is only because we confuse agency (the ability to create effects or products) with consciousness (the ability to have a conception of oneself as active in the world). To put it another way, there is a social life of tourist objects without which tourism would not work. John Law again:

> . . . there would be no social ordering if the materials which generate these were not heterogeneous. In other words, the somatic – the resources of the body – though these are already heterogeneous, are altogether inadequate to generate the kinds of social effects that we witness around about us. For orderings spread, or sometimes seek to spread, across time and space. But, and this is the problem, left to their own devices *human actions and words do not spread very far at all*. For me the conclusion is inescapable. Other materials, such as texts and technologies, surely form a crucial part of any ordering. Law, 1994: 3)

Celia Lury (1997: 76–7) is one of the few contributors to tourist studies who have begun to analyse tourism in this way.

> . . . objects help to comprise tourism; more than this, it is not simply objects-in-motion but also objects-that-stay-still that help make up tourism. It is further suggested that looking at the career or biography of objects, as they move or stay still, will add to what we can say about the lives of people that travel (and then go home), that is, tourists.

What is it that the analysis of objects can add to our understanding of tourism? As with much of the new literature on the social significance and 'activity' of objects, Lury draws on Appadurai's influential book, *The Social Life of Things* (1986):

> Tracing the social and cultural movement of objects, Appadurai claims, helps identify the dynamic, processual aspects of social life, illuminating not simply the small scale shifts in an object's meaning, but also broader transformations in social organisation itself. What I want to do here is to consider both some of the ways in which the capacity of objects to travel and stay still is constituted in and helps secure particular relations of dwelling-in-travel and travel-in-dwelling, and also to suggest that these relations are constitutive of both the very objectness of objects and the organisation of space. (Lury, 1997: 77)

We will pick up Lury's intriguing argument that exemplifies the approach advocated in this chapter (Law, 1994: 23 has called it *relational materialism*) shortly. This will form part of a sequence of other ways in which relational materialism or the social life of things approach can be useful for understanding tourism. First, we will take seriously Appadurai's notion that it is in the biography of objects that their agency and social life become apparent. I will use as an example here the social life of a tourist souvenir, in this case, bark cloth souvenirs from Fiji. I will examine Ewin's claim that cultural efflorescence in Fiji could not have come about without the persistence of bark cloth production for tourism. This is an interesting finding in the light of arguments that claim the opposite, that tourism systematically threatens or destroys authentic cultures. Continuing the theme of identity and especially the link between tourism and nationalism, I will explore the value of the concept *interpellation* as yet another mode in which objects enter our social life and create social effects. This will be useful at a later point in the book where interpellative effects are noted. We will return to Celia Lury's analysis of 'objects of travel'. I will then consider the relationship between objects and the ritual base(s) of tourism. Of all theoretical accounts of tourism my students are normally most inspired by the work of Shields (1990) (and others) on the ritual nature of much tourism activity. This body of analysis has been widely read and applied to many new cases but it still sits alone and is poorly connected to other general accounts of tourism. What is especially intriguing, though poorly realised by its authors, is the material basis of this activity. It will be argued that in common with almost all human ritual activity, it is really very dependent upon ritual *objects*. We will look at a series of examples of this from contemporary heritage sites in the USA in which objects are used to focus attention on national life and belonging, and through an extended exploration of both the rituals of carnival and pilgrimage.

Before that, I want to explore in more detail the place of tourist objects in what we might call a social constructivist or humanist tourism theory. By doing so we will be better able to locate its origins and antecedents as well as to draw contrasts between it and approaches based on relational materialism.

Social constructivist or humanist tourism theory

To repeat an argument from earlier in the book, the two most influential explanations of tourism identify the significance of tourist objects and what they signify to tourists, but that is as far as they go. They do not ask what sorts of relationship tourists have *with* tourist objects, or whether tourist objects engender responses from tourists and whether those responses themselves have implications for new social and cultural forms. Also, they have not considered the cultural ramifications of hybrid tourist forms that combine technical and machinic objects with human counterparts: humans and cars (but see Urry, 1999); families and motor caravans; individuals and video cameras (but see Crawshaw and Urry, 1997); children and games machines (but see Law, 2001); tourism clothing and gadgetry (but see Michael, 2001). This chapter argues that tourists are inextricably intertwined with tourist objects and that this relationship matters or has important implications for tourism behaviour, the experience of tourism, the social relations of tourism and the impact of tourism on the world. This sort of argument is very different from previous explanations and investigations of tourism because they focused only on human social and mental constructions of the world; it was as if tourists were insulated from the non-social, inside their own cognitive self-absorption. So, for example, the explanations of tourism that Rojek and Urry (1997) identified as dominant in the literature suggest that tourism reduces to the search or quest for authenticity missing in everyday modern life. It is the search for a true and Arcadian humanity as opposed to the synthetic, simulated and ephemeral world of modernity. In this, objects can confirm or deny authenticity but they are essentially passive; objects that really only require the tourist to have a brief encounter with them, and even that is largely visual rather than embodied, interactive or performative. Urry's tourist gaze idea also only requires objects to confirm or deny difference and hence provide a pleasurable encounter with otherness, a welcome relief from the repetitive and the everyday. The tourist gaze theory also postulates a relatively passive tourist subject who is exposed to socially specific and differentiated discourses that authorise the nature of particular gazes. This of course links tourism and tourists to the wider notion of social order, domination and power that make subtle but effective 'ordering' moves through popular cultural forms, surveillance and visual technologies as well as through the control of movement. But again, objects themselves are essentially passive providing a vocabulary of meaning and a material manifestation for social discourses – ideas and arguments that in their assemblage and operation are intended or attempt to lead to particular patterns of behaviour and social order.

If you think about it in another way, however, tourism does seem on the face of it to be more *object-* rather than simply *idea-* or *discourse-*orientated. Tourists have an intimate and complex relationship *with* tourist sites, heritage buildings, museum artefacts, art gallery objects, souvenirs and postcards, cameras and videos, foods and drinks, tickets and passports, planes and trains. However it is not just physical objects that we must count because tourism also abounds with commodities, or things that have an exchange value, and these can range from tourism services (guiding for example) culture (for instance rituals performed for a fee) and nature (payment to visit or see natural objects, habitats, species etc.). These tourist things are intertwined in the practice of tourism, we do not merely look at them or search them out. We become *involved* with them. We collect souvenirs and we may even display them in our homes. We make gifts of souvenirs to people and we send messages to people on postcards. As Franklin and Crang (2001) argue:

> Even thinking about the pre-eminent visual and representational practice of photography, it is clear that this is not just promoting or affirming an image of places, but also about things circulating around and with tourists. Thus, picture postcards that circulate among and sustain social networks, snapshots that are composed, posed, taken, developed, selected or discarded, stored or displayed all are, not just symbols but, material practices that serve to organise and support specific ways of experiencing the world (see Crang, 1997). (Franklin and Crang, 2001: 15)

We like to be in an old building, to hear the echo perhaps in an old cathedral or to smell the aroma of an ancient castle. We carry objects around with us that mark us out as visitors and tourists, we have maps in our hands, cameras across our shoulders and we trail suitcases around with us. Some might prefer the pose of traveller to tourist but both can be identified by their tourist things, and their enthusiasm for these things. We actively engage with a whole series of machines that transport us, house us, support us, entertain us, permit us to be creative and protect us. The other day I met a man who said 'for me, a holiday means driving' and in part he meant being in a car, his car; driving his car. What he could see from the car entered into this passion but part of the pleasure came directly from the car, from movement and mobility and the sum total of experiences and outcomes that result from the interaction between a machine and a person, namely *driving* (which is a human–machine hybrid experience). Other theories or accounts of tourism (for example, Wilson, 1992) would tend to emphasise what he could see from his car but what of *driving* itself, the relationship between the machine and the person? In Wilson's own terms the car/tourist has had a major impact not only on the development of a car-based tourism in the USA but also on how tourism objects were framed to be viewed and experienced from car windows, car parks, camping grounds, the non-space of motels and so on (see Augé, 1995). A similar 'object effect' has been noted for the riverboat in the process of nationalisation in the USA (see Sears, 1989).

Tourists like to shop too, and shopping has been recognised as extremely important to contemporary tourism, both to the tourism industry as well as to the enjoyment of being a tourist. Shopping is listed as one of the most common tourist activities and a tourist city would certainly be judged on the basis of its shopping. For Americans travelling overseas, for example, shopping was reported as their second most important activity (Travel Industry Association of America, 1998). Some cities such as Singapore are shopping tourist cities. London and Paris are also shopping tourist cities, in part. However, one is hardly escaping modern society for authentic humanity in the international branded electrical shops of Singapore or indeed finding respite from constant stimulation and change when one buys branded fashion goods from London or Paris. Further, one can hardly tell the *difference* between any shopping centre in the world, particularly in terms of the goods sold, so Urry's central emphasis in *The Tourist Gaze* on a pleasurability that derives from difference would struggle to explain the significance of much contemporary shopping to tourism. So, again could it be that we need to look instead for the sorts of relationships that tourists have with tourist-shopping objects. Should we look instead for the performative, embodied and interactive relationship (and their consequences) with these objects? What is going on when tourists 'pick out' and 'pick up'; when they haggle and bargain; what is it for them to have and to hold and to touch and to imagine the object into their lives? Why do they collect, give and assemble objects and how are the consequences of these *hybrid* activities constitutive of social life and culture?

As tourists we are also very close to a multitude of objects and in part, tourism is all about *attending* to those objects, adopting the correct manner before them, taking sufficient time to see and read them, making sure we are attentive to the landscape and city scapes that they jointly compose. We like to feel the sand beneath our feet, to smell delicious foods, to find seashells and to watch craftspeople at work, making things – to sell to tourists. These are not particularly profound observations, but it is worth making them if only because so many writers on tourism barely touch upon this dimension. For most tourism books the centre stage is entirely taken up with tourists themselves (*their* behaviour, what *they* are doing, what *they* want and why, how *they* vary and change, what motivates *them*) and the places (and peoples) they visit (resorts, sites, regions, tours, cities, villages, cultures, settlements, natural areas and so on). Places are import-ant to tourist studies because these are the natural regions, the planning, commercial and accounting units of tourism. Places have marketing budgets, places have specific tourism associations and departments, tour-ism strategies, tourist surveys and what we could call a touristic- or place-identity. Places are also frequently the measurable units for assessing tourism impacts. Places are also things of course but they are massive amalgams of all the things and what we might call the 'thinginess' of tourism. Places gather these numerous things together into views, land-scapes, cityscapes, marinescapes and postcards provide a device (for dis-courses) to define and frame what is deemed relevant to the visiting tourist.

I am going to argue that this inevitable emphasis on place also inadvert-ently masks the significance of things to tourists and tourism. We may notice here that theories and methods that try to understand tourism from a commercial and economic angle can obscure the cultural content and implications of tourism. Indeed I am going to argue that all manner of objects that are associated with tourism from the most sacred sites to the most kitsch souvenirs and kiss-me quick hats of the English seaside holiday hold tourism together as a cultural activity. I am going to argue that far from being the ephemeral, epiphenomena of tourism, they are central to its very possibility.

However, before I introduce these arguments and materials I want to consider one other reason why tourist studies have been prevented from fully grasping the significance of tourist things. This, I want to emphasise, has to do with conceiving tourism as a predominantly visual activity.

John Urry has argued that tourism is an *essentially* visual activity, an activity in which the objects of the gaze are there just to be seen, to be appreciated for their difference, to be recognised and then left behind in the restless quest for yet more visual novelties. At the extreme, under what we might call *postmodern visualism*, things themselves are potentially redundant as the sign becomes more important than the signified, the things themselves. However, even signs (images, frames, adverts etc.) are things. Of course the tourist industry knows only too well how appro-priately framed visual representations of tourist objects work their magic on consumers. But to note this is not to exhaust the role that objects play in tourism. Indeed, it is to miss perhaps the main significance of things to tourism – it tends to mask their participation in the *social life* of tourism. This is because the tourist gaze tends to render objects passive in contrast to the effect of the mental activity of humans. For example, the visualism of the Romantic gaze emphasised most particularly the significance of the *imagination*, the ability to conjure mentally the meanings and significances of what is seen. Only humans have imagination, only humans can learn to appreciate and develop their imagination though education and intellectual attention and only humans can direct their attention and their imagination (primarily) through their gaze. The visual has been placed in this dominant sensual position precisely because of its special relationship to cognitive, mental or intellectual processes, but in so doing it shifts our attention to the agency of humans as the principal source of agency in the social world. The humanist perspective, and we should note that most western academic perspectives are, or have been humanist for at least 300 years, places humanity at the centre of analysis and privileges humanity in models of agency. Humans in this account are both the most important object of analysis and the proper subjects of history. For a number of reasons this anthropocentric view of the world has come under sustained critique in recent years, a twin prong critique in which both the notion of human privilege and the uniqueness of human agency are questioned. Humanist concepts and theories such as nationalism and nation formation or tourism only seem to call forth or require the activity and agency of humans and in such accounts non-humans are required simply to be inactive symbols, metaphors and metonyms. Their existence and significance are entirely mediated by the social and as Peter Berger once said of animals, they remain mysterious from us and retain their unknowable secrets in silence. Animals, stars, sites and things become merely a linguistic palette for cultural creativity. Pickering defines the humanities as humanist 'inasmuch as they study and theorise a world of humans amongst themselves' (2000: 3). So a humanist perspective also tries to create a world of humans separate from non-humans and to insulate this world of humans from any direct or important non-human intervention. This was achieved initially by the arbitrary classificatory division of academic labour that separated the human from the natural sciences. In this way, we could say that rocks, engines and dogs were properly the domain of natural science while economies, societies and tourists were properly the domain of social sciences. However, this separation was consolidated when Durkheim and the subsequent *social* sciences established the case for a domain of facts that was entirely *social*. Here was a world of social facts, of social institutions, practices, cultures and structures that was focused on, and created by, humans among themselves. There was great excitement about this because it was as if a major discovery had been made, a new dimension of life that had hitherto been hidden. Much work was required to discover and name the manner by which this entirely human world worked, as if one was setting about discovering how a machine or the planets operated; to discover the secret or unseen ways in which human societies worked or how they were socially ordered. Concepts emerged to describe these invisible *social* forces that almost matched those that ordered the physical or natural world such as gravity, electricity and energy: sociologists discovered ideology, hegemony, fetishism, capitalism, discourse, the panopticon and so on.

Among the more influential of these in the history of tourist studies was the discovery by Foucault of the development of new visual technologies of surveillance as a means of maintaining control and order in the dramatically reconfigured urban spaces of the early nineteenth century western city, the early years of mass society. The metaphor for these new technical means of ordering, not through direct physical punishment but through observation and surveillance was the panopticon, a new model prison in which all prisoners can be watched from a single vantage point, and as a result of which prisoners took part in their own self-ordering. Crawshaw and Urry identify the social implications of this technology for tourism in the following way:

> The reverberating economy of gazes that is established is taken by Foucault as a mechanism of surveillance that can then be widely applied. And it is a mechanism that has parallels with photography, as the modern traveller both subjects others and is subject to, an increasingly interiorised gaze. Both the panopticon and photography involve the material production of bodies, of the bodies that are gazed upon and the bodies that undertake the gazing (Batchen, 1991: 25). Crary interestingly argues that Foucault's opposition of surveillance and spectacle seems to overlook how the effects of the two regimes of power can in effect coincide (1990: 18). This is because of the ways in which people become objects of observation, and in particular how vision itself becomes a modality of surveillance and discipline. (Crawshaw and Urry, 1997: 182)

However, visual technology not only promised social order that extends from the control of deviance to the control of leisure/pleasure, it promised truth itself and Crawshaw and Urry offer an illuminating summary of the ways in which visual description and data based on observation became foundational for scientific procedure, debate and the establishment of modern epistemology. The more the visual became the proper means of apprehending the truth of the world in the emerging sciences, the more widely the visual and visual technologies became used and desired generally, in education, art and exploration. This spread widely among the middle and upper classes and gave rise to travel not for scientific purposes but for aesthetic purposes, and a new connoisseurship emerged for buildings, architecture and natural landscapes. The Romantic gaze therefore linked the notion of truth and beauty to the visual sense, but also to the prepared, sophisticated and trained mind's eye of the viewing subject. Paradoxically, the technology of photography was brought into being by the build up of a desire to *fix* the fleeting nature of the gaze and not the other way around. And it is therefore not a mere coincidence that the first major tourism companies and the arrival of photography occurred within a few years of each other, around the year 1840.

This new technical–aesthetic innovation produced ripple effects through the nineteenth century world of art, design and literature and gained an extremely solid place in high culture, the officially recognised domain and standard of intellectual and artistic excellence. Such a pedigree infused touristic practices with an air of cultivated elevation that quickly and visibly created lines of social and cultural distinction among the new middle classes that were emerging as a result of commercial and industrial expansion. In particular the cultured imagination required for tourism could be used to debar or disqualify the uneducated working classes, travelling in larger groups, from appreciating the same touristic spaces. Wordsworth, for example, was particularly against opening up the English Lake District for workers outings, giving this reason for his antipathy. Tourism had become and should remain, poetic. But it was also Romantic, which is to say striving for the very highest standards of civilised behaviour. As connoisseurs, the new tourists sought experiences of the aesthetic sublime; a spiritual experience of the world that could only be conjured by the educated imagination. Above all else it was an intellectual activity or effect and the visual path into it involved 'a prolonged contemplative [look] regarding the field of vision with a certain aloofness and disengagement, across a tranquil interval' (Bryson, 1983: 94, cited in Crawshaw and Urry, 1997: 181).

> The photographer and then the viewer are seen to be above and dominant over a static and subordinate landscape, which lies out beyond us inert and uninviting our inspection (Taylor, 1994: 38–9). Such photographic practices thus demonstrate how nature was to be viewed, as dominated by humans and subject to their mastery; the mode of viewing being taken as emblematic of the relationship of domination of humans over nature, and also of men over women. (Crawshaw and Urry, 1997: 183)

The figure of the aloof tourist, standing away from and frequently above nature or city created a necessary distance or perspective between the viewing subject and the touristic object and although 'the view', 'perspectives' and visually framed constructions have remained a part of tourism, it is questionable whether our understanding of tourism should be based on this as the essential practice. Put another way, one would not want to dispute the foundational and influential nature of the tourist gaze, but we might say that it is only one among many types of touristic relationship with objects and that many others do precisely the opposite: close the gap between tourist subject and tourist object; make the relationship interactive rather than anthropocentric; create hybrid forms and networks of agency between humans and objects rather than a separable world of the human and the non-human; contribute to a heterogeneously ordered world rather than one characterised by a social order.

As we have noted earlier, accounts that emphasise the tourist gaze as the central cultural content of tourism create a distance or perspective between the viewing tourist and the viewed object. Put another way, our understanding of tourism as organised through visualism focuses everything on the viewing subject. It is the tourist who is doing everything while objects are simply the chosen backdrop and the carriers of signs and meanings. This view of the world in which it is only humans who are actively doing things, or at least doing things that are relevant to understanding the social and cultural world, has recently become the subject of some major rethinking in social and cultural theory. This human-focused approach (or humanism) not only privileges the human as the principal agent in the construction and creation of a social and cultural world, it also privileges certain kinds of specifically human forms of agency. For example, the social and cultural world we inhabit (and tourism is a part of this) is thought of as an intellectual construction, wrought mainly through cognitive and symbolic processes, a world that is mapped out, designed or conceived mentally prior to its realisation. Social order, for example, is thought of as an intellectual design or blueprint that precedes its implementation. In this scheme, nature and non-human objects are only of interest in the light they throw on the symbolic construction of the human world, as they are called upon to symbolise or carry social and cultural meanings. In this way a significant amount of sociological and anthropological work has been spent on deconstructing the cultural meanings of objects. The tendency has been to ask questions such as 'what is the significance (for this specific human group under examination) of this pattern or that sculpture, or this mask or that animal or this ritual or that story'? The non-human world of objects then becomes saturated with human meanings that can provide valuable clues about the nature of our social and cultural life. In particular, we have asked how these meanings and the discourses they belong to, establish particular patterns of social order. This seems a perfectly reasonable way to proceed on the face of it, but in recent years the very idea of a singular social order, based on the metaphor of a master plan system of the like that characterises engines and computers, has been effectively questioned. In place of a homogeneous unifying order, of the sort Foucault identified at several earlier stages of modernity, we are now inclined to believe such edifices are unlikely. There is a growing suspicion that something so massive as a social order is unlikely to arise from a single organising cluster of agency or from multiple simultaneous ordering agencies. Rather, we should recognise the messiness of social and cultural life, the incomplete and multiply contested nature of social ordering, the sheer multiplicity of configurations of humans and non-humans and objects that have implications, intended or otherwise, for the way they interact with each other and with orders of smaller and larger magnitudes around them. This is a world full of surprises, unanticipated occurrences and relationships that arise from the heterogeneous and uncontrollable clustering and arrangements of humans and non-humans, and as social scientists we should be attentive to this field of possibilities, and not fixated on discovering the blueprint that explains everything. There is no ultimate explanation, or order to find, only 'orderings', 'explanations'. So these new theoretical possibilities call on us to reflect on tourism with this in mind. The general theories of tourism that groan under the burden of having to explain too much can be laid to rest, or at least unpacked and made to do less (Rojek and Urry, 1997). In particular we can abandon, hopefully forever, the search for singular or megalithic functionalist explanations for tourism, that is to say, explanations that describe how tourism contributes to or relates to a social order. In doing this we are freed up to explore the more heterogeneous and unfolding or open-ended sociology/geography/political economy (etc.) of tourism. Further, this will not be constrained by humanism or an anthropocentric tourism, we are free to examine for the first time tourism as heterogeneous clusters of humans and non-humans, clusters and networks comprised of touring humans and touristic objects.

The social life of souvenirs

Souvenirs are a fascinating class of objects, not only because they enable the recreation of a touristic experience to occur but also because they seem to embody and retain something of the place (and its significance) where they were purchased. This is nowhere clearer than in the case of souvenir objects sold to pilgrims. In the case of 'pilgrim badges' of Thomas Becket sold from his pilgrim shrine at Canterbury Cathedral, these objects themselves were 'often regarded as secondary relics themselves' taking on some of Becket's miraculous powers, to heal the blind for example (Lyle, 2002: 81). However, in the case of Ewins' (1999; 2002) study of bark cloth souvenirs sold to tourists in Fiji it is clear that tourist objects can trace an interesting biography during which they play a critical role in social change.

Bark cloth is a papery material made from certain native plants of Polynesia. In Fiji they are called *tapa*; an onomatopaeic word that refers to the tapping sound made during its production. Before tourism came to Fiji *tapa* was made for clothing, ritual garments and bedding. It was ornately stencilled by patterns that were emblematic of the particular locality of its makers. When steam ocean liners first called in on Fiji local artefacts were frequently bought at markets and this spawned a manufacturing industry of especially small pieces of tourist *tapa*. Ewins argues that tourism is frequently blamed for the 'trinketisation' of local indigenous cultures, part of the process whereby tradition is trivialised, commodified and extinguished. However, Ewins' research reveals that tourist *tapa* in Fiji actually had the opposite effect: it enabled the efflorescence of tradition to stand as a bulwark against forces of change and a weakening of indigenous Fijian culture.

In Fiji, as elsewhere, cheap manufactured cloth quickly replaced the wearing of *tapa* clothing during the twentieth century but tourist *tapa* remained a lucrative source of income for women on islands such as Vatulele. Tourist *tapa* became the main reason why *tapa* continued to be made even though in addition to the small pieces made for tourists, some of the larger pieces continued to be made for ritual exchange (weddings, funerals and other ritual occasions). Tourist *tapa retained* a large proportion of women in certain localities in full time artisanal production, and throughout this period the skills were passed on to new generations.

During the 1980s and 1990s, indigenous Fijians were threatened by a loss of political power to migrant Indian cultures whose power base was in business. The ownership of land in Fiji was dominated constitutionally by

Figure 5.1 *Tourist* tapa, *Fiji*. Source: Rod Ewins.

the pre-colonial chiefs but the value of this land had declined, as agriculture was now less profitable. A profound challenge to their historic, or traditional social ascendency. As a result of this Ewins is able to show that traditional ritual life became more intensified. Not only were ritual occasions more elaborately performed but also more indigenous Fijians, including lower status groups were now performing traditional ritual more frequently. Since *tapa* is central to ritual observations both in terms of wearing it and as gifts, the very fact that the tourist trade had maintained the craft skill base meant that when this new demand occurred they had the resources to switch from tourist production to supplying the local market.

Objects of travel

In an essay of this title Celia Lury (1997) explored the ways in which culture can become detached from place and travel, often enough in the form of the flows and travels of objects. It is the ability of culture to become spatially detachable from place and context of origin through flows of objects that make a touristic everyday world possible. This is not a world where cultures exist discretely in their own separate spaces (one of the assumptions in a great many tourism texts) but they travel and flow, having no cultural epicentre or boundedness. We do not have to travel to other cultures, they travel to us in multiple and infinitely nuanced forms, through objects themselves, through media and advertising, through images on television, internet and print media, through foods, aromas and technologies. Of course not everyone lives in this touristic everyday world (at least, not quite yet); for Lury it is an artefact of what she calls global cosmopolitanism, but, as the name implies, it is an infectious state and has no obvious or permanent boundaries. 'In this way, global cosmopolitanism contributes to the formation of new hierarchies, and transforms the terms of object – people practices in tourism'. In global cosmopolitanism people are *open* to objects, curious and highly interested in objectness and the cultural genealogies and fusions that they permit. In a similar way, Lury argues that objects themselves are increasingly building global cosmopolitanism into them: their 'user friendliness is the quality in objects that reciprocates the open-mindedness of people' (Lury, 1997: 82).

Lury is interested in the way these objects of travel become re-embedded elsewhere as travel-in-dwelling and she cites the manner in which key retailers (Habitat, Benetton etc.) transfer meanings conventionally associated with places and cultures elsewhere to ordinary household objects: such that 'travelling is superimposed *within* dwelling to create objects of travel that dwell' (Lury, 1997: 83). Lury interestingly shows how Swatches are believed by their manufacturers and their consumers to somehow embody Swiss-ness, and as a result of this, benefit from a generalised sympathy towards the Swiss: as their senior executive remarked, 'We're nice people from a small country. We have nice mountains and clear water' (Lury, 1997: 86).

Of course the way in which these 'object effects', as she calls them, work is by drawing on repertoires of experience in tourist–object relationships. So for example, prior to the formation of global cosmopolitanism where we can say that the distinction between 'dwelling' and 'travel' has merged into a new way of life, travellers, trippers and tourists established a variety of relationships and practices with objects that travel. Typically the traveller establishes a fascination for what Lury calls *traveller-objects*. These include arts and crafts and items of historical, political or religious significance 'in relation to national or folk cultures' (Lury, 1997: 78). These are objects 'whose ability to travel well is integrally linked to their ability to signify their meaning immanently, most commonly by an indexical reference to their "original dwelling"'. Their meaning and integrity is based on what Lury calls practices of symbolic binding whereby they are completely tied to their specific place of origin, in many cases they are tied or even prevented by law from being moved from their dwelling. As such, it is often only their image that travels.

In complete contrast, are *tripper-objects*, including mass produced souvenirs, 'found' objects such as pebbles from the beach or 'incidental' objects such as bus tickets, or matchboxes. Their meaning is not given in their places of origin as with traveller objects but in their final resting place, 'as something to be brought home'. 'While the object may have 'personal', 'sentimental' meaning in its final resting place, this is a meaning that is not intrinsic to the object and thus is not publicly valued. Tripper-objects are objects whose object-ness is lost in space, as the binding practices in which place and culture are combined in physical charac- teristics are undone (or rather, never take shape) in the travelling-dwelling practices of tripping' (Lury, 1997: 79).

Finally Lury describes *tourist-objects*, objects that are self-consciously located in *mobility* itself. They are in-between objects, neither meaningful as a result of their place of origin or their final resting place but by their very nature, in between – embodying the very movement of travel itself. They might include clothing such as t-shirts referencing the fact of having visited somewhere, 'through television programmes and alternative health products to types of food' (Lury, 1997: 80).

Of course this is a schematic account of tourist-object relationships and in fact there will be less distinctiveness and indeed, in the biography of individual objects there may even be a degree of switching from one to another. But the point of this is to show how objects undermine the fixity of culture and place in specific spaces and show how they constitute an important range of touristic experiences before, during and after the physical movement of humans themselves. But in addition it shows that the movements of objects and humans are not synonymous, objects do not always accompany humans and they engender effects separate from those of the travellers themselves. Before the arrival of global cosmo- politanism, the shrinic collections of tripper souvenirs in many western households not only brought back memories of place and tales of travel but they were physical manifestations of local social solidarities – they were the annual exchanges of people who might be missed as they travel away from home; those people who were thought about 'while away' from them; those people who could not be left out of gift exchange. Not merely sentimental, they might also describe to attentive visitors, various routes of social mobility as seaside wares were replaced by Spanish castanets or a Swiss cuckoo clock. In these various ways, tourist objects have a life of their own and have a variety of effects on social identity, social and cultural relationships and consumption. They also assisted in ushering in a more generalised global cosmopolitanism where cultures were no longer bound by space and tourism no longer required travel.

Ritual and tourism: heritage, carnival and pilgrimage objects

In this next section we explore the ritual character of tourism. Ritual analysis is useful because it forces us away from megalithic or general theories of tourism to precise practices of specific people in specific times and places; we are forced in other words to see tourism not as an inevitable singularity nor as something that exists independently of the people (and objects) who perform it. Rather, tourism has a performative quality that adheres to, and makes sense only in relation to, those who perform it and the tourist objects, without which it could not function. We can say that almost all types of tourism take a ritual form but that the ritual form it takes varies very considerably as do the objectives or effects of the ritual performance of tourism (Cohen, 1988: 38–41; Graburn, 1983: 11–17, 1989; Lett, 1983; Connerton, 1989; Ryan and Hall, 2001; Jervis, 1998; Jokinen and Veijola, 1997). This becomes clearer when we understand the nature of ritual activity at tourist sites. Most tourism rituals correspond to what van Gennep (1960) called 'rites de passage' or rituals of transition.

> . . . all rites de passage (rites of transition) are marked by three phases: separation, limen or margin, and aggregation. The first phase comprises symbolic behaviour signifying the detachment of the individual or group, either from an earlier fixed point in the social structure or from a relatively stable set of cultural conditions (a cultural 'state'); during the intervening liminal phase, the state of the ritual subject (the 'passenger' or 'liminar') becomes ambiguous, he passes through a realm or dimension that has few or none of the attributes of the past or coming state, he is betwixt and between all familiar lines of classification; in the third phase the passage is consummated, and the subject returns to classified secular or mundane social life. The ritual subject, individual or corporate (groups, age sets and social categories can undergo transition) is again in a stable state, has rights and obligations of a clearly defined structural type, and is expected to behave in accordance with the customary norms and ethical standards appropriate to his newly settled state. (Turner and Turner, 1978: 2)

In traditional societies these were associated with the principal life stages of an individual's life – for example, birth, naming, puberty, initiation, betrothal, marriage, death. All around the world these transitions are marked by rituals that also seem to follow a recognisable pattern. These rituals typically involve the movement of the relevant congregation to a place away from the village or settlement to a special sacred place. These spaces are frequently on borders or margins or they may have some anomalous geographical or spatial feature. Once the ritual begins, the ritual subjects, those who are in the process of transition and often the congregation who accompany them too, enter a liminal state: it is a time and place suspended in between states of being, between the old state of affairs and before the new state that is to emerge. Typically these rituals involve behaviour that is different to, opposed to or inverse from that of everyday life. There are examples of gender and status inversions, mockery of status, extremely free and liberal sexual practices, the use of intoxicants or narcotics to produce an altered state of consciousness; the use of music, dance, songs and chants to produce a specifically different aural environment and embodied foci; altered states of time and the production of ritual time. Once the ritual has been *performed*, things return to normal with the exception that the ritual subject(s) have been altered, typically elevated to a new and higher status. Tourism seems to be a ritual of a similar kind in that:

1. Tourism often involves a period of time spent away from the *mundane* space of the everyday. Indeed the metaphors of 'get away', 'a change' and 'escape' are central to the language and practice of tourism in its formative years.
2. Tourism tends to create special liminal spaces different from the everyday spaces of living and working. They can be ludic, for example a theme park village or seaside resort, or sacred, as in a special national monument or natural or religious site.
3. Behaviour among tourists at these places is often different from their everyday behaviour. They do different things, they often wear different clothes, their time schedule is warped by their performance of tourism; new and different activities often produce a different state of mind (awe, wonder, exhilaration, fatigue, humility, excitement etc.); such states are induced by a variety of objects, texts, performances, devotions, substances or activities; a variety of officiates are often present to guide and contain the ritual activity away from non-congregants. Importantly, like pilgrims before them, they spend a large amount of their time *in devotion* to the objects and places they come to see and the embodied, performed practices associated with them.
4. Upon return to the everyday, tourists often enjoy some sense of transition. This can range from the accretion of additional status that is frequently conferred on the well-travelled (and there is a long association between travel and education in the west and elsewhere), or the consumer of luxury experiences (as Bauman (1998) argues, in a consumerist society an individual's competence and standing are judged in relation to their consumption practices/achievements) or to a spiritual, intellectual or experiential transition to a new, heightened or improved state of mind (this might be the case with pilgrims, those on intellectual, literary or artistic quests or even those seeking sexual or sporting experience). In some cases, travel might involve transition in all three types of sense. In contemporary Japan, a country noted by its reluctance to travel as much as other modern societies, overseas travel is seen as critical to corporate, social and spiritual careers (see Moeran, 1983) and of course, the metaphor *career* also describes a series of life changes.

Graburn (1989) follows the anthropologist Edmund Leach who argued that 'the regular occurrence of sacred–profane alternations marks important periods of social life or even provides the measure of the passage of time itself' (Graburn, 1989: 25; Leach, 1961: 132–6). With this in mind Graburn modelled modern time into periods of work/profane and episodes of tourism/sacred. In this model, point A stood for the profane, B the entry point into tourism/sacred, C the experience of tourism itself, D the departure back to the profane world of work and E the next bout of profane/work time. It is not an elegant model we might say but Graburn is better at locating its truth in the language and performance of American touristic rituals:

> Our two lives, the sacred/nonordinary/touristic and the profane/workaday/ stay-at-home, customarily alternate for ordinary people and are marked by rituals or ceremonies, as should the beginning and end of lives. By definition, the beginning of one life marks the end of another. Thus, at time B, we celebrate with TGIF (Thank God it's Friday) and going-away parties, to anticipate the future state and to give thanks for the end of the ordinary. Why else would people remain awake and drink all night on an outbound plane en route to Europe when they are going to arrive at 6.40 A.M with a long day ahead of them? The re-entry ritual, time D, is often split between the ending-party – the last night in Europe or the last night at sea – and the welcome home or welcome back to work greetings and formalities, both of which are usually sadder than the going-away. (Graburn, 1989: 26)

Graburn (1989: 28) reminds us also that 'a journey is seldom without purpose, but culturally-specific values determine the goals of travel'. It is important to keep in mind that whatever these goals may be at any one place and time, they relate in important and often specific ways to the culture of the tourists and in this way, they have a great deal of autonomy from those who frame and narrate tourist sites and objects. In this sense they are not socially determined and may even be under-determined, as people enter tourism spaces, rather as they entered pilgrimage spaces, 'making it up' largely as they went and for reasons/motives they did not need disclose to others. As Löfgren puts it we might

> [. . .] view vacationing as a cultural laboratory where people have been able to experiment with new aspects of identities, their social relations or their inter-actions with nature and also to use the important cultural skills of daydreaming and mind-travelling. Here is an arena in which fantasy has become an import-ant social practice. (Löfgren, 1999: 6–7)

For these sorts of reasons, I reject claims that ritual approaches to tourism are functionalist (or are inevitably so): to say that people enter ritualised spaces, to say that tourists look for or anticipate transformative experience and to say that we can observe ritual effects of tourism is not to say, as Edensor (1998: 4) argues, 'that the actions and meanings of tourists merely act to reinforce social cohesion'. Indeed, tourism can be and has been one of the ways people transgress, break rules or engage in new forms of experience. The history of sexuality and nudity on the tourist beach in the nineteenth and early twentieth centuries counters any such claim. In addition, Jervis has argued that tourists at Albert Dock found to be mainly 'doing nothing', are not merely doing nothing. Taking an eager, enthusiastic stance to national heritage, is part of what he calls *project*, the approved leisures associated with the progressive and improving character of modernity. Therefore, to stand before these iconic objects of collective memory and significance and to ignore them, and do nothing with them is not only an anti-ritual but a ritual 'of ideological complacency' and wasting time in repetitive bouts of doing nothing 'questions the world of project, of purposeful activity especially work' (Jervis, 1998: 322–3). The accusation of functionality also seems to miss, precisely, the way in which tourism is caught up in the transformative nature of modernity, not tying people to tradition but breaking it. We shall see in Chapter 6 how this was a distinguishing feature of seaside culture in the twentieth century. And by culture I do not mean anything so awkward and general as national culture; rather I mean the heterogeneous and fast changing sub-cultural lifeworlds of tourists. It is also important to consider that in transitional terms the tourist is like the Christian pilgrim: tourism is essentially about individual transition, salvation, redemption but what these mean varies radically from one individual and one sub-culture to another (Urry, 1990: 10). However, there are examples of transitions that involve more than the individual and outcomes that do intend (and result in) social cohesion. Honeymoon tourism is of course related to a major rite of passage. At various times and places, towns and work groups have gone away together and experienced a collective transition. More recently, work-based groups often go away to retreats, frequently luxurious and pleasurable, to achieve organisational change or improved productivity. Some team-based groups in companies are sent on challenging walking or survival courses that are supposed to achieve the transition to trust, cooperation, and effective teamwork. One says 'supposedly' because writers have been extremely cynical about their results. Television series such as 'Pie in the Sky', 'The Bill' and 'Hamish MacBeth' have all used such settings for dramatic irony: to show how they provoke social tension rather than cohesion.

Seen in these ways, the ritual nature of tourism cannot be understood in a purely functionalist way. Individual people may be looking for something in terms of transition for themselves; governments and companies may wish to promote certain kinds of transition, and there may be broad patterns of correspondence in any particular time and place but as Crang (1994) argues, correspondence or symmetry is unlikely in heterogeneous nations with histories of economic inequalities and differential power relations (see Hinchliffe, 2000 for a good discussion of outdoor management training). According to Crang (1994: 344–5) writing on heritage tourism, for example, '[t]hese [heritage] rituals give distinctive opportunities to certain groups to acquire cultural capital' and '[t]he ritual performed is not reliant on the content – for power is inscribed in the very ability to perform the ritual.'

Antecedents to rituals of tourism

It will be useful to try to make some historical connections between the rituals studied by anthropologists, largely outside advanced modernised cultures with the rituals of modern tourism. We can do this by looking at some forms of ritual leisure activity that prefigured modern tourism. The most obvious choices here are the *carnival* and *pilgrimage*. Both of these provide some cultural roots for modern tourism, but they also enable us to understand the connection that contemporary tourism has with ritual.

It is also noteworthy, especially for Chapter 6 on seaside that follows this chapter, that hitherto British ritual spaces were not characteristically set on beaches but inland, in areas central to farming districts, particularly at the level of former land units called 'hundreds', which were pre-Norman land units of administration (Meller, 1976). This is typically where the main carnivals and fairs or revels were held although some were focused around certain churches and villages, for example, Padstow in Cornwall, while others seem to be associated with trade and sacred sites. The earliest glimpses of evidence on English fairs and the carnivalesque date back to the period of the Anglo-Saxon kings. Here we see something of a pattern emerging:

> Fairs had been held probably since prehistoric times, and often on tribal boundaries, for communities needed to exchange their surpluses and special-isms. Some fairs were concerned with a specific commodity: horse fairs appear to have been particularly ancient. A number of places are called long ports, 'port' being Old English for market (thus showing the original nature and purpose of seaports). One such place is Lamport in Northamptonshire. I wonder whether such places were the locations of fairs strung out along a road or street and how many were on ancient boundaries. Fairs were one reason for coming together, another was the holding of annual sports or games, and sometimes the two went together. Brigg Fair in Lincolnshire was held at a bridge, as its name implies, but the place was also known as Glanford, from the Old English gleam, which as well as being the root of our word 'glamour', also meant 'revels', 'festivities', 'games'. Close by Glanford Brigg is Hibaldstow, and stow in Old English means a place of assembly – in this case to visit the resting place and shrine of St Higbald, a bishop of Lindsey. Stow frequently has a religious connotation, but sometimes it is difficult to decide on a religious or secular explanation for the gathering. Bristol means 'bridge stow' and could equally refer to assembly for buying and selling, and assembly to visit a holy place. Again, both could co-exist. Indeed, within a mile or so of each other in Gloucestershire there were in the late medieval and early modern period, annual games at Coaley, a fair at Nympsfield, and a shrine at Nympsfield . . . also . . . Nympsfield means in Old English 'the cleared land of the sacred place' – nemet, a British borrowing – and this can only refer to the Romano–British healing shrine of Mercury at adjacent Uley, whose temple was replaced by a Christian church, probably in the fifth century. (G.R. Jones, 1999: http://www.le.ac.uk/elh/grj1/asl.html)

So, the English evidence seems more or less consistent with evidence from all around the world: important rituals take place on borderlands between specific social groups; spaces between them where trade took place. These spaces of assembly were also overlaid by, or intertwined with, sacred or religious signification. The British evidence laid out above is confusing in its detail but it is indisputable that a characteristic pattern of association existed between these places and trade, religion and periodic social gathering. However, there is also evidence that these places did not emerge in an arbitrary fashion or simply as continuities and accretions from an ancient past. It is possible to identify, particularly perhaps at that time, an organising narrative in their construction as well as links between them.

This was a time long after the order of Roman Britain had entirely collapsed, but it was also the time in which the new order of the Saxon kings was being built – out of which, in the dimly lit figure of King Athelstan, we glimpse the first sight of England *as an agrarian nation state*. In building a large-scale princely state, these kings relied on a systematic gathering of taxes and the maintenance of judicial and administrative order. In order to do this the King and the court had to travel; indeed, even the later Norman kings were more or less permanently on the move. Systematised and legitimated fairs were built into the cycle of this wider national economy and order, and there was a hierarchy of towns that fulfilled other functions. However, there is also some evidence to show that these early foundational kings used religion and ritual, particularly their enthusiasm for the cult of saints, to build nationally orientated religious sentiments, sentiments that were orientated to travel to the various sacred sites of specific (national) saints – as we saw in the case of St Higbald above (Wood, 2000: 175). It is hard to exaggerate the significance of these cults to the coterminous emergence of the nation state and a sense of national culture and cultic tourism (or pilgrimage) at this time. Significant for our purposes here is that the places and spaces of significance in the lives of these saints together with *objects* or relics associated with them become central to the *realisation* of a cult, literally a following. Saints' cults together with their royal patronage (kings in particular visited such places frequently) encouraged pilgrimage and travel on a dramatic scale:

> The cult of saints and saints' relics was one of the biggest currents in the intellectual life of the Dark Ages. It generated a vast amount of comment and speculation in the ninth and tenth centuries: Saints' *Lives*, martyrologies, relic lists, and gazetteers of saints' resting places, not to mention sermons and poems like the *Menologium*, which mentions the festivals observed 'at the behest of the English king throughout the kingdom of Britain': this was all part of the way the divine order was believed to interlock with the earthly. Saints' shrines were focuses of royal power, and their patronage was one way of increasing a sense of unity in the state. (Wood, 2000: 175–6)

This is perhaps most revealed as those parts of the former Danelaw regions of northern England gradually fell to the Wessex Kings. The saints associated with these regions were quickly and emphatically elevated into this cultic order, encouraging whatever residues of ambiguity and hostility towards such territories to be soothed by religious observation and ludic festivities and importantly, pilgrimage travel. The presence of a travelling king and his court and entourage was a spectacle in its own right but through the cult of the saints and their associated festivities, the spectacle was heightened and dominated the annual calendar in all localities. 'In the tenth century, gatherings on the big festival days ran into hundreds and sometimes thousands of people, all descending for a few days on to a small royal estate for a particular saint's day, or for a law-making jamboree, or to witness the hegemonic rituals by which kings kept their thumbs on recalcitrant vassals' (Wood, 2000: 196).

So, even before the Norman Conquest in 1066 we can say that carnivals and pilgrimage were central to English culture at all levels of society. We can now move to describe briefly these two types of pre-tourism in readiness for the subsequent two chapters that will ask first, whether we can analyse modern forms of tourism as rituals, second whether we can identify anything about their ritual nature that points to experiences of transition or potential (Turner and Turner, 1978: 3) and third, whether and how tourist objects are involved in tourist rituals and help secure particular effects?

Carnival

I have used carnival as a generic name for that group of ritual festivities all across pre-modern Europe that are variously called festas (Italy), fiestas (Spain), fêtes (France) festivals/carnivals/fairs/revels (Britain) and so on. There are of course many other synonyms for the same basic activity in other European countries but they all refer as we have seen above, to quite specific forms of celebrating and performing holy days, particularly saints' days. Rather like the aboriginal songlines that describe the places of emergence of totemic ancestors and their subsequent journeys in the Australian bush (see Chatwin, 1987; Fullaga, 2003) inscribing a sacred cartography on the landscape, the saints of the early medieval period also left traces or paths of their saintly lives throughout Europe. These were often former Archbishops or priors of monasteries or other noted holy individuals, and their careers and teaching described specific life routes – where they worked and lived, where they stopped, preached, prayed or performed some miraculous transformation. As with aboriginal totemic ancestors, their journeys and their presence at particular places were believed to hold some continuous significance for the living: some of their saintly power and affect continued to reside in these places but *particularly* in their relics, objects associated directly with their life. Again, in common with aboriginal totemic cults, these powers seem to be most concentrated in particular places and perhaps even more so in artefacts or relics associated specifically with them. While these sacred sites and collections of artefacts became the places of pilgrimage, very often they coincided with trade and annual fairs held in their name. So there is clearly an overlap between pilgrimage and carnival. However, while pilgrimage had very wide catchments of followers of a particular saint's cult (a good example is Thomas Becket martyred in Canterbury cathedral in 1170 who attracted vast numbers of pilgrims from all across the UK but also from France and Holland), the carnival was a ritual belonging to and defined by the restricted congregation of a *locality*.

The carnival is always identified with a particular town, especially in Italy or Spain, or a particular rural district as in the pre-modern carnival in England, and in this way it was a ritual occasion performed by and for a specific local culture. The carnival was, like the social composition of its congregation, an inward looking, insular and self-sufficient affair. As Bakhtin argued, carnival comprised

> forms of protocol and ritual based on laughter and consecrated by tradition . . . which were sharply distinct from the serious official, ecclesiastical, feudal and political cult forms and [ritual] ceremonials. Carnival is a spectacle lived by people who are all participants, actors, not spectators. [. . .] [they] offered a completely different, non-official . . . extra political aspect of the world, of man and of human relations; they built a second world and a second life outside officialdom. (Bakhtin, 1984: 5–7 quoted in Shields, 1990: 89)

It had a number of common characteristics that established it as a liminoid, ritual activity:

- It typically began with a procession to the special place on a specific local Saint's Day (importantly it was an annual, one-off event), a day (or two) when the hierarchical nature of these localities was made manifest, particularly through ritual robes and vestments. At the head of these processions were the ritual objects, typically statues of saints and objects and representations of his/her life.
- Over a specified number of following days, carnivals involved an ordered or ritually prescribed disordering in which there were considerable inversions of roles and practices. There was a heightened party atmosphere generated by more excessive drinking, feasting, dancing and music, but also theatre and games or sports. Critically, much of this behaviour would not be tolerated during the rest of the year.
- Characteristically, carnival involved a ritual language, often derived from market argots and gestures 'permitting no distance between those who came in contact with each other and liberating them from norms of etiquette and decency imposed at other times' (Bakhtin, 1984: 10 quoted in Shields, 1990: 90). Similarly, normal observation of low and high culture within the community was undermined and inverted through the use of the grotesque body, which lowered 'all to the material level of the earth and body, asserting the primacy of life'. This

offers a critical clue to understanding carnival: it is a celebration of 'the collective, ancestral body of all people' (Shields, 1990: 93) and in the specific case of the medieval carnival, the relative isolation and inter-dependence of the communities that gathered to perform them.

- The invocation of a primal grotesque body was achieved partly through a language of lewd gestures and slang and ritual plays, theatre, games and foolery, but also through objects, grotesque statues, masks and costume. Adding to the performance of the grotesque by local people was the mysterious presence (turning up on time and melting away afterwards) of migratory professional entertainers, owners of grotesque side shows (who offered glimpses at freaks of human and other nature, exotic wild animals embodying the idea of monsters, anomalous and mysterious objects), travelling theatre companies and so on.

By the time Brighton, UK was becoming a seaside town, in the mid-nineteenth century, the rural communities that supported these very old festivals and revels were largely urbanised. Those that continued into the nineteenth century, such as the Bedminster Revels near Bristol, were gradually terminated by statute. The Bedminster Revels, a former carnival focused on the ancient Hundred of Bedminster, was banned after a large crowd politically incensed by the failure of a political reform bill, stormed the city at Whitsun 1831, opened the jails, and fought the army on the streets for several days before civil order was restored. As Meller (1976) makes clear, the Revels had always attracted an international and national travelling group of entertainers, sideshows, musicians and theatre. Their annual economy was based on the cycle of festivities and carnivals all across Europe and beyond. When the rural English carnivals dried up many stopped coming and confined their attentions to Europe where they were still tolerated and are still performed to this day, for example Pamplona etc. However, the geography of leisure and entertainment in England had already shifted and differentiated – towards, for example, medicinal spas that had become important, exclusive foci for the affluent aristocracy and emerging commercial classes. These had begun in a rudi-mentary way as early as the sixteenth century (Shakespeare had played at Tunbridge) but by the eighteenth century and the building of elegant centres and cities such as Bath Spa, the leisure industry was becoming more sedentary if still seasonal. By the early nineteenth century most seasides had accreted a considerable semi-permanent assembly of carnival-esque entertainers and sideshows and as Shields argues, the carnivalesque itself had shifted or displaced to the seaside. Shields argues that in this new space, away from the stratified rural societies that gave it meaning and function ('an unlicensed celebration of a socially acknowledged interdependence of all people'), the seaside carnivalesque was nonetheless similar:

Figure 5.2 *The Palace Pier*, Brighton. Source: Ian Britton

The realisation, rehearsal and celebration of this same interdependence are at the heart of the scene of holidaying Commoners who shifted aside the weight of moral distinctions of the Sabbath and propriety to practice carnivalesque forms of unlicensed, commodified, leisure 'attractions' that lined the beach. Particularly through humour, such transgressions deny class barriers founded on moral reasoning. The rowdy fun and mockery of the holidaymakers instigated a heightened level of reciprocity within the crowd from which it was difficult to withdraw and from which no one was exempt. (Shields, 1990: 96–7)

Shields has used the word carnivalesque, meaning carnival-like. It was not the same but its form and ritual nature had evolved into the new spaces and socialities of modern urban cultures. This involved one further elaboration, the new idea of the spectator at the carnival. Jervis puts it well:

When Goethe, discussing the Roman Carnival of 1788, claimed that one participated as 'both actor and spectator', one was perhaps witnessing the fate of carnival in our own time, the transformation of carnival into carnivalesque, into spectacle, but nevertheless still a resource for popular appropriation; not so much the people's second life, but still a distinctive aspect of culture, embodying a distinctive 'form of critical reason' . . . (Jervis, 1998: 331)

Jervis cites Docker (1995: 284): 'the flow of mass culture may possess its own forms of reason, not reason in a rationalist sense, of attention to discrete ordered sequences of information and interpretation, but of sudden juxtapositions, swift contrasts, heterogeneity . . . carnivalesque remains an always dangerous supplement, challenging, destabilising, relativising, pluralising single notions of true culture, true reason . . .'.

In sum, the carnival was a ritual (or as Shields called it, an anti-ritual) of annual renewal of collective social life in the pre-modern period. It was not simply functional to the power hierarchy of the day in allowing the otherwise common people their day to let off steam, it was more complex. Carnival stressed the necessary interdependencies, duties and mutual obligations and social contract of the feudal and post-feudal order; in mocking the existing hierarchy, and posing its hold on power as contingent it asserted the universality and commonality of the people. It pointed always to higher powers, saints, kings, God and the sacred but reminded everyone of their essentially corporeal life on earth. The notion of collectivity that the carnivals embodied was at odds with the emergent individualism of capitalist society, which is one underlying reason why capitalist nations such as Britain gradually suppressed them in that form. The Bedminster Revels showed that they were bad news in theory and in practice. As we shall see it was for similar reasons that the early capitalist societies of seventeenth century Protestant Europe banned or discouraged pilgrimage. However, carnival belonged to the common culture and it could not be silenced or banished. Rather it found new forms in the emergent mass society and popular culture.

Pilgrimage

. . . a tourist is a half-pilgrim, if a pilgrim is a half-tourist.

(Turner and Turner, 1978: 20)

Pilgrimage can be defined as journeys away from the everyday, mundane world of work and home to specific sacred sites formalised, recognised and maintained by major religions. The type of pilgrimage that prefigured tourism in the west belongs to the same social order of feudal or semi-feudal rural societies that characterised much of Christian Europe from the fifth to the sixteenth century. Pilgrimage to places such as Glastonbury in Somerset, UK or Cloagh Patrick in Eire were places of religious pilgrimage prior to Christian adoption, and although they remain principal places of pilgrimage, they were joined by a much larger number of pilgrimages to the shrines and other sites associated with saints, such as at Rocamadour, France from 1193; Canterbury, UK from 1170 or Loreto, Italy from 1294. Even before the Norman conquest of England, the Anglo-Saxon kings of England and others who had the resources to undertake such journeys, made specific pilgrimages to Rome, to the Catacombs and St Peter's. Even though most people during this period were tied to a local economic and religious life, 'Christianity developed its own mode of liminality for the laity. This mode was best represented by the pilgrimage to a sacred site or holy shrine located at some distance away from the pilgrim's place of residence and daily labour' (Turner and Turner, 1978: 4).

> . . . the map of Europe came to be crisscrossed with pilgrims' ways and trails to the shrines of European saints and avocations of the Holy Virgin (varieties of mode of address, such as our Lady of Walsingham) and to churches containing important relics of Christ's ministry and passion. Such pilgrim centres and ways, frequented increasingly by the poor, can be regarded as a complex surrogate for the journey to the source and heartland of their faith. (Turner and Turner, 1978: 5–6)

In the case of pilgrimage what were the rationales and anticipated benefits of such arduous, extended and dangerous travel? First, pilgrimage offered the chance to get away from the mundane world, its 'small grievances over trivial issues [that] tend to accumulate' or the 'store of nagging guilts' (Turner and Turner, 1978: 7). At the same time the trials and tribulations of the journey provide 'a release from the ingrown ills of home'. Second, pilgrimage offered an initiatory quality, a chance 'to enter into a deeper level of existence than he has known in his accustomed milieu' (ibid. p.8). The pilgrim is exposed to powerful religious sacra (shrines, images, relics, liturgies, curative waters, ritual circumambulations of holy objects and so on' (ibid. p.8). Third, the individual moral unit of the pilgrimage 'seeks salvation or release from the sins and evils of the structural world' (ibid. p.8). Fourth, the pilgrim receives a powerful inspiration or guidance into the future. In the final stages of pilgrimage, in or around the shrine centres, the pilgrim is bombarded with 'religious buildings, pictorial images, statuary, and sacralised features of the topography'. Linking these together are often the essential thoughts and feelings of a founder's religion or those of influential followers, but in combination they permit the exhausted but receptive pilgrim to receive 'the pure imprint of paradigmatic structure' which gives 'a measure of coherence, direction and meaning to their action' (ibid. p. 11). Finally, pilgrimage also promised to many, the release from afflictions of the mind or body. Some affliction rituals elsewhere are rites of passage, which transform the patient into 'an adept ready to learn the mysteries of the healing cult' (ibid. p. 12).

As Chaucer's *The Canterbury Tales* makes abundantly clear, although pilgrims may have started off on their own, with their own reasons for completing a pilgrimage, they very soon found themselves on the busy highways of pilgrims' ways, staying at Inns along the route and frequently forming parties of fellow travellers. First, it was safer to do so, but second, part of the liminal space and culture of pilgrimage was characterised by play, games, drinking and merry making – things, one suspects, that made these journeys all the more compelling and attractive in the first place.

One of the intriguing elements of the history of European pilgrimage was its banishment in the major Protestant countries as they emerged from the religious grip of Rome. Religious devotion was not the object of these bans so much as the decorative use of idols and images and the confusion of cults before which the pilgrims bowed and devoted so much time. It was of course associated with Catholicism, but also in the minds of its Protestant detractors was its association with ludic play, which to them was a dangerous distraction from the solemn business of prayer and work. The pilgrims in Chaucer's *The Canterbury Tales* mixed serious religious and spiritual intent with a great deal of play, and that play was of the ritual kind described above, tending towards an especially heightened form of excitability, aided by drinking, sexual freedom, and generalised merry-making. Associated with the pilgrim trail was what we might call today disorderly conduct – and this was of course part of its liminoid phase, a social space or journey betwixt and between the orders of daily life. The attempt to prevent such lapses of order, and indeed to introduce a total regime of Protestant/capitalist social order marks the beginning of what Rojek (1995) has usefully called Modernity 1. Essentially what Rojek argues, following Nietzsche and perhaps also Elias, is that the passions and tensions of life that gave rise to ritual institutions such as carnival or pilgrimage could not be swept under the carpet by the instigation of bans and the introduction of more approved diversions. Crudely, we might say that with pilgrimage banned in the seventeenth century and carnival banned in the early nineteenth century, tourism emerged (very much after the innovation by the religious enthusiast, Thomas Cook) soon after to fill their place. There are good reasons why this came to happen, though the innovations that Cook was to make were hardly inevitable. The approved leisures of Protestant cultures (reading, poetry, art, crafts for example) that resembled work more than pleasure and release, specifically avoided addressing the inevitable tensions and pressures of daily life and of the life course. In Protestant religion, the salvation offered by work and the need for recognition of success added to the pressure to succeed in daily life and to secure a strong, upwardly moving career trajectory. Rojek argues that these passions, tensions and pressures gave rise first to a secretive world of desires and illicit behaviours, tolerable only if practised away from the centres of civil society, hence the development of what Shields identified as the connection between tourism and places on the margin. In addition, of course, such a pressured life produced tensions that were not easily resolved in their place of origin, hence we find the huge popularity of therapeutic spa travel in the eighteenth century. In a different context, why did Thomas Cook get the idea for tourism? He found himself increasingly drawn into his amateur life as a preacher in the religious revivals that accompanied the most pressured and difficult times of the hugely expanding British industrial towns of the early nineteenth century. These religious revivals of nonconformist religiosity existed outside the established churches and as if to emphasise their marginality and potency, they were often held a long way outside towns in the country, on temporary greenfield sites. People travelled long distances to them and there was something about the large numbers of the congregation travelling and assembling together at the destination (as well as the Salvationist tones of the preaching) that produced a powerful liminoid ritual effect. Cook had the germ of the idea of 'a tour' when walking to one such revival on a very hot day. Why not hire a steam train and several coaches at a discount price, and then sell individual tickets to the revival? This proved profitable but Cook noticed something important: the effect of forming a touring party was immensely enjoyable in its own right; he observed a special effect about the collective nature of the journey itself. As Cook elaborated on the revival tours by organising new trips to other sacred sites of the day – the Romantic Lake District, the Scottish highlands, or the Great Exhibition of 1851, he made sure that they maintained that essential ritual form, with himself (and others) the guide officiating. By 1869, Cook had initiated tours to the Holy Land, largely for people like himself, but in this case the differences between tourism and pilgrimage were particularly blurred:

> Low Protestantism did not make much room for traditional notions of pilgrimage; so perhaps being a tourist might actually have been a new, acceptable way for Evangelicals to express a widespread religious impulse. Chaucer has planted in the popular mind the notion that people who were officially pilgrims might have hoped to gain some pleasure from the journey. These tourists, conversely, were people who were officially pleasure seekers, but who longed to derive some spiritual benefits from their travels. (Larsen, 2000: 341)

So the point is that tourism mimics pilgrimage (and vice versa); it was a novel form of ritual that used the performance of travel to secure the liminal spaces of personal and group transition. This helps us to understand some if not all aspects of the *seaside*, a phase of tourism in which pleasurability and rituals of transition were once again reasserted and gained a new universality. However, in so doing, and this is a point that makes reference to the discussion of the nature of contemporary tourism in Chapter 2, the conditions were established for the movement of the ritualised pleasure peripheries to return to the centre, or more correctly perhaps, to lose the necessity for spatial distanciation or differentiation. This is the essential point about Rojek's definition of Modernity 2. Spatial escape attempts become an illusion under the generalised distribution and economy of leisure, and here we might say that new technologies of leisure were called into existence by this desire rather than the other way around. This is particularly the case for a society that during the heyday of seaside was progressing from a producer to a consumer society. Here the distinction

of work/everyday and leisure/holiday is significantly blurred by the distribution of consumerism into both. This is why Rojek was able to argue
that there is no escape through tourism and leisure in postmodern times,
because one is only likely to find the same consumerism, the same emphasis on pleasurabilty that one experiences at home. Theme parks reproduce
the everyday, only, according to Rojek, in a heightened form. And here the
study of rituals of transition does help to identify areas of social and cultural
change; they pinpoint the aims and desires of a society as well as its tensions
and problems.

Some of the aims and desires of contemporary postmodern society are
embodied in the lives of celebrities, and celebrity itself is a specifically
post- or late modern phenomenon deserving serious sociological attention
(but see Rojek, 2001). Think for just one moment how much of our time is
wrapped up in seeing their images, watching them, reading about them
and talking about them. Why is that? The tracings of their working lives
(for example, the *Cavern* club in Liverpool where the Beatles played in their
early days), their homes (Elvis Presley's *Graceland*) and their graves (Jim
Morrison's grave in Paris) have all become sacred sites and places of
pilgrimage for modern tourists. An interesting connection to make here is
the assertion that much popular culture, of the type created by Elvis, The
Beatles and The Doors, is a recomposed form of carnivalesque:

> Again, much popular culture explores the margins, the inversions, the not
> barely respectable, the out-of-bounds. In short, much of this is carnivalesque,
> challenging the harshness of fate and history. The grotesque body returns, for
> example, in forms of popular humour, in wrestling, in advertising. . . . Hence
> carnivalesque parody, inversion and grotesque humour retain an ability to
> unsettle both the defenders of the rational, disciplined zone of project, and the
> modern avant-garde, revealing the truth in Shiach's observation that 'Basically
> "the popular" has always been "the other"'. This may be even more true,
> though, of those elements lying on the far boundaries of popular culture itself,
> or beyond: the hippies, the crusties, travellers, ravers, eco-warriors, and other
> denizens of the nightmare world of the respectable middle classes . . . (Jervis,
> 1998: 330–1)

Although we can think about Rojek's Modernity 2 as a feature of our times,
we need to remind ourselves that forces embodying Modernity 1 have
always been in a powerful position, always moving reluctantly towards
Modernity 2, always behind, conservative. As I write there are conservative
governments in the USA, Australia, Italy and Scandinavia. This is what
gives some aspects of popular cultural celebrity their frisson of danger,
and, also through them, the promise of transition, of salvation: thoughts
that give them an aura of the sacred. Other celebrities embody the everyday, the everyone, you and me struggling with our impossible lives, failing,
hurting. Almost unbelievably this is how many ordinary people reacted to
the death of Diana, Princess of Wales. *Despite* her privilege and her high
birth and marriage, what launched her into sacred celebrity status were her
human failings and human struggles. Memorials to her have appeared

Figure 5.3   *The Beatles Story*, Albert Dock, Liverpool. Source: Ian Britton

spontaneously in official and personal spaces, with the Internet being now a particularly rich ritual space for this kind of thing (see personal memorial below). When Diana, Princess of Wales died, the intention was for her to be buried in the parish church of St Mary's near her family home of Althorp, but such were the fears that it would become a shrine and overrun by visitors (or pilgrims?), that a decision was taken to bury her on the island of the lake in the grounds of Althorp itself. However, as the box below suggests, her resting place in her family home at Althorp has become a de facto shrine.

Box 5.1

This page is just my little 'memorial' to Princess Diana. I have always loved her ever since I can remember seeing her on the cover of People Magazine. *She was beautiful, stylish and no matter what pain she was suffering always remained composed with that famous shy smile. She was a savior to world . . . the sick, poor, unfortunate and even to those who were not. Diana will remain an icon of the world, as we know it today. 'Goodbye, English Rose . . . may you grow in our hearts . . .'*

home.nyu.edu/~jpk4/diana.htm

Box 5.2

ALTHORP SET FOR RECORD YEAR

Dated: 01/04/2001

Althorp House is proving to be one of the most popular visitor attractions in Britain this year – the year Diana, Princess of Wales would have celebrated her 40th birthday. Advance bookings are well up on last year and more than 800 slots have already been allocated to visitors travelling by coach in July and August and weekend availability is now limited.

Jessica Hogan, Group's Co-ordinator at Althorp – the country seat of the Spencer family – said: 'We have received a considerable amount of interest much earlier this year and people are booking even now. We are also getting a remarkable number of repeat visitors who appear to be very interested in seeing how the Exhibition dedicated to Diana, The Princess of Wales, has evolved.'

'Obviously there could be a degree of added poignancy this year because there has been and I suspect there will be a lot more publicity about how the Princess would have celebrated her 40th birthday this year. It is very encouraging to see how many of the new visitors are coming on the recommendation of others who have already been. I think we can honestly say that Althorp House is now well and truly on the map for visitor attractions both for people in Britain and from abroad'.

The facilities for visitors to Althorp have been consistently praised since their opening in 1998. Every moment of each person's visit has been meticulously planned from arrival to departure, ensuring that Althorp fulfils Earl Spencer's ambition of being in a 'different stratosphere' from any other stately home.

New for this year

A new room in the Exhibition dedicated to the work of The Diana, Princess of Wales Memorial Fund, showing exactly where all the money raised has been spent.

A new location for the famous bridal gown and bridesmaids dresses. New captions for the main gallery, which displays 28 of the Princess's most eye-catching outfits showing how she used her unique sense of style to draw attention to the causes she supported.

www.althorp.com/news-media/index.asp

Finally, in addition to what might be called celebrity pilgrimage, we should add that there has been a substantial revival and growth of religious pilgrimage itself, and as with medieval pilgrimage, it is difficult to distinguish it from tourism. So for example, to take the extraordinary revival of the pilgrimage to Santiago over the past twenty years, we can note that the route was 'declared the first European Cultural Route by the Council of Europe in October 1997, and inscribed as one of UNESCO's World Heritage Sites in 1993 (The Confraternity of St James, 2002: 1). Both the route and the Cathedral at Santiago benefit hugely from this revival which grew from around 2,500 pilgrims receiving the *Compostela* (a certificate of pilgrimage) in 1986 to 61,418 in 2001. Over that time the numbers have grown steadily but in Holy Years the numbers more than double (154,613 in 1999). A similar story can be told of the pilgrimage to Walsingham in Norfolk, which in the thirteenth century ranked alongside the pilgrimage to Santiago. This too has enjoyed a massive revival by Roman Catholic and Anglican pilgrims, but in the numerous websites dedicated to it, the commercial touristic content sits alongside the religious content, the assumption being that the two will be combined. Islamic pilgrimage is also a major component of the Islamic travel and tourism industry. Before Saudi Arabia had revenues from oil, it was very reliant on its earnings from the Haj. The two million pilgrims to the 2001 Haj, for example, spent an estimated US$2.7 billion and that could easily grow more if the Saudis lifted national quotas.

In addition, the UN Economic and Social Commission for Asia has recently instigated the promotion of 'religious pilgrims as well as regular visitors' to major Buddhist sites in India, Nepal, Laos, Sri Lanka, Myanmar, Vietnam, Bangladesh and Thailand (Travel Impact Newswire, 2002: 4–5).

Activity box 5.1

In the essentially secular nature of western cultures the notion of the sacred and social identity has diversified into a great range of cultural activities, sub-cultures, spaces and institutions. To some extent the increase in travel and tourism can be attributed to new configurations and patterns of secular pilgrimage. For some, Anfield, the home of Liverpool Football Club will be a place of pilgrimage and not merely the place where they watch Liverpool play. The Second World War has produced massive pilgrimages to war graves and battlefield sites (Lloyd, 1998; Walter, 1993) all over the world. Celebrity, and especially the death of celebrity, produces what Rojek calls the St Thomas effect, 'the compulsion to authenticate a desired object by travelling to it, touching it and photographing it. Fans manifest the St Thomas effect by stalking and mobbing celebrities and in obsessively constructing celebrity reliquaries' (Rojek, 2001: 62). Consider the truly significant objects of your enthusiasm, identity and passion. How relevant and desirable is a pilgrimage to these objects and places? What would you get out of such a pilgrimage and what sorts of activities and objects might be involved? To what extent is it actually possible, commercially exploited or potentially exploitable?

Nationalist heritage and the interpellative nature of national objects

Tourist sites, and spaces of special or even sacred national significance are visited regularly and sometimes repeatedly by tourists. In performing the pilgrimage to these places and through observing the rituals appropriate to them, citizens are making a number of possible performative links to the higher social formation referenced at the site and to which they are *variously* connected. Despite the fact that nations are messy affairs with strange, unequal, contested and often violent biographies attaching to their mixtures of peoples, national tourist shrines often deliberately seek to assimilate all citizens in some way, to underlie the fact of their relevance and connection, no matter how shameful, scandalous or heroic their place in national biographies may be. Indeed some interpretations of history at tourism sites may even reverse negative connotations and seek to show how all have contributed to the national character. Kirshenblatt-Gimblett's (1998) analysis of the new heritage centre at Ellis Island, New York is a good example of this. Ellis Island was an administrative office that sought for much of its life to keep certain types of migrant out of the USA . It was the aperture through which all migrants landing in America had to pass for much of the nineteenth and twentieth centuries and where highly selec-tive policies of inclusion and exclusion were practised. Paradoxically, in its current reincarnation as a heritage centre, its main message now is one of celebration and valuation of the ethnic diversity of the nation and it permits a number of performative links to be made by migrants and their descendants from all national and ethnic origins.

Another good example comes from the Smithsonian National Museum of American History, Washington, where *Within These Walls* was one of its virtual exhibitions for 2001. Occupying the centre of an enormous room, an entire 1760s built house from Ipswich, Mass. was reassembled. Around it was constructed a chronological/biographical path for visitors to follow. The house and its occupants and their things tell an interesting story and we are invited to 'Meet five ordinary families whose lives within the walls of the house became part of the great changes and events of the nation's past, and learn how to look for clues to the history of your own home and neighborhood.' Note how we are invited to make a connection between ourselves and the nation with this move. The visitor can look to their left

Figure 5.4   *Ellis Island.* Source: Barbara Kirshenblatt-Gimblett

and see cut-away sections of the house exposing social spaces and artefacts or look to their right at groups of artefacts, documents, materials and images. As I wandered around this exhibit I became aware of the ethnic and racial diversity of the other browsers and wondered how they would or could make the link into their own personal lives as the exhibition's authors suggested – what would all those histories amount to? In the early period we are told 'Abraham Dodge, a patriot who fought in the Revolutionary War, bought this house in 1777. A few years later, he married his second wife, Bethiah. The Dodge household also included an African American man named Chance, who most likely was a slave during the war.' For me this introduced a tension into the room, a divisive narrative. We the visitors did not possess a common reference to exhibits but one that has continued to divide us in a profound and disturbing way. Such a thought was reinforced by the next exhibit. It spoke of the military foundations of the American social order and also of their social elites. 'This is the regimental coat of Col. Peter Gansevoort, 3rd New York Regiment of the Continental Line, a rare surviving symbol of the sacrifices patriots made.' Looking to my left this tension was reinforced by a small and functional doorway. The inscription read: 'This door led to the unheated attic where the Dodges' African American servant, Chance, most likely slept.' More tension. However as I walked on I came across this: 'The American Revolution transformed this household. By 1786, the year Abraham died, the Dodges were no longer British subjects and slavery had legally ended in Massachusetts. Still, Chance remained tied to the Dodge household as a servant in the transition from slavery to freedom.' The stark division evident from the very first period is transformed by this and we see the exhibit pointing up a national trajectory of civil rights. However, this is also intertwined now with a patriotic theme that overrides social and racial division. We see a picture of a battle by Alonzo Chappell, 1859. It reads: 'Peter Salem was one of about 5,000 African Americans, free and enslaved, who fought the British during the Revolutionary War.'

As with all nation formation mythologies, the best strategy is always to identify the other. In this case various references to the wicked British enable everyone in the room to feel American. Everyone it seemed had fought the enemy to build a free and heroic America. Now we have a bond going between us, except of course that I had forgotten something. I was British.

It is easy to explain how these heritage constructions work their nationalistic magic, providing ways of including and celebrating their imagined community, but how easy would it be without the objects that they typically use and how *do* these objects work such magic? If we focus specifically on the objects themselves, what are they doing? At one level they are part of a coherent narrative, a textual pleading with the visitor to see the world the way they do. A narrative uses props such as objects to illustrate the veracity of its cause and argument. Narratives are designed to speak to a general audience and to implant a standardised account of the relationship between the individual and the nation. However objects can also work in the way they interpellate the person or persons in their presence, which is to say, they can speak directly to them, hailing them *personally*. This is how national memorials seem to work since they typically employ very little narrative persuasion. Instead they rely on embodying an idea that can be directly related to by individuals or crowds. The statue of *Boudicca*, placed on the north side of the Thames, opposite the Houses of Parliament, is a large Victorian bronze of the warrior queen in full flight on her chariot against the invading Roman army. To the British tourist, already dwarfed by the sheer scale and intensity of the Houses of Parliament themselves, this figure interpellates them in a genealogical manner, for is not this queen a native ancestor to all subsequent Britons whose national distinctiveness has been to defend the British Isles against invaders? Interpellation consists of an object hailing an individual, speaking directly and meaningfully to them, binding them into an idea but also a community of others who share a similar relationship. So the interpellative power of objects consists not only of pulling individuals into an idea, it also suggests lines of association and alignment with untold others; it suggests in other words, an identity *and* a corporation. However, it is important to note that in the case of this figure there is clearly a message from the sculptor as well as the positioning of it close to the very heart of a nation, that suggests nationalistic themes. But since the concept of interpellation reveals the role that objects can have in *suggesting* social ideas and corporations, it is not restricted to those objects with specifically targeted effects, such as *Boudicca*. Interpellation occurs spontaneously in the course of everyday life, and is as much the result of an individual's biography as it is the biography of objects themselves. Thus although the constructors of *Within These Walls* could be reasonably certain that the objects chosen would interpellate most visitors, a feat made easier by the suggestive powers of narration, there is generally less control and coordination of interpellative processes. As Crang (1994) makes clear in his analysis of heritage, the designers and interpreters of heritage sites cannot control the pattern and direction of interpellation since they cannot figure in to their constructions the individual biographies of the visitors; it is always underdetermined.

Durkheim realised the power of objects to take a part in the social life of people during his analysis of the totemic cults of aboriginal people of Australia. In the case of Australian aborigines the clan ancestors allegedly emerged from the earth in a period known as the Dreaming, when the earth became animated with life and from when human clans were initiated. Aboriginal clans are seemingly religious or ritual communities as much as they are cognatic communities, because marriage rules, which dictate that clan members must marry outside the clan, mean that clans are not necessarily the day-to-day groups formed by marriage and birth. The multi-clan day-to-day groups or bands are highly scattered spatially and therefore clans tend to meet together only rarely, for special occasions associated with the life of the clan – matters relating to its continuity, death, birth, marriage, initiation and so on. Initially, one theory held that totemism was a misguided attempt to harness and pacify natural powers through ritual observation in nature cults. The social logic of kinship was drawn on to establish links between the key subjects, clans and species. Just as clan members are bound to support and protect one another, so such a relationship was incurred between human clans and natural species. This made little sense to Durkheim who asked why it was that the little, apparently insignificant plants and creatures (for example, the gum tree grub; edible roots and small birds) were the object of such social alliance rather than the really dreadful powers of nature, fire, thunder, flood and wind? For Durkheim there could be only one answer to the riddle: the relationship with the natural world represented by totemism was nothing other than a projection and representation of the clan itself. This is illustrated for Durkheim in the apparent strength of totemic powers vested in different objects. In individual clan animals or plants it was relatively weak, gaining strength in various body parts and fluids, yet more strength in pattern representations and ultimate power in the highly abstract nature of the sacred objects, stones often with highly cryptic minimal marks. For Durkheim these levels of power relate to the relatively insignificant status of an individual clan member as compared with the more abstract and fragmented nature of the clan itself. Totemic powers were at their most potent in their most abstract expression in centralised hidden locations, just as the clan was at its most potent when it was gathered together on those rare occasions to administer the continuity of its social existence. Durkheim wondered at the unequivocal nature of his source material when it described the state of great excitation at clan gatherings: 'The smoke, the blazing torches, the shower of sparks falling in all directions and the dancing, yelling men,' say Spencer and Gillen, 'formed altogether a genuinely wild and savage scene of which it is impossible to convey any adequate idea in words' (Durkheim, 1976: 218).

He considered it plausible that the psychosocial dynamic of the situation gave rise to a sensing of collective powers at work and also of the existence of 'two heterogeneous and mutually incomparable worlds':

One can readily conceive how, when arrived at this state of exaltation, a man does not recognise himself any longer. Feeling himself dominated and carried away by some sort of external power, which makes him think and act differently than in normal times, he naturally has the impression of being himself no longer. It seems to him that he has become a new being: the decorations he puts on and the masks that cover his face figure materially in this interior transformation. . . . And at the same time all his companions feel themselves transformed in the same way and express this sentiment by their cries, their gestures and their general attitude, everything is just as though he really were transported into an environment filled with exceptionally intense forces that take hold of him and metamorphose him. How could such experiences as these, especially when they are repeated every day for weeks, fail to leave him the conviction that there really exist two heterogeneous and mutually incomparable worlds. (Durkheim, 1976: 218)

The undoubtable reality of these experiences combined with the impossibility of explaining them exactly favoured their objectification in an external source:

He does not know that the coming together of a number of men associated in the same life results in disengaging new energies, which transform each of them. All that he knows is that he is raised above himself and that he sees a different life from the one he ordinarily leads. However he must connect these sensations to some external object as their cause. Now what does he see about him. On every side those things which appeal to his senses and strike his imagination are the numerous images of the totem. They are the *waninga* and the *nurtunja*, which are the symbols of the sacred being. They are *churinga* and bull-roarers, upon which are carved combinations of lines having the same significance. They're the decorations covering the different parts of his body, which are totemic marks. How could this image, repeated everywhere in all sorts of forms, fail to stand out with exceptional relief in his mind? Placed thus in the centre of the scene, it becomes representative. The sentiments expressed fix themselves upon it, for it is the only concrete object upon which they can fix themselves. It continues to bring them to mind and to evoke them even after the assembly has dissolved, for it survives the assembly, being carved upon the sides of rocks, upon bucklers etc. Everything happens as if they inspired them directly. [. . .] So it is from it [the totem] that those mysterious forces seem to emanate with which men feel that they are related, and thus they have been led to represent these forces under the form of the animate or inanimate being whose name the clan bears. (Durkheim, 1976: 220–1)

Summing up his analysis Durkheim realises that the social reality of the clan could not be grasped without the intervention of these totemic objects. 'In a general way, a collective sentiment can become conscious of itself only by being fixed upon some material object; but by this very fact, it participates in the nature of this object, and reciprocally, the object participates in its nature' (Durkheim, 1976: 236). In this way, paradoxically, social groups, societies and cultures are not so much held together by ideas as by *objects*, that permit them to *think* of social collectivities and to perform them through rituals. Now although we have strayed a fair distance from the subject at hand, contemporary forms of tourism, it should be clear that tourist objects enable similar types of connection and performance to be made. Perhaps, it is through the action and performances of tourism that contemporary cultures have a chance to reflect upon and perform their collective sense[s] of identity, their connections to space, ethnicity, nation, lifestyle group and so forth.

Further Reading

Crang, M. (1997) 'Picturing practices: Research through the tourist gaze', *Progress in Human Geography*, 21 (3): 359–74.

Kirshenblatt-Gimblett, B. (1998) *Destination Culture: Tourism, Museums, and Heritage.* Berkeley: University of California Press.

Law, J. (2001) 'Machinic pleasures and interpellations', Centre for Science Studies and the Department of Sociology, Lancaster University at www.comp.lancs.ac.uk/sociology/soc06711.html

Lury, C. (1997) 'The objects of travel' in C. Rojek and J. Urry (eds), *Touring Cultures.* London: Routledge.

6

Objects and rituals of seaside

SUMMARY

- The English seaside
- Blackpool observed
- Ritual clothing
- From swimwear to surfwear
- Seaside devotions
- Health and curative rituals
- Rituals of dance
- Rituals of sensation and fantasy
- Conclusion

I intend to use the term seaside as a general term for what is otherwise and variously referred to as 'the pleasure beach' or 'sea, sand and surf holidays' or coastal resort tourism or more latterly, after Lencek and Bosker (1999), 'the beach'. I think there is something quite general about all of these to justify a general term although it is important to recognise that they do not denote the same cultural activity across time and in different places nor are they the same in terms of cultural practices between nations, ethnic groups, class, age and so forth (see for example, Preston-Whyte, 2001). Some authors rightly emphasise leading dimensions of change in touristic practice and technologies, tourism has been postmodernised by these means and we need to track those changes (see Rojek, 1993, 1995 and 1997 for the most innovative and useful discussions of this). However, it would be misleading in a book on tourism to imply that seaside has supplanted, faded or died somewhere back in a chronological history of change. Seaside is still a dominant form of tourism and not merely on the new pleasure peripheries of South East Asia, Mexico, the Caribbean, Bali or Australia. The seaside towns of the USA and the UK, for example, have been through a turbulent period of change as they faced new competition but even they are remarkably resilient, morphing into new lives for fashionable nostalgias and kitsches; homes for theme parks; new and desirable locations for weekend villas, condos and spaces of retirement and as centres for conferences and conventions. At the same time many have continued to provide a relatively cheap holiday for workers and the unemployed. As an example, the most famous seaside of them all, Blackpool Pleasure Beach *is still* Britain's most popular tourist attraction. It is visited by over seven million people annually and has more hotel beds than all of Greece, including its islands (Roodhouse, 2001), and its range of clientele has remained very wide. Further, despite British heliotropism (which might be defined as a preference for sun holidays abroad), according to the UK Day Visits Survey a total of 81 million day trips to the seaside were made in 1998 (www.staruk.org.uk). At the opposite extreme perhaps, in the state of Florida a recent survey of beach visits in 1995/6 revealed that 84 per cent of Florida residents visited the beach at least once and that these visits might include anything up to fourteen different types of activity. The fact that Lencek and Bosker's (1999) book, *The Beach* became an international bestseller reveals the continuing relevance of the coast as a tourist destination. Even *water* itself has been a remarkably resilient component of leisure and tourism, as Anderson and Tabb (2002) in their new book, *Water, Leisure and Culture* make clear.

In this chapter I am going to concentrate particularly on the seaside's development because it was an early manifestation of modern consumer culture, and, as it evolved, it offers a good opportunity to examine it as a new (ritual) form of pleasure tourism and also a good baseline against which to judge how and why it has changed. In its early days as a mass seaside holiday centre (as opposed to the earlier 'medicinal' seaside that preceded it) it was a wonder world, a 'dreamland'; a utopian promise of the future brightness and consumerism of a post-depression, post-war world. Seaside, I will argue was an important ritual of transition into the new world of consumerism, spectacle and pleasure. However, the more that everyday life borrowed or styled itself on the seaside (producing universal all year round access to pleasure) the less specific seaside resorts were able to reproduce that rapture, breathlessness and euphoria. Seaside and the subsequent routinisations of pleasure after the style of seaside, produced a second, blasé period of connoisseurship; a more socially stratified, spatially extended, rarefied, and measured set of expectations and ritual. Seaside then became just one of very many alternative types of pleasure. However it remains one of the most important, precisely because it retained its basic ritualistic formula: it maintained its liminoid space of the beach, its ritual devotion to the sea, the sun and the body and its unhurried basic structure as a ritual of passage. When people say they need to get away, when people conjure an ideal holiday or break, in their imaginations seaside is still a dominant evocation.

This chapter will first of all account for the emergence of the mass seaside and then analyse its changing social and cultural form in terms of rituals of passage or transition. It will also distinguish seaside from the carnival and pilgrimage that preceded it. Its ritual form and ritual frames of analysis require attention to the entire sequence of the holiday, taking in dimensions and elements that many accounts leave out. Hence for example, I will investigate closely the ritual and machinic effects of new technology such as steam trains and also the interpellative effects of ritual objects such as deckchairs, swim suits and seaside hats. Whereas the ritual basis of early seaside forms can be located in emergent consumerism and also to a degree nationalism and a new erotic of the healthy body (a body routinely in danger of ill health and disease), later, more contemporary forms relate to a continuing emphasis on the body albeit to changing technologies of the 'sustainable' body (a body requiring constant and regular attention especially in relation to new dangers of stress, change and ontological insecurity).

The English seaside

The English seaside and all the subsequent seaside type holidays that it spawned is a curious but important cultural space of tourism. I am going to argue that it not only demonstrates the ritual nature of tourism very well, but that it points to the origins of such tourism rituals in nationalism and an emergent consumer society. So this claim links up with the discussion in Chapter 3 where it is argued that tourism is intimately linked with nation formation and modernisation and what we might call performative rituals of nation and consumerism. According to Shields 'the seaside [the popular, mass seaside of the pleasure resort circa 1920–1960] was a ritual in name only, for many of the structuring codes of the nineteenth century [therapeutic seaside resort] had been removed' (Shields, 1990: 86). Although we can certainly agree with him that things had changed, it is also possible to suggest that the seaside holiday was not a weakened version of the water-cure resort but an entirely different activity in the same space. Whereas the latter was very clearly a ritual of purification and health, with many of the universal ritual codes and practices observed everywhere (see Shields, 1990: 83–6) the former was very clearly not. Whereas in the latter visitors became client–patients and developed communitas among themselves as fellow initiates, the former were defined almost by the fact that there were no specific ties. So why and how was it that these crowds were notoriously gregarious? And although not as orchestrated as the water-cure rituals of the 'medicinal' beach they were still clearly ritualistic. But about what? Shields offers a clue:

Seaside resorts such as Brighton gained a real cultural significance for *the nation as a whole* as old religious feast days were augmented by factory and town holidays and finally by statutory vacations and the Bank Holidays Act of 1871. . . . Bank holiday crowds attracted entertainers from the inland fairs that were increasingly restricted (Stallybrass and White, 1986). London stallholders introduced what came to be seen as 'typical' seaside food, the Punch and Judy shows and other attractions. (Shields, 1990: 86)

Shields (1990) and Fiske et al. (1987) make the observation that like all 'betwixt and between' ritual spaces, the beach marks the boundary between nature and culture. Such structuralist accounts that use and associate binary opposites such as centre/margin, nature/culture, respectable/disreputable, order/disorder and so on are dubious often because they tend to reduce social life to an orderly pre-given logic and to ignore the spatial and temporal specificities of people and cultures. As it happens, it is also clearly the case that for Britain (and many other places) the beach marks the national boundary. As we shall see below, the beach or more properly the coast and its ports was an ancient borderland area, a borderland of a nation that had become predicated on overseas commerce and trade. It was an anomalous social space populated on the one hand by a migratory culture of mercantile men of more than simply national origin, and it was serviced on the other by a culture of pleasurability – pubs, brothels and other entertainments. Ports and coastal hinterland were temporarily occupied by men away from home, resting from long and arduous voyages and with money in their pockets. Their spoils of war, piracy and commerce were important to the national interest and their rest and recreation in the liminoid port were exempted from the norms of censure in everyday life. While this is very important and prefigures and critically informs any story we can tell about 'the seaside', the naval and mercantile ports are only one beginning to the story of seaside.

We also need to ask why and how did the beach and the seaside reproduce a form of cultic assembly that had died and was less tolerated elsewhere? At one level we can say that the carnivalesque seaside followed on the heels of the more ordered, mannered and medicinally orientated bourgeois coastal resorts. It was a question of social emulation, fashion and the economy of distinction perhaps. This is no doubt part of the answer. However, while the seaside holiday took over the same space and many of the same activities, we should be careful to identify the differences. While the coastal health spas were a *therapeutic* activity timed for maximum effect in *winter*, the seaside holiday lifted from antiquity the *spring/summer* season of *ludic* activity. Where the coastal spa resorts were exclusive and celebrated the luxury of travel and social segregation of the wealthy, seaside holidays were gregarious spaces of the common people, they pulled everyone into a common frame regardless of class, income and background. Perhaps this was a ritual acknowledgement of interdependence as Shields suggests, but this somewhat abstract, not to say vague, notion may be bound up in a more inclusive answer: the seaside was a ritual of *national* life. How can this be? How can these disorderly, spontaneous and essentially hedonistic assemblies be linked to nationalism and nation formation?

First, the seaside holiday was significantly different from the coastal spa in its very origin: the former was an artefact of the highly individualised leisure class whereas the latter was based on a significant gain for the nation as a whole: the gradual provision of national holidays and later national legislation establishing paid holidays. The early days of workers' paid holidays were confined to a select number of paternalistic companies and mill towns leaving large numbers of workers elsewhere unable to participate in the seaside (Davies, 1992: 40–2). It was not really until the nationally instituted *public holidays* by an Act of 1871 that a day in late spring (Whit Monday) and another in high summer (August Bank Holiday Monday) encouraged day trips and overnight stays at the seaside on a truly mass scale. We have to avoid assuming that this new social institution was attractive to everyone and that it automatically replaced traditional, more local leisure activities. Inevitably it was the young, the single and the unmarried who pioneered the seaside holiday as a social practice in their respective families, neighbourhoods and localities. It was they who brought back news of what Shields (1990) calls the 'aliveness' of these new ludic spaces. These new excitements also have to be understood as part of a general mood of their day, and the more hedonistic behaviour of the beach has to be understood alongside a view common among employers and legislators that fun, freedom and pleasure were good for people and especially good for the nation.

Nations are abstract socialities that combine two seemingly opposed features. On the one hand a looseness and weakness of social ties between their millions of citizens who are largely strangers to each other, and on the other, the tendency for a welling-up or effervescence of very strong feelings within the individual and spontaneous (though often short-lived) bonds of affinity (or enmity) between citizen strangers. The effervescence of bonds of affinity between strangers in the crowd is a feature of many ritualistic activities that galvanise around nationalism. One can think for example of sporting occasions, as when Uruguay plays Argentina at soccer, or Germany plays England. Here of course nation objects (scarves, hats, team shirts etc.) play a part in this. 'Wartime spirit' is the metaphor frequently used to describe other such moments, as when a spontaneous spirit of cooperation and affection grips people in national adversity: a bushfire in Australia, a terrorist tragedy in New York. It is interesting to recall how the stars and stripes garnished everything and everyone almost immediately after the events of September 11.

From the 1850s until well into the twentieth century, but especially from the 1870s onwards, the entire western world was gripped by nation formation fever as we saw in Chapter 3. An important part of that fervour was the establishment of national spectacles, which as Urry (1990: 25) observes, were 'often promoted and *rendered sacred* by royal patronage' (my emphasis). The link between national ritual, royalty and nation formation was being made not for the first time, as we saw above (pp. 116–18) in relation to the nation building Anglo-Saxon King Athelstan. Moreover we have already seen the figure of the Prince of Wales remaking Brighton in this manner, culminating with the completion of the spectacular Royal Pavilion in 1823. However, Royal visits were made to many other seaside resorts (Margate, for example). In addition as Urry shows for the UK, other spectacles include Trooping the Colour on Horse Guards Parade, London; The royal tournament (from 1888); the first Varsity match in 1872; the first Henry Wood Promenade concert in 1985 (now called *The Proms*); the Highland Games (1855). In addition to Christmas, Easter and New Year's Day national holidays, the USA has a further eight, all of which relate to moments or events of national significance or formation. This association between holidays (and their associated peaks of tourism) and nationalism is generally poorly identified in the tourism literature, particularly its important ritual content. However, it affirms the significance of what Billig (1995) called 'banal nationalism'.

Davies' study of leisure in working class Salford and Manchester from 1900 to 1939, for example, shows that family holidays were unattainable luxuries throughout the period. Desire for the seaside deepened through the tales of those who did make the journey – children on charitable outings through the church, relatively affluent teenagers and the unmarried travelling by themselves, older couples whose unmarried children contributed to a wealthier domestic economy, older men on pub 'outings'. Even where children were taken to the seaside 'day trips were often the norm' (Davies, 1992: 42). How did the seaside outing sit in the imagination of these poor industrial cultures? Davies (1992: 42–3) is quite clear: '[S]easide holidays, like gramophones and wirelesses, were status symbols which appear to have sharpened feelings of relative deprivation in working class neighbourhoods during the interwar decades. Some families were enjoying new levels of affluence, but those trapped by the poverty cycle or unemployment were often acutely aware they were missing out.' In a consumerist society, as Bauman (1998b) argues, tourism becomes a model metaphor for the successful consumer, and as consumption became ever more significant in judging individual worth and status, *not* to travel and tour became the source of an intolerable indignity. This unevenness and inequality of access to the seaside combined with its status as one of a growing number of approved pleasures by the national elite resulted in the holidays-with-pay movement of the 1930s and culminated with the 1938 Holiday Act which extended a week's holiday (or in some cases, two) to a majority of workers (Urry, 1990: 26–7; Durant, 1938: 231–2). The immediate effects of this legislation were not felt until after the war 'when the number of UK holidaymakers was expected to double, from 15 to 30 million annually' (Urry, 1990: 27).

Reproduced below is a webpage explaining the origins of contemporary holidays in the USA. It is interesting to think about these as commemorating moments in nation formation, and their annual observance as ritual performances of national identity.

Box 6.1   Contemporary American Holidays and Nationalism

UNIQUELY AMERICAN HOLIDAYS

Eight other holidays are uniquely American (although some of them have counterparts in other nations). For most Americans, two of these stand out above the others as occasions to cherish national origins: Thanksgiving and the Fourth of July.

Thanksgiving Day is the fourth Thursday in November, but many Americans take a day of vacation on the following Friday to make a four-day weekend, during which they may travel long distances to visit family and friends. The holiday dates back to 1621, the year after the Puritans arrived in Massachusetts, determined to practice their dissenting religion without interference.

After a rough winter, in which about half of them died, they turned for help to neighbouring Indians, who taught them how to plant corn and other crops. The next fall's bountiful harvest inspired the Pilgrims to give thanks by holding a feast. The Thanksgiving feast became a national tradition – not only because so many other Americans have found prosperity but also because the Pilgrims' sacrifices for their freedom still captivate the imagination. To this day, Thanksgiving dinner almost always includes some of the foods served at the first feast: roast turkey, cranberry sauce, potatoes, pumpkin pie. Before the meal begins, families or friends usually pause to give thanks for their blessings, including the joy of being united for the occasion.

The Fourth of July, or **Independence Day**, honors the nation's birthday – the signing of the Declaration of Independence on July 4, 1776. It is a day of picnics and patriotic parades, a night of concerts and fireworks. The flying of the American flag (which also occurs on Memorial Day and other holidays) is widespread. On July 4, 1976, the 200th anniversary of the Declaration of Independence was marked by grand festivals across the nation.

Besides Thanksgiving and the Fourth of July, there are six other uniquely American holidays.

Martin Luther King Day: The Rev. Martin Luther King, Jr., an African-American clergyman, is considered a great American because of his tireless efforts to win civil rights for all people through non-violent means. Since his assassination in 1968, memorial services have marked his birthday on January 15. In 1986, that day was replaced by the third Monday of January, which was declared a national holiday.

Presidents' Day: Until the mid-1970s, the February 22 birthday of George Washington, hero of the Revolutionary War and first president of the United States, was a national holiday. In addition, the February 12 birthday of Abraham Lincoln, the president during the Civil War, was a holiday in most states. The two days have been joined, and the holiday has been expanded to embrace all past presidents. It is celebrated on the third Monday in February.

Memorial Day: Celebrated on the last Monday of May, this holiday honors the dead. Although it originated in the aftermath of the Civil War, it has become a day on which the dead of all wars, and the dead generally, are remembered in special programs held in cemeteries, churches, and other public meeting places.

Labor Day: The first Monday of September, this holiday honors the nation's working people, typically with parades. For most Americans it marks the end of the summer vacation season, and for many students the opening of the school year.

Columbus Day: On October 12, 1492, Italian navigator Christopher Columbus landed in the New World. Although most other nations of the Americas observe this holiday on October 12, in the United States it takes place on the second Monday in October.

Veterans' Day: Originally called Armistice Day, this holiday was established to honor Americans who had served in World War I. It falls on November 11, the day when that war ended in 1918, but it now honors veterans of all wars in which the United States has fought. Veterans' organisations hold parades, and the president customarily places a wreath on the Tomb of the Unknowns at Arlington National Cemetery, across the Potomac River from Washington, D.C.

In Chapter 5 it was argued that the former *inland* fairs, festivals or revels (which organised a carnival experience on holy days) had faded during the nineteenth century as a result of the depopulation of the countryside or were discouraged or banned where they were accessible and politically threatening to the fragile new order of industrial towns such as Bristol. The festivals or revels belonged to very different, essentially parochial and complexly intertwined, inward-looking rural social networks. Although they were large gatherings they were the gatherings of a district social network comprised of criss-crossing ties of kinship, clientship, patronage and village identity. The festivals and revels were also essentially associated with low culture and a state of relative regional independence and isolation that characterised proto-national formations outside the capital and courtly institutions (Gellner, 1983; James, 1996).

Critically, the social networks of the carnivalesque were preoccupied within their own cultural orbits; they had their own taste traditions, local customs, dialect and geography and were typically suspicious or hostile to outsiders and foreign culture. Indeed they might even be cast as the cultural opposite to tourism. Gellner argues that as new communications and technologies broke down the relative isolation of the provincial life they also exposed it to the expanded universalistic interests of high culture and national markets. The growth of the printed word, radio and transport together with the creation by high cultural institutions of new national geographies, biologies, cultures and histories made a world beyond the districts of the festivals accessible and relevant. Although in the UK people had been extremely mobile for a very long time, travelling great distances routinely for trade and work, the nineteenth century opened up every locality to the emerging modern nation state. The network of railways in particular made everywhere accessible, but to most people in many inland manufacturing towns, the first conceivable 'end of the line', the nearest frontier to a world beyond the industrial order was the coast – which had been transformed into a leisure space by the maritime economy and then bourgeois health spas. The inward-looking and self-absorbed cultures of the pre-nation-building period of the nineteenth century were also disturbed by the 1871 provision of national holidays. These bank holidays were new, universal and coterminous; and their arrival coincided with an era of affordable rail transport.

So, the coast was first colonised by the relatively affluent whose holiday adventures became the source of envy and emulation in working class neighbourhoods (Roberts, 1984: 99). However, bank holidays soon became routinised around day trips to the seaside that in turn paved the way for a seaside holiday, particularly after 1945. To say that the carnivalesque festival had shifted in some way from the interior to the coast is to make more of the fact that some of the peripatetic entertainment businesses that had frequented the revels and fairs relocated in a permanent way to the emerging coastal resort towns. Some of the noise, foods and entertainments of the rural fair had made their way there, including the emphasis on bawdy, less civil behaviour. Whereas the carnivalesque festival was predicated on a relatively fixed and interdependent rural social network, the seaside holiday grew to be characterised by the opposite, an almost amorphous mass of strangers. While they lacked the strong ties of *gemeinschaft* or community, this crowd generated its own form of excitement around equally powerful sentiments: they all owed their presence at the seaside to the granting of holidays to all citizens, regardless of their social or economic status. Miraculously it seemed, the nation had decided everyone was to experience days or even weeks of fun and respite from the tyrannies of work and routine or what Turner and Turner (1978) called 'the mundane'. Importantly, the crowd of seaside strangers liberated the holidaymaker, albeit temporarily, from the moral world of industrial village or neighbourhood. At the seaside their reputations and status, their woes, wrangles and problems with others were set aside or suspended in an edifying limbo. At the same time, the presence of everyone around them had its origins in a weak tie that bound them all to a feeling of communitas. The social relationship that bound the seaside holidaymakers, however loosely, was citizenship and nation. But, these were not rituals of citizenship or celebrations of nation. In the same way pilgrimage was not a ritual of belonging to a religion *per se* but of individual redemption, so the seaside holidaymaker was also seeking an individual experience of transition and renewal. Pilgrimage was not a collective ritual but a rite of passage, for the individual ritual subject (although it could be a group ritual it was mainly individual). A crowd or community of *fellow travellers* of course is central to the practice of rites of passage, as Turner and Turner (1978) make abundantly clear. At the seaside then, it was this commonality and greater unity that permitted the extraordinary, promiscuous gregariousness associated with the crowd. Perhaps this was the cause of what Shields refers to as the 'aliveness' of places like Brighton.

Finally and very obviously, although missing from almost all accounts of the anthropology of seaside, over the entire period of its emergence, almost naked nationalism had characterised the sentiments of daily life – these were the life and times of an intense period of nation formation across Europe and the USA. Moreover it found expression through a sequence of wars, producing new forms of sociation and cooperation (as well as new social spacialisations) among stranger–citizens, churned by the mobilities and mobilisations of war, military organisation and social lives and wartime economies. Although the spontaneous and vivid sociability of seaside holidaymakers has this social and economic background, we are still left with the problem of accounting for its particular form. The argument I shall make here is that seaside behaviour was ritualistic, specifically, belonging to that group of rituals called rituals of passage. Sociologically, seaside holidays resembled more pilgrimage than carnival and although that might seem counter-intuitive, the one playful and superficial, the other sombre and serious, it must be remembered from Chapter 5 that pilgrimage was in fact characterised by a great deal of mirth, playfulness, drinking and debauchery, as Chaucer's *The Canterbury Tales* make very clear. Equally, it can be shown that seaside had its more serious side, particularly the manner by which people sought life and health affirming activities. As with pilgrimage, seaside was particularly rich in ritual objects and these play an important role in defining its ritual space, performing ritual devotions and effecting ritual transition.

As with the Aborigines at their *corroborees*, special objects at the English seaside enabled this sociality and this affective community to coalesce. In many ways the seaside holiday began with the relatively new steam train. But the steam train was also a key component of the ritual experience. As with all ritual occasions, participants enter a liminal or liminoid space. The train's moving carriage describes a non-space (see Augé, 1995) that is always in motion between two fixed locations, particularly in this case, between the everyday or mundane and the holiday site or sacred place. In addition, this liminal space and tourists' experience within it is administered and governed by ritual specialists (the station masters, the guards, ticket collectors, drivers etc.) and in a sense they deliver the tourists from one stage or ritual state to another. Finally, passengers enter a passive state, relinquishing control and agency to the massively powerful machine. We are now so habituated to rail and other machinic travel that it is possible for us to underestimate the dramatic effect it had on people in the early years of steam. However, Law (2001) reminds us of the interpellative nature of our relations with machines, and also the machinic pleasure these interpellations involved. What does this mean? To say that objects such as machines interpellate us means that they call out to us, hail us or address us and create in us particular subjectivities in relation to them. In a nutshell they make us feel different, or at least they bring out in us a particular subjectivity, state of mind or being. Law speaks of how fighter aircraft interpellate some men into heroic subjectivities and how this generates a machinic erotic, a series of pleasures that accompany or derive from that interpellation. Law also talks about a common way in which many, but not all people are interpellated by the experience of flying in passenger jets. Many people are interpellated by the aircraft during the take off sequence, after which the interpellative effects tend to fade, though not disappear altogether. 'Some are simply terrified, sweating as they grip the armrests, knuckles white. Others simply seem to be oblivious to what is going on. Perhaps they have flown two hundred or five hundred times before this year. . . . Yet others are thrilled' (Law, 2001: 6).

> Crushed together inside a cabin, and belted into our seats, we can hardly move and have not the slightest possibility of controlling anything. But all the while huge physical forces are working their best, or their worst, upon our bodies – are experienced in or by our bodies. There is a heaviness that is irresistible, a weight that binds us to our seats, together with the knowledge or the fear that if something goes wrong there is nothing to be done. Our bodies will be broken beyond repair. (Law, 2001: 6)

Recognise any of this? What is important for the subjectivity that jet aircraft interpellate is this loss of agency to the machine. It creates fear to be sure but there are also what Law calls machinic pleasures. These would seem as applicable to the early steam train travellers as they do to twenty-first century air passengers. The first pleasure Law talks of is fatalism: for with the inability to act come the pleasures, the luxuries of fatalism, of waiting, of waiting for the machinic, the natural, the divine, to act on and through the body. Fatalism 'is its own form of comfort, this distribution into passivity'. The second pleasure is 'being cared for, of being looked after, of being held up, in the belly of the monster or by the wings of the divine . . . there are the pleasures in trusting enough "to allow" the distribution of agency out of the body into other materials, the hands of the carer, the belly of the technological whale, or a machinic mother'

(Law, 2001: 7). Third, Law argues for the pleasure of non-responsibility, 'that is, of not being required to take responsibility for anything, for others, or, indeed . . . for oneself'. We can readily appreciate how the steam trains of the past with their massive machinic presence and raw power – and many people were quite scared as the train pulled into stations – provided similar experiences to those experienced by jet travellers.

In a similar way then, the train performed an important first step: it removed the tourist very rapidly and dramatically from the mundane everyday world; it placed them in a liminal in-between space; and it created a new inverse subjectivity: as against the world of work you are now fatalistic, cared for, free of responsibility. It was an exciting and transformative subjectivity that prepared the tourist for what lay ahead: the strange but exciting prospect of a week of public play.

As the massive steam locomotives pulled into stations with the incredible noise and blasts of steam, some mouths may have become dry among the waiting passengers, notably those non-regular users. As the train picked up speed, speed that was totally off the scale of all other embodied or machinic experience, the passengers for whom this was not a routine may have experienced these same machinic pleasures of passivity, a loss of control but at the same time a fatalism, being cared for and trusting, but also a temporary loss of responsibility. These were (and still are) powerful subjective states and in the case of holidaymakers they find parallels in other ritual occasions where those undergoing the ritual are rendered passive, delivered into the control of others, transformed from one state to another.

The early experience of rail travel suggests that this may all have been more significant than we might assume today. Some of Cook's first tours of the 1840s and 1850s were reported to be overwhelmingly exciting for the passengers, and a measure of the excitement can be gauged by the fact that train loads of tourists attracted large crowds of onlookers too, and frequently arriving trains would be met by brass bands and marched to a dinner or lunch at the town hall (Withey, 1997). As we travel today, the experience of liminal or non-spaces has shifted to the automobile/motel (see Urry, 1999; 2000: 57–63) and the aircraft cabin/airport lounge. Increasingly we form a hybrid social and technical system, which is 'a machinic complex constituted through the car's technical and social linkages with other industries . . . road building . . . hotels, roadside service areas . . . suburban house building; new retailing and leisure complexes; advertising and marketing . . .' (Urry, 2000: 58). There is certainly an associated machinic pleasure to automobility and we are interpellated in a number of ways, into a home from home, literally a new way of living in the liminal, in-between space of the car with its associated narratives of luxury, comfort, insulation from 'the road', its pollutions and its risk. As with the luxurious interiors of the steam train, automobility takes place in a space modelled on a sitting room, with comfortable chairs, the possibility

Figure 6.1   *Steam Train at Rothley, UK.* Source: Ian Britton

of light entertainments, convivial intimate conversation. At the same time, the automobile provides a panoramic view of the in-between space, crushed and fragmented as it is, into the speeded up (and speeding up) nature of automobile time. While drivers maintain a greater degree of agency over the individual car, this is marginalised by the overall machinic assemblage of 'the road': we are still as much in the grip of traffic as steam train passengers were in the rail network. And anyway, if we take average car loads, the growth of taxis and coach transport, most passengers of automobility are passive, trusting, cared for and 'delivered' by their car.

Blackpool observed

Much of this ritual atmosphere is apparent from the accounts of holidays to Blackpool in 1938 by the Mass Observation team of researchers working in a northern mill town (dubbed 'Worktown'). They already knew from their observations and interviews that Saturday 29 June 1938 had been planned and dreamed of ever since the dark days of January and February. Most of the town were off to the seaside and many to Blackpool. When the day finally arrives excitement builds as massive crowds descend on the train stations; there is a crush 'for Worktowners on holiday prefer to travel by train – partly for the convenience of fewer stops, and partly because trams and buses are part of everyday, workaday life. What everyone wants, according to the Blackpool publicity bureau (closely linked with the railroad company) is to get to fairyland as fast as possible. "Come to Blackpool by rail" adverts advise and promise "A journey without anxiety"' (Cross, 1990: 58).

Everyone was dressed up, the men in new suits, women wearing coats and hats 'the scene is a parade of Sunday Best . . . the children as well, all carefully polished, are continually reminded to stay that way' (Cross, 1990: 58). A period of silent waiting, and standing about on the platform gave way to nervous excitement as the time drew close. Here is the sequence of observations:

> A group begins to sing and their mood spreads infectiously across Great Moor St. Station to children and adults alike. One child, on the opposite platform, *'hearing the singing, began dancing about; one pretended to play the banjo. Men with accordion played 'Horsey, Horsey'. Some people sang. Accordion played 'Count Thy Blessings, Name Them One By One'. Everyone singing'.* (Cross, 1990: 59)

Once aboard the train, the mood was again sober and quiet 'for the first part of the journey there is almost always restraint and silence. Girls read *Woman's Own*, *Passing Show* or *Silver Star*; men smoke; and the train moves on to stops at Chorley and Preston' (Cross, 1990: 60).

> Then things begin to change, Preston is the door to the Fylde, a wide flat plain, roughly square, of pastoral land lying between the rivers Wyre and Ribble. Beyond Preston the traveller sees meadow landscape unlike most Northern scenery. . . . Inside the train, the mood changes; the travellers are now bound together as 'fellows' by this common rallying point. The restraint clearly visible at the outset has dropped from sight. *Without thinking, observer hands a woman passenger a cigarette and passes them around. All men take one including a man who has slept until now, and who suddenly comes to life. One of the women, competitively hands around sweets to women only . . . sound of accordion being played is now audible. Then singing. Female voices, pleasant and tuneful. . . . Accordion struck up a hymn. Three people singing in next carriage. Young man and two girls join in. 'Jesu is friend to all'. Then accordion played 'Daisy, Daisy'. Everyone sang.* (Cross, 1990: 61)

How did seaside tourists emerge from the train? What did they do, where did they go? It was a very different social space that daytrippers alighted onto. Most especially it was a ludic space, a place essentially for play and pleasure. The train journey had involved the pleasures of passivity, but beyond the station, trippers had to be more active: they had in one sense or another to perform a role, which of course was not easy, partly because it was a public performance and partly because they were unused to doing it. However, the seaside offered a liberal and lateral space for individual experimentation, and people literally performed their way into the role by improvisation, copying role models. Of course like all ritual occasions, the initiands were in a process of transformation and change. The Mass Observers sensed this moment as important and tried to capture it. Here are the diary accounts of two arriving tourists:

> We emerged from the station, Blackpool Central, me feeling like a schoolboy again for it was as a schoolboy I had last been to the seaside and my wife's cheeks glowed with the salt air of the incoming tide[which] provided the first sense that we were going to have a beneficial holiday.

> Emerged Central Station. Felt elation of being in Blackpool, breathed deeply and saw sea on left with sun on it, tide out. About to ask for Tower when I saw top of it poking over roofs of buildings ahead. . . . Did not look in any shops but walked straight towards the Tower

> [the tower is] the Mecca of our journey. (Cross, 1990: 61)

Mass Observers had agreed to follow twenty people off the train for the first hour. Of these none went to the sea. 'Many only look at the sea, being far more intrigued by the shops – such as the "World's Greatest Wool-worth's" where some people go straight off the train . . . new visitors spend forty minutes to two hours there' (Cross, 1990: 61).

So this evidence suggests that the train did indeed play a significant ritual role, *as a tourist object*. First it was the mode of transport associated with the non-mundane; it was by its very nature special. Second, it removed them from the mundane everyday and let them down in the liminal world of the resort, referred to as 'fairyland' or even 'Mecca'. The train was literally betwixt and between; in constant movement between ordinary and sacred places. Third, it provided a space of fellowship for the traveller, and indeed the richly ritual behaviour of communitas was recorded even on this relatively short journey. Within that space there was food sharing, singing, music, playful foolery and joking behaviour – largely between strangers. Fourth, as the railway advert claimed, the train provided machinic pleasures; it was 'a journey without anxiety' and marked for the first time, a ritual space and time where work and anxiety were to be replaced by pleasure and rest. Fifth, it altered their subjectivity, inverting it and creating a heightened sense of self: the man becomes the schoolboy; the couple began to experience 'beneficial' qualities; while another felt 'elation'.

Seaside railway stations had the added frisson of also being the end of the line. We have very little evidence of attitudes to and feelings about the coast among the ordinary person, save that the vast majority had little knowledge and experience of the sea or the coast. However, the fact that on national holidays the entire population of factories and cities left their homes for the national boundary played no small part in the nature of this as a ritual occasion or pilgrimage. As Shields (1990: 96) notes 'there was a genuine reaching out to embrace the social totality of the *national* holiday (his emphasis)'. Shields underlines the significance of the coast as a place on the margins, and draws a universalistic association between marginal places and marginal or disapproved of behaviour. It was as if a blind eye could be turned to the less acceptable forms of behaviour providing it was placed at some distance from the centre. This resonates with the sort of analysis of ritual instigated by van Gennep and elaborated by Turner and Turner: borderland spaces set at some distance from the everyday are typically chosen for rituals of passage. However, to argue this in the case of Brighton and other seaside resorts is to ignore two rather important points. First, seaside tourism began with the medicinal beach and seaside spa bathing owed its origins to the expansion of water cures. A large part of pilgrimage is concerned with individual redemption and the restoration of order, and health was centrally implicated in this. Christian pilgrims sought among other things cures for their ills and their illnesses and other forms of pilgrimage seek cures and transformations of fortune. The healing qualities of waters, particularly of specific springs, pools and lakes have a long history dating back at as least as far as ancient civilisation, and the medicinal spas of early modern Europe have to be understood in this context even though they acquired a veneer of scientific endorsement in the eighteenth and nineteenth centuries. Part of that endorsement was the mineral and other measurable qualities of the water and so even though many of the new spa resorts were in marginal spaces a great many others were not. On the other hand they required that most of their clients travelled some distance to them. Although much can be made of the sexually charged ludic atmosphere of the spa resorts, one must not confuse the ancillary entertainments and pleasures formally and informally associated with them with the client's core motive and the social tone they expected: many people were there to be cured, they were wealthy and the resorts were managed in a rather sedate, not to say formal, manner. Second, seasides had acquired a 'marginal', lewd and disreputable character long before 'the seaside' but this was clearly not related to their distance from the social centre but to their association with the masculine world of navy and mercantile cultures. Mercantile cultures were almost entirely male and ports consisted largely of several ships' companies of men at any one time, many of them unmarried or living away from their wives and families. Ports were places of rest and recreation from wars, the stresses, discomforts and deprivations of sailing. These were places of bars, hard drinking, entertainment, prostitution and men behaving badly. This was considered good for morale within the navy and to a degree a blind eye was turned to it. But it was not only the ports that built up this kind of service economy. Some places such as Deal, Kent were anchorages for sail ships that needed to be serviced as they waited for better weather. In addition, the national defence front lines were on the coast. While it was always hoped that the navy would protect against invasionary forces it was also true that army camps were located strategically, especially around the southern coast. Brighton in particular was the base for one such army camp, and the fully deserved reputation of towns catering to a similar concentration of men away from home was ably used by Jane Austen in *Pride and Prejudice* as a place of sexual indiscretion and social ruination. So, while many might have been relieved to have these liminal spaces away from their back door, on the nation's margins, the implication in Shields' account that such spaces have some social authorship seems unrealised. I would stress more 'continuity in discontinuity' and hybridisation of these spaces. It was a matter of minor adjustment for prostitution and other entertainments together with the liberal moral economy of the coast to move into new visitor markets. Within that milieu, boarding houses, inns and hotels were routinely more tolerant and so when the seaside emerged, characterised as it was by a greater gender balance, the visitors were able to exploit these spaces of sexual freedom. As Shields shows, Brighton extended this economy to organised sexual indiscretions among Londoners giving rise to the economy of the dirty weekend and divorce. However, this has to be judged against other seaside resorts such as Blackpool, where intensive research has shown that accommodation spaces were highly regulated by a respectable class of boarding house landladies, with most refusing, for example, to give rooms to single women. More generally, as we will see in Chapter 9, the 'sexual' reputation of Blackpool was not realised in practice, even if there was a sexually charged atmosphere. In what other ways did seaside resemble rites of passage such as pilgrimage? These can be organised under the headings of ritual clothing, seaside devotions, health and curative rituals, ritual dancing and music and rituals of sensation.

Ritual clothing

One almost universal response to ritual transition and performance is to change quite dramatically one's outward appearance. Ritual garments, especially headwear, special ritual objects and motifs all combine to achieve this effect. Sure enough among those participating in seaside we can identify special dress codes that signal (or even demand) belonging to this generalised ritual engagement. In England and the USA seaside outfits have always involved more festive, outlandish and risqué designs than mere summer fashion/wear (Lindsay, 1983; Lansdell, 1990). Seaside clothing was graded spatially to match the graded spaces of the beach itself: in particular, smart but ludic holiday outfits and swimwear (see Fiske et al., 1987). Holiday outfits were bought specially for the seaside occasion, were worn on the journey, and could be augmented during the holiday by seaside fashion boutiques. These were typically very colourful and bright with regular design motifs – stripes, the navalesque or nautical, eccentric hats and so on. Eccentric hats, emphasising the essentially party ritual form, could be taken to extremes by purchasing cheap plastic or felt authority character hats – naval officer, pirate's hat, policeman's helmet or the ubiquitous and unsubtle 'kiss-me-quick' hats. At Blackpool in the summer of 1937, young men and women wore 'a light cap with alternating blocks of red and white or blue and white, with tassel and peak on which were written slogans like: COME UP AND SEE ME SOME TIME and UP THE OLD NARKOVIANS. (Narkover is the 'college for crooks' made famous by film and stage comedian, Will Hay (Cross, 1990: 161).) These sorts of clothes not only mock the establishment and authority, but they establish those present in a topsy-turvy world where normal relations are inverted, a world of anti-structure where the individual is free to engage in experimentation and alternative or new identities and embrace improving or purifying experiences (such as pleasure, healthiness, exposure to sun and ozone). The promenade and other ritual objects and spaces were established in all seaside towns not only to stroll beside the sea, but also to be seen in these sorts of clothes, and to make immediate, promiscuous and intimate contact with fellow revellers. Again, at Blackpool in the 1930s, the massive crowds and 'crushes' seemed by themselves to encourage episodes of extraordinary, spontaneous play. Here is Cross commenting on one such 'crowd phenomenon':

> Late in the summer of 1937 long chains of young men held up traffic at Belisha crossings, went right through Noah's Ark in formation and silted up the entrance to the pleasure Arcades . . . sometimes these groups were of mixed sexes (with women riding on men's shoulders), always below the age of 25 and numbering 8 to 22. Others would join who clearly did not know any of those participating. (1990: 162)

It is no accident perhaps that one of the pleasure rides in the Fun House was called the *Social Mixer* which 'hurls and swirls strangers together' (Cross, 1990: 162), an experience that chimes well with the diary entry of one mill worker who described the crowd as 'an animated mass of bustling, laughing colour. Young folks, old folks, all out for anything – and the sky's the limit' (Cross, 1990: 161).

These contacts might be sexual where appropriate (see Chapter 9 for accounts of the sexualised nature of conversation between strangers at seasides), but non-sexual contacts tended to be, or were encouraged to be, overflowing with friendly familiarity. The promenades were dotted with all manner of more semi-private objects/spaces where such intimacies and friendships could be extended and elaborated – tearooms, gardens, kiosks, booths and shelters. Such spaces enabled the masses to break down into smaller assemblages and to replace generalised with reciprocal forms of social exchange. As with the clothes, the promenades were also highly decorated, usually with maritime symbols in bright colours, augmented by garish displays of flowers.

On the liminal beach itself, holiday outfits were discarded for swimwear, regardless of whether swimming, dipping or paddling was intended. There were no inevitable clothing arrangements for entering the water or even swimming, but it was generally true that over time, in most places,

Figure 6.2   *Blackpool Sea Front*. Source: Ian Britton

swimwear tended to push accepted boundaries of decency and modesty to the limit; it went as far as it could go and a little further. All around the world, the beach became the subject of regulation and moral outrage not simply because sea bathing and sunbathing were more effective with less clothing worn, but because the naked body interpellated sexually charged subjectivities. As Lansdell argues, 'the bathing costumes of the 1920s for both men and women showed, almost year by year, an increase in the amount of skin exposed and a decrease in the weight of fabric used' (Lansdell, 1990: 63). By the 1930s men's full-body costumes of the earlier period had given way to 'trunks' that differed only from contemporary designs in that they covered the navel and were variously belted; by 1938 two-piece women's costumes had been introduced in the USA and Europe and were on sale in Bond Street, London (Lindsay, 1983). Indeed, this tendency is still a part of the seaside ritual, and in contemporary times of course, bids for topless and nude bathing provide the critical and ultimate boundary. In Australia, as Booth's (2001) book on beach cultures demonstrates, the seaside was not a separable space from the suburb, since most Australian cities were built along the coast. For this reason, beach culture was not conducted away from the everyday and evidently did not establish the same degree of licence to suspend norms of propriety and public decorum. This is quite clear from a history spanning the entire twentieth century where 'residents' fought long and bitter battles with the bathing cultures of the beach. So, for example, the earliest forms of essentially naked bathing by young men and later by those clad in the early swimming costumes became subject to a daytime ban between 6.00am and 8.00pm. When this was widely disregarded, the beach was gender segregated in an attempt to maintain morality. By the beginning of the twentieth century the beach was the subject of a major battle: those who saw the sun and sea as a commendable environment for physical and moral improvement (largely beach culture itself) and those who saw it as sexually depraved and morally dangerous (largely residents and moral guardians in the church and local conservative institutions). The so-called battle for daylight bathing was eventually won, but not without punishing requirements to cover the body in a manner that defeated the ease of swimming and the object of devotion before the sun. So began what might be called the battle for the naked body and Australia seemed dogged by serial rounds of restrictions on bathing attire tolerated widely elsewhere followed by heroic acts of civil disobedience. In the middle was the figure of the 'beach inspector' who had to decide, often in very difficult legal circumstances whether an individual had transgressed local by-laws or gone beyond the point at which they had been stretched by local precedent. Fines were levied, new campaigns on both sides ebbed and flowed but eventually by the 1940s, Australians were finally wearing what had been acceptable in Europe for many years with barely the same degree of fuss. One Australian solution to the problem was for bathing and surfing to move away to more secluded spots, but this failed because the suburban beach was a commons and local swimmers and surfers used it as part of everyday life. The Australian case demonstrates the peculiar and powerful culture of (English) seasides that occupied spaces on the social margin, and particularly their ability to create liminal spaces of sexual freedom and practice. By the last quarter of the twentieth century there were a wide variety of nudist beaches near most English seaside resorts, including one at Brighton, a mere stone's throw from the pier. The international trend towards sexual liberation and the body sculpted by regimes of fitness, dieting and toning, had also influenced Australia but the same conflict between beach-goer and anguished and morally outraged resident reappeared and fumed unresolved through the 1970s right up until the present. So for example, Reef Beach on Sydney harbour has undergone several periods of 'optional' and 'clothed only' periods as the battle raged on, typically involving debates at the highest political level (Booth, 2001: 55–64).

In the properly marginalised English seaside, bathing dress codes were free to invoke two standard features of human ritual behaviour: the inversion of everyday norms (in this case the norms of clothing modesty where effectively everyone parades in underwear); and a heightened sense of, and tolerance for, public displays of sexuality. However, notice here that it is the norms and styles of common swimwear that enable these transgressions to occur and to be seen to occur. One is interpellated by one's own and others' swimwear into a sexualised subjectivity. All ritual occasions tend to use such clothing props to align people into a commonality and to mark the social boundaries of the ritual. This was emphasised by the Mass Observers in Blackpool in 1938, who noted that many (if not most) wore costumes without going into the water. Indeed on three afternoons in late summer, they counted around 8,000 people on the beach and only between 8 and 63 in the water itself (Cross, 1990: 91) and detected from interviews with Blackpool traders and vendors, a decline in swimming itself. This is persuasively the case from the proprietor of bathing vans (mobile changing rooms wheeled onto the beach) on the best site who said 'There used to be three bathing sessions, before breakfast, after breakfast and afternoon, but now there's only the afternoon' (Cross, 1990: 91–2). In addition, the open-air bath 'was never used as such'.

Here are the notes of one observer who was on hand to see and record this vignette:

> Eight women disrobing amongst crowd. Bathing costumes under skirts. One takes hers off, but others shy. Proceed to lift each other's skirts off, while others resist, run away screaming. Young man takes photo. Eventually all run towards water, dancing on the way. (Cross, 1990: 91)

From swimwear to surfwear

Swimwear has remained a remarkably stable feature of seaside and the contemporary 'beach' culture. However, as swimming became eclipsed by the cult of surf and surfing from the 1950s onwards, ritualistic beachwear and beach objects became more elaborate. This had its beginnings in the USA and Australia but has been successfully marketed around the world. In Australia this generalised surfing culture began as a youth sub-culture, the unremarkably named '*surfies*' (whose culture developed at some distance from the more conservative surf life saving associations that dominated most suburban beaches). By the late 1960s surf culture expanded away from its exclusive serious core and was propelled into mainstream Australian culture by the media. 'All the mass media and channels of publicity have thrown their weight behind the surfies: the Sunday newspapers carry surfing supplements, disc jockeys plug surf music remorselessly, the advertising agencies flatter and glamorise beach life. They know what the coming thing is' (McGregor, 1967: 285). During the 1980s and 1990s 'surfwear' domi-nated clothes worn on beaches and on coastal holidays, and the big three Australian companies Rip Curl, Quiksilver and Billabong grew to dominate this growing global market. Rip Curl for example began in 1969 when two enthusiasts in Torquay, Australia began making their own boards. By the late 1990s they were producing branded clothing and accessories with corporate Licensees in the USA, France, South Africa, Indonesia, Brazil, Argentina, Chile and Japan, with an estimated turnover of $150 million (Stranger, 2001: 212). But these cult surf companies are only a small proportion of the total surfwear phenomenon: '[m]ainstream manufac-turers soon appropriated the surfing style and began producing under their own labels; or alternatively by purchasing existing surfwear companies. Also, many, if not most surf shops, once cult enclaves intimidating to the outside world, began to change their focus from the surfer to the more lucrative mainstream market for authentic surf culture brands' (Stranger, 2001: 214). Today most of the main hub airports include one or a number of such shops and they are practically the only word in beachwear available for the tourist bound for resort destinations. The point I want to stress here is that 'surfing' and the cult of the surf has become the new manifestation of the ritually mantled and performed cult of seaside. Ritual clothing has expanded to wet suits, T-shirts, caps, jackets, shorts and a wide range of accessories. As Stranger (2001: 218) remarks, 'the mainstream consumer can purchase a T-shirt which declares "Only a Surfer Knows the Feeling" irrespective of whether they are a fully initiated surfer or merely consumers of style experiencing to some degree the surfing aesthetic'. Such is the evocative nature of contemporary seaside in its *surf* manifestation, that it has become something of a postmodern metaphor for the good life, and surfing wear has become dominant everyday leisure wear everywhere.

Shields (1990) notes that the English seaside carnavelesque rituals tended to flatten and dedifferentiate social difference, producing a homo-genisation of swimwear. Everyone had to participate in the rituals of the beach, and this was achieved by adopting the ritual code of dress. In surfwear this has been amplified. However, the appropriate dress was simply the first stage.

At seasides there were a range of activities that have parallels at pilgrim-age sites: relatively long periods of time spent in devotion before ritual objects. We do well to remember here a contrast with some rather estab-lished understandings of tourism as essentially *restless*, constantly on the move. As we will see, seasides slowed the body down and made it fre-quently still; it was a restful body, frequently dozing off, napping, lying down; it was a contemplative body staring out to sea or at the hypnotic effects of the crowd or the fantasy of a book or a beautiful body (Jane Desmond's (1999) material on 1930s surf beaches in Hawaii shows how the beach and surfing offered opportunities for sexual experiences as well as 'sights') . The architecture of the seaside was dominated by the provision of seats, and our faithful band of Mass Observers in Blackpool did not fail to measure how well they were used and for how long.

Seaside devotions

On the liminal commons of the beach all citizens had rights of passage and impermanent occupancy. These were above all commons protected by national statute, where all were equal before the law (Walton, 1983). Anyone from anywhere could be a part of the beach. Indeed in the case of the UK where space and accessibility were highly privatised and restricted, it is hard to think of other spaces that might be used as gathering places on national holidays. Beaches became special liminal places rendered ludic and festive by the economy of national holidays. Some companies began suggesting a seaside break for their workers, but then it was encouraged powerfully by national organisations and finally legislation. In many ways the movement for national paid holidays resembles the actions of those kings and their archbishops who supported and encouraged pilgrimage. In the case of both, an external body (the church, government) encouraged individuals and small parties to leave the mundane world of the everyday and travel to a place of sacred significance.

To what extent does the seaside holidaymaker replicate these aims of pilgrimage? It is fairly clear that the intentions of the holidays-with-pay movement and other organisations promoting the seaside and other holidays identified the importance of getting away from the everyday world of work, neighbourhood and city. An unremitting life of work was seen as unhealthy and unproductive; simple time off work would still leave the individual vulnerable to other obligations and chores and the city at this time was particularly polluted, dirty and for many a grim environment. Simply to get away, to do something different even to face different challenges on the tourist road characterised the sentiments of the seaside break.

Second, although the seaside holiday of the interwar and post-war years can be seen as artificial, shallow and insubstantial – by its very nature – we need to appreciate that in fact it was an exciting experience. Pure pleasure spaces such as these, spangled and noisy and designed to deliver you into a state of elation contrasted so dramatically with the industrial landscape of work. It is instructive here to think of stained glass windows in cathedrals and churches. To us now they seem unedifying and perhaps a little serious, if not moody. However, when they were first innovated and built into the medieval cathedrals they took people's breath away; the spectacle produced excitement and the sensation that this was a very special, exalted place. Seasides buzzed with these special objects, magical piers, amusement arcades, entertainers, funfairs, coloured lighting at night, parks and gardens, monuments such as Blackpool Tower or the Wintergardens at Bournemouth. But was this a deeper level of existence? In some ways it was. The material life of an industrial worker through the first half of the twentieth century was extremely basic. Sophistication and depth could be measured by access to luxury and the time to luxuriate. The seaside had depth and excitement for those who craved and dreamed of consumption and the things money could buy. It was no accident, for example, that the giant Woolworths superstore was situated across the road from the Central station of Blackpool nor that this was the first port of call for most arriving by rail. Further the seaside had depth in terms of social activities that could not normally be considered: café lunches, hotels and guesthouses, sports, such as tennis, swimming and golf. In a consumer society fixated on the luxurious lifestyles of celebrity Hollywood, it is quite easy to see that all this was more than charming, it was sacred, magical, amazing; but also personally transforming and therefore similar to salvation. Turner and Turner (1978: 3) argue that liminoid rituals of this kind are about transition, what is 'going to be' but also 'what may be'. It is hard not to imagine tourists of the mid-twentieth century as being excited by the speed of technological and consumer change. Real wages did grow, consumer power grew dramatically even during the 1930s, the world of goods expanded and it was possible to be drawn into utopian dreams of a consumer future. For all its kitsch glamour and carnivalesque borrowings it still held the promise of a leisure future that was more fun, more exciting. Indeed Durant's (1938) discussion of leisure in the late 1930s reveals that government and planning rhetoric contained a clear intention to model new urban leisure policy on the seaside. In other words, the seaside was a metaphor for the consumer society just around the corner. During this period the numbers of people who could imagine the fixed place of holidays and leisure in their lives steadily grew. For many of these their first glimpse of a more pleasured life was made at the seaside; the seaside was replete with symbols, architectures, objects and texts that provided an imprint or paradigm structure of a new kind of lifestyle based more on leisure and pleasure. The sheer proliferation of exhortations and encouragements of these objects interpellated a leisure subjectivity and this was confirmed through *devotion*, of which more below, and the crowds of fellow passengers. So much of this seaside consumer excitement relied on the imaginative and speculative world of the future; in this sense we can understand seaside as the promise of a brighter dazzling and more pleasured future. This theme of a futuristic landscape

The emotional intensity of liminoid rituals such as pilgrimage or seaside is also based on the effect of communitas: 'Symbols that originate in elevated feeling as well as cognitive insight, become recharged in ritual contexts with emotions elicited from the assembled congregants . . . the quality and degree of the emotional impact of the devotions (which are performed day and night), derive from the union of the separate but similar emotional dispositions of the pilgrims converging from all parts of a huge sociogeographical catchment area' (Turner and Turner, 1978: 13). Finally, there is an unmistakable sense in which the seaside holiday was seen as *therapeutic*. Seawater and the ozone gas it gave off continued to be viewed as healing and beneficial to health. All manner of illnesses (but especially lung diseases) and convalescence were treated in institutions by the sea throughout the twentieth century. The therapeutic nature of seaside compounded water cures and therapy with heliolatry. As Gibson (2002: 279) nicely put it, 'UK tourists are heliotropes – they travel towards the sun'. These elements, sun, air and water offered seasiders *exposure* to a therapeutic environment, and like pilgrimage that exposure needed to be extensive and enduring. What enabled such a long period of exposure was a series of devotions, that took place in the crowded space of fellow congregants. The therapeutic objects were the sea, the sun, the air and the water but the beach was cluttered with all manner of objects that permitted that devotion to take place.

Part of the ritual practices or devotions of seaside was to be on the beach, to occupy for long periods a part of this special space and, especially, to forgo usual norms of privacy and personal space. On the beach one spent a period of time in very intimate contact with others. One not only changed one's clothes in such public propinquity, but one also lounged or pottered about in a state of semi-nudity. Certain objects made all this possible. Important among these were deck chairs. Hired off the beach for the day, these tended to not only legitimise the claim of a particular area but they also directed the temporal presence of the seasider: they were there for the duration, as were most others. Apart from being festively striped or coloured the deckchair also permitted different body poses by being able to sit forward or recline. Forward positions permitted the focused attention to the sea, to sea air, and the ceremonial life on the beach. Reclining positions allowed rest if not sleep and exposure to sun. Deckchairs also authenticated membership of the seaside congregation, enabling and encouraging free and easy social exchanges between people. In cultural terms deckchairs derived from the more luxurious or even decadent cruise liners but they translated onto the anthropology of the beach. On the cruise ship deckchairs were laid out in lines on the assumption that the fellow passengers sought communitas in the liminal space and time of the deck. The deckchairs also enabled the passengers to access the transformative potencies of sea air, fresh air and sun; the chairs were designed to enable *exposure* of the body to these elements.

The Mass Observers at Blackpool discovered that people spent an average of two hours at a time sitting on deckchairs but there were also other seats built into the promenade that they studied. They discovered, for example, that there were five such seats facing seaward for every two facing inland, which meant that people's bodies were directed predominantly at the sea. Fifty per cent of those sitting on these in the afternoon were 'sitting, looking about' while most of the others were either described as 'talking' or 'smoking'. It was a seaward, sea-orientated stance and although those on the hard seats only spent an average of twenty minutes there, groups that were followed over the course of a day were found to rest for around 10 per cent of their time. The pattern of the day consisted of small periods of movement, followed by small periods of rest. Movements themselves were related to making sure that all parts of the pleasure beach and the town had been visited, usually with a rest taken in each station. At any one time in September there were 10,000 people on Blackpool beach while on Bank Holidays they numbered nearer 40,000. Those sitting or lying on the sand stayed between one and three hours and activity depended on the condition of the sea and the time of day. A turbulent rising tide produced great excitement among the crowd as groups of people danced among incoming surges attempting to stay dry. However, '[J]ust before tea time on a typical afternoon . . . 50 per cent were sleeping or snoozing, 25 per cent were looking, 10 per cent playing, 10 per cent supervising children and 5 per cent talking' (Cross, 1990: 94). (For other contemporary data on beach activities see Maas et al., 2000.)

In the water, seasiders at most resorts paddled and swam, often in groups or huddles. We saw earlier that in the early summer of 1938 (June) the Mass Observers did not find large numbers in the water at Blackpool, but this is not surprising given its northerly position. Bathing could be prolonged or literally a dip, but it was essential to bathe in some way at most seasides. The practice of drinking seawater terminated with the medicinal beach resorts, but the period of time spent in the water increased. So also did the variety of bathing activities. On the medicinal beach, patients were dipped rather like a baptism into the cold winter water. Once this had been done the treatment terminated for the day. On the seaside beach, new technologies of bathing in the warmer summer water came into practice. Swimming was a relatively new technology and most people of the period had little access to swimming pools or swimming instruction, but it was developing. There were different swimming strokes, there was long distance swimming; there was underwater diving as well as diving from boards and anchored platforms. A variety of objects came into bathing practices, balls, inflatable devices and so forth. Fishing from piers and promenades became very popular at this period, as did the study of rock pools and marine life.

Towards the end of the twentieth century the beachside devotions shifted increasingly towards the sun as the aspect of devotion, and besides merely health being the sought after transformation, exposure to the sun gave a more tangible and visible result, the 'tanned look'.

[the beach] gradually became an axis of consumption and transformation. The cult of the suntan exemplifies this. Successful tanning requires the consumption of sun-tan lotion and the abandonment of work. It is quintessentially, a transformative activity. Often, the process literally involves the shedding of skin to acquire a new look. Display and appearance determine tanning activity. If as Baudrillard (1985: 126–34; 1988) intimates, postmodernism is a social consciousness organised around an economy of signs rather than an economy of commodities, the tan is one of the most accessible and universal signs. It instantly conveys health, leisure, vigour and sophistication. (Rojek, 1993: 190)

To Rojek's list of signs we might also suggest 'Modern' itself and 'Holly-wood', one of its key metaphors for cultures influenced by western television. Although fashions do change, the 1990s, for example, enjoyed a pale-skin phase from time to time; it is interesting to consider the centrality of the tanned look in popular culture from the 1960s onwards. One of the reasons is without doubt the status that the tan conveyed: it stated that you were part of the travelling cult, a pilgrim, transformed each year by exposure to the sun in faraway resorts. However, this was under-written by a far more powerful influence from the everyday: western television and film is dominated by the bronzed look of Californian 'whites', and the same body is used to advertise most things on offer. In this way, there is yet another association between tourism and consumption: whenever we become exposed to new and desirable things, they are almost always mantled in a touristic aesthetic, if not a setting. However, the classic seasides of the mid-twentieth century were more generally focused on transformations of health itself.

The new cult of the surf that now dominates seaside and beach experi-ences is a more active and muscular set of devotions but as we will see in a section dedicated to understanding what is going on in the performance of surfing, we can identify an even more sophisticated slowing down of the body culminating in expanded moments of ecstasy. However, that section properly belongs in Chapter 8 where I discuss and account for the emer-gence of more embodied forms of tourism and their special relationship with 'nature'.

Health and curative rituals

It is possible when looking at the seaside holiday to see only the carnivalesque surfaces and to read these, as Shields did, as a weakened or emaciated version of the rural original. Certainly they look insubstantial and inconsequential. They have the look of throwaway, meaningless or even of vacuous pleasure seeking. But there was a seriousness too. Prior to the holiday season, the Mass Observers studied the holiday desires of Worktowners. Rest and relaxation and health themes were particularly prominent in their thinking, and the search for the therapeutic benefits of the medicinal beach had not completely disappeared. Despite the outward appearance of fun and excitement, health was the single most prominent theme to seaside Blackpool in 1938. First, it had 'become the main theme of Blackpool's publicity' and 122 out of 365 of the Mass Observers' correspondents 'liked Blackpool because it was healthy' (Cross, 1990: 76).

And the moment they step out of Central station, they become aware that Blackpool assumes their inherent unhealthiness. In every amusement area there are posters, shops and stalls, such as this one, offering as drinks: Back and Kidney Mixture; Aspro Mixture; Constipation Mixture; Tonic Pick-me-up; Hot Peppermint for Indigestion; Stomach and Liver Draught; Black Drought. . . . Sudden death or disease is stressed on postcards too (and ill health cards outnumber healthy cards by two to one); ill health themes in music hall jokes are the single biggest category, 13 per cent of all laugh-raisers. (Cross, 1990: 77)

Of 281 people interviewed by the Observers, 43 per cent said they liked Blackpool for health reasons and 56 per cent for pleasure and amusement reasons. In terms of the places they liked three types overshadowed all others: 34 per cent liked the sideshows; 13 per cent liked dancing and 10 percent liked the Tower. However, when we look at the sideshows themselves we find that health and cures form a substantial component of them. 'The holiday maker is interested in the score or so of medicos, especially the "health lecturers" with sessions eight to fifteen times a day. Of these fifteen were herbalists (several using snakes as props) and the rest were astrologists and preachers of varying kinds.' Clearly then, despite the playful appearance of seaside holidaymakers, a very large proportion were concerned with the health-giving properties of seaside, both in anticipation of their holiday in the winter and during their time away. Seaside towns marketed themselves as health resorts and orientated the tourist towards their health-giving properties, the sea, the air and the sun. Their architecture and facilities were designed to maximise the amount of time tourists could devote themselves to health-giving exposure and encouraged many businesses to practise the theme of cure and well being. Its ultimate expression at Blackpool was *The Rejuvenator*, a tableau in the autumn Illuminations:

The Rejuvenator looks like a ship's turbine into which three old people enter, a man in a bath chair wheeled in by another old man in a beard and a lively old woman with a smile on her face and strutting gait. Printed on the long cylindrical machine is 'BLACKPOOL FOR REJUVENATION'. Behind this is a tank on a pedestal, marked OZONE. At the other end of the machine comes a dancing stream of 9-year old children. (Cross, 1990: 81)

This is surely the perfect metaphor for seaside as a rite of passage and a very modern one at that. Far from following the usual cradle to grave sequence of *rites de passage*, the transition on offer at Blackpool was to defeat aging, to return tourists rejuvenated. Although seaside subsequently evolved into a number of different themes and spaces, the enduring modern theme equating pleasure with health has persisted to the present. However, seasides offered a range of pleasurable experiences that typically also focused on body and performance. As we witness a major contemporary revival of jazz music it is instructive to consider its transformative role in popular culture, particularly through its presence at seasides of the twentieth century and the new dance craze it engendered.

Activity 6.1

Using the internet it is a relatively easy task to compare the emphasis given to health at seasides in the mid-twentieth century (reported above) to those of the present day. Select five seaside resorts that have produced a website and do a brief content analysis of its marketing. How many themes do they emphasise; how is healthiness portrayed (if at all); how do pictures and graphics support these themes? Count the number of times words like 'health', 'fitness', 'excitement', 'fun' and 'fantasy' are used. How are people shown relative to the sea, the sun and the air? Compare the contemporary arrangements for devotion with those discussed above. To what extent do these resorts emphasise relaxation, slowing down, entertainment, sex, drinking, dancing and promenading? What new activities have been recruited into seaside?

Rituals of dance

The rhetoric of the holidays-with-pay movement and the discourse on the benefits of pleasure that brought the public holidays in 1871 was also never far away from an emphasis on healthiness, and here the connection between the healthy and 'fit' body and the healthy nation was explicit. Some of this can be attributed to the Romantic movement that if anything tightened its grip on national imaginations during the early part of the twentieth century. After all, Romantics idealised Roman (and Greek) civilisation with its emphasis on bodily strength, fitness and training and especially the beautiful body. They also cultivated spaces of pleasurability, hedonism and recreation in the context of specific beliefs about their benefits to the individual and the nation. Ancient Rome instituted no less than 173 '"nefarious" and other rejoicing days' and this may have prompted or contributed indirectly to new legislations for leisure (Flametree, 2002). Rojek (1995) reminds us that Nietzsche idealised the passionate and pleasure-seeking nature of classical civilisation, but more importantly he saw the inhibition of passion and pleasure as unhealthy and impossible to prevent. Rojek's analysis of leisure and modernity divides into two critical periods, Modernity 1 and Modernity 2. Modernity 1 is characterised by the search for a rationally ordered and controlled society; it is a society that was ambiguous about pleasure and leisure and sought to control it via promoted rational recreations on the one hand and suppression and control over hedonistic, purely pleasure-seeking leisures on the other. In trying to suppress, in particular, the pleasures of the body it succeeded only in creating craving and desire and their satisfaction in the illicit pleasure trades.

Modernity 2, by contrast, is characterised by the collapse or relaxing of Modernity 1 or rather the recognition that modern social life is essentially about change and flux; a state of disorder. With this understanding comes a realisation about the impossibility of stamping order over it or finding 'management' solutions; also that overly ordered regimes are unhealthy, unproductive and ineffective. Writers such as Baudelaire and Nietzsche sensed this through their interest in the *experienced life* in modernity. Nietzsche used the classical Greek gods Dionysus and Apollo as metaphors to express the tension between order and freedom as practised in modern life in the early twentieth century. Apollo the god who represented order and self-discipline and Dionysus the god of wine who represented 'sensuality, abandon and intoxication' (Rojek, 1995: 80).

> The relish of the passions and the contact with beauty which are so essential for personal and social health and creativity are blocked by the habitual requirements of civil society. Modern life echoes with the sigh of self-denial. We are dully aware of Dionysus' call to open ourselves to experience, to embrace the pain and joy of life and to act guiltlessly, but instead we meekly surrender to the conventions of respectable society. (Rojek, 1995: 80)

In the interwar years these essentially Romantic leanings to the Dionysian impulse became routinised in everyday life. We have to remember, for example, that the 'devils' music' or jazz spread very rapidly across America and into Europe after the First World War. After 1918, jazz and dancing to popular dance bands established new pleasure spaces in British town centres where before there had only been the over weaned approved leisures of the suburban chapel halls with their emphasis on suppression of sexuality and surveillance (Meller, 1976). Prior to jazz, dance had been a highly controlled and restricted activity, overseen by parents or other community moral guardians. When jazz arrived and the ballrooms appeared in the downtown areas, with buses and trams or the underground available to transport people in from the suburbs, an entirely new leisure space was created. Dance before jazz certainly contained an erotic aspect but it was repressed. By its own definition jazz and the dance forms it inspired produced an unrepressed erotic culture that by its very performance questioned the stifled nature of other areas of civil life (Meller, 1976).

Box 6.2

When the new sound of jazz first spread across America in the early twentieth-century, it left delight and controversy in its wake. The more popular it became, the more the liberating and sensuous music was criticized by everyone and everything from carmaker Henry Ford to publications like the Ladies Home Journal and The New York Times. Yet jazz survived.

Advertising for the TV series The Devils Music, PBS (2002)
www.pbs.org/wgbh/cultureshock/beyond/jazz.html

But this was no permissive society, as Box 6.2 above suggests, it was opposed by an even more powerful Apollonian reaction, which, as Rojek notes, produced a deviant leisure culture. Ostensibly this was populated by the young who also, not surprisingly, adopted other potentially harmful practices such as cinema going (for a contemporary account of the cinema as a moral problem see Henry Durant's *The Problem of Leisure*, 1938). Equally, the seaside, and most other tourist spaces, were not homogeneous leisure spaces. The seaside consisted of different age cultures, classes, tastes and political opinions and it was in perpetual tension between Apollonian and Dionysian impulses. All around the world for example, there were local feuds over bathing in the sea, bathing dress codes and particularly, the seaside behaviour of the young. The Romantic emphasis on the healthy, athletic body was taken up by nation building (ordering) discourses and practices. It found expression in state-organised youth movements that were to channel youthful exuberance and sensuous pleasure into forms consistent with a military state. There was an undoubted erotic element to the Hitler Youth movement and other movements of its kind. They sought freedom and space on the margins through camping, walking and exciting sports as well as through competitive sports. This ordering of leisure, attention to the body, to fitness and beauty, to a cult of the beautiful, fit body found a good deal of expression at the beach. But, as Rojek argues, such things could never be contained, in this case merely as a national asset or investment. To repeat, a great many of the seaside congregation had been in military or para-military organisations or youth organisations. Communal fitness, exercise and attention to the body were endemic features of this period, but once the ordinary body had become the object of special importance and technological attention, it was prone to other orderings because specific regimes of the body could be challenged, mutate, evolve under the influence of competing claims, such as from discourses of the sensual body: from jazz, from the cinema, from television. And of course these were also characteristically present at the seaside.

It is hard to find any studies of the seaside that investigate the place of dance, music and stage but these were also fundamental to the experience. Daytime and evening entertainment maintained the intensity of the liminal space, especially if, during the day, rain prevented devotions on the liminal beach. Summers produced a summer season where musicians, comedians, and actors moved to the coast to be with their new mass audiences. Television (and film) centralised entertainment and the creation of celebrity, but during the summer, celebrity acts could be seen live. The presence of celebrity, as with the presence of royalty before, underlined the sacredness of seaside places, and provided yet more spaces of devotion. Seasides also produced audiences of sufficient size to stage major national and international musical acts and in this way seasides were far from parochial. Seasides were also the conduit for new music, dance, and comedy. The comedy was always raunchier than the TV; the music always louder and more intense, the opportunities to dance and drink longer than at home.

This was well illustrated by George Formby's show at Blackpool in 1939 where 'the breast of a living female [was] fully exposed for the first time in the city' (Cross, 1990: 182). Dancing and dance band music was a central component of Blackpool resort life. If the beach dominated the day, the night was dominated by its main ballrooms, such as the Tower, where by 9 o'clock in the evening some 5000 people were observed by the Mass Observation exercise in 1937. The atmosphere was hot and sweaty and dancing and drinking seemed to be undertaken in equal measures. Clearly, the view of the revellers was that the band quality was much better than they could expect in *Worktown*, and indeed, two tiers of spectators above the dance floor were there to hear the music as much as watch the spectacle of dance below. The Observers were interested in the social practice of picking up partners at the dances and recorded a great many of them. Interestingly, only one observed request for a dance was refused and there was a general lack of formality and surveillance: as Cross summarised, '"picking up" and "getting off" was accepted, normal behaviour' (Cross, 1990: 174). At the Winter Gardens another team of Observers did a census of the ballroom and analysed the dance styles. Sixty-seven per cent of the people in the ballrooms were women and, depending on the dance step, anything from 13 to 57 per cent of the couples were females dancing together. On average 82 per cent of couples were mixed. Diaries kept of the week in Blackpool show that dancing by unmarried adults was the principal activity, practised every night and frequently in the afternoons as well.

Typical accounts of seaside emphasise its daytime activity but dancing was a central and demanding physical activity in the 1930s. Most of the ballrooms played from around 8.00pm until 11.30pm and the dance styles were fast and complicated. The relative ease with which dancing partnerships could form in conjunction with the fact that most people were total strangers added a frisson of excitement to the pleasure, and the successful format of the ballroom as a place of sexual encounter is attested by one Observer who on leaving the Tower at 11.30pm 'counted fifty-nine necking couples on way home . . . about a mile of promenade' (Cross, 1990: 179).

The ballroom was clearly a place of fantasy and social encounter. As a fantasy it most clearly simulated the cinematic world where heroes and heroines danced the night away to impressive big bands, and a world ordered by the fantasies of chance romance. Pairing up and the creation of romance were ritualised at the ballroom and participation was free and easy.

> The dancer is aware of the social value of dancing, and they know that in the ballroom they have an opportunity of getting to know people which is lacking on the promenade during the daytime. So the boys and girls who have failed to 'get off' in the course of the day make another attempt in the Tower and other ballrooms at night. The ballroom sanctions approach without intro-duction. (Cross, 1990: 174)

The accounts of the Observers at Blackpool are valuable not so much for identifying the prodigious sexual activity in ballroom settings, but for making it quite clear that it was an expected and called-for performance. Just as people were expected to become semi-naked on the pleasure beach, they could expect to find dance partners and have their advances received amiably in the ballroom. At the end of the dance a very large proportion had paired up, and could look forward to varying degrees of sexual activity in the public spaces of the night-time beach. It is the atmosphere of expectation, participation, freedom and licence in the ballroom that makes it so typically ritualistic, typical of rituals of passage found anywhere in the world.

Dancing has continued to be a central night-time activity at seaside and beach holiday resorts, and we can see in the social tone of Blackpool ballrooms much of the later and even contemporary informalities of the disco and club. Music and alcohol remain central provisions; strangers can be approached without introduction and they remain focused around the 'pick-up'. What has changed is the scale and openness of the seaside ballrooms. From the 1960s onwards, the mass ballrooms gave way to more intimate, themed and socially stratified clubs and discos. In addition, the remaining spaces of sexual surveillance terminated with the demise of the boarding house as the main provider of accommodation. Paired couples no longer needed to linger in the shadows of the piers and promenade, and the public ritual of 'necking' seems to have declined with the growth of private spaces in hotel and apartment rooms, and the so-called sexual revolution(s) of the later twentieth century. Sex and tourism is explored in greater detail in Chapter 9.

Rituals of sensation and fantasy

It needs to be acknowledged that seasides tend to come in two main kinds, both of which were distinguished in the early twentieth century as indeed they are today, although in a changed form. The first is what we might call spectacular seasides, large centres with a very considerable emphasis on spectacular pleasures, entertainments and elements of fantasy. These include the major seaside towns of Blackpool, Morecambe, Margate and Great Yarmouth in Britain and Coney Island, NY and Redondo Beach, LA in the USA. They were predominantly mass holiday venues and largely, although not exclusively, working class. If they were not exclusively working class, we can say that they were inscribed with a populist social tone, and as such they maintained a claim to being a ritual spectacle of the common people. These were the forerunners of Disney-styled theme parks (for a good discussion of these see Rojek, 1993; Bennett, 1983; Hannigan, 1998) and in many respects these aspects of seaside are now detached from the sea and the beach, and the rituals of health and restfulness that they grew from. They are still very often on coastal sites, as in Florida and San Diego, USA or the Gold Coast in Australia, but they are clearly separable and placed in major inland cities. City-based theme parks are now so normative and their fantasy component so widely diffused in the city (from theme parks to theme malls to theme shops, eateries and cafés, entertainments, and so on) that Hannigan (1998) is able to suggest the notion of *Fantasy City* as a metaphor for the contemporary metropolis. This of course feeds into the major theme of this book, that increasingly, we find the objects and leisure of tourism right on our back door step and do not have to travel to be a tourist. As a result, tourism has become an everyday experience, and even though we now make many trips away from home they are no longer confined to 'holidays' or what Rojek (1993) means by 'escape attempts'. As he argues, 'the distinctions between the world of duty and the world of freedom have lost much of their force experientially and therefore are of dubious analytical value' (Rojek, 1993: 169).

The second type of seaside is what we might call the sedate seaside. These places have always tried to be quieter, smaller, socially exclusive and holding more steadfastly on to the transcendent qualities of nature–health. These have not developed a technological interior to the sea but have arguably increased the use of the sea by new technologies, sailing, power boating, diving, fishing, marine cruising, water skiing and so forth. So these places have built marinas and encouraged investments in high quality restaurants and cafés, all commensurate with the pursuit of rest and the slowing down of 'fast time'. Very often the sedate seaside resort was associated with its opposite spectacular seaside, so Douglas, Isle of Man was to Blackpool as Broadstairs, Kent was to Margate. It is worth mentioning before looking more closely at the development of the spectacular, that the sedate seaside has been remarkably resilient, despite the competition from overseas tourism. With greater access to the coast by car and fast highways, these places can be reached very easily for weekends and short breaks and increasingly they have been transformed by second home purchase. This is also symptomatic of the routinisation of tourism in everyday life, where the seaside becomes a second home or where home (or simply time) is split between city and pleasure periphery.

Figure 6.3 *Jungle River Ride.* Source: Ian Britton

We have already noted above that key seaside towns accreted the remaining fragments of the peripatetic entertainment and sideshow cultures of the carnivalesque. Towards the end of the eighteenth century these travelling family enterprises settled finally on the coast, where, along with summer visiting Romany travellers (specialising in palm reading and other oracles), money was made from the growing numbers of medicinal tourists. As the numbers grew, more elaborate investments were made, switchbacks, steam driven rides and other fantasy attractions were built but there were elements of continuity between the culture and rituals of carnival and these new developments.

The carnivalesque was characterised by almost universal elements across Christian Europe from the medieval period onwards, if not before. We have come across these in Chapter 5 so I need only summarise them here. Broadly speaking these elements comprised ways of constructing an 'other' or 'upside-down' liminoid world of reversals, inversions, anomalies and monsters. These constructions of course helped to create the liminal 'in-between' world that was suspended between the routines of everyday life, but as we have seen, the emphasis on elements such as the grotesque body helped to establish the point, in ritual enactments, that the carnivalesque was a ritual of a particular interdependent sociality – ultimately, everyone was reducible to a common state of flesh and blood regardless of everyday observations of hierarchy and rank. So in a way, although the carnivalesque was centrally concerned with social reproduction and renewal, it did so by emphasising the social interdependencies and tensions as well as the transcendent powers and human conditions affecting all. The embodied subject was laid very bare in the carnivalesque and this is a key recurring element as we have already seen.

On the pleasure beach of mid-twentieth century Blackpool there were acres of themed amusements that in various ways conformed to these characteristics. One of the smallest and one of the most concentrated was the Museum of Anatomy in which the grotesque body (mainly pickled body parts) could not be more clearly exhibited. There were eight exhibits showing masturbation and its (putatively bad) effects, there were no fewer than 52 exhibits of venereal disease; three of circumcision; anomalies such as a human pregnant male and there were 51 exhibits of pregnancy and childbirth of which 22 were abnormal. Another small and bizarre sideshow exhibited a live transsexual lying in bed (doing nothing) with a same sex partner. Over and around this was a steady stream of on-lookers. It is hard to imagine.

Although these were highly popular, the Mass Observers' detailed analysis of the other spectacles showed that the monstrous and 'other worldly' spectacles were gradually giving way to worlds more resembling those of the industrial workers. So, for example, in order of descending age since first introduced there were Fairyland, the Grotto, Noah's Ark, Ghost Train and Fun House. In analysing the constitutive elements of these 'worlds', Cross (1990: 107–9) argues that 'what is striking is the declining curve of interest in the rural scene or the water scene' whereas 'replicas or suggestions of the industrial scene from which the Worktowners have just come have intensified; the cave motif has continued strong; distortion, principally by the aid of mirrors, has become increasingly popular'. In analysing this developmental sequence they also notice that the purely passive and visual was giving way to a more active and tactile/kinaesthetic experience:

> In Fairyland, the journey was made in a dragon from which you passively saw the tableaux. So too in the Grotto, but the range of distortion in the things seen increased. In the labyrinth of Noah's Ark you felt things as well as saw; you could not avoid feeling them. Same in the Ghost Train. The Fun House differed from all of these because you could select, go where you please, avoid what you please . . . (Cross, 1990: 109)

In the USA, early twentieth-century public amusements followed similar logics but included some path-breaking modern innovations, most notably by Frederic Thomson. In 1901 his 'trip to the moon' (yet another 'other world') was 'a participatory fantasy experience'. After experiencing the sensation of flying to the moon, patrons were then transformed into extraterrestrial tourists: shopping, viewing a 'moon calf' and sampling green cheese (Kasson, 1978; Hannigan, 1998: 27). In association with Elmer S. Dundy, Thompson set up Luna Park at Coney Island, New York. Billed as the electric city by the sea, its ornamental architecture was lit by 250,000 light bulbs, but this was nothing compared to the permanent and live spectacles they enacted:

> Themed areas included an Eskimo village, the canals of Venice and a Japanese garden. [They] supplemented these displays with live entertainment shows, the most spectacular of which were disaster spectacles: 'Fire and flames,' in which a four-storey apartment building was burnt down; recreations of the Johnston (1889) and Galveston (1900) floods; and the eruption of Mount Vesuvius, including the destruction of a replica Pompeii. (Hannigan, 1998: 27)

The Mass Observers did indeed anticipate the way spectacle display parks were heading. Increasingly, they were attentive to the worlds of modernity and modern consumerism, in other words they were related not to rituals of social reproduction and renewal as with the carnivalesque, but to rituals of transition: the experience initiates the participant into the new themes, technologies and experiences of a changing modernity. If day to day life in modernity was a line of flight towards multiple other 'future' worlds, the idea of *an* (i.e. singular) other world lost its currency: from now on the other world came at us from the future and via channels of consumerism. In Tony Bennett's later (1983) analysis of Blackpool this point was made of The Pleasure Beach – for almost all of its twentieth century history:

> From its earliest days as a seaside resort the by-word of Blackpool recurring again and again in its publicity brochures, has been *Progress*. In the pleasure beach . . . pleasure is resolutely modern. Its distinctive 'hail' to pleasure-seekers is constructed around the large mechanical rides, unavailable elsewhere in Blackpool and packaged for consumption as a manifestation of progress, harnessed for pleasure. (Bennett, 1983: 146; 140)

A further point not to be missed is the close connection between the seaside and national events that celebrated modernity and consumerism, particularly the great exhibitions. In addition to their adherence to and adoption of modernist architectures, they were centrally constructed around displays of modern technology, an 'appeal to America, to the future and to a super-modernity . . . the appeal to modernity was becoming the dominant form of "barking"' (Bennett, 1983: 144).

It is worth quoting Bennett at length here in order to establish this general point and it should be remembered that this was more or less true of most other seaside resorts:

> Since the 1930s, the architectural modernity of the Pleasure Beach has been updated from time to time. In the 1950s Jack Radcliffe, designer of the Festival

of Britain in 1951, was commissioned to give it a new look – largely by superimposing an American jazz and glitter on Emberton's clean white facades. In the 1960s most of the new rides were stylistically indebted to innovations pioneered in world fairs and exhibitions. This was merely following a time-honoured pattern of development for Blackpool as a whole – the Tower was modelled on the Eiffel Tower constructed for the Paris Exhibition of 1889; the giant Ferris Wheel which dominated the Winter Garden sky-line from 1896 to 1928 was based on the one designed for the Oriental Exhibition at Earls Court in 1895, in turn modelled on the first Ferris Wheel exhibited at the Chicago World's Fair in 1893. In like vein, the chair-lift (1961) was inspired by the one used at the World Fair in 1958, the dome of the Astro-Swirl (1969) was based on the design of the American Pavilion at 'Expo 67' in Montreal, and the Space Tower (1975) was a smaller replica of an exhibit at Lausanne in the early 1970s. Since then, the Pleasure Beach has acquired a series of rides derived from American amusement parks, many of them still with futuristic references – the Revolution in 1979, and in 1980, the Tokaydo Express and the Starship Enterprise. (Bennett, 1983: 145)

Following Benjamin, Rojek (1997) argues that the culture of capitalism in its consumerist phase involves a phantasmagoria, 'the dream world of commodity capitalism'. A similar idea has been expressed by Campbell in his assertion that in the powerful imaginary of Romanticism was sown the foundation for a new dreamlike world of anticipation for new goods, new technologies, new experiences of consuming. As Rojek argues, 'the market is not only the showplace for commodities, it is also the material register of our inner fantasies and dreams . . . it can be argued that tourism is a concentrated instance of the phantasmagoria of capitalism . . . escape experience is packaged in an intensely commodified form' (Rojek, 1997: 58). However Rojek also follows Goffman (1967) in understanding leisure forms such as tourist attractions as spaces of controlled excitement, and indeed part of their packaging is to mark themselves off quite distinctly from the non-ritual spaces around them. Part of this controlled excitement seems to consist of uninterrupted and safe forms of ritual play: the rides and attractions are said to be dangerous with monstrous and blood curdling names but they are paradoxically very safe, they are 'riskless risks' as Hannigan (1998: 71) put it.

At one level tourists seem abundantly happy to visit theme parks such as at Disney or other film studio theme parks where the exhibits and worlds are nothing other than the characters and things that they already know and where a major attraction is the 'opportunity' to purchase associated merchandise, a means of deepening and concretising their association with transcendent consumer brands and products. Is there much of a difference between a Disney key ring and the tin-lead ampullas of holy water sold at Canterbury in Chaucer's day? Probably not, except that the modern consumer of a key ring is less prone to the sensing of aura than the fourteenth century pilgrim, even though in both cases what is purchased is a copy of the original. The modern consumer makes up for auratic quality deriving from a limited number of wonders with an unlimited supply of consumer creations and their reproducibility. In the case of celebrity, which is increasingly itself the object of themed attractions, the auratic possibility is far stronger, as indeed the zeal for it is more religious and devoted. Its current voguishness may be understood in relation to the collapse of aura in consumerist societies: Marilyn Monroe, Princess Diana and John Lennon are refreshingly one-off.

Equally several authors including Harvey and Rojek argue that the seemingly absurd eclecticism of those theme parks which mix or compress space and time by having mixtures of historical moments and geographical domains jammed together on a small acre site, are nothing other than the way the world is experienced by modern consumers. As Rojek (1993: 164) says, 'simultaneity and sensation are at the heart of the postmodern experience': the world we live in *is* simulation or a world socially constructed for tourists (and others) by what Rojek in a later paper has termed indexing and dragging. Indexes refer to the set of possible visual, textual and symbolic representations to an original object, while dragging refers to the agency by which elements from different indices may be assembled to create a new value (Rojek, 1997: 53–4). Places, for example, can now be evoked as much by novels and films set in them as by what actually happened there. So these are strange new worlds that are not other to us but symptomatic of us as an essentially transformative culture, and these sites are compelling because they interpellate new subjectivities, that can yield to and participate in a more simulated, negotiated and constructed world. We would and do soon tire of these worlds given to us as attractions; they must continue to usher in novel interpretations, technologies, information, simulations and hybrids: they must relate powerfully to us as consumers and provide, as Rojek argues, a sense of who we are becoming in a concentrated form.

Conclusion

Seaside is a fantastically rich terrain for the anthropologist and sociologist and what has been suggested here is only a brief summary of what can be said about it. I have suggested that seaside has been a complex and changing ritual space in modern society. In its popular phase in the earlier part of the twentieth century, but especially as it gained pace from the 1930s onwards, it contained aspects of a national ritual pilgrimage, not to celebrate nation but, like earlier Christian pilgrimage, to provide individual transition and redemption. The cultural steps of this modern ritual of passage in which the metaphor of rejuvenation was used, was rich and complex. I outlined how the liminal space of ritual and communitas was created by subjectivities interpellated by stations and especially trains and how ritual transition was enacted through a variety of highly ritualised performances of devotions in an overall slowing down to restful tempos.

The form that transition and redemption took began with an emphasis on health and consumption. Seasiders entered a hyperreality of consumption that initiated them into the new world of consumerism. However, seaside at this time was still other to the unhealthy world of the industrial town and a transition into better health and youthful vigour was also anticipated and in various ways performed. The theme of consumerism and sensation developed from the spectacular seaside to a range of theme parks and other 'world' attractions to the extent that we can expect it all around us. The metropolis can be renamed fantasy city and fantasy spaces of consumerism abound. From its earliest days at seaside the phantasmagoria of capitalism began to fill the imagination of industrial workers, and as producer society gave way to consumerist society, dream worlds of longing and anticipation and especially excitement provided the context for elaborate ritualised displays and attractions. Seaside and theme parks provide a transcendent experience similar to pilgrimage, and for common reasons both are distinctly object orientated. Ritual objects and arrangements of magical objects still focus the mind of the pilgrim, and part of that magic world can be taken away in the form of souvenirs. The more blasé forms of beach holiday maintain the devotions of rest and health. Transition is still a feature of the restful body. It is soaking up sun and changing colour, signalling quite specific positive metamorphoses in a consumerist society. However, as we shall see in Chapter 8 on tourisms of body and nature, new technologies of the body are designed to slow down time and produce yet another liminoid experience and to effect another transformation of touristic ritual space.

Further Reading

For an excellent general account and history of 'the beach' in western cultures see Lencek, L. and Bosker, G. (1999) *The Beach* (London: Pimlico). There is also a particularly good new account of the beach in Australia by Douglas Booth (Booth, D. (2001) *Australian Beach Culture – The History of Sun, Sand and Surf* (London: Frank Cass). For a more specialised understanding of water in tourism see Anderson, S.C. and Tabb, B. (2002) *Water, Leisure and Culture*. Oxford: Berg. The best theoretical work that locates seaside within the broader currents of a developing leisure aesthetic in capitalist societies is Chris Rojek's *Ways of Escape* (London: Routledge, 1993). There are also some good analyses of specific seaside resorts that are a rewarding read: for Blackpool, UK try Cross, G. (ed.) (1990) *Worktowners at Blackpool: Mass Observation and Popular Leisure in the 1930s.* (London: Routledge) and Bennett, T. (1983) 'A Thousand and One Troubles: Blackpool Pleasure Beach (in *Formations of Pleasure*. London: Routledge and Kegan Paul. pp. 138–55). For Brighton, UK see Shields, R. (1990) *Places on the Margin* (London: Routledge). John Urry's study of Morecambe is also excellent (in *The Tourist Gaze*, London: Sage, 1990). The classic analysis of ritual and tourist draws on Turner, V. and Turner, E. (1978) *Image and Pilgrimage in Christian Culture* (New York: Columbia University Press) and is worth reading in full.

7

Objects and rituals of heritage

SUMMARY

- The arrival of heritage tourism
- Romanticism and consumerism
- The dissolution of high culture
- Heritage and economic restructuring
- Theorising heritage
  - landscapes of nostalgia
  - heritage and the tourist gaze
  - heritage and authenticity
  - heritage and the anti-modernist turn
  - heritage as performance
- Conclusion

This chapter aims to provide a general understanding of heritage tourism. As the title suggests I will continue to organise a framework for this understanding around the social life of the objects that are so central to heritage and also the social life and performativity of the tourists who pay good money to see them. I will continue to denote the social life of tourists at heritage sites as in various ways *ritualistic* because much of the evidence shows that heritage tourism involves a considerable degree of ritual behaviour as it embodies what Rojek (1993) refers to as the 'cult of nostalgia' (see also Horne, 1984; Jervis, 1998; Crang, 1994). However, this evidence points in the direction of a diversity of ritual effects rather than a singular 'outcome' or function. To put these ideas together it is possible to say that one of the effects of heritage objects and installations is to interpellate new, contested and possibly transitionary subjectivities among tourists who come before them. In some cases tourists come in order for this (known and desired) effect to take place, in which case they resemble pilgrims who travelled to achieve specific transformations of self: spiritual redemption; self renewal and /or improved health. So for example, those who pay to watch the Royal Tournament, a ritual display of national military capability, frequently do so in order to reaffirm or perhaps celebrate national pride and identity. Museums as national showcases typically permit the generation of this subjectivity. The Smithsonian Museum of American History, for example, narrates the development of America as a nation in multiple ways, but also through its displays of objects of consumption it showcases a chronology of modern American ways of life. As we have already seen with the case of *Within These Walls*, the exhibition appeals to the American in all of us, regardless of background and culture. It is assimilating and reduces the significance of difference. Many British heritage tourist sites do the same, hailing what Crang (1994: 345) called 'the imaginary Briton'. As we will see, this view of a singular account of heritage and those academic accounts that rest on them are problematic, but the design and intended effects are often built into both the social construction of heritage as well as the pre-scripted anticipations of the tourist.

In other cases, tourists are less specifically motivated, or perhaps not motivated at all, but enter heritage sites out of curiosity, idleness or boredom. Nonetheless, much of the research on heritage shows that a range of effects take place; that tourists are sensitive to the spaces of heritage as liminoid; that they are less passive before the objects than performative, in other words they are doing something with the site, not merely passing through and taking in the site visually; that heritage speaks with them not (simply) in a linear manner delivering a script (or discourse), but producing 'an effect' or what Crang (1994: 346) calls *utterance* through the intersubjectivity of the interpreted objects and the subjectivities of tourists. Even when tourists at heritage sites appear to be doing nothing, wasting time, ignoring the invitation to be inspired or interpellated, we must still ask what they are doing. Jervis (1998: 322–3) reminds us, for example, that in modern societies where there is a sense of linear time that invites or even demands some productive use of time and the delivery of social or individual progress, to engage in doing nothing is to radically challenge what he calls *project*, the moral trajectory of modernity, which places great emphasis on the 'good' use of time.

The chapter will be organised into three parts. First a broad account of the emergence of heritage as a form of tourism. Two phases will be distinguished and accounted for: first the heritage of national high culture and nationalism and second a heritage of popular culture, a diversification of heritages of everyday pasts, cultures and places. Key aspects of these developments will be set out, including a statistical overview and trends in the industry.

Second, I will briefly review the principal theoretical accounts of heritage tourism. Here we revisit some of the earlier theoretical themes as they are applied to heritage: the tourist gaze, the demand for authenticity, and the arrival of postmodern 'spectacle'. In addition, we will look at some other accounts of heritage that appeared from outside tourism studies, principally those that view it as pathology of various contemporary 'presents'. Most of these accounts have one thing in common: they attempt to produce a general account of the causes, structure and impact of heritage sites, as if heritage itself was a given, acknowledged and taken for granted 'thing' existing independently of how individual tourists experience it. Anthropologists sometimes distinguish between this sort of approach (which they call etic) and others that draw on the way the world (or, say a heritage site) is *experienced* by specific people in time and space (which they call emic). We will conclude by reviewing recent phenomeno-logical research on heritage that produces emic accounts of heritage as the privileged domain of performance and experience. We will take as examples some recent work by Mike Crang, Barbara Kirshenblatt-Gimblett and Tim Edensor. One of the benefits of these approaches is that the everyday subjectivity of the tourist is seen as interpellated by and inter-active with the objects of tourism: heritage is the result or effect of this interaction; lines of significance and meaning traced between objects and subjectivities. Here the politics of arrangement and display meet and react with the everyday subjectivities of tourists, whoever they are.

The arrival of heritage tourism

As we have already seen in Part One, tourism as a form of consumerism cannot be easily disentangled from the conditions of early and later modernity that gave rise to it, modified it, and continue to change it. Part of those conditions, particularly in the earlier phases, but continuing also, was the emerging global network of nation states as the organising totality of specific economies, cultures, social infrastructures and so on. Nation states were new, brand new, and lacked self-confidence and a past that could provide people with a sense of who they now were (because nation states collapsed the distinctiveness of localities, regions, ethnic differences and even former pre-modern state structures) as well as a sense of social solidarity (where they 'belonged' and with whom they 'identified and belonged'). Nation states could not function on the formerly dispersed and relatively autonomous and independent localities and local cultures. They relied on greater flows of people and things but they also created overarch-ing or universal national languages, modes of communication, literatures, histories, transport networks, national educational curricula, national geographies, natures and so on. Nationalism created a tremendous enthusi-asm for things national; places, sites, cities, shrines, capitals, exhibitions, malls, natural areas and folk cultures. Since nation states had no prehistory they had to be fabricated as hybrid assemblages, and a good deal of this drew on constructions of regional, folk and low cultures that allegedly preceded them. Once assimilated into narratives of national emergence they became mantled with high culture; they were painted by artists, used decoratively on national objects or emblematically in national badges, anthems and regalia, written into national histories and mythified through stories, songs and music. Occasionally, as in Norway, an entirely new hybrid national language was constructed from the various regional dialects and introduced into schools. However, nationalism was not simply an artefact of the work of high culture. Nation formation together with the churning and changing nature of modernisation *disturbed* localities and traditional cultures. The disruption was not only spatial displacements, migrations, diasporas and economic restructuring and so forth, it also disturbed the ontological security and identity of modern citizens, creating an ontological vacuum into which nationalism and a cult of nostalgia often flowed.

All of this assemblage, gathering together, hybridisation and reconfiguration of identity around the idea of nation created a *national character* and identity that for almost everyone derived only in part from their immediate daily life: so much of national life and culture was elsewhere. It was both centrally important to everyone and yet out of immediate reach. As with the great religions, nationalism established travel and tourism as an integral part of national life. Around key sites of national significance and performances of national pageant and ceremony there was, and still is, an unmistakable aura of the sacred, and visitors to them undergo similar if not identical experiences to the religious pilgrim. As we have seen, nationalism was the spread or universalisation of a national high culture, but nationalism and culture had to be performed, they were not simply a set of ideas that could be read about or taught. Most of us know that the experiences of nationalism can be very powerful, moving the body and the spirit in profound ways, but these powerful emotional responses are less evoked by texts and thought than by performance and staging. The effervescence of collective sentiments, of whatever kind, tends to surface around performance and the identification of collective objects, particularly those that arouse a sense of genealogy, of collective pasts. We have already seen its ancient form in the Australian aboriginal *corroborees* as analysed by Durkheim, but they resurface regularly, even in the modern world.

At one level nationalism was performed through military and public service; at another it was taking part in national life, national civic occasions, the national cultural calendar, national sporting interests, but also visiting places of national significance and taking and celebrating national holidays. It was only in this way that citizens could be acculturated into the increasingly national nature of organisations, companies, public services, an economy based on the commonalities of citizenship.

So part of the explanation of heritage derives from the powerful influence of nation formation and nationalism but also the modernisation that nations took on as a project. An excellent illustration of this is the relationship between schools and national museums. Schools are an integral part of museum life outside of the summer season, indeed museums are now dependent upon them, which is why so many cannot follow the high tech, 'edutainment' models of the theme parks: school trips could not afford them (Hannigan, 1998: 98–9). National museums tend to be free or at least affordable (subsidised), underlining the significance of binding citizens to a common understanding of a national past, and not just the significance of education per se.

But this is only part of the story of heritage; another thread of the plot unwinds from the development and spread of Romantic thought and experience, resulting in a new and important phase of what I want to call anti-modern consumerism. Yet another part of the story derives from the fact that high culture collapsed as a dominant ordering mechanism of modern and national life, creating a new and contested anthropology and history of western cultures – an anthropology that the culture and media industries were in a good position to establish as popular culture. To these we need really only add a third and final ingredient: vast areas of the western world lost their economic livelihood as a result of neoliberal economic restructuring in the 1980s. Heritage tourism turned out to be a major economic strategy in the quest to create new jobs as well as preserve cultural identities that in many places were founded on an industrial, rural-industrial or maritime past.

Romanticism and consumerism

The authors of Romanticism were also in part the authors of the heritage trail. As Rojek (1993: 145) concludes, in their work we 'find evidence of a strong aesthetic and ideological association with the past as a place of peace and splendour'. However, according to Campbell (1995), in their ritual devotion to objects of nature and historic places they inadvertently created the conditions for modern consumerism, and an argument I want to construct is that an anti-modern consumerism of the late 1960s and 1970s created the conditions out of which the past could be more widely consumed as a leisure commodity.

Campbell argues that Romanticism spawned a generalised and compulsive consumerism in modern societies; a desire to consume things produced by developing the skill of *longing*, being able to conjure up the *pleasure* of possessing something in the imagination, and then being ultimately prone to disappointment and seeking further pleasurable fantasies. Romanticism privileged pleasure and the pursuit of pleasure through the identification and appreciation of beauty: it was a consuming passion.

Figure 7.1 *The Ruin of Corfe Castle, Dorset, UK.* Source: Ian Britton

However, Campbell argues that it was not stabilised aesthetically or materially or rooted only in the objects of beauty that held the nineteenth century imaginary.

> Labelled self-illusory hedonism, [Modern consumerism] is characterised by a longing to experience in reality, those pleasures created and enjoyed in imagination, a longing that results in the ceaseless consumption of novelty. Such an outlook, with its characteristic dissatisfaction with real life and an eagerness for new experiences, lies at the heart of much conduct that is typical of modern life, and underpins such central institutions as fashion and romantic love. The Romantic ethic can be seen to possess basic congruence, or 'elective affinity' with this spirit, and to have given rise to a character type and ethical conduct highly conducive to the adoption of such attitudes. In particular, Romantic teachings concerning the good, the true and the beautiful, provide both the legitimation and the motivation necessary for modern consumer behaviour to become prevalent throughout the contemporary industrial world. (Campbell, 1995: 206)

This is ironic of course, because this consumerism was not an intended outcome of the Romantic ethic, in fact quite the reverse. It was in many ways against the growing industrial capacity for machine-made goods and mass production, favouring instead, the arts and crafts traditions of production. However, as Campbell argues, Romanticism remained a dominant intellectual current for much of the twentieth century and beyond and in that time, various new manifestations renewed the basic foundation for consumerism. Bohemianism, as manifested in its original Parisian base, produced a 'dynamic upsurge in cultural consumerism' and the 'fashion capital of the world'. Beat and later hippie bohemian movements concentrated in California became involved in the 'most advanced experiments in consumerism'. Indeed, Campbell (1995: 206) argues that 'it is possible to discern a close correspondence between outbursts of Bohemianism and periods of creative consumer boom'. So, is there any link between the arrival of heritage tourism and an outburst of bohemianism that prefigured it? I am going to argue that there is.

In the post-war, which is to say the post-1945 boom period up until the late 1960s, Romanticism that had been a dominant cultural force in the first half of the twentieth century was put in abeyance. The war had been an exciting period for design and consumption but importantly, the war produced a renewed enthusiasm for technology and for consumerism. Shortages of everything and restrictions on the production and consumption of luxuries, during and immediately after the war, produced a longing for consumerism. The austerity of the interwar and wartime years in Britain was disturbed also by a contrasting consumerist US economy and its high visibility after the USA joined forces with Britain and her European allies. American consumerism in the first half of the century had embraced modernism, modern design and technological development. It was bright and new and used new materials innovatively for practical and luxurious purposes. In contrast the interwar years in Britain were dominated by the arts and crafts movement and its emphasis on natural material, natural colours: browns and muted natural tones being dominant. After the war the drabness of British products and consumer weariness of them produced a new movement inside British design and industry: new, young designers were employed throughout the entire cross-section of domestic consumption, fashion, architecture and engineering. Culminating in the 1951 Festival of Britain, an essentially modern design consumerism was established across mainstream British taste. Identical types of transformation took place in Scandinavia, Italy and elsewhere in Europe. For the next twenty years or so, an essentially modernist idiom dominated most areas of social life. Not only in terms of fashion, domestic interiors and consumer durables but also in domestic architecture, car design, housing, town planning, tourist resorts and social policy. What was new about this modern idiom? First, it was experimental and predicated on using new technologies and design to improve and progress human material life. TV improved on radio; cars improved on motorbikes and cycles; electrical inventions such as vacuum cleaners improved on the broom. New materials and their application were part of this experimental ethic. Concrete and steel fabrication that had transformed New York in the first half of the twentieth century (confirming its leadership in glamour and aesthetic appeal) promised new solutions to enduring housing shortages in Europe. If repeated attempts to recreate village Britain proved too expensive, why not build villages in the sky? If vast areas of slum housing stock were worn out and unsuitable (they were cold, draughty, damp and rotting even if they were salvageable) and worse, built initially for profit rather than for social function and progress, then why not bulldoze the lot and build a better, planned environment for the future? Such was the enthusiasm for 'high' modernism that most towns and cities were utterly transformed. However, social policy went beyond housing policy, and the new experimental mood affected education, family policy, youth policy, crime policy and so on.

By the late 1960s and early 1970s, however, this experimental mood and much of its products and policies were in the midst of critical review. The last of the New Towns such as Milton Keynes in the UK were just beginning life at this time among a barrage of criticism. A new word, 'tradition' came into its own as the victim of modernism, and alongside it traditional freedoms were seen to be under threat now from an interfering modern welfare state (see Finnegan, 1998). Planners and visionary architects were now dubbed as the new blight in society or blot on the landscape. New and liberal social policies, educational theory and law-making came under similar forms of attack. In sum, nervousness spread about modernism, and its relentless search for the experimental and new created failures and a sense of ontological insecurity. Ontological insecurity is a term used by Giddens to describe one of the destabilising social effects of modernity: people began to lose a sense of the norms and routines that 'traditional' ways of life once provided (see Franklin, 1986 for a discussion). It was apparent that a relentless procession of new things, new developments, new lifestyles and change (family structure, position of youth in society, racial and ethnic immigrations, cities, schools etc.) engendered a feeling of loss as well as rootlessness. If there was only ever the new and if the new always supersedes the past it meant that traditions, cultures, technologies, genealogies, ways of life were in a permanent state of decline. While this is a general feature of modernity, this particular period was a distilled and purified version that resulted in a variety of anti-modernist experimentations and a new anti-modernist period of consumerism. Heritage tourism was part of that experimentation and consumerism.

Heritage sites emerged after the massive consumer boom of the 1960s to 1970s, which was heavily influenced by Romantic themes. In many ways the new heritage tourism industry came in on the heels of a preceding 'heritage-style' consumerism of the 1970s. Despite the prevalence of a new Modernism in the 1960s, typified by Jackson (1998) as 'the new look', the experimental period of art and design was followed by a period of intense questioning of the new: the Beatles terminated their mod look and traded it in for a nostalgic drift into working class origins (brass bands become a refrain in much of their work after their modern period), and an idealisation of non-western, particularly peasant life styles and transcendental religion. Moods and tastes swung backwards: art deco styles of the late Victorian period became vogueish; the backward looking arts and crafts movement of William

Morris and associates established itself across a new decorative art world culminating in such companies as Laura Ashley and Habitat (Jackson, 1997; 1998; MacCarthy, 1982; Franklin, 2002a). Handicrafts were the motif of the day; high streets everywhere saw the introduction of a new, heavy (medieval) pottery look, often with a potter working somewhat self-consciously in the shop space itself. Hand-weaving, spinning, toy making, indeed an entire raft of historical crafts came to dominate the consumerism of the 1970s. Added to this we can identify cognate heritage consumer innovations: classic among these were The Campaign for Real Ale in the UK, which rediscovered and remade historic beers and ciders; the movement to save historic varieties of plants, fruits and vegetables and the specific form in which health food stores were reconfigured in the 1970s (away from modern manufactured health foods and towards historic and peasant 'wholefoods'). There were performative aspects of what might be termed heritage consumerism: adult classes for historical crafts (pottery, print-making, weaving, spinning, jewellery-making etc.) burgeoned; historical re-enactment societies were formed in which craft skills developed around costume, weapon-making and use, historical cuisines, home brewing. The historic re-enactment societies also staged historic re-enactments, specific events, battles, feasts and gave participants new names, titles and characters with which to imagine and live their re-enactment character. This historical consumerism ramified into all aspects of life in the 1970s and 1980s. Pubs that had been modernised and given the modern 'new look' in the 1950s and 1960s were stripped back once again to their historic roots and filled with old junk, reproduction 'traditional' furniture and decorated with horse brasses, old tools, old photos and prints. A similar fate awaited many British homes, and this was given added performative poignancy during the intensive years of gentrification (although more correctly it was not gentrification but restoration) of late nineteenth century homes in the UK and elsewhere. The new generation of new home buyers were involved in the quest to find, install and assemble period fireplaces, tiles, lighting etc. This too was heritage activity. As Hewison (1987: 135) noted in the late 1980s, 'The house is no longer a machine' but 'an antique for living in.' An important but often missed element of heritage consumerism is its appeal to anti-science/green consumers who began to make their presence felt in the 1970s and then very powerfully through the 1980s and 1990s. The reason is quite straightforward: heritage production is by hand rather than machine; uses natural materials rather than synthetic; is built to last rather than be disposed of; it protects jobs and preserves craft skills and is biodegradable and relatively unpolluting of the environment.

The proliferation of heritage tourism after the 1970s relates in important ways to consumerism rather than previous modes of *displaying* history. First of all, it is clearly related to pleasurability: notwithstanding its educational pretensions, heritage aims to please and give pleasure and does not rest simply on dry forms of display in the auratic treasure houses of

Figure 7.2 *The Shambles, York.* Source: Ian Britton

national museums. This is a key argument in Rojek's (1995) analysis of themed heritage centres that appeared in the 1980s. Second, it is endlessly creative and fashion conscious and orientated towards commercial viability and success; not here the rock steady icons of nation that accrete the patina of sacredness simply by doing nothing except laying claim to the status of *permanence*. Third, its concern with beauty, truth and goodness takes it way from the grand and singular narratives of national heritage, emphasising instead, pluralism, heterogeneity, choices, conflict, dissonance and contingency (Ashworth and Ashworth, 1996). Just to take the significance of restoring the Victorian housing stock in the 1980s, it is clear that the performance of restoration takes place in specific local and particular contexts. Within the genre of British row housing there was a distinctive range of local and regional types that found their contexts in particular industries (for example, coal mining villages built to model housing specifications) regions (slate roof tiles in Wales, Kent peg tiles in Kent) and traditions of building in cities (fire wall divisions and ground rents in Bristol; yellow brick in London). Around the need to understand and restore the specific and local built environment there emerged, or at least greatly expanded, the activity of local history itself (Crang, 1994: 348–9).

In sum, it has been argued that other forms of mainstream consumption became 'heritagised' before the principal wave of heritage tourism. However, this was met and strengthened by another stream of cultural change: the further dissolution of a dominant high culture.

The dissolution of high culture

Prior to the 1960s, art history, literature, music and indeed most cultural forms were marked off or differentiated from popular or low culture. High culture had an auratic quality that was supported by elongated exposure and success in the academy; through virtuosity in recognised canons of work; through public performance, publication and recognition by a professional elite and in many instances by appointment or patronage from the crown or aristocracy. High culture was wedded to the notion of perfectible forms of beauty or knowledge or truth; the aesthetics of high culture in the nineteenth and twentieth centuries were also modelled to a degree on classical antiquity and this provided the grounds for thinking that culture was absolute, invariable and off limits to all but those (the elite) in a position to nurture it through specialised and expensive dedication.

Prior to the 1960s, various organisations (for example, the UK Industrial Design Movement) and artistic movements (Dadaism, early surrealism, constructivism, and expressionism) sought to close the gap between this high culture and popular culture. These were revolutionary and experimental ideas that did not so much break down the distinction as lead to the systematic application of art and artists to the production and design of objects of the everyday (see Franklin, 2002b).

According to Harvey there were several currents of change in and around the 1960s that were to essentially dissolve the distinction between high and low culture. Although the cultural traditions from each side of the divide were to continue (there are still classical and pop radio programmes for example), the tendency from the 1960s onwards was to bleed into each other: the Beatles mixed orchestral with Victorian dancehall and African American R&B; Andy Warhol sold paintings, at Sotheby's and Christie's, of repetitive images of tins of Campbell's soup and the serious matter of American or French history could be informed by the lifeworlds and habits of ordinary people (Le Roy Ladurie, 1978; Boyer and Nissenbaum, 1974).

During the 1960s, the high and low cultural worlds began to collide and merge: 'there were innumerable points of contact between producers of cultural artefacts and the general public: architecture, advertising, fashion, films, staging of multi-media events, grand spectacles, political campaigns, as well as the ubiquitous television (Harvey, 1989: 59).

In addition, around the turn of the twentieth century there were movements within the art and design world that wished to democratise and popularise art and design so that it could embellish and enrich the lives of everyone and not just the social elite (Franklin, 2002b). Progress was made in this direction through national organisations to promote industrial art and design and to introduce it into the sphere of mass production. In this way for example, and unbeknown to many people, the young Henry Moore and Graham Sutherland produced designs for curtain material

(Franklin, 2002b); Graham Sutherland and many others produced posters for London Transport. Likewise, Venturi argued that architects should learn their trade by studying popular places such as Las Vegas and Disneyland and living spaces such as industrial suburbs, to blend what they could do with what 'the people' seemed to like (Harvey, 1989: 60).

Putting these sorts of trends together Daniel Bell (1978: 20) drew attention to the emergence of a new cultural labour market where the creative and rebellious impulses of modernism had become institutionalised, largely around media, film, television advertising and publishing (Harvey, 1989: 60). Access to this labour market was no longer barred by social advantage: the expansion of education, art schools and universities in the second half of the twentieth century permitted relatively easy routes into artistic and formerly high cultural careers.

This last point underlines the significance of new youth cultures from the 1950s onwards. Youth cultures were relatively affluent and 'actively used fashion to construct a sense of their own public identities, even defined their own pop-art forms, in the face of a fashion industry that sought to impose its taste through advertising and media pressure' (Harvey, 1989: 60). Also significant here is the relative ease with which new and affordable technologies could copy, mix, fuse and reproduce art forms that were hitherto inaccessible to ordinary people. New cultural forms emerged as a result of these technologies, techno music being the exemplar, but computers have done much the same for art and design. These new cultural forms become attached to their producers and followers producing a mass of relative and contingent cultural forms, where both *popular* and *high* lose all sense of meaning. Instead, the proliferation of sub-cultures based on permutations of ethnicities, styles, class, gender, age, region, sexuality, city, locality and so on start to become more important than the broader bands of identity such as class and race that had previously typified cultural stratification. Youth cultures became a model for how almost everyone could find and develop a separate cultural space for themselves. The birth of these sorts of postmodern social identities and bandings, no matter how ephemeral or fugitive, were similar to the birth of the nation itself: they lacked a firm definition of themselves or the means to assert their presence. A new period of sub-cultural efflorescence was established by the 1980s, and an intense interest was expressed in this new anthropology of postmodernity, or, as Maffesoli (1996) called this new period in advanced western societies, 'the time of the tribes'.

Just as the press (and other media), academia and the general public wished to see and understand the new configurations of contemporary social life as 'culture', 'the past' and 'pasts' were to be interpreted along similar lines. Under the new academic banner of cultural studies, studies of class, for example, had to be unpacked into class cultures and so began a major new project: the reconstruction of historical class cultures, historical gender studies, historical ethnicities and so on. Methodologically, local and oral history became the templates for the recovery of these pasts, and as they surfaced in and through journals such as *History Workshop Journal* and many others like it, the conditions arose for more popular and elaborate disseminations of this material. The conditions were ripe, in other words, for exhibition, display, interpretation and naming the newly uncovered cultures and their pasts. It was a new archaeology that could connect the living with their immediate forebears in a history that they made, though not always in conditions of their own choosing.

Jervis sums this up very nicely:

> There is a focus on experience as plenitude, and the challenge posed by this to representational strategies in the arts, together with the way this enforces a concern with the ordinary, everyday world; there is an increasing self-consciousness in the arts, a 'reflexive turn', in the twin senses of an interest in which techniques to use, and the medium itself (words, paint, surface), along with what this in turn suggests about our capacity to grasp experiences of space, time and the present, and the sense of self embedded therein; and there is the 'return of the other', an interest in the way experience and its presuppositions necessarily open up 'other' dimensions of gender, culture and the unconscious. The implications of these shifts are profound: multiple perspectives become necessary in a world that is multidimensional or fractured, ever shifting in our experience of it. (1998: 263)

Heritage and economic restructuring

At a time in the 1980s when consumerism swung into an anti-modern phase, favouring the widespread consumption of traditionally made and traditionally designed goods, and at a time when a heightened sense of importance was becoming attached to local cultures, neoliberal politics cut state support for the post-war welfare economy, cities, nationalised industries, regional policy and continued levels of rural provision of services. Judd (1999: 35) spells out the sudden and bleak manner by which this was ushered in in the USA and its immediate consequences for tourism: 'Upon assuming office in 1981, the Reagan administration moved rapidly to reduce or eliminate all urban policies aimed at helping distressed cities. To make up for the loss of federal funds, President Reagan's first National Urban Policy Report observed, "States and local governments will find it in their best interests to concentrate on increasing their attractiveness to potential investors, residents and visitors"'. The 1980s became characterised in the USA as an era of heritage production: the US National Register of Historic Places, for example, recorded an increase in places listed from 1,200 in 1968 to 37,000 by 1985 (Urry, 1990: 106). The upshot of Thatcher's early years in power was an economic restructuring that took out much of the UK industrial infrastructure, plunged most industrial towns and cities into recession, terminated some longstanding major industries such as ship building and closed down mining and steel towns, often overnight. In addition to this, heavily subsidised sectors of the rural economy had their subsidy removed leaving them exposed to declining commodity prices. On top of this, urban councils had significant parts of their income removed through policies requiring them to sell off the housing they had built in order to rent. Although economic restructuring was highly uneven in countries such as Britain, the USA and Australia, there were few places left completely unscathed and most were left in a desperate scramble to generate new jobs. The major cities in America entered the scramble for the highly lucrative conventions trade but even they had to augment their cities with new attractions and urban heritage themes were a universal area of new investment among them. Since most of the smaller cities and capital cities in Europe were not in areas of great scenic beauty or coast, one of the most highly successful and ubiquitous strategies was to market their past as heritage. The UK is outstanding in the way it managed to market its rather outsized capacity for history: in 1989 Harvey could report that in Britain a museum opened once every three weeks. By the 1990s, as a 1996 survey showed, 37 per cent of foreign tourists said visiting heritage sites, including castles, monuments and churches was an important reason for coming to Britain (British Tourist Authority, 2002: 1).

Urry (1990: 104–17) provides a useful summary of how this process impacted in the UK during the 1980s:

- The local state were prime movers in generating urban heritage because they inherited vast areas of derelict land, attractive inner city buildings and waterfront; because private capital was small scale and often fragmented; because funding for tourism could provide amenities that the local people can also use; because a vibrant and attractive leisure scene is important in attracting other employers and key employees; because creating tourism jobs was considerably cheaper than other alternatives (£4,000 per job in tourism, versus £32,000 in manufacturing).
- Some places, such as Hebden Bridge have made heritage the basis of a successful local revival; some regions such as the North, the Midlands and Wales have made substantial moves to develop tourism while others such as Scotland, the South East and Northern Ireland have been less proactive; central government has assisted cities to develop a heritage industry through Tourism Development Action Plans.
- By the end of the 1980s there were at least 41 heritage centres; 464 museums including industrial material and 817 with collections relating to rural history; of the 1750 museums which responded to a 1987 questionnaire half had opened since 1971; there were 500,000 listed buildings and over 5,500 conservation areas; 56 per cent of new museums were privately developed; in the 1980s more people visited museums and galleries than visited the cinema and more visited heritage buildings than visited the theatre; visitors are dominated by the middle class (three to every one working class visitor).

- While some places such as Wigan Pier Development and the Albert Dock in Liverpool were major and complex developments relating as they do to both the sense of profound and total loss of industrial identity and to the availability of character buildings, Urry reminds us that many were small and narrow (a pencil factory, a shoe museum, a chemical industry museum). However they all 'work' because they provide a link between a place and its past.

Urry's updated second edition of *The Tourist Gaze* (2002) confirms that the trajectory of growth in heritage has continued: new museums in Britain open once every fortnight; some new domains of heritage have expanded, for instance, there are now 78 museums devoted to the (much beleaguered British) railway; and there are 180 water- or windmills open to the public. Some places thought unlikely centres for tourism have thrived: Urry (2002: 94–5) notes that the former woollen mill town of Bradford, once the provider of holidaymakers to the resort of Morecambe, increased its share of visitors from 1.5 million to 5 million during the 1990s. Somewhat ironically perhaps, 'environmentalists have sought to preserve the largest slag heap in Britain, which British coal wanted to remove' (Urry, 2002: 95).

Theorising heritage

Theorising the confusing terrain of heritage is important because while heritage might appear to be just a discrete set of self-standing, self-evident, niche tourism businesses – and that is often how the tourism literature makes them appear – you should already be aware that it relates to significant and broad currents of social, economic and cultural change. Heritage became so deeply embedded in places such as Britain that people joked about the island collapsing into one giant heritage theme park with Heathrow or Gatwick as the entry gates. Such is the significance and impact of heritage across the world that a fair degree of theoretical orientations have surfaced over the past twenty years or so. Much of it addresses one or more of the following types of question:

- Why did heritage arise, what causes it?
- What is heritage?
- Whose heritage is referred to?
- What is the relationship between heritage and history?
- What is the social impact of heritage?
- What is happening when tourists visit heritage?

In this section I will set out briefly the main types of theoretical explanations of heritage tourism. To an extent there are overlaps in these but they all have something distinctive and useful at their core. These are the landscapes of nostalgia school (a term coined by Crang, 1994: 342); heritage and the tourist gaze (referencing the work of Urry and followers); heritage and authenticity (referencing the work of MacCannell and followers); heritage and the anti-modernist turn; heritage as performance (referencing the work of Crang, 1994, 1997; and Edensor, 1998, 2001).

Landscapes of nostalgia

This was one of the earliest theoretical forms of explanation of heritage and is most comprehensively set out in Hewison's 1987 book, *The Heritage Industry* (but see also Wright, 1985; Wood, 1974). At the outset I want to make it clear that although this title makes it seem applicable to the general rise of heritage across the world, it is in fact addressed specifically to heritage in Britain, indeed heritage in this theory results from peculiar and specific characteristics of Britain at a conjuncture towards the end of the twentieth century. This is a strength and a weakness of the book, and the general approach. Its strength lies in the realisation that heritage in the UK relates specifically to British events, politics, economy and history. But as a general theory of heritage it is clearly inadequate: since this occurred on both sides of the Atlantic more or less simultaneously, following many of the same forms and applications, we would expect heritage to have some critically general attributes, but Hewison's account of the UK simply does not translate into the American experience.

For Hewison and others of this school, heritage emerged in Britain in the 1980s because a cultural hiatus had been reached: the British sense of importance and greatness was based on its industrial past, not simply for being the cradle of the industrial revolution, but for maintaining a presence as an innovator and for living so extensively off its industrial skills. Its greatness as a nation was built and sustained by this industrial character, but in the 1980s almost this entire industrial infrastructure and its cultural embeddedness was torn apart and lost, seemingly, forever. According to Hewison, the 1980s focused sharply a set of self-realisations for Britain: Britain had lost its way, lost its former greatness and status in the world: 'the slow decay of industry and national prestige had eroded national self-confidence. The national psyche was gripped by "cultural necrophilia"' (Crang, 1994: 342). According to Hewison, it was the political right, particularly the neoconservative forces of Thatcherism that seemed to require this displacement culture. 'Neoconservatism needed a protective illusion of how Britain was once great, rather than face Britain's current powerlessness in an uncertain world' (Crang, 1994: 342). For Hewison this nostalgic obsessiveness blocks out the present and the ability to project into a future, or as Crang (1994: 342) nicely puts it, 'a fear *for the past being destroyed* becomes a fear *of the past destroying the future*' (original italics). Hewison was certainly onto something. He makes some sense of the particular way in which the new heritage tourism grasped an industrial theme in the UK. It becomes 'a symptom of a nation immersed in nostalgia and living in its past; concerned with manufacturing heritage rather than manufacturing goods' (Herbert et al., 1989: 1, cited in Crang, 1994: 343).

The problem for Hewison is that precisely the same kinds of heritage emerged in the USA at the same time, a time when the USA was never more confident of its global domination, stature and future. So heritage tourism does not correlate seemingly with an uncertain and diminished present or future. Of course, as we have seen, economic restructuring of a profound kind did affect the USA and the UK and this left cultural voids and absences in the heart of towns and communities which had hitherto anchored their identify and lifestyle on the mining, manufacturing or farming of particular products in particular ways. The disappearance of cultures in the west was already prefigured by a general concern with cultural disappearance in the non-western world. The long running Granada TV series *Disappearing World* was a globally successful series that depicted evocatively, the disappearance of cultures in the Third World. The idea of the west, or modernity itself, was a steady state of change, and we reckoned our present civilisation to be wrought from a dizzy set of difficult transformations. More importantly, the foundational ethic of modernity, the notion of continuous progress, was predicated on continuous change and cultural flexibility. In the first part of the twentieth century, depressions wiped out industrial and rural communities without trace, with barely a flicker of sentimentality remaining. These places were caught up in tragedies and people responded largely by waiting out the depression or migrating to where similar if not exactly the same sort of work was available. This was continuity and change. However, in the 1980s the western industrial capitalist infrastructure in the form it had always been experienced change with little continuity. Many areas affected most by deindustrialisation faced two crises: how to recreate lost jobs in the locality (migration was less of an option since similar work had evaporated generally) and how to prevent a culture from disappearing completely? Hewison rightly noted how, in Thatcher's Britain, icons of Victorian industrial strength became heritage monuments at the same time as massive industrial complexes of the present were bulldozed. Hewison mentions Consett, the integrated steel mill in northern England that was closed down overnight in 1980. Deindustrialisation in England up until then had been a piecemeal affair, and often-obsolete buildings, technologies and works were abandoned and became ruins long before renovation. However, the speed and pace of deindustrialisation in Thatcher's Britain invoked the fear of political reprisal if it remained visible. For this reason the plant at Consett, as elsewhere, was razed to the ground and sown over with grass. Deindustrialisation could be rewritten as greening. The immobility of labour, the solidarity of community combined with this neoliberal scorched earth approach to a livelihood and culture provoked not nostalgia as championed by the right as Hewison puts it, but memorialisation, committing to sacred memory, the body of a dead and dying culture. This is one key point. Its twin is that a public already existed to mourn the death of cultures, communities and ways of life, and so part of the success that Urry documents in such seemingly 'unlikely' places as Bradford may be put down as much to this as to clever marketing campaigns.

Urry also makes the point that industrial heritage was often driven by amateur plebeian movements, eager to preserve old canal boats, old sailing boats, steam technologies and so forth. The steam rallies in Britain date back to the early 1970s and although less emotive in their enthusiasm, the enthusiasts were nonetheless memorialising their past, finding it difficult to let go of the bodies and frames of the machines that were intertwined in their lives, childhoods and dreams. In addition, as Law argues, there is an identifiable machinic pleasure in the seemingly self-running nature of steam engines, evoking a perfected and visible machinic order.

Hewison also fetishises industrial production and unreasonably poses it as a future option for advanced economies in the 1980s when clearly it was not. Heritage can be easily recast as an important part of the service and leisure orientated economy of the 1990s and 2000s. I have already demonstrated how heritage consumerism, repackaging the past for the present had become a dominant form of retail production at least a decade earlier and there is no reason why fashions, styles and designs will not circulate endlessly, borrowing heavily from pasts, mixing, fusing etc.

Hewison is also hard on heritage tourism as a form of 'bogus history' but as Crang argues, whom does history belong to? Whose heritage is it and how is heritage created? Is the sneering at heritage merely sour grapes expressed by those who used to possess it as masters of high culture? As Crang puts it, 'the commentator becomes an anti-tourist asserting education over entertainment, accuracy over evocation, depth over surface' (Crang, 1994: 343). Surely, heritage was also a part of the reconfiguration of history teaching. Urry (2002: 102) asks the pertinent question: how do you find out about the past, how can you do this adequately and evenly without heritage? This view is supported, presumably, by survey evidence that shows that nine out of ten people support the use of public funds to preserve heritage (Urry, 2002: 96; see also Prentice, 1995 on the role of heritage in formal education).

Hewison is also heavily concerned that an authentic true and rigorous history is being cast aside in order to simply titillate and entertain. Some historic tourism forms are not serious historical projects; Main St at Disneyland is clearly one, but then how many film and TV formats use historic themes playfully? On the other hand, heritage sites do tend to bring serious professional historians who might otherwise work predominantly within their own professional circles and journals, into the public mainstream, refreshing school history and providing new lines of communication between the academy and the public. Indeed heritage has produced a new labour market for professional historians.

Crang points out that in fact whatever heritage interpretation and design may wish to convey in terms of serious historical points, it is not at all clear that this is what tourists will carry away with them or even that this is how tourists interface with heritage sites. By creating personal links and community associations '[n]on academic users can create different phenomena that fail to register on the contemplative stare of the "official culture". Heritage is not comprised of "empirically self-evident objects"' (Crang, 1994: 343).

Finally, returning to a point made above, Urry argues that 'the critics of the heritage industry also fail to link the pressure for conservation with the much broader development of environmental and cultural politics in the 1980s and 1990s'. Heritage here is literally genealogy, a chance to showcase local culture, to create social identity, and to have some say and control over how others, especially tourists, understand local people. Urry cites a study by McCrone et al. (1995) that shows the significance of heritage to the development of Scottish nationalism in the 1990s. On a smaller scale but no less significant, MacDonald shows how 'heritage is put to more radical use' in a heritage centre on Skye, Scotland: *Aros – The Skye Story*:

> *The Skye Story* has been constructed by a particular group of local people, young fairly successful Gaelic speakers who are making a living from their 'Gaelicness'. It is a story they tell themselves about themselves (Geertz, 1985: 448). This is a story of a distinctive local historical experience; a story of continued Gaelic resilience in the face of outside threat. It is a story, which, I have suggested, the heritage format (which does not rely on originals) may be well suited to telling, though it is certainly neither uncontested nor without its problems. . . . The heritage centre and cultural tourism more generally *can* be a way of telling the people's story, and of helping to make sure it will be heard. (MacDonald, 1997: 173, 175)

Heritage and the tourist gaze

For Urry, tourism (in all its forms) is an essentially visual activity, the sighting of objects carrying meaning beyond them to a key series of authenticating discourses. Tourists collect the sign values reflected off the surface of tourist objects and in so doing access a world of difference from the everyday, for that is held to be pleasurable in the anticipation as well as in the present.

> Minimally there must be certain aspects of the place to be visited which distinguish it from what is encountered in everyday life. Tourism results from the basic binary division between the ordinary/everyday and the extraordinary. Tourist experiences involve some aspect or element that induces pleasurable experiences, which by comparison with the everyday, are out of the ordinary.

... But potential objects of the tourist gaze must be different in some way or another. They must be out of the ordinary. People must experience particularly distinct pleasures that involve different senses or are on a different scale from those encountered in everyday life. (Urry, 1990: 1–2)

It is never entirely clear in *The Tourist Gaze* why difference generates pleasure, whether tourism pleasure *needs* difference from the everyday or indeed, whether tourism is necessarily and always about or directed to pleasurability. To these, as those who have read the earlier chapters will anticipate, we have to add another problem: whether there is anymore such a thing as a separable world of the everyday and a touristic other. In the second edition of *The Tourist Gaze*, this observation is acknowledged through the work of Bauman. On the penultimate page Urry concedes an important point:

According to Bauman, the good life has come to be thought of as 'a con- tinuous holiday' (1993: 243). There is thus no separate tourist gaze since according to Bauman this is simply how life is lived for the prosperous one- third within the new global order. (Urry, 2002: 160)

If we can take as given that the prosperous one third of the global population make up the majority of modern tourists, this in effect means that the tourist gaze disappears, or at least becomes absorbed into a more rarefied everyday. This is the essential thesis of this book, although I will go further to say that even those who are not in the prosperous one third, have their lives substantially organised around tourism and do not need to physically travel in order to experience the extraordinary as part of their everyday.

The tourist gaze idea was useful, however, in directing our attention to the way heritage museums were organised; the effort being made to direct and organise both the movements of the tourists and the relationship between the object, its sign value and its authenticating discourse. Critical here is the authenticating discourse of education in combination with national curricula, high cultural norms and national museums. High cul- ture and nationalism valued highly a continuing interest in education, at an individual level (say as parents) and as a strived for quality of citizens. Such was the gravity of high culture and the auratic nature of national objects (national museums, monuments, etc.) that people were drawn to them rather in the manner of pilgrims, and Urry draws on the work of Horne (1984) to link the organisation of the gaze, the significance of the act of gazing and the semiotics of nation (see especially Horne, 1984, part 5, which underlines the centrality of nationalism to tourism throughout Europe and the former Soviet Union).

Whereas in the days of Horne's 'great museum', it is implicit that the opposition between the everyday and tourism corresponds to the opposi- tion between the provinces and the capital, the arrival of heritage makes the distinction less clear. This is because heritage occupies ordinary, everyday spaces; they might be former work places and spaces but they are essentially in ordinary places. Bradford, Wigan, York, Newcastle and the former coal villages of South Wales are ordinary, everyday places. Of course this is their charm, and we have to note that with the collapse of high and low culture we are more tuned in to the aesthetic value of the everyday. This is true to the extent that the ordinary objects of an ordinary contemporary person work just as well as a spectacle as those of a Tudor, Roman or Viking person:

> Or closer to home, imagine that the contents of your apartment are removed – everything in your medicine cabinet, kitchen cupboards, wardrobes, your refrigerator and sofa, vacuum cleaner and radio, socks and laxatives – and installed in a local museum. Christian Boltanski effected precisely such a removal at the Baden-Baden Kunsthalle in 1973 and more recently at the New York Historical Society in 1995. (Kirshenblatt-Gimblett, 1998: 49)

Also, the anti-auratic nature of the everyday objects of heritage do not create the same sense of distance between the viewer and the viewed, and with the closure of distance the erasure of *difference* is effected. As Crang (1994: 351) notes people use their own lives to make sense and create meaning out of other people's everyday. Heritage sites then form markers that are not about didactic history, rather markers of family events '. . . [h]eritage performance is made to fit in with these domestic journeys rather than historical appreciation . . .'

> Amid the background of period photos was the very camera used (or maybe not). 'That's like mum's,' said a young girl. The mother was beckoned over and sure enough she still had a similar camera. She blushed and explained how long she had saved for the camera and was one of the first people in her area of rural Devon to have one that was so modern. She began to add details about the small prints that she got then. This interactive process of inter-pretation moved far beyond an exhibit of the rise of seaside holidays. Yet it returned to it, as the woman spoke of how she had had few seaside holidays, because the war had meant beaches had barbed wire and tank traps on them. (Crang, 1994: 350–1)

So in a sense, as we shall see below, heritage tends to be more open than directable, more familiar than auratic and more open-ended than circum-scribed by an authenticating official. As Meethan argues, 'consumer research underlines the point that people are not simply caught in a web of significations or signs and symbols over which they have no control. At an individual level they often negotiate the significance of heritage' (Meethan, 2001: 108).

Urry acknowledges that tourism involves senses other than the visual, but with heritage tourism the distance or perspective created between the viewing subject and the auratic object is not only narrowed, it is often extinguished: heritage tends to be extremely tactile, performative, and multi-sensed. A recent trip to the infamous penal colony at Port Arthur, Australia, ostensibly to see the last remaining working panopticon or model prison, coincided with the opening of a new visitor centre. In this state of the art installation, almost everything involved a multisensual *experience*. Even our subjectivity was disturbed because we were required to draw a card, on the back of which was the identity of a former prisoner who we were going to embody and 'follow' during the visit. From then on the visit was one of embodied interpellation: I/we became, quite easily, early nineteenth century convicts and we entered their world, the sounds, smells even the dark, visionless world of their solitary confinement. It reminded me of the Big Pit heritage site in South Wales, (a former coal mine) where the guide asked us to turn our lights off and experience the total darkness of the underground.

Heritage and authenticity

A great deal has been written about the connection between tourism and authenticity, indeed in a recent book on tourism, the chapter on heritage is entitled 'Authenticity and Heritage' (Meethan, 2001). This is all the more surprising since it sets out to do little more than show that it has had 'a pervasive and negative effect on the analysis of tourism at all levels' (Meethan, 2001: 111), a conclusion which is nonetheless sound. The connection between authenticity and tourism generally dates back to MacCannell's *The Tourist* (1976), a valiant attempt to analyse the exotic subjectivities and devotions of the tourist as they emerge from the mass tourisms of the 1950s–1970s. According to MacCannell, modern tourists embodied a major anxiety of this period: that the churning, changing modernity with its obsession for the new, synthetic and unreal had taken western humanity into a topsy-turvy world of make-believe, invention and fantasy. The antidote was the quest for the more solid ground of traditional societies, pre-modern historical periods and the unsullied nature of the wilderness. 'Tourism is seen as a metaphysical search for completeness, for the authenticity of "primal" social and cultural relations, a pilgrim's progress of the alienated' (Meethan, 2001: 91).

Now this thesis is centrally touristic, it properly involved the quest, the pilgrimage and travel over greater rather than smaller distances from the everyday. This makes it very different from the anti-modernist thesis that simply tried to pull a slower, older, modernity back into the everyday, the so-called traditional modernity as resurrected by William Morris and associates in the late nineteenth century. As with *The Tourist Gaze, The Tourist* emphasised the fundamental difference between the everyday and the object of tourism, the authentic.

To a degree there was some plausible sense in this. After all, Americans were beginning to take a great interest in the various pre-industrial cultures around them: Arctic tourism was established and growing, visits to Mexico and further south were also becoming more developed and trips to the cradle of American civilisation in historic Europe also promised the visitor a glimpse at the real. I always try to imagine that group of Americans crowded around the guide at the top of the steps to the Propylaea listening to the guide say '. . . and here is the beginning of so many architectures and art, and there on the hill of Pnyx, is the beginning of the use of the word "democracy", and down there, in the foundations of Pericles' Odeon, is the beginning of sport' (Horne, 1984: 13). What can they have felt but that they were standing on the spot where the real world began for the west, this is where true and good values were cradled into existence, and where we tourists come from is a land where this has been lost. This fictional construction has been followed up by a considerable amount of research on how tourists behave at these sorts of sites (see Edensor, 1998, for a good review) and it is true, that at least a significant number treat these sites as if they were sacred, and as if they were themselves pilgrims to a shrine of great significance. MacCannell's emphasis on tourism as pilgrimage and tourist sites as sacred is a widely accepted wisdom and much elaborated by solid research since 1976 (see for example Cohen, 1988: 38– 40 for tourism to other cultures; Horne, 1984 for tourism to historic sites; Shields, 1990 for tourism to marginal places; Herbert, 2001 for pilgrimage to literary places). Herbert's study of tourism to Jane Austen's Chawton and Dylan Thomas's Laugharne found that 51 per cent and 39 per cent of tourists (respectively) described themselves as 'fans' of the author – substantial numbers of others were partners, children or friends who were presumably dragged along by the fan. But in addition, MacCannell provided a useful means of understanding how these sacred places are sacralised by naming, framing, elevation, enshrinement, reproduction and souvenirisation of sacred objects and replication of further relatable sites (the pub where Dylan Thomas drank might become The Dylan Thomas pub, for example).

However, while all this seems an entirely plausible, sound and fruitful analysis of tourism, its reliance on the authentic becomes questionable. For Urry (1990: 11) authenticity may be a sufficient reason for sacralisation and pilgrimage but it is not a *necessary* reason. That authenticity is different from the everyday is enough, in Urry's mind, for an object to become of interest to tourists, but all manner of inauthentic objects will do equally well. He reminds us that some tourists actually enjoy the fun and playfulness of heavily constructed fakes and synthetic surroundings. Even tourists to the most sacred of places, such as Canterbury Cathedral or St Peter's Rome, often end up buying fake images of them as souvenirs, but these bought items of kitsch reproduction are often used in the homes of the pilgrim or those gifted by them, as mini shrines in their own right. At these domestic shrines to secular and religious icons, it is not entirely clear where the everyday ends and the touristic begins and whether as objects carrying some of the aura of the sacred, they transform into 'authentic souvenirs' conveying all the otherness and power of their place of origin. A similar confusion or hybridisation of the authentic and the inauthentic centres on so-called tribal art and artefactures made for tourists. As Shepherd (2003) notes, a typical western reaction is to see artefacts made for use as authentic while those made for exchange are seen as inauthentic, literally, copies, fakes.

In terms of seeking living authentic cultures, again, much has been written, and the front stage/backstage metaphors are well worn. MacCannell made much of the tension between local people wanting to protect their privacy from invasive tourists and their wish to take their share of the tourist dollar. Front stages were erected to protect the backstages of life, and this became the staged authenticity of the Hawaiian hula dancers, the Spanish feast, Eskimo dancing and so on (see Meethan, 2001: 99–113 for a good summary). It seems that most anthropologists see very little value in the distinction between authentic and inauthentic culture. There is culture, cultural fusions, cultural change, hybridisations, and all are legitimate 'authentic' *cultural* processes. Signe Howell claimed in 1995 that it was time to ditch the 'moralistic preoccupation with authenticity and single origins' (Howell, 1995 in Meethan, 2001: 110).

The search for authenticity in the non-western world has resulted in the proliferation of heritage everywhere. Heritage there has been criticised in much the same way that Hewison criticised heritage in the UK: tourism lays to waste and destroys true culture in the same way historical heritage was seen to destroy true history. This sort of criticism was mounted in the bourgeoning 'sustainable tourism' and can be found to varying degrees in the work of Turner and Ash (1975: 197); Prasad (1987); Britton and Clarke (1987); Boniface and Fowler (1993); Mowforth and Munt (1998). In various ways these authors point up problems of commodification, cultural pollution, psychic exploitation and capitalist exploitation. Cultural pollution appears to be keenly felt by western tourists to Asia and elsewhere: areas of intense western presence in Thailand for example are eschewed by a great many western tourists (O'Connell Davidson, 1995) feeling that only places unsullied by the presence of the west are worthy of their journey or quest. Inevitably perhaps, this cliché has now been visited in fiction. Two works of fiction that deal with such a tension between an authentic search for culture and its pollution at the hands of Australians and Germans exemplify this: Gerard Lee's *Troppo Man* (1990) and Inez Baranay's *The Edge of Bali* (1995) (see Huggan, 1997 for an overview of this genre).

Against this barrage of pessimism there are many detractors who see tourism as a positive influence on local cultures. Holloway (1989: 179), for example, argues that tourism can lead 'Not only to tourists and locals alike widening their horizons but also to regeneration in awareness and pride in their culture and traditions among the population. But for the advent of tourism, many of these traditions would undoubtedly have died out.'

Further Graburn (1976), Mieckzkowski (1990) and Cohen (1993) have all documented the central place of tourism in preserving cultural art forms from annihilation, and Boissevain (1996) and Ewins (1999) argue that tourism has functioned to maintain if not extend local cultural life 'disrupted' by modernisation and travel. For Boissevain, tourism encourages backstage rituals of *intensification* to be maintained. As with many forms of ritual activity these intensify local solidarities around cultural practices. 'Back-stage rites of intensification are increasingly important for maintaining solidarity in communities that are . . . overrun with outsiders. I would suggest that the scale of these back-stage celebrations will continue to grow as the relative importance of cultural tourism increases' (Boissevain, 1996: 17).

One has also to bear in mind Cohen's (1988) corrective that the need for authenticity varies according to the type of tourism under consideration. According to him, it is central to *existential* forms of tourism and unimportant to those seeking mere *diversions*. It is more important in *experiential* tourism (those seeking to experience, well, experience itself) than in recreational tourism (where the object is fun, pleasure, play). Although much evidence points to the sober-minded middle classes dominating heritage tourism, it is by no means dominated only by Cohen's existential tourist. We have to factor in those who traipse around all the tourist sites in the locality where they are staying; we have to factor in children, school parties. We also have to understand that those heritage sites are increasingly trying to combine educational seriousness or some other serious message as, for example, social identity on Skye or the formative influence of convicture on Australian culture, with entertainment and pleasure. As these projects develop and extend, the primacy of the authentic becomes diminished.

The notion of the authentic belongs to the differentiating and discriminating nature of high culture, and as high cultures of varying kinds have collapsed into various kinds of popular cultures that are both localised and globalised, it has become an illusive quality. To a degree, of course, all cultures at all times have been fabrications; after all if people themselves don't make them who does? Anthropology, sociology, history and even the biological sciences have been largely responsible for (inadvertently perhaps) essentialising cultures and environments so that a proper, true and authentic state or reality can be identified from its opposite. It is almost certain that recourse to authenticity will pass into history itself as this truth becomes more widespread. Heritage tourism seems set to be a part of this dissemination rather than a bulwark to it.

Heritage and the anti-modernist turn

We have already dealt with this way of viewing heritage above and a summary will be provided here only in order to remind readers of its core argument and how it differs from explanations of heritage as the quest for authenticity.

The anti-modernist turn that I have argued is an explanation of the heritage phenomenon is not to be confused with nostalgia for a more perfect past. Nor is it associated with the sense of decline and a lack of self-confidence associated with MacCannell's account of authenticity and tourism. Anti-modernism is less an anxiety of what we have become than a fear of relentless change, a churning of identities, the erasure and criticism of pasts, the perennial creation of an unfamiliar world. In a phrase, it is the fear of the shock of the new. Anti-modernism was not born out of a lack of confidence and a need for displacement repositories for national pride; in fact, it was a very radical move against the hegemonic and heroic modernism of the 1960s.

In the 1960s, modernism was a bright and wonderful part of everyday life: it brought new technologies, new leisure possibilities, better medicines, the building of a new democratic base, new universities and colleges, new towns, new transport systems but above all it was fun, enjoyable. Things were getting better; the 1960s brought the mini car to a mass market in the UK and Europe; young people bought them and indulged in a fast changing world of fashion; new homes were built to modern designs away from the vile smoking chimneys and grim monotony of the Victorian terraced house. The modern world lived in suburbia, travelled more, began to eat out; it was a time of the seemingly impossible: the affluent worker. So when the Beatles and many others started to question modernism, began to recommend Indian mysticism, vegetarianism, rural living, crafts and an entirely opposed way of life to a generation eager to listen, it was a radical step, some would say courageous, creative and daring. Indeed, as I have already argued, it began life on the cutting edge of fashion, making its way to the mainstream via records and film, via the new designer shops of Habitat, Laura Ashley and Heals; via neo-beatnik fiction and poetry and through rock festivals and pilgrimages to the unmodernised world.

What was new about this also sets it apart from 'the quest for authenticity': whereas the notion of authenticity needs experts, official organisations and the apparatus of high culture with which to construct an auratic authentic other to contrast with the alienated everyday, anti-modernism was the opposite. Anti-modernism thrived on the grass roots and it was legitimated by its radical, hip, revolutionary, anti-bureaucratic stance. It was a culture epitomised by bohemianism. It was experimental with drugs, music, food, religion, politics and so on, because it was out to change the world for the better; certainly, it was not hiding the future in the past. However, it was interested in what was worth claiming from the past and what was worth memorialising for the future. Critically also, it was informed by the new environmentalism and this was fiercely anti-technology and anti-science, at least in its defining years.

So, since it was attempting to name a new world of popular cultures, it was also keen to recreate the past in its own likeness. Working class history was reworked as popular class cultures and retrieved and retraced (for example see Clarke, Critcher and Johnson, 1979). After anti-modernism had established itself as a mainstream current in the high street, the night school class and the bourgeoning world of new cultural activities, it was a relatively small step for popular archaeological histories to be a source of widespread interest. But as Urry argues it also merges seamlessly with existing plebeian movements, the boat and steam engine restorers, the rescue of obsolete agricultural machinery from oblivion, the seemingly endless desire to collect and to display (see Pearce, 1995). Finally, and most importantly, by the late 1960s and early 1970s capitalist production and modes of consumption entered a disposable phase. Unlike the 1930s or the 1940s, the western world was piling up with things that had been superseded or simply gone out of fashion. The problem before was getting commodities at all, now it was managing their disposal. The disposal of things was morally charged and new circuits of exchange emerged to channel disposed goods to the poor or needy. For the first time ever-larger numbers of relatively poor under-graduates were scattered across the UK struggling to make temporary homes until the first salaries kicked in. They made a virtue of necessity and developed an aesthetic based on the consumption of the past and this style had reached such a pitch by the early 1980s that London companies began to import the higher-quality American second hand clothes that were sold at high prices in Covent Garden by shops such as *Flick*. Soon after Next opened shops that sold what were, in effect, reproductions of these fashions. However, along with a familiarisation with clothes from the 1920s to 1950s came an interest in the other artefacts from charity stores and jumble sales, building to a generalised aesthetic for the 'retro' during the 1980s–2000s. We have to remember that charity shops and car boot sales are all related to a similar concern with objects of the past.

So in effect, heritage was always taking place alongside this generalised interest in the everyday objects of modernity and part of its appeal was the generalised expertise and connoisseurship that sedimented around ordinary practices of consumption, collecting, disposal and re-use. Almost everyone had a point of departure with heritage because it was largely a popular cultural form, and in the absence of their own experience heritage recalled their genealogy: their parents, their grandparents and great grandparents.

The everyday nature of the anti-modern turn meant that it could not be opposed to heritage in the way that the modern everyday is opposed to the authentic in MacCannell's account. Heritage of course is everywhere in the modern west. It is in people's homes (restored, gentrified, retrofied etc.) it's nearby as part of the local tourism industry, it's where you travel to as part of *their* tourism industry – almost anywhere in the world.

Box overleaf: *Men Behaving Badly*, From *The Good Pub Guide*, Scene 3 (Nye, 2000: 192)

Activity box /.1

Scene 3: Inside the Crown

Seconds later. Tony, Gary and Ken are obediently sitting at bar stools in the gutted, dusty interior

Ken
Yeah, at first the brewery wanted to rename this place Mobiles, the pub for people who like using their mobile phones in public places. Then they were going to turn it into a Showaddywaddys theme pub called Shawaddywaddys. Um, then they thought about a darts theme pub called Tossers

Tony
Yep, I could go with any of them.

Ken
But then the brewery decided to recreate the Crown how it was. I found an old black-and-white photograph of here before the war.

Tony
What was it like?

Ken
Terrible apparently. Lots of people killed.

Tony
What was the pub like?

Ken
It had the authentic pub feel that people are now looking for as we approach the end of one millennium and the beginning of a new millennium. And there'll be horse brasses. To preserve the authentic pub atmosphere. Pink ones.

Tony
I always wondered, what are horse brasses for?

Ken
Nobody knows

Tony
Oh.

Activity box 7.2

It has been a central argument in this book that tourism has ordered more and more of our lives, our localities and cities, our modes of consumption, our leisure time and indeed, everyday life. It is worthwhile taking time to consider how this touristic logic has been applied to specific activities, places/spaces and institutions. A good example is the English pub but one might investigate cafés, shops, malls or city centres. English pubs have been extensively redesigned in the past twenty years and the logic of their restructuring has followed touristic models. Pubs have been themed, heritagised (or museumised), rendered more desirable by niche groups (families, singles, gays, women and so on). Because pubs are an old cultural artefact and institution of British life, they have been particularly easy to restore to various stages of their own past or theme in line with iconic aspects of local history. Simon Nye, the writer of the TV comedy *Men Behaving Badly*, used this trend for pub makeovers to disturb the blokey haven of *The Crown*, Gary and Tony's local. Such disruptions have occurred everywhere and this makes them accessible for researching some interesting questions. What proportion of pubs have been restructured in these ways? What objects beside horse brasses establish them as 'authentic'? To what extent does this sense of authenticity refer to the former industry and culture of the locality, and to what extent do these pubs harmonise with other local touristic themes and narratives? To what extent do reconfigured pubs create a different, touristic atmosphere? Do they discourage a stable set of (mainly male) 'locals' and attract a shifting, more restless and mobile (touristic) clientele?

Whereas the notion of authenticity generates the figure of the modern pilgrim and devotions to sacralised pasts, did the anti-modern turn obviate the need for ritual? We shall investigate how heritage is visited in the final section, but there is no obvious reason why objects and accounts that memorialise the lives of local cultures should not be enrolled into the collective conscience as sacred objects. Following Durkheim (1976) we would say that the notions of god and of the sacred were nothing other than manifestations of ourselves, and this is likely true to a degree with heritage objects. But why objects, what special sacred powers can they possess? On this point Durkheim was particularly perceptive. Concluding his epic analysis of Aboriginal totemic cults he writes:

> For the emblem is not merely a convenient process for clarifying the sentiment society has of itself: it also serves to create this sentiment; it is one of its constituent elements. . . . In a general way, a collective sentiment can become conscious of itself only by being fixed upon some material object; but by this

very fact, it participates in the nature of this object, and reciprocally, the object participates in its nature. (Durkheim, 1976: 230; 236)

Potentially then, heritage objects can perform this ritual of social identification. It is necessary to say *potentially* because unlike the clansmen and women of aboriginal Australia, the visitor to heritage is not already constituted in any stable sociality, at least to the degree the Aboriginal clan was at one of its specially convened *corroborees*. Nor do the crowd visiting heritage constitute a congregation except perhaps when they are loosely and temporarily together in a room or as part of a guided tour. But again, even in a highly individualistic society there are ties that bind, ties of locality, class, generation, consumption and style, ethnicity and so on and there are objects that perform those ties. To a greater or lesser extent heritage is imbued with the sacred; it is at its most magical, we might say, when it performs links with other people, cultures, places and times.

Heritage as performance

Most of the accounts of heritage considered so far have been concerned to account for the arrival of heritage as a late modern form of culture and cultural tourism; to explain why everyday pasts should suddenly compete for our attention and money and why social, economic and cultural conditions favoured their almost universal spread. However, this is not the end of the story by a long way. Generalist theories of tourism such as those offered by Urry (1990), MacCannell (1976), Graburn (1989) generated an interesting decade of empirical investigation over the course of the 1990s and 2000s that in turn has informed new theoretical works. Among these, one of the most promising new approaches is what can be called tourism *as performance*. This takes the focus away from the producers, marketers, framers and providers of heritage tourism and onto tourists themselves. Although the generalist approaches always conceded that tourists varied in the way they appropriated and consumed tourism, they did still cling to the idea of tourism as a cultural given, a socially constructed 'thing'. No matter what the range of variations might be, tourism was always a manifestation of a definable social and cultural form. More recent attention given to the tourists themselves has contested this singular nature of tourism. Radically, many of the new writers have taken a phenomenological turn; they argue that tourism cannot exist independently of the tourists who *perform* it. This is because there is not one identifiable transcendent thing that is heritage. To say this is to do no better than Hewison who claimed there is a single and true history. Rather, like history itself, there is not one heritage but heritages. These are multiple and contested versions of cultural pasts and these are constructed or made not by the makers and constructors of sites (they tend to set narrative lines as if they were reconstructing a singular and general former 'way of life'), but by the people who come to see them. It is only among these people that different lines of meaning, relevance and truth connect with the artefactures and objects in heritage sites through lived lives, cultural absences (through exclusion, discrimination or inequality) and variable cultural landscapes of memory. These connections are performed through their embodied presence at heritage sites, their mode of engagement, their conversations, their surprise, delights, sadnesses and angers. They are not merely absorbing signs from these objects and making sense of them through socially constructed narratives, but being interpellated directly to them through their life histories and experience. Or not, as the case may be, because the general theories also presuppose a general effect of heritage on the tourist, and, empirical research has found that in many cases tourists are bored, disengaged or mildly or weakly entertained. Or, alternatively, they are found to oppose, query, or stray away from the 'interpretation' and direction offered by the site. Numerous new terms are circulating. MacCannell (2001) offers the term 'the second gaze' to denote the way many tourists wilfully ignore the proffered direction. He uses this to underline the independence or agency of tourists in the face of attempts to order and manage the 'gaze'. Similarly, Bruner (2001: 899) suggests the notion of 'the questioning gaze' 'to describe the tourists' doubts about the credibility, authenticity and accuracy of what is presented to them in the tourist production'. He also underlines agency, 'active selves that do not merely accept but interpret, and frequently question the producers' messages'. Meller's research on visitors to the redeveloped heritage space of Albert Dock in Liverpool reveals a similar independence or agency 'what is most significant is what these visitors are *not* doing', and that 'the most important thing that visitors to the Dock are not doing, is anything in particular'. That is, they wander around in a relatively aimless fashion (Jervis, 1998: 322–3, quoting Meller, 1991: 107–8).

So, heritage cannot be defined in advance of, or independently of, the tourists who perform it. It is a quality, rather like genealogy, that traces out from any given ego/person, not people in general and not 'situations in general'. This approach has a great many advantages and is becoming something of a new orthodoxy. It forces us away from the form of 'tourism scholarship' whereby 'scholars tend to work within the frame of the commercial versions of their sites' (Bruner, 2001: 881). What happens in tourism sites is not circumscribed by the site itself or the interpretations of its objects or the manner by which tourists are organised in and through the site. Instead heritage is an artefact of the *interaction* of a multiplicity of tourist subjectivities constituted away from the tourist site and the particular configuration of objects on that site.

Michael Crang (see for example, 1994; 1997) has produced some of the most theoretically elegant expositions of this approach that are also nuanced by acknowledging the *political* content to heritage. His (1994) account shows heritage to be as much a political object as a leisure object. We have already noted the place of heritage in the process of nation

formation and nationalism (frequently topped up by rituals of identification and intensification) but the politics of heritage operates at a number
of levels, as we shall see.

Crang begins his analysis of heritage by reconceptualising heritage as an
'object'. Attempts to understand heritage often begin by making the fatal
error: to construct a typology. What is so wrong with this? After all do we
not understand the world by first classifying it into its constituent pieces?
Well yes, except that this move conceals one very unfortunate consequence. Instead of casting more light on or explaining the phenomena in
question, explaining what they are, it simply serves to give the class itself
an air of reality (a reification) that it may not deserve. The operation does
not explain all the phenomena under investigation but gives them a false
sense of belonging to a singularity. But in a sense, they appear to be
explained by virtue of belonging to a particular class of phenomena.
Obviously however, nothing has actually been explained and worse, a
potential diversity of opposed and conflicting phenomena are presented as
the opposite. This is essentially Crang's first message. He puts it very well:
'in such an approach the empirical object is treated as an unproblematic
entity' (Crang, 1994: 343). '[T]he reactionary tendency to reify heritage is
seen less as a result of misleading versions of history than as a result of
their organisation. This organisation is like a map that is used to attempt to
project its own selective order back onto heritage experiences.' His metaphor of map is a good one, 'such maps reveal the order behind the
experience of the world. They inscribe Others and values on places,
projecting an order onto the world' (Crang, 1994: 341).

In this way all the singular, contested and very specific moments of
political history become detached from their context and placed into a
unified field, they are all heritage, they are all part of *our* past, they are all
equivalent and exchangeable. Indeed, they can be arranged into routes and
trails rather like the medieval cult of saints: they are all instances of a
singular (English, now) sacred Christianity.

But, Crang asks, can we all fall before the sacred objects of heritage
equally, do we really all belong to this cult? The answer is, of course, no:

> However this apparent equivalence serves to euphemise power relations,
> because these practices fit only into certain fractions of the population. High-
> status groups may find a sepulchral hush, a marker that one is in the presence of
> exhibits that demand a feeling of awe. Low status groups tend to be intimi-
> dated by, bored by and reject such situations. [. . .] The practice of responding
> to such situations is not universally known. Moreover one can suggest that the
> traditional museum and its subject position are so heavily allied to the dominant
> culture and its legitimate modes of expression, that what is crucial is less the
> 'call' and more the ability to 'hear'. (Crang, 1994: 344)

Against Hewison, Crang cites Merriman (1989: 158) to note that these
devotions at museums correspond to rituals of transition, orientated to the
future and what can be: 'the practice appears as part of a positive attitude

to the future not as a compensatory, nostalgic gesture due to social dislocation' (Crang, 1994: 344–5).

Crang contrasts the high culture museum with the everyday nature of heritage tourism: here surely there is the chance for democratisation? There ought to be a plurality of appeal and ability to relate to the display, but the *singularity* of heritage often blocks this.

> Heritage phenomena call for different practices. There is less a focus on 'dead exhibits' extracted according to scientific categories. Instead the focus is on the human use of exhibits. Objects become emplotted in affective tales that appeal in terms of connections to the everyday – bringing abstract stories and everyday experiences together. With increasing social pluralism museums cannot rely on shared, implicit taxonomies and have to turn to such narrative appeals to answer challenges to their relevance. But what subject position is being hailed in this performance? The 'over' swift answer is that one is interpellating 'The Imaginary Briton'. The stress on a shared humanity, as a common denominator amid social diversity, tends to occlude relations of oppression from the experience. The visitor is encouraged imaginatively to identify and understand, and is drawn into a new politics of leisure. (Crang, 1994: 345)

In these ways, all heritage sites have a common appeal to the common person; all such places can be placed on the same map. However Crang argues that these designs and such maps cannot control 'how these places are performed, the events that occur through them and how they are used. . . . Beyond the map is the multitude, the heterology of practice that in using heritage produce qualitatively different experiences. The existence of the "Imaginary Briton" is limited by the multitude of ways sites are appropriated and used and by the ability of visitors to construct their own paths around sites, to reorganise space-time narratives, individual journeys, to suit themselves' (Crang, 1994: 345–6).

So there is unintended agenda that takes place in heritage sites because however well mapped and organised and appealing to all, whoever walks in brings something that sparks off new performances:

> The practices that animate heritage operate at the intersection of the participants' life-stories and the stories told by the displays (de Certeau, 1984). Each time heritage is performed it is open to alteration . . . the way heritage appeals is to invite the actor to take the proffered readings of the past and reorder or domesticate them into a story that makes sense to the actor. To each exhibit, people bring a host of metonymic others – personal resonances that are set off, memories and connections triggered by the display. (Crang, 1994: 346)

Participants' *performances* are based on these sorts of experiences but also on what he calls their motions, the way they negotiate the spaces of display with their body: to dawdle, skim, to wander. Crang terms these performances '*utterances* of these places . . . overlooked in many accounts – by commentators and designers' (Crang, 1994: 346).

Crang wants to underline the diversity of heritage journeys themselves as well as the utterances at any one. He provides examples of this diversity as well as the performative options and strategies. These examples include the high-tech sites and tours that compress time and space, a world of instantaneity and velocity where 'heritage sites compete to divide and establish their place in the geography of national history'; a heritage of local history societies and their exhibitions, pamphlets and books 'mobilised as part of a struggle to preserve communities from these external forces; to write the history of areas so they will never again be a blank slate for redevelopment' (1994: 349); a neoconservative heritage that reappropriates struggles re-presenting them as industrial idylls, as perfectly ordered and harmonious as the steam engines that animate them; and day-tripping to heritage where research shows that performance takes place predominantly through conversations between parties of visitors and particularly through the domestication of material into special events within family biographies; 'heritage sites then form markers that are not about didactic history, rather, markers of family events' (Crang, 1994: 351).

For Crang, heritage cannot be independent or irreducible to these diverse performances, and yet it is constructed as a transcendent signifier, appearing to be organising them all onto a common field or map, where they are all instances of the celebration of an imaginary Briton, the nation no less.

> That is the multitude of heritage practices are often not seen as ends in themselves. Rather they are seen as celebrating or experiencing parts of a wider theme. '*Our* great island story' is constructed as a field of rituals whose performance makes such an abstract discourse concretely present to 'us'. The rituals are made into a whole by this heritage-qua-thing. In the case of oral history and right-wing narratives, the journeys can create a sense of originary wholeness that organises these experiences. This is a Thing created in and by these practices yet appearing to organise them. It provides a Map that combines these experiences. (Crang, 1994: 352)

Conclusion

Crang's analysis not only undermines generalising and essentialising theorisations of heritage, it also reminds us that despite the fact that tourism seems to be about the difference, the non-everyday, and travel away from home, this is an illusion. Heritage is a serious business of the everyday because it is concerned with who we are, how we will be and how we make sense of the cultural world we find ourselves in. Heritage can be dangerous to the extent that it does not hail all people equally, and those it leaves out are vulnerable and marginalised. On the other hand heritage sites such as *Within These Walls* and *Ellis Island* offer some hope, even if in the case of the latter one has to suspend one's disbelief. Heritage can attempt to hail everyone, even if the call is louder for some than others, because where multicultural nationalisms hold sway, history can be represented in its own image, a projection of a utopian present on the past. And if the ritual form of heritage is a particularly potent mode of social solidarity and transition, it may possess the potential to do more than all the speeches, and all the written words.

Further Reading

Crang, M. (1994) 'On the heritage trail: maps and journeys to Olde Englande'. *Environment and Planning D: Society and Space* 12(3): 341–55.

Coleman, S. and Crang, M. (eds) (2002) *Tourism: Between Place and Performance.* Oxford: Berghahn.

Horne, D. (1984) *The Great Museum.* London: Pluto.

Kirshenblatt-Gimblett, B. (1998) *Destination Culture: Tourism, Museums, and Heritage.* Berkeley: University of California Press.

MacDonald, S. (1997) 'A people's story: heritage, identity and authenticity' in C. Rojek and J. Urry (eds) *Touring Cultures.* London: Routledge.

Meethan, K. (2001) *Tourism in Global Society.* Basingstoke: Palgrave.

Urry, J. (2002) *The Tourist Gaze*: Second Edition. London: Sage.

Part 3

The Embodied Tourist

8

Tourisms of body and nature

SUMMARY

- Recent theorisations of society, nature and the body
- Surfing
- Climbing
- Ecotourism
- Naturism
- Tasting the world, touching the world
- Wine tourism

In this chapter I am going to argue that 'nature' and 'body' are not only relatively new and important themes of the 1990s and 2000s but for the first time they are linked in many new and interestingly touristic ways. Whereas, for example, many early tourisms emphasised the disembodied subjectivity of the gazing tourist and the (ethnic, folk, bathing, native, local, animal etc.) bodies of the Other as objects of their gaze, increasingly in recent years it is their *own* bodies that many tourists attend to, as tourists. In other words, although the visual gaze is still an important part of tourism, tourists are increasingly doing things with their own bodies, with embodied objectives such as fitness, thrill, spirituality, risk, sensual connection, sexuality, taste (olfaction and degustation) and what I will presently refer to as 'inscription' and 'flow'. Of course, more recent thinking about the body emphasises its visceral *naturalness*, in addition to its cultured, social and cognitive aspects (the gazing tourist is essentially a thinking, imagining, decoding and aesthetically appreciating subjectivity), and we have seen, for at least twenty years, the idealisation of nature and the natural, particularly with respect to the body and health. The thera-peutic benefits of contagion with nature have extended from natural foods, diets and medicines, fabrics, births and so on, to many overlapping spheres of leisure and tourism in and with nature. Western forms of tourism and travel have a long track record of visiting areas of 'natural beauty'; of beautiful and 'unspoilt natural landscapes', but the dominant structure of this was tuned into the visual and aesthetic attributes of nature rather than to nature *itself* or as we might say, a 'natural world' and its various surfaces and interactive possibilities. Although most people today would find the notion of natural beauty and the implicit attractiveness of natural land-scapes unproblematic, or even self-evident or normal, it is important to understand that this was not always so; that it is far from inevitable or 'natural' or even in leisure terms, stable.

The point above is made abundantly clear in Keith Thomas's *Man and the Natural World* (1983) where he discusses the nature of western cultures in England prior to the Romantic movement's sudden, dramatic and influential enthusiasm for touristic consumption of wild nature in the eighteenth century. By contrast, '[I]n Renaissance times the city had been synonymous with civility, the country with rusticity and boorishness. To bring men out of the forests and to contain them in a city was to civilise them . . . Adam had been placed in a garden, and Paradise was associated with flowers and fountains. But when men thought of heaven they usually envisaged a city, a new Jerusalem' (Thomas, 1983: 243–4). The Romantic movement drew its inspiration from the idealisation of nature, particularly from ancient Greek sensibilities, but these essentially urban societies loved not wild untamed nature but the *pastorale*, the relatively ordered land-scapes of the shepherd, goats, vineyards, olive groves and landscapes of bountiful agriculture. It was an aesthetic idealisation of a largely urban society. Early modern Britain, by contrast had neither the sophisticated civil society of ancient Greece nor a mannered and civilised farming landscape; it aspired to the former but was largely mired in close and contagious relations with an isolated rural life. Hobbes famously described the lives of people in nature, that is to say pre-civilised peoples living in close proximity to nature, as 'solitary, poor, nasty, brutish and short' (Williams, 1992: 155) but these views can be counterbalanced by those of his contemporary Locke, who saw nature as harmonious, ordered and good, offering humankind a model by which to govern its affairs. Else-where, Williams analyses the use of the word nature in the language of Shakespeare, writing in the sixteenth century. He finds a mix of meanings but together they indicate a contradictory tension, and ambivalence:

> from nature as the primitive condition before human society; through the sense of an original innocence from which there has been a fall and a curse, requiring redemption; through the special sense of a quality of birth, as in the root word; through again a sense of the forms and moulds of nature which can, paradoxically, be destroyed by the natural force of thunder; to that simple and persistent form of the goddess, Nature herself. . . . What can be seen as an

uncertainty was also a tension: nature was at once innocent, unprovided, sure, unsure, fruitful, destructive, a pure force and tainted and cursed. (Williams, 1983: 186–7)

This ambivalent attitude should not surprise us because we find it throughout the anthropological record. Elizabethan England may have had a long Christian antecedence but what we also know is that folk beliefs about the powers and mysteries of nature were still alive and well, fuelling for example, periodic intensities in the activities of witches (witchcraft) who were believed to commune with and invoke the powers of nature.

By the mid-nineteenth century England was wealthy, intellectually sophisticated, largely urbanised and its poets could praise the beauty of both town and wilderness. Wordsworth is the Romantic poet of the Lake District, but he is also the one who wrote of the view from Westminster Bridge, London: 'Earth has not any thing more fair'. Views and viewing and the aesthetic judgement of landscape that could be honed and refined in the process was the dominant way in which nature was consumed by early tourism, and its domination lasted until relatively recently.

Wilson's (1992) description of tourism in the USA in the middle of the twentieth century is a visualism dominated by the view through the windows of the motorcar. The roads and parkways constructed during the depression years to open up the wild mountainous regions and the forests of the interior to domestic tourism were constructed in such a way as to afford views, panoramas and vistas to the driving tourist and lookouts and picnic spots to the parked tourist. The landscape was purified of former hillbilly farms, cultures and their tumbledown buildings and the 'hill-billies' themselves were consigned to visitor centres where they could find work and, particularly, entertain the tourists with their dance, music and (suitably sanitised) dress. Species cleansing followed ethnic cleansing: weedy and non-native trees and bushes introduced by human settlement were removed and 'proper' native species planted in their place. At special photographic lookout spots, new maps and diagrams and dioramas assisted the viewing public to orientate themselves in a purely spectacular form of consumption. The essential touristic tool apart from the motorcar was the camera.

Mountains and ranges of high ground were a preferred landscape of the Romantic movement and these dominated the sorts of natural landscape that interested tourists throughout the twentieth century. Constructed as a natural place by 'Grand Tour' English tourists of the nineteenth century (Pimlott, 1947), Switzerland, the European Alps and other upland areas were major beneficiaries of this tourist gaze throughout the twentieth century. A similar tourist construction was effected by Thomas Cook for Scotland and Wales following his successes in the Lake District, so that in fact there were very few highland areas that were not in many ways becoming dependent on tourism income. The critical point here is that upland areas afforded spectacular views and created the most dramatic differences of perspective between the viewing subject and the natural object(s). According to Urry and MacCannell, of course, the tourists were in the pursuit of something at these places; signs of Swissness, or Scottishness or wilderness in the case of Urry; and the authentic or primeval nature in the case of MacCannell, but we must be careful not to be swept away with postmodern thought. There carried through into modern tourisms, the notion of the *natural sublime*, which does not signify something else or reference a transcendent authenticity. Rather it moves the person experiencing it in spiritual terms and this moving of the spiritual subjectivity is not merely ideational, arising from imaginative thought, but an embodied feeling, as the word 'move' indicates. Tourists were moved by awesome natural forces, as were their Romantic predecessors. At Interlaken, the hub of Swiss Alpine tourism, Simmel (1997b: 219) described how the tourist was able to access mountain tops without climbing from as early as 1895; in addition waterfalls could be viewed from inside mountains, and there were the spectacles of wild rivers and glaciers. Indeed the U-shaped valley of the Aarne could be imagined to be the result of tremendous glacial forces.

Even by the late 1980s, when Urry was writing *The Tourist Gaze*, it could still be the case that it was the *visual* aspects of nature as countryside that were the real draw. This was the legacy of Romanticism given a substantial fillip by the new universities and colleges of the post 1945 period that were still in the grip of the Romantic aesthetic (Budd, 1996).

Hence in *The Tourist Gaze* (1990: 94–100) Urry talks of the 1980s growth of 'nature' or natural forms of consumerism as arising from the new service class, the creative and powerful new middle class fraction dominated by the university-educated baby boomer generation. Urry also invokes the neo-rustication of architecture and a new ruralisation of the British housing market alongside major growth in memberships of organisations that conserve or protect 'countryside'. Despite this Urry argues that 'there is indeed a relationship, albeit complex, between postmodernism and the current obsession with the countryside' (1990: 97) and that this renders the visual even more central to tourism:

> To the extent to which contemporary appropriations of the countryside involve treating it as spectacle, even a 'theme', this can be seen as a postmodern attitude to the countryside, to be contrasted with an approach that emphasises its 'use'. (Urry, 1990: 98)

But why such a fascination with natural spectacles and themes? Urry suggests that because of a generalised disillusionment with urban modernity, particularly among the new service class, many sought a new space and a mode of appropriating it away from contaminating modern influences. They sought above all an absence of a planned, regulated space; they sought vernacular architectures, winding lanes and minimal social intervention. This explains why only certain sorts of countryside were attractive to the natural tourist gaze. Urry quotes Cosgrove's (1984: 98) assessment of this aesthetic:

> the landscape idea was active within a process of undermining collective appropriation of nature for use. It was locked into an individualist way of seeing. . . . It is a way of seeing which separates subject and object, giving lordship to the eye of a single observer. In this the landscape idea either denies collective experience . . . or mystifies it in an appeal to transcendental qualities of a particular area.

Urry's analysis of the late 1980s was sound enough: this visuality and anti-modernism were clearly evident. However, we must be very careful about the generality and universality of these claims. Urry (1990) and Rojek (1993) both emphasised a postmodernisation of leisure and tourism by the early 1990s; however, both of these writers were clearly influenced by key theorists of the day, particularly Foucault and Baudrillard, and were keen to use them to explain what they took to be leading edge areas of postmodern change. 'Meaning has been replaced with spectacle' argues Rojek, 'and sensation dominates value'. 'What evidence is there in contemporary leisure forms to support this assertion?' (Rojek, 1993: 136). Rojek finds plenty of examples in theme parks, and other display/thrill-orientated leisures based on new leisure electronics and the engineering of simulation, but Urry's trawl is less than convincing for nature-based tourisms.

Apart from mentioning working class agitations to access walking, cycling and climbing in the countryside in the 1930s, Urry scarcely mentions those who might 'use' rather than view the natural world in their leisure and tourism. Was he correct to sideline this area of activity? Certainly no empirical evidence was marshalled either way. It seems that had he looked beyond the rather narrow preferences of the new service class he would have found a more complicated picture. For example, Savage et al. (1992: 116) looked more broadly at the British middle class and found that the managerial middle classes were considerable and extensive 'users' of the countryside:

> They seem more prone . . . to seek 'escape' in the form of modified versions of country pursuits earlier adopted by the landed aristocracy. For the managers at least, the pursuit of a cleaned-up version of the 'heritage' or 'countryside' tradition seems apposite.

Savage and others have discovered that the commercial, private sector, middle classes in Britain were getting into shooting, fly fishing, deer stalking and an otherwise consumptive appropriation of nature, much of which was commodified for tourism in places such as Wales, Scotland and Ireland as well as a fast growing international market. According to A.A. Gill writing in *The Times*, 'A recent survey of City gents . . . found that shooting is now their favourite, number one recreational pastime, ahead of golf . . .' (Gill, 2001: 7). Another middle class fraction of the service class that Savage et al. called *ascetic*, the relatively low paid public sector professionals at the vanguard of new modes of consumption, also favoured a more embodied consumption of nature, preferring walking and camping. Moreover, holiday and vacation versions of all of these activities have grown strongly in the past twenty years, as has angling tourism among the British working classes (and there were 3.3 million such anglers in 1994, representing 7.2 per cent of the population over age 12).

Again, how universal could this emphasis on a natural gaze be? Certainly if Urry had looked at Germany, Scandinavia, the Netherlands and the USA for example, it would have been impossible to reach such a conclusion. In Scandinavia, for instance, most people spend the summer months in their rural cabins, typically in the forests and mountains of the interior. 'Second homes in the countryside are commonplace – because in this huge but sparsely populated area they are affordable – and to be able to get away from it all among the birds and bees is, for many a craving as strong as any addiction. . . . In a recent survey, people of all ages and walks of life were asked to describe themselves to outsiders in a couple of words. A remarkable 86 per cent gave the same reply: "Forest people"' (Scanorama Magazine, 2001). This claim is supported by the Norwegian anthropologist Hylland Eriksen (2001), who specifically identifies the Scandinavian cabin culture as a closer relation to nature and a synchronisation with natural rhythms:

> One puts the watch in the drawer and leaves it there until it's time to leave for the city. . . . The children go to bed at a later hour than usual, dinner is served as a result of mounting hunger, berry picking and fishing last as long as one feels like it and so on. (Hylland Eriksen, 2001: 157)

During the winter cabin life is dominated by muscular activities, notably cross country skiing where great distances are covered over a completely different winter cartography of forest and mountain trails. In addition, in winter and summer seasons there is a more or less continuous sequence of gathering, fishing and hunting activities based around expeditions to cabins.

A similar picture can be painted for the USA, although camping and commercial lodge tourism came to replace the privately owned wilderness cabins. The USA is one of the few places that have surveyed this sort of tourism over a significant period of the twentieth century and so we have good trend data. Family holidays to forest camping sites have been a major form of summer tourism since the 1950s and although the long trips undertaken have employed an essentially visual form of consumption en route, the camping activities themselves are characterised by a more muscular and use orientation. All manner of sports, swimming, hunting, fishing, walking and boating constitute this form of tourism. In the USA, there was also a more masculine form of tourism to camps and cabins in the wilderness dictated by the appropriate seasons for different species of animal. These rituals of American masculinity attended to the bonds between 'buddies' and between fathers and sons and are very evenly spread across the nation, despite the great distances travelled from some states. In 1955 21 per cent of the US population over 12 years of age fished, hunted or did both and this steadily rose to 26 per cent by 1985 (USA 1991: B-7). If we factor in that almost all of these were men, then we can reliably estimate that around half of all men were involved in this sort of activity by the time visualism came to dominate tourist studies.

The antecedence for this consumptive orientation to nature in the USA has threads that connect modern touristic hunters and anglers to traditions of food gathering in colonial times. However, the major impetus for it came afterwards as part of the American Romantic imagination. In the USA tourism orientated conservation braided into two very different and opposed types of consumption of nature in the last quarter of the nineteenth century. Cartmill has epitomised them as 'tender-minded Romantics' and 'tough-minded Darwinian types':

> From the very beginning, the American conservation movement has encompassed two rather different sorts of nature lovers: tender-minded Romantics who want to preserve nature because it is holy, and tough-minded Darwinian types, who want to preserve it because it is healthy. For the Romantics, nature is an open-air chapel in which one can commune with the Infinite and make friends with the forest creatures; for the Darwinians, nature is a kind of vast exercise salon, in which one can get rid of bodily flabbiness and spiritual malaise, work up a glorious appetite and polish off a couple of those forest creatures for supper. These views are not mutually exclusive, and most nature lovers hold both to varying degrees; but there is a tension between the two attitudes, which sometimes breaks out over such matters as hunting. (Cartmill, 1993: 149–50)

In the 1880s tender-minded Romanticism was institutionalised in the USA in the form of the introduction of 'nature study' into the public school curriculum 'in the belief that boning up on birds, bugs and woodcraft would not only teach American school children some natural science but instil in them an appreciation of nature's beauties, a respect for her creatures, and a reverence for her Author' (Cartmill, 1993: 151). In addition, the subject of a proper relation with nature became the centre of heated national debates. So, for example, the popular anthropomorphising literatures by reformed hunter William J. Long incensed established naturalist John Burroughs, the emphatic Darwinian who also held Cartesian views on animal nature. At the same time Burroughs had notable exchanges with the Romantic founder of the Sierra Club, John Muir, described by Cartmill as 'a bounding, arm-waving ceaselessly preaching mystic who saw the western wilderness as holy ground "where everything is wild and beautiful and busy and steeped in God"' (Cartmill, 1993: 150). Such was the public and national theatre for these debates that eventually no less a figure than President Theodore Roosevelt weighed into the fray on the side of the Dionysian impulse:

> He was a devout conservationalist, but his view of man's relationship to nature was thoroughly hierarchical and Darwinian. An enthusiastic imperialist and a staunch believer in the superiority of the Anglo-Saxon race, he was also a renowned Great White hunter who devoted much of his life to killing large animals throughout the world and writing books recounting his adventures. He favoured the preservation of America's wild lands because he thought the wilderness inculcated 'fighting, masterful virtues' and 'that vigorous manliness for the lack of which in a nation, as in the individual, the possession of no other qualities can possibly atone'. When Roosevelt travelled west for the first time to meet John Muir and go camping with him, Muir promptly asked, 'Mr President, when are you going to get beyond the boyishness of killing things?' (Cartmill, 1993: 153–4)

Cartmill is at pains to point out that the contested natures of recent years derive from these earlier (and continuing) debates and practices, but what is important here is that it seems that there never was a purely visual way of consuming nature in a touristic manner even if a powerful lobby pushed strongly for one. Arguably, Thoreau's *Walden* (1965; first published 1854) and Leopold's *A Sand County Almanac* (1949) are the two most influential popular philosophies of nature in the USA – even today – and to an extent they both recommend an embodied relationship, but it is interesting that the settings of their retreat to nature, Walden Pond and Sand County, were not the wild west natures of the Romantic imagination but relatively ordinary places not far from civilisation. Moreover, Thoreau's simple and sustainable life very close to Concord, Mass., which celebrated fishing as much as vegetable raising and Leopold's great enthusiasm for bird hunting on lands wasted by bad farming, describe an essentially use orientated natural aesthetic in America. Significantly as Thoreau's chapter 'Winter Animals' and Leopold's extensive passages on wildlife make clear, they explicitly advocate a closer sensual knowledge of nature through having direct contact with its sonic, textual, olfactory and visual presences; in other words, it is the opposite of the Romantic gaze of the tourist and resembles more the culturally proximate setting of the social anthropologist. That is, to appreciate nature fully, one has to get in to the thick of things, not view it from a safe distance.

Similar currents were at work in the nascent tourism and travel industries in Europe. Thomas Cook, for example, was a great admirer of nature and nature study and included it on his guided tours of upland Europe, but more significantly perhaps, as Withey (1997) makes clear, as a guide himself Cook worked his tourists very hard in the muscular sense, maintaining a very rigorous not to say difficult regime of hiking with which only the physically fit could keep up. Simmel began his 1895 essay *The Alpine Journey* by questioning the ultimate value of building funicular railways up to viewing places that had hitherto been accessible only to climbers. Although he appreciated the benefits it brought to the physically challenged, he wondered if something important had been lost in making the alps a spectacle for the masses:

> Alpine journeys had a pedagogic value in that they were a pleasure that could only be had by a self-reliance that was both external and internal to oneself. Now there is the lure of the open road, and the concentration and convergence of the masses – colourful but therefore as a whole colourless – suggesting to us an average sensibility. Like all social averages this depresses those disposed to the higher and finer values without elevating those at the base to the same degree. (Simmel, 1997a: 219)

As we will see below, Simmel was typical of his generation in their doubts about the civilised metropolitan life and he advocated, in his famous essay of 1910 *The Adventure*, the means of rupturing the rhythms and routines of the everyday – and this could take the form of a love affair, gambling or dangerous high risk sports (Simmel, 1997b).

Despite this influence and the significant leisure practices it encouraged, throughout the western world the tourist industry was predominantly *organised* around the provision of visual natures until quite recently. As Urry cogently recognised, tourism was highly organised around the production and maintenance of views of natural landscapes and townscapes and viewing life was elevated over experiencing it for oneself. In part, this was a function of the Romantic aesthetic as translated into a commercial popular form, but also, it was more practical and cheaper in the context of a growing mass market. When travel itself was still a marvel and views constituted the biography and milestones of any journey, it was perhaps enough to sample an exotic world from the safety of distance, and here Boorstin's (1964) notion of the protective tourist 'bubble' is important. We can see this, for example, in what I have elsewhere called the zoological gaze. Until well into the 1980s, zoos and wildlife parks concentrated most of their energy and innovation on the display of animal bodies. It could be said to be a predominantly architectural and aesthetic problematic (see Hancocks, 1971; Mullan and Marvin, 1987; Franklin, 1999). However, in tracing transformations in zoos in late modernity one thing became very clear. Both zoo managers and visitors were to become less *anthropocentric*, seeing their relationship with nature as more than simply about *their* leisure and amusement. Quite suddenly, zoos began to change: they became more *zoocentric*, existing more for the benefit of the animal bodies in captivity (by emphasising an appropriate natural environment for the animals rather than purely display criteria) and the species they represent (by making zoos part of conservation or breeding programmes to restock endangered wild populations). This chimed well with a more reflexive, decentred audience. A good example of this can be seen in the various transformations of the killer whale displays at Sea World at San Diego. The original display was pure entertainment and spectacle; the visitors were referred to as a show *audience* and the animal bodies were those of performing bodies, rather in the manner of a circus. However, this went through two transformations, here is the first.

Mullan and Marvin are able to trace the gradual elimination of the circus content at Sea World by comparing Cherfas's (1984) account of the 'Shamu – Take a Bow' show with the 1986 show they saw called 'Celebration Shamu'. In the earlier show, Shamu their killer whale is exhibited as a sensation that the audience are invited to *experience*. The killer whale is not juvenilised but admired as an animal. According to the show commentary: '*We may never really understand, but we can experience all of his strength and agility*' . . . '*Combined with an intelligence*' . . . '*And in it there is a beauty, like the finest gymnast or ballet dancer*' . . . '*And there is a spectacle.*' . . . '*Focus your attention on the centre of the pool*' '*In one fleeting moment – diving, leaping, spinning.*' . . . '*Natural grace, beauty, power*' (Cherfas, 1984: 48). In the 1986 show less attention was drawn to these physical and mental attributes. 'The emphasis was still on experience but now much more so in terms of a changed understanding and a concern to establish a relationship with the whales' (Mullan and Marvin, 1987: 21). Here the commentary specifies how that relationship should be: 'We mustn't forget that at one time so little was known about these magnificent creatures that killer whales were hunted and shot for the sheer pleasure of it and in some parts of the world it still occurs. We like to believe that because of marine zoological parks such as Sea World the public has turned fear into fascination and is going to respect the killer whales and *even love one* like Shamu or Kandu' (Mullan and Marvin's emphasis: 1987: 21).

Mullan and Marvin (1987: 22) argue that the notion of friendship changed from one where the trainers were able to cross the species barrier in order to act alongside the animals in 'Shamu – Take a Bow' to one of *mutual* understanding in 'Celebration Shamu':

> To the accompaniment of soft and mellow music the trainer drifts gently around the pool with the whale and a prerecording of his voice drifts with him. 'At times it's a quiet moment that Shamu and I enjoy together when we are just lying still and not doing anything at all. I'll touch him and he'll look up at me and I'll know that he's thinking just as much about me as I am about him.' (Franklin, 1999: 79)

The second transformation not only deepens the zoocentric content encouraging empathy and closeness, it also brings the tourist physically closer too.

In a manner that seeks to deny any crass touristic front-staging, the new Shamu for 1996 is called 'Shamu Backstage'. Here the killer whales are no longer a 'show' and visitors are no longer an audience. The promotion material refers to them now as 'guests', suggesting a warmer, closer relationship. Indeed this is precisely what Sea World wants them to experience.

Instead of watching the trainers' relationship with Shamu, they are to have one themselves, backstage. Instead of a pool, a 'naturalistic habitat'.

'Shamu Backstage', a 1.7-million-gallon naturalistic habitat, debuts in 1996. Eight different interactive areas provide guests with the opportunity to give visual, audible and tactile signals that whales associate with specific behaviours. Guests are able to help with feedings and interact during play and training sessions. Guests may also view killer whales underwater through a 70-foot-long acrylic wall. (Franklin, 1999: 80)

From viewing to interacting with killer whales and from audience to guests at Sea World, in the 1990s and 2000s tourists have begun to find themselves engaged with the natural world in entirely different ways. The list of other examples might include wildlife trails with guides through local habitats; nocturnal flashlight walks; walks through forests and canopy top walks along specially constructed gangways; diving and snorkelling in marine parks and tropical reefs; activities that encourage a close exposure to the physicalities and natures of water, rivers and oceans (rafting, canoeing, fishing, surfing) forest (bush walking, camping, hunting, cross-country skiing) or snow (skiing, sledging, dog sledging, snowboarding etc); activities that generate excitement and risk (bungee jumping, climbing, paragliding, hand gliding, reef surfing etc.) activities that provide long and close exposure to particular environments (bush walking, survival tourism, orienteering) and activities that are designed to have a low impact on delicate environments (various forms of ecotourism). If we go to Swiss alpine tourism websites these days, these sorts of activities dominate the itinerary and it is not easy to find information on purely visual, spectacular activities, although it is implicit that the more embodied activities take place against spectacular backcloths. I personally went to Switzerland on summer holidays in the 1970s, and according to my diary as a 12 year old boy, I listed the following activities, almost all sight seeing: a ferry ride across Lake Thunersee; a visit to the Tranmelback falls; a funicular ride to Kleinescheideg and view of Eiger; a ski lift ride to the Jungfrau glacier; a drive to Grindlewald, a drive to Berne (museums and city centre sites), a trip to a clock factory; watching the mid-summer folk procession. We liked to think we had exhausted pretty much what summer tourists could do in the Bernese Oberland, but compare what is on offer these days from just a Grindlewald centre alone (see Box 8.1 below).

Box 8.1   Activities at Grindlewald, Switzerland

Summer:
Bowling, Figure skating, Fishing, Fitness, Golf, Gri-wa-ki (children's programmes), Hiking, Horseback riding, Jogging, Mini-golf, Mountain-

biking, Mountaineering centre (includes Canyoning, Bungee-Jumping, Flying Fox, River-rafting, Paragliding, Spider-Highway), Paragliding, Places of interest, Regional Pass, Sauna, Sports centre, Swimming, Tennis, Wellness.

Winter:
Tobogganing, Wellness, Winter hiking, Snow-shoe hiking, Snowboard schools, Snowboarding, Skiing nurseries, Night skiing, Children's ski school, Climbing, Cross-country skiing, Curling, Devalkart, Figure skating, Fitness.

So why has there been such a dramatic shift in relationships with nature in recent years? There are probably at least five sorts of reason:

1. Most visual sites were constructed and paid for from federal, state or local government budgets and access was free to those who could travel to them. Some, like Europe's elderly funicular railways, were built as a business but most were free and designed to bring tourists into local accommodation, food providers and retail centres. As manufacturing and income from primary industries declined, many such regions became more reliant on income from tourism and so new enterprises took advantage of the more active tourist emerging in the 1990s. These were more value-adding services such as guiding, training, leading, children's programmes, often paid for by the hour, day or trek.

2. Muscular tourisms became dominant as part of a generalised concern with exercise and fitness, particularly as a more significant component of health and well-being. Although a younger generation pioneered many of the new activities it is among the ageing populations of the west that they are most evident. As we will see below, the treatment of disease by standard medical practitioners became a smaller and smaller proportion of the overall health economy: increasingly the key issues were to do with treating non-disease problems such as obesity; stresses; headaches, migraines and other non-disease related pain conditions; mobility and fitness and a range of depressive and allergenic disorders. Fitness and exercise are estimated to become a much greater part of health and well-being regimes in the twenty-first century and here again, the difference between the everyday and the holiday becomes blurred. Whereas the spa health resorts were predicated around a *cure*, more recent attention to fitness and exercise is orientated to an ongoing *state of health*, a permanent fixture in daily life. Golf is a good example here. Golf provides an active and healthy state of mobility and exercise for

many people and golfing tourism or the provision of golf courses in tourism resorts is increasingly common.

3.   Scenic tourism had become overpowered by numbers leading to frictional problems such as overcrowding, queues, traffic congestion, crime and rising prices at iconic sites. A good example of this is the annual congestion caused by the massive numbers of Winnebagos and other motor homes converging on national parks in the USA. Similarly in recent years, the Lake District in England has started to lose whatever is left of its reputation as an isolated and wild landscape with significant traffic jams forming regularly during the year as the M6 motorway feeds into its narrow winding lanes. The narrow range of key sites are still very important but their sustained popularity has created an equal and opposite tendency to avoid them. The *Lonely Planet* guides and equivalents are critical here since they provide the new tourist with updates on congestion and other problems as well as being a broker for alternative options.

4.   Many of the new exciting, high risk, bush walking and other muscular leisures are predicated on a global economy and the globalisation of information. Although many of them can be undertaken close to home, they have expanded strongly into the principal purpose for travelling. Most are still orientated to the marginal and accessible remote mountain areas – in order to glide, climb, snowboard etc. As accessibility and transport costs have declined a much wider geography of muscular tourism has developed, with activities specific to single sites operating as a draw card rather than generalised activities around a particular region or country. A good example of this is the scattered geography of bonefish fishing, allegedly the most powerful of all game fish. The bonefish has an enormous and wealthy following of fly fishermen from all around the world, and they typically pay a great deal of attention to just one small locality for an entire trip. The same is true of climbers of course for whom specific, named climbs live in their literatures and folklore, and surfers who travel long distances to surf specific breaks on a specific reef. Bush walking, bird watching and outdoor magazines are continually referencing specific walks/habitats in remote and exotic places in this characteristic way.

5.   Environmentalism has contributed a great deal to the changing patterns of tourism in natural areas. First, it has created a reflexive, decentred tourist as opposed to the anthropocentric tourist focused purely on entertainment and spectacle. The reflexive environmentally sensitive tourist is concerned about such issues as sustainability, impact on local species and habitats as well as issues to do with protection and conservation. The 1990s saw a considerable amount of drama attached to the innovative modes of direct action politics among environmental groups, particularly in relation to road building in the UK, logging in Australia and a variety of wildlife campaigns

in the USA, and to a degree this generated something of a travelling culture of green activism. Environmentalists have been very sensitive consumers of tourism, eschewing for example, those tourist concentrations along ecologically sensitive coastlines that produce overwhelming pollution and degradation. At the same time, they favour visits to ecologically balanced and sustained areas and projects where tourism can be linked, productively to environmental benefits. A good example of this is highlighted by Weaver and Oppermann (2000) in their excellent *Tourism Management*. This centres on 'debt-for-nature swap' schemes successfully implemented in Bolivia, Ecuador, Costa Rica, Madagascar, Zambia and Ghana. Crudely, a western-based NGO purchases part of the debt owed by a developing country in exchange for agreements to preserve an area of environmental significance. The western NGO then transfers its rights over that debt to an NGO in the developing country, who exchanges it for revenue earning bonds from their national government who pays them in local currency. That income is then used to fund environmental protection projects and when the bonds mature, the money is used to endow the local NGO (Weaver and Oppermann, 2000: 301).

The Kakum district on the central coast of Ghana contains some of the best natural beaches and coastal rainforest in West Africa, and is home to endangered animals such as the forest elephant. The government of Ghana, with advice from domestic and international NGOs, decided that nature-based tourism would provide the best vehicle for obtaining revenue for the area without disrupting its natural environment. Otherwise the area seemed destined to be clear-cut and used for cash crop production, as had happened in most of the surrounding area. . . . Accordingly, a 140 square kilometre area was established as a national park, and debt swaps were arranged by the Smithsonian Institute and Conservation International to provide funds for a number of tourism related initiatives. These include:

- an inventory of the area's resources and their tourism potential
- interpretive training services and the development of local museums
- environmentally sensitive interpretation services
- increased community involvement in tourism planning
- integration of agriculture with tourism

[. . .] In 1997 some 40,000 visitors came into the park, which provided employment for over 2000 Ghanaians. (Weaver and Oppermann, 2000: 301–2)

The inspirational work at Kakum and other similar places is a reason why tourism is considered to be a potentially useful 'clean green' industry, and clean green destinations such as New Zealand and Norway have been major beneficiaries of this kind of tourism. As environmental consumerism has begun to make itself felt in the developed world with major growth in organic farming, for example, it is to be expected that environmental tourism will continue to grow. But how exactly do green consumers consume nature? This takes us on to the sixth and final point:

6. It would seem consistent with the concern for sustainability and 'low impact' that green tourism would favour a purely visual 'look but don't touch approach'. However, this would ignore a strong realist streak in environmentalism that does not value the human imagination, intellect and refinement (elements that some Romantics held up as the thing that separated us from nature) or see nature as a pure poetic construction of the human mind. For realists, nature and ecology are very real, immanent and relevant. They argue that despite their intellect, and perhaps to a degree because of it, humans have become distant and removed from nature and in so doing have lost sight of the webs of life that sustain the entire planet. Worse, humans have disregarded the future in favour of short-term profits and the natural world has been wickedly destroyed. This misanthropic tendency in environmentalism is a feature of twentieth century writing on nature issues (see Franklin, 1999: 54–5) and it drives a need to atone and rekindle a more appropriate relation with nature, but particularly a tendency towards rites of purification (see Alexander and Smith, 1996, for a good discussion of this) and transition: how can we become better people and establish a proper relation with nature? Here we are, once again, back on ritual ground and we should expect to find more embodied, material- and technique-orientated practices taking place in liminoid natural settings. Of course the problem is, how to go about this task as fully rational, modernised, secular individuals, with very little sense or experience of ritual life. It is clearly very difficult but people seem to have done what people everywhere have always done, they made it up as they went along. So, for example, at one end of the spectrum, there are those who wish to return to a moral way of being in the world in which humans and non-humans are related, relate to each other and are bound morally to each other. Clearly, various forms of tree-hugging and tree atonement rituals are pertinent here (Rival, 1998). Similarly, neo-paganism is growing strongly in western countries and this in various ways seeks to harness natural forces in the world and to become once again in tune with or a part of nature. As it was revived in the twentieth century modern west, witchcraft or Wicca was quite openly a hybrid of eastern mysticism, spiritualism, theosophy and western mysticism, but it crafted a unique ritual approach to the natural world including using natural settings for ritual, stripping the human body of its clothing for many ritual occasions, reviving medicinal herbalism (the so-called 'craft of the hedge') and the use of ecstatic rituals (as in the Wiccan 'drawing down the moon'), an embodied trance where the participants' sense of self and of their environment are temporarily

fused in an experience Csikszentmihali (1988) has called 'flow' (of which more later). More generally, rituals celebrate the changing seasons, attempt to attune with nature, attempt to attain self-realisation, to teach new initiates and to practise magic and healing (Hume, 1997: 113). The Pro-*Earth First!* Donga tribe, famous for their interventions against new road building in the 1990s was also inventive and eclectic in efforts to place ritual back into their lives:

> Some dongas were neo-tribalists with a complex mythological commitment to the land, believing that Twyford Down was the site of King Arthur's Camelot. Such heterogeneous beliefs, combining diverse pagan myths, came from a wider travellers' community and incorporated a rich sense of ritual practice (Lowe and Shaw, 1993: 112–24). (Wall, 1999: 71)

Clearly, these are extreme cases but I am going to argue that we can find expressions of similar embodied and ritualistic orientations to nature in many mainstream forms of tourism. We will look very carefully at some interesting examples from surfing and climbing; from ecotourism; from naturism and sex tourism; from what the Japanese tourism industry calls '*jibun no hada ni snaka suru*', to participate with their own skins, and to the tourisms of taste and degustation, food and wine orientated tourisms. But before we turn to these case studies, it is perhaps useful to look briefly at some of the new ways social scientists have begun to revise the way we theorise the relationship between society, nature and the body. The new theoretical work on these linked questions can, in turn, be used to help understand these new forms of tourism (for a fuller account see Franklin, 2002a, chapter 7).

Recent theorisations of society, nature and the body

In recent years, many theorists have grown sceptical about the separability of nature and culture, that we can and should distinguish two different and opposite worlds. It might seem odd to even put it like this; you may well think that the two are inextricably intertwined and interdependent, because in many ways we do experience it as such. Think about food for example, where does culture begin and nature end? Think of your dog or cat. When I think of my dog I cannot separate the functional contributions of her genetic make up and her evolutionary origins from the bodies of the European wolf, together with the affordances of their bodies and their social make up etc., from her *co-evolutionary* origins as a symbiotic and emotional partner of my own ancestors, our genetic make up and the affordances of our bodies (and their limitations) and the cultural-technical worlds we have created (in hunting, pastoral, fishing, farming, industrial types of societies). Is the dog nature or culture? The answer is inextricably both. However, think also of this: where in the university or in any kind of scholarly research are phenomena considered cultural and natural at the same time? When have you ever been asked to account for something using both scientific and cultural theory? Chances are you have not. Unfortunately a long while ago it was decided that culture and nature were incommensurately different orders of reality; both were coherent orders in their own irreducible terms, and thus we have been saddled with the social sciences and the natural sciences. University degrees recognise this absolute boundary with its binary of Arts and Sciences, and even where you can take courses in both they are internally validated by either one or the other. However, this line of reasoning is beginning to crumble away and very new ways of understanding the world are beginning to come into view. So, for our purposes, we can ask if tourism is an exclusively cultural phenomenon, or, is it an exclusively cultural phenomenon in all of its manifestations? The renewed and strengthened presence of natural objects and the body make this unlikely. Some recent tourism texts, such as Meethan (2001) or Judd and Fainstein (1999) avoid this important question by subsuming tourism into a purely commercial world; the world (cities, natures, histories, cultures even) is increasingly commodified as tourist products and as commodified 'things', they are simply consumed by tourists; 'like any other product', they often say. However, this does not answer our question, it merely poses it in a different way. We can ask: how are these so-called commodities consumed? All the while it can be kept simple, with answers such as 'through a quick visit, maybe the taking of a photo or a quick look at it'. Where tourism amounts to not very much more than flicking through a glossy magazine, the illusion of shallow, symbolic consumerism is kept intact, but what if there were more *substance* to it than that? What if tourism leaves residues other than souvenirs?

Thrift's recent (1995, 1996, 1997, 1999, 2001) work on the body and nature offers some useful clues. He not only suggests a further set of reasons why contemporary tourists may seek out a more embodied nature tourism but he offers some useful ways of understanding how the human body *engages* with the natural world.

Thrift's analysis of time and contemporary forms of engagement with nature rather pre-empts Hylland Eriksen's (2001) advice for us to find ways of slowing down the 'fast time' of contemporary life. What is fast time? It is worth hearing Hylland Eriksen out in full:

> . . . the unhindered and massive flow of information in our time is about to fill all the gaps. Leading as a consequence to a situation where everything threatens to become an hysterical series of saturated moments, without a 'before' and 'after', a 'here' and 'there' to separate them. Indeed, even the 'here and now' is threatened since the next moment comes so quickly that it becomes difficult to live in the present. We live with our gaze firmly fixed on a point about two seconds into the future. The consequences of this extreme hurriedness are overwhelming; both the past and the future as mental categories are threatened by the tyranny of the moment. This is the era of

computers, the Internet, communications satellites, multi-channel television, SMS messages, email, palmtops and e-commerce. Whenever one is on the sending side, the scarcest resource is the attention of others. When one is on the receiving side, the scarcest resource is slow, continuous time. Here lies a main tension in contemporary society. (Hylland Eriksen, 2001: 2–3)

Acceleration removes distance, space and time. This was once the main criticism against the steam train – the passengers lose the ability to enjoy, the landscape and their minds become hurried in an unhealthy way. Today the criticism is levelled against the jet plane, the Internet and mobile communications. When that which used to be remote is no longer remote, that which used to be near is no longer near either. (Hylland Eriksen, 2001: 149–50)

So, 'fast time' robs us of the present and it speeds up our lives; things pile on top of us; it is allegedly stressful and unhealthy and in any case we never have time to do things like 'far-sighted work, play and long term love relationships' (Hylland Eriksen, 2001: 50). As a matter of fact, Hylland Eriksen recommends among other things, that other people do what Scandinavians do, leave the world of fast time and spend a significant period in a wilderness, in the slow time of nature (although we should note that travel away from the everyday is not necessarily to escape fast time and indeed Hylland Eriksen recommends changing many home-based practices in order to concentrate on the present). Thrift (1995, 1996, 1997) on the other hand suggests that strategies like this and many more besides (especially body techniques) have been around for some time and may account for the considerable increase in recourse to a more *active and sensual* engagement with the natural world. Before we look at that we need to understand the revolutionary way in which the body and the world are starting to be understood by philosophers, geographers, sociologists, psychologists and others – almost as a separate new field of study.

Thrift begins his analysis by engaging with approaches that 'escape the traps of representational thinking of the kind that want, for example, to understand nature as simply a project of cultural inscription (as in many writings on "landscape") in favour of a kind of thinking that understands nature as a kind of complex virtuality'. He draws on Deleuze (1988); Ansell Pearson (1997, 1999); Margulis (1998) and others to suggest that the human body and other natural objects do not stand as separable bits, with discrete lines of interaction between them, but exist in assemblages, multiplicities and co-evolving 'blocks of becoming'. Nature is nothing much more than a sequence of these blocks of becoming, and humans are as much involved in them as any other kinds of object and organisms. Indeed the implication of globalisation is that we are involved quite critically, and tourism is not, of course, quarantined from such assemblages. Think of National Parks as an assemblage, for instance.

In wishing to get away from the cognitive world of the representations of nature, Thrift reminds us that 95 per cent of embodied thought is non-cognitive. This carries all sorts of implications but particularly for our understanding of the relationship between thought and action or doing. Our bodies are often doing things before we have really thought them through cognitively, and our bodies are particularly engaged, through their various organs with other objects and life around us. Many tools we use, for example, and our techniques for using them expertly evolve outside the direction of conscious thought and cognition. For this reason, the body is able to make *anticipations* and *intuitions* in the environment around it, because different organs are locked into relationships with all manner of external connections. As Thrift argues, these anticipations and intuitions are material and embodied and not just spiritual.

Equally, Thrift argues, 'we need to escape the constructionist view of the body as simply an inscribed surface, in which the body is reduced to what Gil (1998) calls a "body image"'. This makes several errors: 'the body becomes a static signified to be filled with signs'; the body 'becomes divorced from other things, from the object world'; and the body is '*located* in space but does not produce space' (Thrift, 2001: 41).

Next, Thrift uses his idea of the 'go-faster world', the world of fast time we have already encountered, to suggest that people have effectively resisted it through developing 'body practices that value the *present moment*, rather than spearing off into the future' (Thrift, 2001: 41). These body practices are predominantly focused on the sixth sense, kinaesthesia, and 'based on the interactive *movement* and subsequent awareness of body parts', as 'an interaction of all the other senses', but clearly more than simply a sum of the individual senses. Thrift lists several types of body practice that allow us to 'separate out and value a present orientated stillness.' First, contemplation or contemplative techniques as a form of body performances, together with rituals, some prayers and other religious technologies 'which concentrate time' (Thrift, 2001: 42). Contemplative techniques transmuted into new more muscular forms: 'a series of body practices which stressed sensory appreciation through more complex control of the body'; for example, Alexander technique, the Feldenkrais technique, Biogenetics and Body-Mind centring. These emerged first in the nineteenth century but have multiplied in the twentieth century and particularly since the 1960s. Second, photography fixed a still contemplative gaze, especially through social rituals that organise the body and the environment in a specifically new constructed time and space. Finally he details how the academic study of gestures, body language, symbolic interactionism and so forth leaked out into everyday culture to inform what he calls 'a whole new corporeal curriculum of expressive competence' (for instance, body language training, and cultural awareness training).

What Thrift is doing here is alerting us to a genealogy of practices that have increased our knowledge and control over the body during (and in relation to) periods when fast time was churning our lives and changing everything. Far from producing a disenchanted world in the west, devoid of 'magic, the sacred, ritual, affect, trance and so on' other related practices associated with the 'vitalist turn' (renewed attention to the doctrine of a principle of life; that this principle operates through all organisms and materials) have made the west rebound with them. We have already mentioned neo-pagan and new age practices, but we need to note that they are by no means restricted to a small minority. In their many manifestations, experiments and cults they are now mainstream. One only has to see how much shelf space is given over to them in bookshops to appreciate this.

Thrift also includes other areas of ritual initiatives and he speculates that 'there may have been a multiplication of these performative spaces of affirmation, in which mystical experiences can be brought forth and animated through the power of body postures, repetitive movements, schedules of recall and spatial juxtaposition' (Thrift, 2001: 44–5).

> Western societies have evolved more and more bodily practices which are a means of amplifying passion and producing 'oceanic' experiences: music, dance, mime, art and so on, which very large numbers of the population participate in. (Thrift, 2001: 45)

And finally, Thrift alerts us to the dramatic growth of body therapies (dance therapy, music therapy, massage therapy and so on, 'which try to harness and work with emotional energy on the grounds that movement causes emotion' (Thrift, 2001: 45).

All of the foregoing must be recognised as influential on how we 'consume' nature – although of course it also shows how feeble a concept like 'consumption' is relative to the complexities of our interaction, and Thrift uses the term 'apprehension' instead. The contemplative and mystical developments 'form . . . an embodied "unconscious", a set of basic exfoliations of the body through which nature is constructed, planes of affect tuned to particular body parts (and senses) and corresponding elements of nature (from trees and grass, to river and sky . . .' (Thrift, 2001: 45). In turn, these capabilities, Thrift argues, generate 'a new form of vitalism, a stance to *feeling* life (in the double sense of both a grasp of life, and emotional attunement to it) which explain many of the strong, sometimes even fanatical investments that are placed on the "natural"' (Thrift, 2001: 46). A biopolitical domain emerges from all this and is enhanced by three sorts of development.

Some kinaesthetic spaces and the practices they engender become privileged and powerful. 'As walking becomes a natural practice to be indulged for its own sake, so, against the background I have outlined, it can be a means to contact the earth, to be at one with nature' (Thrift, 2001: 46). Bird watching might be another here, and a very significant one in the biopolitics of the UK, the USA and Australia. The RSPB in the UK is a very powerful body and the policing and surveillance of illegal acts against birds is manned by incredibly well-equipped and enthusiastic volunteers. Birders in most states of Australia have banned duck shooting.

Second, walking (and birding too) involves what Thrift calls a 'style of the body location in space' and these produce those anticipations and expectations noted above. 'There is, if you like, a genetics of movement which the body slips into through constant practice. There are "dance floors of nature"' (Lingis, 1998: 87) (Thrift, 2001: 47). As a result of this activity, the body 'attends to configurations of objects which are in line with its expectations and which produce particular exfoliations/spaces and times' (Thrift, 2001: 47). In a sense, these configurations and objects in them are artefacts of the body and its style of body location.

Finally and importantly, Thrift argues that nature 'pushes back' by way of confirming the embodied exfoliations 'for example, our experience of walking is validated by its effects on the body, from sweat to heart rate to muscle stretching'. Markwell's study of the experiences of eco-tourists at nature sites was narrated, as we will see, by the 'push' that nature gave them. As Thrift argues, 'the body-in-encounter, fixes "symbolic" thought as affect, mood, emotions and feelings' (Thrift, 2001: 47). Clearly, this is experienced in a wide range of nature based tourisms but it is routinely obscured by keener interests in the 'push' or impact that humanity has on nature and natural settings. In an interesting research note, Bauer (2001) has enumerated the many ways in which the natural world 'pushes' on the tourist body. The first she talks about is air pressure itself, encountered in high altitude travel as well as in jets. Temperature, of course, pushes on us resulting in extremes of hyper- and hypo-thermia and both are encountered as tourists push out into more extreme climates, particularly if they are attempting to engage in equally extreme physical activities. Queensland, Australia has both an extreme tropical climate and a relatively new appeal to global tourists; nature poses quite a risk to anyone there, but especially tourists. Bauer cites recent medical research to show that 38 per cent of hospital admissions of overseas visitors were due to injuries and poisoning, whereas only 15 per cent of Australian interstate visitors were admitted for these reasons. In another study of guests on tropical island resorts, 'of the 317 clients with skin disorders, 10 per cent were due to sunburn, 20 per cent due to bites and stings and 30 per cent due to cuts. Even in more moderate climates such as Malta, 24 per cent of British tourists reported having suffered sunburn or sunstroke (Bauer, 2001: 302). Sun-related illness is very extensive. The mildest form is syncope that merely causes headache, dizziness or fainting. When the body core rises above 38°C medics begin to talk of heat exhaustion although Australians call it 'going troppo'. Effects include 'decreased coordination, nausea, vomiting, muscle cramps' while at core body temperatures of 39–41°C victims suffer hallucinations, irritability, muscle cramps and eventually coma with or without convulsions. . . . Damage to brain cells is possible' (Bauer, 2001: 302).

Water and water-related risks are also very significant. A 1983 study of 346 surfers over a two-year period recorded no fewer than 337 injuries and similar results were found for windsurfing. The push of nature here is on the muscular-skeletal system (especially the spine) but most commonly on the skin, as waves push and scrape surfers across jagged reefs: 41 per cent of injuries are lacerations; 35 per cent are soft-tissues.

The tourist body is also open to attack and disease from a wide variety of micro and macro animals and plants, and in some cases this risk is increasing (Bauer, 2001: 304–7). Warm seas can be particularly hostile to bathers in the form of jellyfish stings; bats and dogs in South America endanger nature tourists with rabies; there are 3000 snake bites annually in Australia and an astonishing 30,000 deaths from snake bite in India; malarial mosquitoes and other tropical insects and parasites are endemic. As with almost all of these tourist natural hazards the tourist body is either less adapted or less knowledgeable and therefore more at risk, but part of the lure of less civilised places is their less sanitised environment. It is not surprising, given the enormous value attached to the wild, clean, pristine and natural that so many wish to experience such places directly and in a relatively unprotected manner. This provides a good introduction to the first of our case studies, surfing.

Surfing

Surfing and body boarding are now ubiquitous features of the beach all round the world, arguably taking over from the previous concentration on swimming. For Lencek and Bosker, authors of the late 1990s book *The Beach*, surfing was the ultimate expression of human adventures with the sea because it placed the body not only in this watery element but used the body to sense its power and to tame it:

> Addicted to the adrenaline gush and endorphin highs produced by the glide of fibreglass across water, these surfers were, in every sense of the word, New Age explorers of the sea, crossing aquatic boundaries and tangling with a tumultuous realm that man had never dared to enter. Unlike fifteenth- and sixteenth-century explorers, who travelled thousands of miles to uncharted, far-off beaches, modern surfers ventured only a few hundred yards off shore. But in this circumscribed parcel of sea, the technology of modern surfboards made it possible for surf enthusiasts to engage with nature in an entirely new way: to play 'chicken' with the powers of the sea.
>
> They flocked to the beaches of California, Hawaii and Australia to harness the power imparted to the breaking surf by wind, planets and currents for a blistering journey to the shore. It was exploration in every sense of the word, creating an intimacy with the sea that would have dazzled the Romantics of the nineteenth century. For the first time in the history of beach athletics, it was possible to blaze through a pipeline of water so dense and powerful that only the most courageous would even contemplate the journey. They navigated Brobdingnagian waves with more speed and alacrity than had ever been possible. (Lencek and Bosker, 1999: 259)

For a while surfing was viewed as either part of the organised leisure world or dismissed as yet another hedonistic space of postmodernity. New studies of surfing however are beginning to make the sorts of connections between nature and the body that Thrift refers to. In seeking to analyse the dramatic growth in high-risk sports such as surfing, Stranger (1999; 2001) argues that it is not danger per se that motivates the surfer but thrill. The intensity of the kinaesthetic exercise involved in surfing techniques in combination with the intensity of the challenge locks the surfer into what he calls 'an ecstatic moment'. Here again, we find the interface between nature and the body as intensifying a sense of the present. Stranger is able to call on analysts of religion such as Maslow (1970) who talked of a similar 'peak experience' that 'is said to involve feelings of oneness with the universe; distortions of time; intensely focused concentration; non-judgmental cognition; ego-transcendence; and fearlessness'. Stranger also notes a literature on play and sport where similar phenomena are reported, particularly in the so-called whiz sports (surfing, windsailing, skateboard-ing, sky diving, extreme skiing etc):

> . . . the ecstasy or the 'going out of oneself' seen in whiz sports . . . the sensation of being at one with the environment, and the feeling of entering an altered state of consciousness have become familiar notions. Time and space are one and the same; the event seems to unfold in slow motion. (Midol and Broyer, 1995: 209, cited in Stranger, 2001: 136)

Stranger refines his understanding of these peak experiences by developing Csikszentmihali and Csikszentmihali's (1988) concept of *flow*: '*flow* theory argues that the achievement of these ecstatic moments – which they call "optimal experience" – can be understood in terms of a harmonious match between challenge and skill' (Stranger, 2001: 138):

> Whenever we are fully functioning, involved in the challenging activity that requires all our skill, and more, we feel a great sense of exhilaration. Because of this, we want to repeat the experience. But to feel the same exhilaration again, it is necessary to take on a slightly greater challenge, and to develop slightly greater skills. (Csikszentmihali, 1988: 367)

Stranger explains how *flow* produces this ecstatic moment using some of his respondents' own descriptions. 'In surfing this union between the surfer and the wave can occur when the nature of the breaking wave is such that the surfer's abilities are pushed to the point where they have to perform automatically:

> When you abandon yourself to the rhythm of the wave and become part of that rhythm, you get that arrested time. . . . The ecstatic moment is increased in intensity with an increase in size and critical nature of the wave. (Lynch Interview, 1995, in Stranger, 2001: 139)

Figure 8.1 *Surfing.* Source: Mark Stranger

Stranger argues that the degrees of difficulty force the surfer to act quickly 'and /or with such intensity of focus that there is no time/room for conscious decision making and the surfer *loses consciousness of self as separate from the act of surfing the wave*' (Stranger, 2001: 139, my emphasis). Other researchers have come across this, for example, one of Martin's (1991: 112–13) respondents had this to say:

> When you're surfing big Waimea [Bay], you can't be thinking about anything – except the moment. Which means that you're just there, in harmony with the universe. . . . If you've got that moment, that's all you need. If you know that feeling of being here, now, you're set.

Notice common themes here, the push of the wave, the switch from cognitive to sub-cognitive thought, the focus on, and attention to, the 'present' and feeling at one with the objects of nature. However in addition to this, surfing has established a large number of sacred sites and these provide for a very significant international traffic by a growing world following. For Stranger the achievement of flow depends critically on the 'actions having significant meanings for the participant'. Trivial activities cannot generate flow and rational instrumental objectives (for example, what it can do for you such as catharsis or character building) have the 'potential to inhibit flow' (Stranger, 1999: 269). For Stranger, what warrants and permits flow in the case of surfing is aesthetic reflexivity which Lash described as central to contemporary culture: 'with its emphasis on the body and the physical experience as part of the reflexive self, aesthetic reflexivity enables the sensual and emotional experience to be recognised as inherently worthwhile' (Stranger, 2001: 143). This generalised reflexive aestheticisation with its emphasis on sensuality and physical experience can adhere to any number of activities, some entirely novel (even though adopted from another culture initially) like surfing or skate boarding, others less new, such as climbing.

Climbing

As with the section above on surfing I will draw mainly on one recent study, in this case, a brilliant essay by Neil Lewis (2000). As with surfing we can detect that climbing is yet another example of embodied activities in association with nature that *appeal* to contemporary cultures. Certainly the climbing tracks laid out on gymnasium walls and the ubiquity of outdoor climbing adventure courses for school and college kids are all relatively new. In many ways, climbing and mountaineering (the activities, experiences and organisation) are seen as model ways of interacting with the natural world and are promoted eagerly. Johnson and Edwards (1994: 459) argue 'that mountaineers with their long-term relationships with specific regions and peoples, complex motivations structuring their presence and activities, and lengthy history as a distinct cultural community, represent what ecotourism is striving for'. The travel section of *The Times* newspaper of April 7, 2002 reviewed what is clearly becoming a bourgeoning industry under the heading of 'high adrenalin activities': 'from paragliding to caving' it argues 'it has never been easier to try a high adrenalin activity in Britain' (www.thetimes.co.uk).

Lewis's essay is on adventure climbing which is a peculiarly British and dangerous form in which the climbers use no ropes and no bolts to save them from a fall. Naturally, it is a dangerous and high-risk sport that not all or even very many would want to participate in, but as an extreme form of something, it is particularly useful for our purposes here. Climbing is active and extremely athletic as with many sports, but what is of special interest is its interface between hands and nature; it is an activity predicated on *touch*, tactile technologies, rocks, crevices, overhangs, tree roots as well as aching tired muscles, confounded strategies and the haunting presence of death.

For Lewis, modernity has always undermined or felt ambivalent about a fully sensuous embodied stance to the world, preferring a more passive, mediated ocular body to his *climbing body*, which is organic, self-determined and tactile. First and foremost then, climbing represents a form of freedom: 'consequently freedom becomes a form of embodied awareness: a choosing to sense and, more specifically, a choosing to feel and *touch* an environment . . . it is to exert an existential freedom: for *how we choose to make sense of the world significantly constitutes its reality'* (Lewis, 2000: 59, original emphasis). Lewis is also influenced by Simmel's essay 'The Adventure' and notes that while the metropolitan life suggests

Figure 8.2   *Climbing*. Source: Ian Britton

reservation, spectatorship and a spiritual life removed from the personal-
ity, the adventure emphasises immersion, participation and spiritual depth
(Lewis, 2000: 70).

Lewis works on the difference between the metropolitan body of
modernity and his *climbing body*. He argues, using Bauman particularly, to
show how in sanitising death in the modern west, and by isolating and
marginalising death – and the dying – we simultaneously avoid recog-
nising our bodies, our mere mortality. Against that the adventure climber
who explicitly exposes his body to death and the site of the death of others
is 'compelled to comprehend our organic nature . . . to experience the
body as it ages, as it sways from moments of illness to fitness and back
again, as it desires and is desired . . . as it is satiated through pain and
pleasure' (Lewis, 2000: 61). So, this is another recurrent theme, active
relationships with nature prevent us from withdrawing from the world,
and they expose us to ourselves; literally, nature reveals things in us that
we cannot see or merely think. Here the idea of performance is critical,

especially the idea that we can only become what we have performed, and not the other way around.

The rest of Lewis's essay, the really important bit, is the anthropology of climbers' hands. Touch, we are reminded, is the senior sense, not vision, as the expressions 'to be in touch', or 'to lose touch' imply; touch is also of course the most direct experience, the most unmediated acquisition of embodied knowledge (Lewis, 2000: 70). 'Climbers' we are told *'feel'* their way up a route via tactile navigation' and this point chimes well with another, that kinaesthesis does not require sight, one can know where one's body is in the world without seeing and here touch is the key. The hand itself is a conduit of much required knowledge about the world and almost everything about a climb.

Lewis also talks about the way the body becomes inscribed by climbing and also by particular climbs. 'The practice of climbing trains or cultivates the body towards a better configuration for climbing' and the best techniques for climbing are learned through climbing itself. The climbing body physicalises itself through climbing, and all climbs inscribe themselves on the body through the aches, injuries, scratches, and cuts etc. that are entailed. These are not mere epiphenomena: 'through its very engagement with nature, the climber becomes natural'. And, as with the rather less adventurous nature tourists we are about to meet, these inscriptions provide moments of remembrance and identity.

Ecotourism

Less esoteric are the sorts of tourists who enrol in 'nature tourism' – adventure attractions that are beginning to become established globally. Ecotourism is a very recent concept and it emerged predominantly through that very intensive episode of heroic environmentalism and the emergence of global environmental governance in the 1980s. Although tourism to natural areas had started long before that and gave rise to concerns about its impact on fragile and rare ecologies, it is also true that a reformed version of tourism to natural areas was considered a useful and sustainable industry that would provide an alternative source of income to more environmentally destructive industries (especially logging) and degradation (industrial development, mining, urbanisation etc.). Ecotourism became a buzzword as a result of this tourism agenda and especially the report 'Our Common Future', produced by the World Commission on Environment and Development in Brundtland, 1987.

So, we can say that nature tourism was given a considerable boost through its connection with environmentally correct and sustainable new forms of tourist development. Through the protocols and ethics of sustainable development, new tourism companies were able to form and access protected areas, national parks and specific sites as never before.

With estimates of growth in ecotourism between 20 and 30 per cent per year by the mid-1990s (Shackley, 1996), some have argued that it is the fastest growing sub-sector of the global tourism industry (Cater, 1993; Buckley, 1994). In the Galapagos, for example, actual growth in ecotourism was 20 per cent per year between 1980 and 1991. Most of the research on ecotourism is driven by scientific and environmental agendas and to date there has been relatively little understood about the *experience* of ecotourism. That is starting to change, partly as a result of the need to understand in finer details the relative benefits of tourism to such areas (see Norton, 1996; Markwell, 2001).

Markwell has recently analysed three examples of these in the East Malaysian state of Sabah, Borneo. He asks whether these experiences on organised tours actually achieve what they claim: to 'allow the tourist a closer involvement with nature than is usual in their everyday lives' (Markwell, 2001: 54). Using a detailed ethnographic approach, Markwell has produced some useful data on the changing nature of the touristic experience of nature. Three important conclusions were reached. First, that tourist organisations promise close contact but the structuring of the tour ritually and technically serves to create a distance between the tourist and the wild:

> The combination of material interventions in the landscape and a system of rituals served to discipline and domesticate much of what is promoted to tourists as 'wild nature'. Human interventions in these natural landscapes, such as walking trails, fences, lookouts, hides and boardwalks not only civilise the landscapes, but also established, in most cases at least, clear boundaries which demarcated the wild from the tourist. (Markwell, 2001: 54)

Second, however, tourists are not firmly confined to, or bound by such boundaries and they permeate them through a variety of practices and experiences:

> A greater congruence of mind and body seemed more evident during those times when the tourists were experiencing places relatively free of the mediations provided by the tourist industry, when fantasy and imaginative interpretations of place were evoked. Indeed, a number of participants felt that one of the factors contributing to their enjoyment of Supu Caves was the experience of scrambling over jagged limestone and tree roots. A sense of discovery, wonder and playfulness was experienced, while the cloud forest on Mt Kinabalu elicited childhood memories of enchanted forests inhabited by goblins. The imagination seemed to be liberated and the interplay between fantasy and reality and the interconnections between nature and myth are clearly evident here. It was at times such as these, when the material interventions required by both the tourism industry and protected natural area management were least obvious, that it could be argued that the tourists . . . experienced something like Turner's (1973) concepts of liminality and antistructure. (Markwell, 2001: 54)

Finally, as the above suggests these sorts of experiences are 'not only ocular . . . but truly corporeal':

> Data were obtained which suggest that the embodiment of the tourist experience was strong and palpable. . . . The tourist body played an important role in how tourists experienced (and remembered) nature at these sites. Their bodies were stressed and sometimes placed under considerable strain, particularly during the climb of Mt Kinabalu, but also during other times during the tour. Bodies ached, leg muscles became sore, throats were parched, skin perspired and smelled . . . (Markwell, 2001: 55)

It was also clear from Markwell's account that the body became the focus for discussions and ongoing updates as if the tour and the terrains they were traversing became inscribed on their bodies. Unlike the visual tourist who sees in a disembodied manner, these tourists had to use their bodies as tools for travel and as a sensual interface with nature itself: 'the body is taken for granted until it is placed in novel and physically challenging situations . . .' (Markwell, 2001: 55).

Markwell's study is useful, not only in identifying the relationship between organised nature tourism and the experience of nature, but also in pointing up the close relationship between nature and body in these new kinds of tourism. Such experience also focuses the mind on the tourist body and encourages a form of accentuated attention to it. Naturism or nudity is another example of this sort of activity and here again there is a connection between attention to the body and natural environments. As with almost all of these activities we can say that they had much earlier antecedents, activities pioneered by minority intellectual, Romantic or bohemian sub-cultures. But in recent years, aesthetic reflexivity of the sort Lash describes, has encouraged a more embodied, sensual aesthetic that has broken down modernist taboos on the body and sexuality. Hitherto, the body was to be covered and sexual urges to be contained or in the case of 'deviant ' sexualities, suppressed. It encouraged both compliance and a hidden secretive world of the grotesque body. However with increasing self confidence since the 1960s, aesthetic reflexivity has encouraged far greater confidence in celebrating and exposing the body, ultimately in ritual shedding of the clothes that indicate inhibition. We will look briefly at this next.

Naturism

It is not immediately apparent why nudism, which includes the 'social nakedness' of organisations like British and American naturist organisations, the cultic nakedness of the mythopoetic men's movement (where nature forms a backdrop for 'natural masculinity'), and erotic nakedness associated with gay and lesbian sex as well as within mainstream heterosexuality, should find nature and natural settings so significant. In order to understand why this is so, we shall turn to a recent paper by Bell and Holliday (2001) that not only charts the history of naturism but also usefully analyses the *different* ways in which nature and naturism articulate.

To begin with then, a brief history:

> The emergence of western naturist movements in the early twentieth century has to be located within a broader cluster of cultural re-orientations towards nature. The aesthetic and romantic appreciation of the countryside, which in Britain emerged from Romanticism, spilled over into a number of embodied engagements with the natural landscape at a time when mass urbanisation and industrialisation were affecting the nation's population – and psyche – to an unprecedented degree. (Bell and Holliday, 2001: 129)

In late Victorian England these engagements were often described as 'the art of right living' and included organisations and passions dedicated to such things as folk songs, peasant crafts, vegetarianism, land reform, theosophy and communal living. By the interwar years, Britain and Germany describe two quite different though related cultural trajectories. In Britain, the body was implicated in an enthusiastic exposure to the elements generally (although largely through sports and rambling and cycling), but there was something of a class schism when it came to nudity. Artistic, bohemian and largely middle class experiments took place with naturism, largely nudity in rural and coastal 'retreats', but this became highly lampooned by lower-middle class and working class cultures for whom such things were more or less exclusively comedic: '. . . the bawdy humour of saucy seaside postcards and music hall smuttiness – as Matless (1995: 115) puts it, there were particularly strong "English undertows that pull[ed] bodily exhibitionism into nudge-and-wink-territory"' (Bell and Holliday, 2001: 131).

The idea of the aesthetic naked body of course was a Romantic import from classical antiquity, and although this inspired all forms of national Romanticism, it was rooted more strongly in Germany. Evidence for this is cited by Bell and Holliday (2001: 129, citing Anthony, 1998): 'the art of right living much more readily embraced *mass* naturism, especially in the youth movements; it is estimated that, prior to its outlawing by Hitler, there were as many as 3 million social nudists in Germany in the 1930s'.

> In opposition to the decadence and degeneracy perceived as rife in the city, the German life reformers looked to the national landscape, transplanted some ideas from Greece, and built a cult of the countryside and of the natural (national) body which embraced social nudity with fervour. Importantly, a distinction was drawn over the appropriate location for nakedness, marking a differentiation in the symbolic meaning (and reading) of the nude body: 'nudity was only acceptable only when seen in an unspoilt natural setting: meadows, gardens or against the backdrop of the sea' (Mosse, 1985: 51) – in the city, or indoors, or on a stage, the naked body became lewd and sexual; in the country it was only *natural*. (Bell and Holliday, 2001: 130)

In this way, naturism became non-sexual and British naturist organisations found themselves having to surround naturism with rules and proscriptions that outlawed any hint of a sexual content. Thus, it became a fiercely (married-) family-orientated activity, singles were banned and today sexual jewellery and photography of any kind is proscribed. The ban on photography (and the general prudishness of official naturism) related to various ways in which naturism was used as a cover for the manufacture and marketing of pornography. Official naturism therefore became marooned in respectable and discreet middle class circles.

Bell and Holliday note that nudism was once again practised by the counter- and hippie cultures of the 1960s, and indeed, in many places in Europe it has melted into previous public naturist practices, especially in parks, forests and beaches, producing a generalised 'cool' attitude with little philosophical thundering or organisation associated. Most of this is sun and warm weather oriented during daylight hours, but after dark these sorts of places have become eroticised, naked, sexualised spaces, particularly for gay men.

Outdoor sex is not confined to gay men however, and Bell and Holliday (2001: 134) remind us through such studies as Douglas et al. (1977) that outdoor sex is widely, if discreetly practised in mainstream America – in choice natural settings but also in back yards and beaches. As Bell and Holliday argue there is a long association of the natural world with the erotic, as a world of unrestricted animal sexuality and reproduction, as other to civilisation, as places away from the knowing and censorious eye.

It is with respect to the latter that gay men have eroticised many city parks, woodland areas and beaches for themselves – and indeed, this has served as a model for the geography of gay tourisms, with their own beaches, resorts and international destinations.

Finally, nature and nakedness are linked in the highly ritualised nature of the mythopoetic men's movement, which is growing rapidly in recent years, as a means of celebrating and reconfirming their gender identity, widely reckoned to have been battered into confusion by the success of feminism.

In sketch form, the movement's key concerns lie in rediscovering and celebrating 'deep masculinity' as a response to the softening effects of feminism, white collar alienation, and postmodern urban living; tapping historically and transculturally into sources of masculine strength; reaffirming via naturalisation the duality of the sexes and the social roles attached to each side of that duality; and . . . *locating* a space for rituals of deep masculinity: in the wilderness. (Bell and Holliday, 2001: 135)

This movement is therefore predicated on the touristic form and is a part of what we might call New Age tourisms that focus on both the body and the natural world.

Tasting the world, touching the world

Another field of tourism that involves an embodied sensing of nature has to do with taste itself and food and drink have become a major component of contemporary travel and in some instances the predominant reason for travel. This was not always the case however. Pimlott (1947) reminds us that when the English visited Italy on their Grand Tours of the eighteenth and nineteenth centuries, specialist cafés, restaurants and hotels grew to provide their preferred 'English' foods and beverages. Even as late as the 1960s it was not uncommon to find tourists packing food to take with them, and even now English-styled pubs, fish and chip shops and restaurants are common in working class holiday resorts in Spain. The English were not the only tourists who feared foreign food:

> The first Japanese tourist this author ever met was in Athens, Greece in the summer of 1967. He and all the others in his party of twenty-five, carried three pieces of hand luggage. Of these . . . two were filled with food! The first Japanese tourists abroad were chary of sampling foreign cooking and took with them as a precautionary measure, green tea, dried seaweed, pickles, instant noodles and various other Japanese delicacies. (Moeran, 1983: 97)

This should not surprise us because sociologists have found 'taste' to be bound up with what Bourdieu (1984) called social 'distinction'. People use foods that they eat to distinguish who they are, to define themselves, often distinguishing themselves from others as they do so. This is evident at the level of class and regional differences in France – and elsewhere. However, it is at the national level that one sees social distinctiveness being promoted and performed. As part of nation building, as we have seen, disparate regions, ethnic and language groups were often thrown together, and part of the nation building work was to find ways of forming a commonality, a corporate identity: 'Claims for a national food are inseparable from claims to a national identity. . . . Eating, it could be argued, is one of the ways in which the relations between a nation and individual are embodied' (Peckham, 1998: 174).

Peckham (1998: 173–4) argues that national diets emerged in relation to nation building projects. She shows how a Greek cuisine became standardised in the twentieth century for example, and she quotes Elizabeth David who noticed that '[after] the 1914 war patriotic Frenchmen began to feel that the unprecedented amount of tourists . . . was threatening the character of their cookery far more than had the shortages and privations of war. . . . It was at this time that a number of gourmet-minded men of letters set about collecting and publishing the local recipes of each province in France'.

So in the twentieth century we can imagine two things starting to take shape, first a more self-conscious acknowledgement and celebration of national food, dishes and diets among most nations, and second, an increasing degree of foreign travel, where the most intimate sense of who you are is challenged by the threat of intimacy with that of the Other.

Of course, it was the social elites who broke the ice first, largely through the filters of bespoke, trustworthy restaurants or through social or business visits. The French *Michelin* guide and Gault-Millau guide and in England the *Good Food Guide* and Egon Ronay's were one of the very earliest post-war manifestations of this. Gradually, in the travelling classes, the elite language of international travel began to use the language of food as metaphors of nation, and this too, solidified national reputations around food and drink. By the 1950s, as we saw earlier, the symbols of Mediterranean or Mexican foods and drinks became more freely used in the decorative arts of northern Europe and the USA, becoming metaphors for luxurious travel itself. Before long, to complete the chain of transformations, eating the food of the exotic other became a metaphor for the properly touristic. In order to say you had truly been to a place, it was not enough to have merely seen its surfaces and taken photos of key sites: the real acid test was whether you have eaten its food, literally consumed, a new and exotic place.

> In travel guides foreign cultures are likely to be identified first and foremost with the foods to be tried and avoided; to travel involves the risk of becoming sick. Conversely, international cuisine is promoted and consumed as a touristic experience, so that a meal at an Indian, Italian, Greek or Chinese restaurant becomes a substitute for travel. (Peckham, 1998: 172)

Of course consuming other places through their food in one's own home town is consistent with one of the main themes of this book, namely that tourism is now part of the everyday, and one does not need to leave most cities in order have touristic experience.

By the 1980s, the Japanese had fully embraced this postmodern habit:

> Nowadays, however, they prefer to travel alone or in small groups of friends or relatives. They want to experience not sights but action, to 'participate with their owns skins' (*jibun no hada ni snaka suru*). . . . It is suggested [by holiday brochures] that [tourists] can be party to the smells, to the laughter, to the fun of an evening in Taipei, Barcelona or Los Angeles. He can 'melt' [*toke-komu*] into his surroundings, not 'just as passing traveller, but in touch with the lives of local people'. As the Japan Travel Bureau's catchphrase goes: 'Travel is contact' [*tabi wa fureai*]. 'Contact' is the vital word. (Moeran, 1983: 96)

The embodied experience of tasting and eating a nation or place, or people is a very complete and performative activity; it's the most intimate of contact, full of surprises, pleasure and indulgences, typically embellished by the presence of national waiters, often in costume and occasionally with background or live national music. Tourists know to put particular foods on their itinerary. 'Japanese tourist brochures are full of tips on what to eat where: Macao is billed for its Portuguese cooking, Penang for its fresh fish, Vienna for its coffee, Paris for its raw oysters,

Geneva for its fondue . . . and food – from Alaskan salmon to Hawaiian pineapples – is frequently advertised as one of the better forms of gift to take back home' (Moeran, 1983: 97).

From the consumption of 'national' foods, there have been connoisseur-led travellings for more rarefied palates. Obviously one direction has been to 'discover' regional cuisines and specialities. Another has been to open the 'home' of particular foods: so Dublin is the home of the global beer favourite Guinness, and Dublin makes no small thing of the fact; Brighton is the home of seaside rock; and the Highlands and Islands are home to whiskies. The concentration of distilleries and wineries in particular districts has given rise to whisky and wine tourism and this can provide an organising theme for an entire holiday in specific countries. As this developed spontaneously by wine and whisky pilgrims, so the wineries themselves diversified into the tourist trade. So besides organising 'degustation' (France) and 'cellar door sales' (Australia) wineries invested in the conference trade, letting rooms, fine restaurants, tea-rooms, children's entertainment and so on.

As global tastes refine and become ever more proficient within and now across (through a bewildering range of fusions) national styles, tourists are now increasingly hunting down cafés, brasseries and restaurants of great repute and fashion, and again, trips to these can become one organising theme for a metropolitan long weekend break. We should note that this refining taste also belongs, more generally, to the aesthetic reflexivity that underlines most forms of embodied competence in postmodern times. We can sense this in the incredible transformations in knowledgeability and sensitivity to global wines for example. The food and drink pages of the weekend papers have expanded immeasurably from the 1960s and sophisticated food and drink television is now an established favourite, often as with Rick Stein, for example, organised around travel and food. In this context it is interesting to reflect on the changing nature of food guides. For example, in 1972 for the very first time, Egon Ronay thought it possible to give restaurants scores on a linear, better/worse basis:

> For fourteen years we have appraised the cooking in a restaurant according to how well it achieved what it set out to do. No comparisons were implied. But good cooking has spread spectacularly, the public's judgement has grown more sophisticated, and we find our former concept outgrown . . . we find ourselves able to apply absolute measures more easily. (Ronay, 1972 cited in Mennell, 1996: 283)

Wine tourism

There is probably no limit to the capacity of humans to refine and expand their ability to taste and smell the world around them. I was recently on a Qantas flight to London reading an article from the in-flight magazine that in all seriousness contemplated the future of air tourism: a form of tourism where the object was to experience different airs, and the associated fragrances of the landscape. I would have dismissed it as madness were it not written by a respectable wine writer, who saw in air a possible extension of a growing new form of tourism to taste wine. As we all become more and more concentrated in large cities and ever more anxious about air quality, this might just come to pass. Certainly, we can point to the growth of understanding and interest in wine, which, among the British and Americans at least, would have been unthinkable fifty years ago. In the last section of this chapter I will trace out some of the main elements of wine tourism, leaving the reader to ponder whether this could, or indeed has, extended into other modes of taste tourism.

According to Hall et al. (2000), wine tourism has become a major tourist business worldwide. The Napa valley in the USA, for example, attracted some 5.1 million visitors in 1996 generating US$600 million and around 8,000 tourism jobs. In Australia wine tourism attracted 5.3 million visits and was estimated to be worth A$428 million in 1995 but anticipates being worth A$1.2 billion by 2005. Italian wine tourism grew from 400,000 visits in 1993 to 2.5 million visits in 1996 (Hall et al., 2000: 25).

In traditionally non-wine drinking countries such as Britain, consumption of wine has increased by 400 per cent since 1970, from 3 to 13 litres per capita per year with annual rates of growth in the 1990s approaching 10 per cent. Eighty-six percent of wine is sold to the highest socio-economic groups (A B and C1), a combined taste group that also dominates the bulk of overseas travel (Hall et al., 2000: 180). This correlation is no accident because it is largely through travel to favourite wine drinking locations in Europe that wine drinking has grown in popularity. That experience produced a critical mass that became very interested in food and drink, providing an opening for a very vibrant food and drink journalism and TV from the 1980s onwards. British wine taste is very eclectic 'with exports from all major New World, as well as traditional countries rising, with the exception of Germany (Hall et al., 2000: 181).

One of the most intriguing changes in British cultural life has been the intense fascination with the language and poetics of wine tasting, but it has arguably opened up an experiential tastescape lost for at least two hundred years. However, it is not just in Britain, but America, Australia and increasingly through Asia.

Among the more ardent wine drinkers in the world, wine has become an everyday experience, easily accessible and in bewildering variety. This, of course, is an example of the reverberation of tourism, producing reverse flows of export goods initially experienced through tourism, back into everyday life. As connoisseurship developed and as more and more private cellars were laid down, the availability of cheap access to wine-producing regions provided the right conditions for a formal wine tasting industry to take shape.

Most tourists organise themselves, more or less as part of the claim to connoisseurship, but for others there are now professional wine tourism companies. Arblaster and Clarke Wine Tours of Hampshire, England, was founded in 1986 and organises tours for private individuals, wine clubs and corporate parties to every major wine producing nation in the world. The company has grown consistently in a manner reminiscent of the first ever Cook's Tours. Thomas Cook was a great enthusiast and liked to accompany and guide tourists himself. In a similar way, Arblaster and Clarke employ *Masters of Wine* to accompany all of their tours (Hall et al., 2000: 16–17).

Wine tourism has also grown around relatively new phenomena, wine roads and wine festivals. The notion of distinctly marketable wine areas and districts was first muted by the French in their 1855 *Classification of the Wines of the Gironde* in preparation for the 1855 Paris Exhibition. However, it was in Germany that the first tourism to wineries by road was initiated, the so-called *Weinlehrpfad* (instructional wine path) derived from practices that began in the 1920s, but by the latter years of the twentieth century all eleven German wine producing regions had their *Weinstraben* (wine roads) (Hall at al., 2000: 2). Wine roads and trails are now to be found from Hungary to the Barossa Valley in Australia. Wine festivals are yet another elaboration of this organised response to the twin growth of tourism and wine consumption. The UK wine producers in the Southeast are linked to three 'Gourmet Trails' in which other foods and food outlets are arranged into maps and guides for independent travel.

Although one might expect international tourists to constitute the biggest single group of wine tourists, the visitor demographics at cellar doors say otherwise: only 3 per cent of visitors to Victorian (Australia) wineries were international tourists, only 9 per cent at Augusta-Margaret River and 8 per cent at West Auckland, New Zealand (Hall et al., 2000: 122). These data are of course limited, and we might expect larger numbers in Europe, but nonetheless, they highlight the extent to which these tourism industries are supported very considerably by local and national visitors, as with many other tourism industries.

Wine tourism, therefore, is an established activity that stamps the notion of taste onto landscapes, or *winescapes* as Peters (1997) put it. It is a fundamentally opposed notion to the tourist gaze since wineries certainly do not correspond in every case to pleasingly beautiful rural locations, but derive their appeal in embodied moments of degustation and reference heterogeneous natures in terms of soils, climate, oak barrels, but also human contributions such as winemaking skills and foods.

Activity 8.1

The examples given above may in many cases be a relatively new means of penetrating and engaging with nature through tourism but there are many more. It is a good exercise at this point to choose another example and research how it engages with nature, whether or not it has taken on aspects of flow, excitement, therapy, trance, and whether or not it encourages a multi-sensing of the world or is confined to the visual sense. Similarly, does its promotional literature emphasise the slowing down of time, escape, and ecstasy? To what extent have these activities generated a touristic following of their own and what sorts of places have benefited from their development?

Further Reading

Bell, D. and Holliday, R. (2001) 'Naked as nature intended' in P. Macnaghten and J. Urry (eds) *Bodies of Nature*. London: Sage.

Desmond, J. (1999) *Staging Tourism: Bodies on Display from Waikiki to Sea World*. Chicago: University of Chicago Press.

Franklin, A.S. (2002a) *Nature and Social Theory*. London: Sage.

Hall, C.M., Sharples, L., Cambourne, B. and Macionis, N. (2000) *Wine Tourism Around the World*. Oxford: Butterworth-Heinemann.

Macnaghten, P. and Urry, J. (eds) (2001) *Bodies of Nature*. London: Sage.

Mullan, B. and Marvin, G. (1987) *Zoo Culture*. London: Weidenfeld and Nicolson.

Veijola, S. and Jokinen, E. (1994) 'The body in tourism', *Theory, Culture and Society*, 11: 125–51.

9

Sex and tourism

SUMMARY

- Sex at Blackpool pleasure beach
- Sexualising tourism
- Sex tourism arrives
- Sex tourists
- Sex tourism for men *and* women
- Sex workers
- Conclusion

Sex has been a part of tourism for a very long time, but according to Veijola and Jokinen's (1994) playful paper that sets up a fictional theoretical discussion between themselves and Urry and Rojek – on a beach – 'the body has been absent from the corpus of the sociological studies on tourism' and 'the analyst himself has likewise lacked a body' (Veijola and Jokinen, 1994: 149). As part of this discussion, the two authors (who want to argue an embodied, phenomenological position against the visualism of Urry and Rojek) engage in topless sun bathing and at one point are rudely interrupted by a naked man 'or to be more precise, his sex' whose volleyball has landed between them. Rojek and Urry meanwhile, are imagined to be sitting away from this embodied (and passionate) beach scene, under sunshades, on deckchairs deconstructing what seaside postcards *mean* with Ovar Löfgren (see Löfgren, 1999). Their point in writing this very witty paper is that the tourist gaze is impossibly abstracted from 'tourist events and encounters, in the duration of time and [the] sexed body' (Veijola and Jokinen, 1994: 149). As we saw in Chapter 6 the naked body and the ritual conventions of the beach interpellate a sexualised subjectivity, not merely the recognition of signs. Whereas the recognition of signs may have consequences for thought, and is not unrelated to action, Veijola and Jokinen seem to argue that sexualised subjectivities have consequences for passion, arousal and sex itself. This is surely an aspect of tourism we cannot ignore.

At a general level, we can say that if tourism comprises an important part of ritual life in late modernity, then we should not be surprised to find sexuality so ingrained in the aspirations and practices of tourists, because a heightened sense of sexuality and playfulness typically accompanies human rituals. In the case of western societies that have generally surrounded sexuality with all manner of taboos, injunctions and rules, it is little surprise that for most of the history of tourism, sexual encounters were widely hoped for and encouraged. This was certainly true at the seaside town of Blackpool in 1939 when a team of 23 observers set out to study what they called 'the image and reality of sex in Blackpool' (Cross, 1990: 180). This study is all the more interesting since this was part of the wider Mass Observation exercise in a nearby mill town (*Worktown*) whose workers came to Blackpool, almost exclusively. The authors of the study of sex in Blackpool are thus set in the context of a detailed knowledge of sex back in their home town. To my knowledge this is the only empirical study of sex and tourism in the modern 'Fordist' period.

Sex at Blackpool pleasure beach

According to Gary Cross, 'the couple is the preponderant Blackpool unit' and 'sex in Blackpool is especially good for study because here it is bound to be more overt, for there is little opportunity for secrecy or home privacy in the supervised setting of the boarding house'. Although it might seem to be pushing the ethical boundaries of research these days, the team of Mass Observers had already been quite systematic in studying public sex in the back streets and lovers' spots in *Worktown*, turning car lights on lines of 'necking' lovers in order to count them systematically (Cross, 1990: 188). In Blackpool, observers also appeared to go in for participant observation: 'Altogether as a result of exhaustive research and many pick-ups by observers themselves, we scored only four records of copulation [in 1937]' (Cross, 1990: 189).

Reading their account it is hard not to notice their sense of disappointment at the relatively low level of sexual activity in Blackpool in comparison with what they knew to occur when the street lights went out (after 11.00pm) back in *Worktown*.

> . . . the back street is the locus classicus of unmarried love in Worktown; here are the results of turning car headlights on back streets in the central Blackpool area. The back street behind Vance Road: seven couples necking against the wall and in the corner of doorways. In the other back street, on the other side

of Vance Road, are five couples. There is none of the *vigorous* activity that Worktown streets show at the same hour . . . (Cross, 1990: 188; my emphasis)

This 'vigorous activity' evidently included full sexual intercourse ('as common in winter as in summer') which took place in the back streets where there would be 'closely linked couples, standing, one or two in every back street' (Cross, 1990: 183).

Their disappointment was not due to a lack of thoroughness or commitment:

> Observer units combed the sands at all hours, crawled around under the piers and hulkings, pretending to be drunk and fell in heaps on couples to feel what they were doing exactly; others hung over the sea wall and railings for hours watching couples in their hollowed out sandpits below. With wild cries observers set out, fortified by a meat-pie supper, speeding through the night in a car to the extreme southern boundary of the town. Here a traditional sex area Number One, the sand hills, famous as the scene of alleged seductions and assaults. . . . Typical of the difference between truth and legend was an incident at 1.00am, when a band of weary observers stopped for coffee at an all-night stall on the promenade. The stallholder, an old hand in Blackpool, said that it was disgusting the way some of the young people went on, that right now there were thousands on the sands, and the largest part of them stay there right through the night. In fact, there were three. (Cross, 1990: 185)

Their apparent disappointment has to been seen in relation to the otherwise overtly sexualised nature of the seaside *during the day*. This began for many with the brochure for Blackpool, produced by the local council:

> In the Blackpool holiday pamphlet, unlike that of Brighton, sport, entertain-ment and environment are subordinated to the charms of the girls in the bathing dress. Seven of the fifty photographs published in the 1937 pamphlet feature specially posed groups of girls shown playing leap frog, picnicking, riding donkeys, and playing ball on the beach. Their sex appeal is in their frankness and healthiness, reminiscent of the photographs of film stars published in fan magazines. Whatever they are doing they display more vitality and personality than one would find in a hundred Worktown girls. They wear the latest bathing suits, chiefly the brassiere and shorts type which is rarely seen in Blackpool. (Cross, 1990: 181)

Once in Blackpool the atmosphere is sexually charged. There are phallic sculptures along the front and the Tower looms phallus-like over the proceedings, but 'Blackpool's sex appeal is firmly based on the body'. Sweets such as 'Mae's Vest' and 'Sally's Whatnots' were clearly sexualised bodies; there were machines offering peeps at 'intimate scenes'; there were thousands of smutty postcards; states of undress and undressing extended from the beach to the theatre and side shows (shows were observed and reported in great detail: here is a sample for the George Formby show of 1939):

Men and women in rich costumes of eighteenth century France. Behind, the wrought iron gates of a manor house. Gauze rises to show a fountain-well. . . . Another curtain rises. Red suns are glowing; chandeliers descend from the ceiling, on which stand lovely girls, breasts naked, nipples upstanding and red. (Cross, 1990: 182)

Undress, nakedness and exposure were a feature of theatre shows but they continued into side shows such as in the Fun House, where for one shilling 'holidaymakers could see the undies of ordinary live girls . . . where air currents blow up skirts', but more generally, 'for the showman a little "dirt" draws the crowd' (Cross, 1990: 183). This carnivalesque atmosphere saturated and sexualised the public performance of people themselves. For example, groups of men and groups of women followed each other around, smiling suggestively and joking loudly. One of the team of observers, the wife of an Oxford don and Labour Party activist was constantly propositioned by men as she stood 'observing' outside the Tower, here are some excerpts from her notes:

Middle aged man in a bowler and mackintosh: 'Will yer come to bed with me love? 'Ave yer done it before?' Very tall man fairly well dressed: 'Are you all alone sweetie? Come along with me and I'll give you a real good time. Come on, don't be shy. You don't want to be alone tonight do you?' Man, 30, wearing mackintosh and cap. 'Come with me lass? I'll pay for you but you'll have to give me a cuddle. What about it lass, come on.'

Finally, and almost unbelievably, watching the courting, kissing and otherwise sexually engaged couples on the beach late at night was evidently a major draw for men of all ages:

Watchers are not youths only. For older men of scopophilic tendencies, the sands at night are a happy hunting ground. Whenever a couple get down on the sands in the dark shadows of the Central Pier, they very quickly have a ring of silent, staring individuals around them less than two yards away, apparently immune from rebuke. (Cross, 1990: 187)

As if talking about a colony of seabirds, Cross muses that 'this tolerance naturally helped observers in their study' (Cross, 1990: 188).

In sum the Mass Observation team found that Blackpool was highly sexualised and that this carried over into sexualised performances in both formal and informal situations, but although it was infused into day and night time activities, for most it was predominantly comedic and voyeuristic, and even for most of the mill girls and their boys it rarely went beyond petting and flirtatiousness. Prostitutes were conspicuous by their very low numbers, and most of these were outsiders restricted to propositioning punters, including the Mass Observers (of course) on the sea front. Why was this? Cross argues that for the mill girls going further than necking was far too risky with a boy they did not know and have some means of controlling. Control and confidence were greater at home and sex on the street more likely between long-term partnerships and couples saving for marriage. However, the mill girls did leave the pubs more or less drunk and in theory were more at risk if men pressed their suit too hard. It seems they did not.

> Evidently the males are also careful or merely flirtatious. We think this is so because, for the average young Worktowners, Blackpool does not offer a special outlet for sex. This he can generally satisfy as well in Worktown. Both men and women go to Blackpool for the things they cannot get at home – oysters, sleep, sea air, the Big Dipper, Formby in person, a first-rate dance band, variety and no factory. The tension of sex, often as severe as the tensions of time, money and work is a thing from which for one week you try to get away. (Cross, 1990: 190)

Sexualising tourism

Between the 1930s when we see these first and valuable glimpses of ordinary people away on holiday and the present, a great deal has happened to change the nature of sex both at home and away. To begin with, those tight knit industrial communities did not last very long after this study; the war kept most very busy, but afterwards new technologies, new markets and competition from cheaper overseas locations saw many such moral communities split away and change. From the 1950s onwards, relative income rose considerably, particularly among a new and affluent generation and they began to take far more leisure and freedom, looking for more out of life than a factory career: social mobility, further education, travel. This and subsequent generations began to live away from home before marriage and this was hugely enhanced by the expansion of further education colleges and grants and scholarships for living away. In the 1960s, the so-called sexual revolution encouraged more sexual experimentation and sexual activity before marriage and in addition, the pill and other contraceptives made this a safer and longer-term possibility. Sex continued to sell tourism, and with the demise of the cold English seaside holiday and the global growth of the warmer sun holiday in the Mediterranean or tropical climates, based around the resort hotel, sex became a more normative part of tourism. A typical post-Fordist strategy in tourism is to segment the market into specialised niche areas, and sex itself became one of the ways tourism markets segmented. So, for example, new holiday packages exclusively for young and single people made the probability of sex an attractive selling point. Gay, lesbian and older age group packages were also marketed with clear erotic subtexts.

Recently Ryan and Robertson (1996) reported that, for example, 13 per cent of students in a survey reported having sex with someone they met on holiday. Summarising most other recent research on holiday sexual relations, Ryan and Hall (2001: 60) reveal that between 8 per cent and 24 per cent (depending on the sample) report having had sex with a new partner on a recent holiday. As Oppermann argues, 'many tourists experience sexual encounters simply because the occasion arises or because they meet like-minded people' . . . or, they 'might simply feel lonely and sexually deprived' (for example, people on conference travel). Ryan and Robertson (1996) found that 10 per cent of their student sample packed condoms.

Travel affords anonymity and respite from surveillance, duty and obligation (as well as engendering loneliness and sexual deprivation), but also the freedom for fantasy, imagination and adventure. However, sex and sexualities are also embodied practices and one of the more important ways in which we express ourselves through natural performance. We can lose ourselves in ecstatic moments during sex just as much as the surfer or the skydiver can through their physical experience; sex is also potentially exciting and 'dangerous' and for this reason Simmel included sexual adventures, affairs and the like, alongside his concept of *the adventure*, which was otherwise about mountaineering and other dangerous, risky and exciting alpine sports. In the next section I can do little more than summarise some of the key features that research on the subject of sex and tourism has revealed, but you will notice that I follow (the late) Martin Oppermann's injuncture to recognise that the notion of 'sex tourism' does not exhaust the range of sexualities and sex that are significant to tourism studies.

Activity 9.1

Is there an intrinsic relationship between sex and tourism, or at least the conducting of courtship and establishing new sexual relationships at some distance from the everyday world? Even if such activities are not exclusive to tourism and travel it is surprising how many examples one can find. Take, for example, the recent Bridget Jones books . If you think about these books, going away to touristic locations is often evoked for the perfect sexual encounter – even Bridget's mother discovers this association. Of course, the Bridget Jones books are a contemporary comedy loosely based on Jane Austen's *Pride and Prejudice*, but considering that the former were written recently and the latter early in the nineteenth century, it would seem, on the face of it, to be something of an enduring association. To what extent do stories in film and novels draw on this relationship and how do these literatures assist you in understanding *why* tourism travel and sex have become so closely associated?

Sex tourism arrives

As Oppermann (1999: 251) says, 'While some countries may be more renowned for the availability of commercial sex, sex tourism exists everywhere . . .'. Men (predominantly) travel from more developed countries to less developed countries in Asia, Africa, Latin America and the Caribbean for sex that is either not available or more expensive or qualitatively less pleasurable at home. But this is not restricted to men, because there is now a stream of discreet travellings by affluent western women to places in the Caribbean and Africa, where sex with local men is explicitly anticipated. However, Dahles and Bras (1999) also note similar relationships developing between local beach boys (who develop an 'entrepreneurial romance' style) and western women tourists in Indonesia. According to many recent analysts, sex is not motivated purely by the 'consummation of commercial sexual relations', and there are 'complex processes by which individuals choose to seek sexual gratification, first within prostitution and secondly as part of the tourist experience' (Oppermann, 1999: 252; citing Kruhse-Mount Burton, 1995: 192).

Certainly sex and tourism is not confined to wealthy international male tourists travelling to exploit poor local women, although that is common enough. But we know that prostitutes travel too and sometimes they are the international tourists, working the conference venues, international hotel districts, casinos and resorts. In Germany for example, 'the large share of foreign prostitutes actually means that in many sex tourism settings it is the prostitute who is the business tourist, an aspect of sex tourism that deserves more attention' (Oppermann, 1999: 262). Oppermann also reminds us that white slavery was common well into the twentieth century with young women abducted and sold into foreign brothels. Similarly, not all prostitution is heterosexual and there is an enormous complexity in the diversification of sexual desires and services. Further, sex tourism is not confined to the sexual services on offer to clients: red light districts are routinely listed as attractions in most tourist cities, and this voyeuristic tourism may be a prelude to further investigation or a sexualised end in itself. In addition, there are all manner of sexual spectacles that encourage a mild form of sexual voyeurism. Ryan suggests that Sydney's tourist-packed Mardi Gras and similar events in San Francisco and Auckland have a strong voyeuristic, sexualised quality, particularly among the largely heterosexual crowds (Ryan, 1998). Nor is prostitution all of a piece, indeed it is precisely because prostitution in some parts of the world varies from the (often) sordid 'brief' and unelaborated nature of client–prostitute relations in the west that men are particularly attracted to sex-centred travel to specific places (Thailand, Vietnam, and the Philippines for example) where this is not the case. Studies of prostitution have found that a lot of men who use it are dissatisfied and wish for more warmth and attention, intimacy and understanding (see for example, Kruhse-MountBurton, 1995: 193). For the prostitute in most western economies, '[a]n important skill is to be able to bring a man to orgasm as quickly as possible. The narrow nature of the exchange is more than evident to the punter as well as the prostitute and a man would no more expect a prostitute to cuddle or stroke him, or act as his companion after sex than he would expect a plumber to do so after fixing a leaking pipe' (O'Connell Davidson, 1995: 48).

O'Connell Davidson (1995) and Kruhse-MountBurton (1995) have both documented what they call open-ended or non-contractual prostitution. In this, the relationship between prostitute and client is less explicit and less organised around the performance of a specific service for a specific charge over a specified time period. Instead, highly skilful 'sex workers' blur the commercial or economic nature of the relationship by encouraging something more approaching a holiday romance or affair; where the relationship might be for the duration of the man's holiday; where the relationship more closely resembles boyfriend–girlfriend amiability, attentiveness, love and romance; where the economic exchanges are less specifically orientated around sex acts and services and where in many cases the economic obligations continue after the man leaves. Typically, for the duration of their relationship, the man pays for everything and so the sex worker's living is made simply by accompanying him over a 24-hour period of each day. In addition, they typically ask for gifts of clothes and other things and they may also ask for cash to help sick or needy relatives. Frequently they keep in touch and may share time together on subsequent trips, and it is on the basis of a continuing moral tie that many men continue to send gifts of money. Indeed, O'Connell Davidson shows that there is range of relationships between western male tourists and Thai prostitutes (and non-prostitutes too) from marriage itself (and there are many agencies to facilitate this) through extended consortation arrangements of the sort noted above, to the very common 24-hour stays in clients' hotels, shorter sessions of a few hours or even fellatio performed on sitting clients in at least one Pattaya bar (O'Connell Davidson, 1995: 46–7).

The extraordinary diversity of sexual experiences on offer in places like Thailand resulted from former (contradictory) policies aimed both to attract the military rest and recreation trade, which began during wars in the Asian theatre, and moral policies aimed to restrict and control it. There are thus a great many settings – bars, clubs, theatres, massage parlours, escort agencies, discos and so on – where sex workers are based, in addition to the street and beach areas. Sex workers of huge diversity are to be found in great abundance and these include child, transvestite and homosexual prostitutes.

O'Connell Davidson underlines the 'bottom line' fact that this trade and the tourist trade from the UK, Australia, the USA and elsewhere that came afterwards is attractive not only because the women are different but because it is cheap, very cheap by comparison with prices in their own country. As she says,

> [i]n Thailand, a prostitute can be rented for almost twenty-four hours for as little as 500 Baht (around £18), a sum that would barely secure a man a ten minute blow job in Britain. The cheapness of sexual services (as well as accommodation, food, drinks, travel and other services) furnishes a single, working class British man with a level of economic power that he could never enjoy at home, or in any other European country, and all the sex tourists I interviewed commented on the fact that, in Thailand, they 'live like kings' or 'playboys'. (O'Connell Davidson, 1995: 45)

The sex tourism trade in Thailand, for example, has been growing steadily, particularly since the early 1970s. Truong's (1990) study of the economics and development of the sex trade in South-East Asia shows how the proportion of men to women entering Thailand as tourists grew from 66 per cent in 1977 to just under 75 per cent in 1986 – a period when tourist arrivals grew from just over one million to just under three million. By the 1980s, it was estimated that there were between 500,000 and 700,000 prostitutes in Thailand, which represented 2.3–3.2 per cent of the female population or more disturbingly, between 6.2 percent and 8.7 percent of the female population aged 15 to 34 (Truong, 1990: 181). By the late 1990s Thailand had 'well over one million prostitutes' (Weaver and Oppermann, 2000: 291).

The impact of 'sex tourism' to places such as Thailand, the Philippines, Vietnam and elsewhere has been profound. Such is the money to be made from prostituting teenagers and young girls that many parents have sold them into the trade in return for a cash loan. Such debt bondage ties the girls on very unfavourable terms to particular bars or clubs where they are at great risk from violence, abuse and infection (see Seabrooke, 1996).

Sex tourists

Just as sexual service varies in Thailand and elsewhere, so too do the tourists themselves. O'Connell Davidson found three broad types among the British in Thailand. The first were skilled or unskilled single working class men she calls 'Macho lads'. They often travel in small groups and 'for these young men, Pattaya is a kind of macho theme park with beer, motorbikes, Go-Go bars, kick boxing, live sex shows, pool tables in English style pubs and guaranteed access to dolly birds to posture with and fuck' (O'Connell Davidson, 1995: 43). Then there were what she calls 'Mr Averages', skilled manual workers, self-employed or junior/middle management, who pride themselves in being 'an ordinary, respectable bloke'. They are interested mainly in 'simulating some kind of emotional or romantic relationship with either one woman or a series of women rather than a large number of anonymous sexual encounters' (O'Connell Davidson, 1995: 44). Mr Averages claim never to visit prostitutes at home and do not see themselves as 'punters' in Thailand. Finally, there are 'Cosmopolitan' men from higher socio-economic groups, who describe themselves as travellers or 'in Thailand on business' but who will spend a few days in Pattaya for 'relaxation'. They use prostitutes but only in a 'worldly wise' manner and claim never to visit prostitutes elsewhere in the world.

Part of the self-deception involved in these sexual economies is that experiences are refracted through complex transcultural differences. The men perceive, quite correctly in many ways, that the girls they meet are more civilised, refined and cultured than the women they typically meet socially at home. They are, in their view, the beautiful Other but also the 'aesthete', refined in the arts of self beauty, poise and style that are again seldom encountered at home. The Macho Lads and the Mr Averages describe places like Pattaya as fantasy lands precisely because they have access to a Hollywood lifestyle for a few weeks with an unlimited number of willing, compliant and beautiful young women. They also mistake the *art* of Thai prostitution for a perfect, or ideal femininity that defers to their wounded sense of masculinity.

O'Connell Davidson is interested in the cultural worlds of these British male tourists, who are in many ways casualties of their own looks, their lack of sexual attractiveness to women at home in relation to norms of masculinity and their perceived problems with forming longer term attachments with women at home. The playful, tender and affectionate approach from Thai sex workers together with the men's relatively height-ened economic power in Thailand gives them 'a greater sense of power over their own bodies . . . [s]ex tourism also frees men from other aspects of the body's power over them ' (O'Connell Davidson, 1995: 53):

> Cultural definitions of beauty turn many people's bodies into prisons, making their sexual desires unattainable, and it is certainly the case that large numbers of sex tourists are either physically repellent by European standards (I have never seen so many enormously overweight men together in one place before), or disfigured or disabled in some way, or too old to be considered sexually attractive.

So, O'Connell Davidson seems to be suggesting that sex tourism in 'notorious' places such as Thailand is not simply one of the least savoury ways in which the most developed countries exploit the less developed. Clearly, the implication is that only a subsection of culturally wounded and sexually failing men are 'catered for' in these places, and certainly, their tourism points to problems experienced with women at home.

> Macho lads complained that English women are 'hard work', that going to discos in England is 'a waste of time'; Mr Averages bemoaned the fact that 'pretty' English women know they are pretty and demand the world (they want to marry you then soak you for every penny when they divorce you); a Cosmopolitan Man told me: 'I'm 48, I'm balding, I'm not as trim as I was. Would a charming, beautiful, young, woman want me in England? No. I'd have to accept a big, fat, ugly woman. That's all I could get.' (O'Connell Davidson, 1995: 52)

For these sorts of reasons O'Connell Davidson (1995: 53) rejects psycho-dynamic theories to explain their behaviour. As she says, 'one could equally well argue that there is nothing very individual or distinctive about these particular men's desires, it is just that they are less well equipped (in terms of economic power, physical appearance and/or social skills) . . . to achieve the degree of access to British women they would like.' At this point it is worth reflecting back to those mill girls and boys in Blackpool in 1939. The Mass Observation team found that the majority of men could find a partner in the close knit industrial communities they came from and did not expect a more sexually charged time from their holiday. Perhaps, as a result of their reliance mainly on *visual* data, their own observations did not lead them to instances of casualties of love and courtship, those too unattractive to be successful. However, in many parts of the industrial world, women were not employed past a certain age and became dependent on finding a husband. In this way, perhaps most men with a regular job *were* attractive as husbands even if they were not attractive per se. On the other hand, the close-knit nature of communities and factory lives made it possible to meet potential partners in a way the more fragmented workplaces and more privatised neighbourhoods of today may not. Today women have greater work and career equality and finding a husband does not rank so highly and urgently as it once did; and arguably there is now a more intense sensitivity to body and beauty than perhaps there was in the 1930s. This means perhaps that finding a partner has become more fraught and frustrating even for those with the average charms and looks. That so many can sympathise with the man troubles of someone so obviously attractive as Bridget Jones, reveals something about this tension.

Sex tourism for men *and* women

Which is not to say that all sex tourists to places like Thailand correspond to the very specific characteristics of the British men O'Connell Davidson interviewed. Thai sex venues attract men from all over Europe, the Middle East, Australasia and Asia and clearly their cultural backgrounds and gender relations 'at home' would enter into any analysis of their desire for sex tourism. However, at a general level we can say that throughout the world sexual taboos are often stringent, freedom of sexual access is often obstructed and difficult and the attainment of sexual pleasure is often blocked by social, economic or physical intervention. At the same time, the media and cultural forces of globalisation pour out a steady stream of suggestions and images that sexual pleasure, fulfilment and fantasy are not only desirable but also properly attainable, healthy and good. Here is the Dionysian impulse being projected onto a global screen and all forms of repression and denial of the body are being eroded.

We can begin to see this perhaps in the growing literature on relatively wealthy middle class women who travel on their own or with friends to exotic African and Caribbean venues where a similarly 'open-ended' sex trade has developed with local attractive young men. Pruitt and LaFont (1995) use the interesting euphemism 'romance tourism' for this activity, a term not applied to men when they are the affluent tourists sexually exploiting local youth. Dahles and Bras use a similar euphemism to describe the beach boys who have sex with western female tourists, they call them 'entrepreneurs in romance'. To an extent, this is understandable, particularly because the men involved are usually fully adult, free agents as opposed to the (often) debt-bonded sex slaves, children and very young teenagers in Thailand and elsewhere. But still, it is interesting that when affluent western women are doing the exploiting it is not seen in quite so sordid terms as when it is unattractive working class white men. Pruitt and LaFont (1995) make it clear that the women they studied found their power in these circumstances to be part of the reward:

> The economic and social status the women enjoy provides them with a security and independence that translates into power and control in the relationship. Some of the women enjoy the control they have in these relationships and express a preference for keeping a man dependent on them. (Pruitt and LaFont, 1995: 427; cited in Opperman, 1999: 260)

As Oppermann observes, the more women increase their economic and social standing around the world 'one might expect more and more female sex tourists and consequently more male sex providers serving female tourists' (Opperman, 1999: 260). And again, with these sorts of relationships, neither side likes to consider it prostitution and indeed it is so diffused in courtship and partnership behaviour that it neither 'looks like it' nor even feels like it. This is all the more so because of 'traditions' of mistressing and toy boys among affluent European circles. And this is not at all new, nor even particularly well hidden. For example, readers of Henry Fielding will recall that his hero, Tom Jones, found himself the long-term sexual plaything of a wealthy countess when he was down on his luck visiting London.

Albuquerque's (1998) research in the Caribbean identified four types of female sex tourist: *neophyte first timers*; *situational sex tourists* who have sex with local beach boys and others if, and when (ever) the situation arises; *veterans* who travel to these places specifically for the sex and *returnees* who visit a man encountered on previous visits. Similar results from Barbados are reported by Phillips (1999: 190–1). According to this research, Ryan and Hall (2001: 60) argue another parallel with male sex tourists: '[t]hus like O'Connell Davidson's pictures of males who are balding, ageing and overweight, so too a similar picture might be painted of the female sex tourist. Just as Thai bar girls target their "partners", so too do beach boys. The parallels and complexities of who is exploited and who exploits exist regardless of the gender of the sex tourist; and equally it may be said, any picture painted of these complexities says as much of the researcher as well as the researched. Are . . . all sex tourists really so physically unappealing?'

Sex workers

Finally, what about the prostitutes themselves and prostitution more generally? How should we evaluate ethically and politically these complicated social relationships. On the one hand, we might act along with the Dionysian impulses and say that liberating the body sexually has to be a good thing and that we should not censor or seek to ban the sex industry, only regulate those aspects of it that are illegal or contravening of human rights (see Ryan and Hall, 2001, chapter 6 for a full discussion of these issues). On the other, we might act with more Apollonian vigour and seek to curb it as far as possible on the grounds that it is producing intractable problems (rising HIV/AIDS; sexual exploitation of young children; slavery and debt bondage; reproducing economics and relations of dependency and inequality; patriarchal domination and so forth). Another view holds that whatever one might want to do on ethical and political grounds the current market for sex will be too difficult to regulate; that too many people and organisations have a finger in the pie (from taxi drivers, to bar owners, to clubs, theatres, resorts, hotels, local law enforcement agencies and government).

Similarly, how should we view the lifestyle and lives of the sex workers? There seem to be three broad views here. Again, according to Seabrooke (1996) and others, we might view prostitution as necessarily demeaning, exploitative and dangerous – whatever the circumstances, but perhaps especially where poor developing countries are targeted by richer developed countries. This was a widely held view about the sex tourism trade until recently. A second, and more recent view is that the sex tourism industries are so diverse, and within them the lives of prostitutes so varied that such a sweeping view is misplaced. Some women *are* duped into travelling to what they think will be better-paid work in a foreign country but on arrival they find themselves having to pay back debts through enforced sex work. *Equally*, some children *are* stolen and locked up in brothels, away from the eye of the public or regulating authorities. However, we know that a large proportion of sex workers in Thailand, for example, are voluntary prostitutes who do this work because they prefer it to other forms of work and lifestyles. Many of the bar girls in Thailand like the life they lead; they stay for a considerable time in the exciting touristic centres, eating at good restaurants, sipping drinks beside pools in luxury hotels and being bought fine clothes and gifts. They are, to a degree, independent free agents and although they may not always relish every man they spend time with, not all of them are so very bad. After all, as the research we have cited has found, many of the men fall in love with them and their relationships are at least tender and cordial. They also earn more money than they would otherwise; they are able to buy good new clothes and maintain themselves in styles and fashions of their choosing; and they are able to drink, party and take drugs commensurate with a lifestyle they enjoy. The beach boys are similarly calculating free agents whose lifestyle aims attract them to an association with wealthy tourists; in addition to the money, gifts and high life, there is also the chance of an invitation to travel themselves, to visit 'girlfriends' they met on their beach. In other words, there is a strategy, benefit and lifestyle that attracts young people into being 'providers'.

Conclusion

From surfing to wine tourism via eco-tourism and sex adventures and adrenalin sports, part three has explored the bourgeoning dimensions of embodied and sensual tourisms. These tourisms are predicated on the relatively new and diverse technologies of and attention to the body. These examples show that even though the visual tourist gaze is still a major feature of tourism, there is a trend towards more active, muscular and sensual objectives. Thrift offered some useful explanations of these new trends as well as the manner by which the body produces new apprehensions and spaces of nature. In a postmodern world bombarded by images and signs and the technologies of 'fast time' people have sought to resist it through developing body practices that value the *present moment*, rather than spearing off into the future. If tourism explanations offered by most theorists agree that tourism is predicated on a restlessness, movement and a fleeting attention to the tourist moment, then these activities point in the opposite direction: they seek to extend and savour the present moment by slowing down time. This was seen in a variety of ways, in climbing, in eco-tourism, in surfing (through the concept of flow) and in wine tasting where the experience is unhurried, studious and where the ultimate pleasure is the length of time a wine stays on the tongue. Importantly, this analysis is consistent with a major theme in this book, that touristic practices have a ritualistic and performative dimension in which tourists experience transition and change. In these activities, we have seen how nature is inscribed on the body, how moments of ecstasy are reached and how the technologies of the body enable sensual and muscular exfoliations that reach out to natural objects. These are tourisms that go beyond the naïve hope for better health that our Blackpool holidaymakers anticipated in the late 1930s, or for a cure for illness among nineteenth century spa-goers. These were relatively passive tourists in comparison to some of the tourists we have met in this chapter. To repeat a line from earlier in this chapter, these new tourist practices with their emphasis on the body and physical experience constitute an aesthetic reflexivity that enables sensual and emotional experiences to be recognised as inherently worthwhile. They are worthwhile because they generate transformative and pleasurable effects, carving a liminal space away from the tyrannies of fast time.

Further Reading

Dahles, H. and Bras, K. (1999) 'Entrepreneurs in romance', *Annals of Tourism Research* 26 (2): 267–93.

Kruhse-MountBurton, S. (1995) 'Sex tourism and traditional Australian male identity' in M.E Lanfant, J.B. Allcock, and E.M. Bruner (eds), *International Tourism: Identity and Change*. London: Sage.

O'Connell Davidson, J. (1995) 'British sex tourists in Thailand' in M. Maynard and J. Purvis (eds), *(Hetero)Sexual Politics*. London: Taylor and Francis.

Ryan, C. and Hall, M. (2001) *Sex Tourism*. London: Routledge.

Seabrooke, J. (1996) *Travels in the Skin Trade: Tourism and the Sex Industry*. London: Pluto Press.

Truong, T-D. (1990) *Sex, Money and Morality: Prostitution and Tourism in South-East Asia*. London: Zed Books.

10

Conclusion – A world of tourism

Now everything arrives without the need to depart.

(Virilio, 1999: 20)

It is a cliché to say that we live in an ever-changing world but sorting out how it has changed and how it has a bearing on the way we live our lives remains a permanent challenge for sociologists, anthropologists, geographers and historians. I began this book by questioning the wisdom of some explanations of tourism, such as that of MacCannell (1976) writing in the mid-1970s and Urry (1990) writing at the end of the 1980s. Although there are many others we might mention, we can single these two out in particular because they established such a firm grip on the future direction of thinking, researching and writing about tourism. This is because these texts were written as, or at least *became* general theories of tourism. They became authorities, standard reading, course books and benchmarks. However, that such great books should last forever is asking too much because they, like everything, were creations of a different world from that of the present; in at least two ways. First, they were written when the world and the tourism that took place in it were different. The modernity of the 1970s was a good deal less travelled and mobile than the world we occupy for example, though that mobility was just 'taking off'. Indeed, it was the very possibility of more and cheaper international mobility that was at least influential over the sorts of things people went to see and wanted to see. Crudely, we can say that in the 1970s it became possible for the swelling ranks of affluent Americans and Europeans to travel *outside* their nation states and geographical regions. As they did so they revisited the sensibilities of the Grand Tour of the nineteenth century, when only the intrepid travelling upper class could afford the time and the journey. In particular, they made contrasts with the simpler, less hectic and less changing worlds outside the modernised west, favourable contrasts that gathered pace to quite a crescendo of self-doubt and panic about the liquid nature of modernity – constantly becoming less solid, constantly in flux, leaving nothing as it was. In sum, it produced an anxiety of authenticity, and an ethic of conservation and a Romantic orientation to cultures of the Other. In this way, we can understand MacCannell's *The Tourist* to be anchored in a general feature or concern of the day. These characteristics of permanent liquidity and flux we now seem to accept, or at least many of us do, and we see them as inevitable and even exciting. Bauman (1998a; 2000) argues that as children of consumerism we crave and need change; we don't want satisfaction, we want to live in a constant state of desire – for new things to consume, new technologies, new experiences. We do not idolise those who live outside the modern west in quite the same naïve, inexperienced way; we see them desperately scrambling over the border from Mexico to the USA, we see them dangerously mounting the undercarriage of fast trains bound for London via the Channel tunnel, we see crumbling, dangerous ships overloaded with refugees from Afghanistan or 'boat people' from south-east Asia. We know that they are not only running away from troubled times and unreliable economies in their homeland but that on balance life is better and more peaceful in the west. Many of those Romantic places that were travelled to by the 1970s tourist questing for the authentic are now too dangerous or as likely sullied by civil war, economic depression, famines, religious oppression or, equally common, their inhabitants are resentful of what is for them the metaphor of the west, the *affluent tourist*. 'We' do not live in places dominated by 'us' any more; other cultures are all around us in cities teeming with difference and differentiating so quickly we do not have time to appreciate precisely how things have changed or make new social arrangements (see Bauman, 2001). Moreover, some of the things that signalled the authentic lives of others are freely available in every city in the world because cities and their incredible ethnic diversity have become the places where the world outside now flows.

But we got bored of the authenticity debate quite a long time ago both as consumers and as academics (see Howell, 1995, for example) and we now accept that everything has a claim to authenticity; everything has a unique cultural content, even fakes. More than that, the hyperreal world as explored by Baudrillard (1983), Eco (1987) and as applied to the analysis of leisure and travel by Rojek (1993; 1995) is now the normative world we live in. It is a world of fakes, reproductions, fusions, hybrids and so forth and computer-driven simulation electronics enable (almost) everyone to be quite creative within this graphical, visual infinity. We don't mind this sort of thing because it cannot be exhausted; it is a parallel universe in which we have more mobility and agency, where everyone is creative, everyone is an artist, authentic, original. The Internet has made us 'supertourists' speeding around the world faster than any machine could possibly travel and we have become sated with viewing the world in this way: it can make seeing the real thing something of an anticlimax. Was the object's website better than the object itself, we might ask? Samuel Johnson was perhaps the first to anticipate the problem we have today in deciding the value of a mere sight. When James Boswell asked him on October 12, 1779 'Is not the Giant's Causeway worth seeing?' Johnson is said to have replied: 'Worth seeing? Yes; but not worth going to see' (*Columbia World of Quotations*, 2002: 31288).

John Urry's *The Tourist Gaze* has to be understood as arising from the life, times and tourisms of hyperreality. As we have seen, Urry was particularly inspired by the work of Foucault who raised the visual apprehension of the world and visual technologies from intellectual obscurity to centre stage. The command and use of vision and surveillance were key ways in which modernity was articulated and ordered, and his all-seeing panopticon metaphor inspired a useful re-analysis of tourism (see Urry, 1990 and especially Crawshaw and Urry, 1997). *The Tourist Gaze* was written at a time when the sign and symbolisation of an object were becoming ever more significant than the thing itself, an observation that gave his book a critical distance from *The Tourist* with its emphasis on the authenticity and aura of the object itself. Urry placed tourism into an economy of signs, an analysis of postmodernity that preceded his successful and influential book, *Economies of Signs and Space* that he co-authored with Scott Lash. This view of modernity enabled him to reinterpret what was happening at tourist sites and what tourists were doing at them. Tourist spaces were ordered by the manipulation of signs, relating visual information to key discourses that warrant their use. Robin Hood country, around the city of Nottingham, UK is replete with all manner of signs pointing the tourist along the Greenwood trail, and the master discourse is of course the stories of Robin Hood.

However, of course, the modern cafés and recently renamed pubs that bear the name of Robin Hood's this or Maid Marian's that are all fakes since in this case the discourse itself is a story. The sliding of signs away from their authenticating objects and their replication in multiple forms is precisely what happens at tourist sites and centres and they are organised in such a way that tourists can line them up in their sight, photograph them perhaps and leave. Here we can move to Urry's explanation of tourist behaviour. In focusing on a restless wish to see, record and move on, Urry attributes a shallowness to the habits of tourists. They were collectors of signs, a fact hardly to be missed by the obsessive snapping of every view and the consumption of tourist souvenirs to authenticate their presence before the appropriate signs of iconic places. The essential motive of the tourist was to get away from the everyday in order to experience the pleasures of seeing new and unusual things, but once seen the pleasure ebbed away very quickly, producing a characteristic restlessness. This restlessness derives from at least two factors. First, since it is the visualisation of objects of tourism that is critical, requiring a relatively brief time span, the essential work of the tourist is over very quickly at any one site. Parallel to the work of sighting is the cognitive assembling of the object into its master discourse and then the gathering and filing away of the experience in the form of photos, postcards and other souvenirs. It is

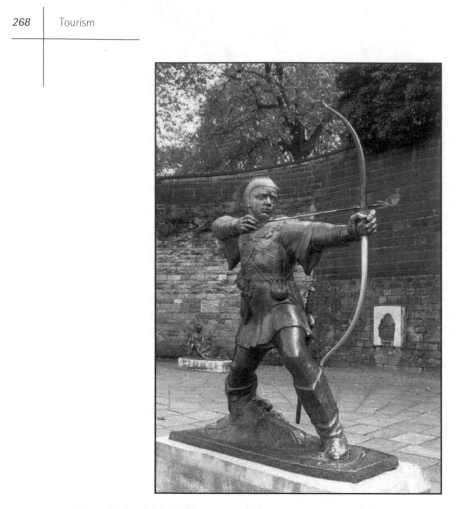

Figure 10.1 *Robin Hood statue*

work that can be done on the run in the interest of maximising the collection. Second, this restlessness relates to the general conditions of consumption in postmodernity, particularly as a result of the proliferation and reproduction of objects, signs and simulations. Magazines are flicked through, TV channels switched and hopped between and shopping also involves this overloading of information and things vying for attention.

So, Urry's *The Tourist Gaze* can be situated in the intellectual and cultural currents of its time and has continuing relevance to the degree that this culture of tourism persists. However, in this book I have made several criticisms of his approach and its continuing relevance. There are three that I want to pursue here in summary form. The first is that the tourist gaze is only a partial aspect of tourism, even in the early 1990s when the book was first received. We have seen in various chapters that sighting objects and the restless itinerary were only one dimension of tourism and others were very different. The more recent interest in the sociology of the body has focused attention on the other senses and other embodied activities. Seaside and beach holidays were analysed in closer detail in this book as a result of these insights. Here we saw a different tourist, a dancing tourist – literally, dancing each night away and many afternoons too; the dancing tourist was also a drinking, drunk and occasionally a disordered tourist; we saw a sexual tourist working hard at finding partners and enjoying the frisson of holiday romance and sex; we saw a devotional, restful tourist attending to the health and looks of their body in the slow time of sunbathing, sitting on deckchairs, taking in the sea air; we have seen the interpellated tourist experiencing the embodied sensations of nationalism or ethnic identity or the recall of personal and family memory, or the pleasures of the tourist machines, steam trains and jets that frighten us but which at the same time, take over responsibility, offering a regime and space of care and extending a fatalistic trust in them.

All of these activities challenge the centrality of the gaze and call into doubt the general claim that what tourists seek is the pleasures of the new and unusual. So, my second criticism is that tourists are doing more than being pleasured by the new and unusual, and it seems to me that in a great many cases, they are seeking some sense of personal change, growth or transition. Over several chapters, including those covering tourisms of nature, seaside, and heritage, I have argued that the individual anticipation and *performance* of transition is a common feature of tourism, and in this sense, it is more like pilgrimage than carnivalesque. I have therefore placed more emphasis on rituals of tourism than many other accounts. Ritual performances link the tourist body with tourist places and objects; I have shown how tourists become involved in devotional behaviour before a great variety of objects that have become personally meaningful to them. With seasides and beach holidays, the tourist body has devoted itself to the sea and sun, seeking the transition into health, vigour and vital appearance. Ritual clothing appropriate to the cults of the sun, surf, serious walker, climber and so forth help mark off the devotee from the mundane world from which they are temporarily suspended and even the less obviously focused forms of tourist wear clothing marking them out as tourists. The performance of heritage tourism is highly varied, but as Crang (1994: 344–5) argues, the educated elites cultivate ritual competences to enjoy it: 'These rituals give distinctive opportunities for certain groups to acquire cultural capital . . . the practice appears as part of a positive attitude to the future not as a compensatory, nostalgic gesture to social dislocation'. Again, these sorts of contemporary ritual are typical of rituals of passage generally, they are about individual transition and change, they typically involve promotion or improvement and they are future orientated (Jervis, 1998).

However, we can locate specific forms of ritual enactment to different problems and pathologies of their period. Thus the medicinal tourisms of the spa towns and medicinal beach resorts related to health anxieties in a period prior to the dramatic control of diseases such as tuberculosis, venereal diseases and many skin diseases. As we have seen, mass seaside holidays of the twentieth century were complex activities; the belief in the restorative benefits of the seaside continued in a much stronger form than is often portrayed, and places such as Blackpool addressed illness as a central activity. However, just as ritual devotions to heritage deliver cultural capital to the social elites, Blackpool and places like it delivered an advanced and magical world of consumerism to those largely embedded in the social relations of producer society. As Tony Bennett (1983: 146) argues, '[f]rom its early days as a seaside resort the by-word of Blackpool, recurring again and again in its publicity brochures, has been *progress*.' Aside from initiating the mill workers to the bright lights of advanced technology and superstore consumerism, new technologies were utilised to give experiences of machinic pleasure in the liminoid spaces of the white-knuckle ride: 'for the most part, however, the Pleasure Beach addresses – indeed assaults – the body, suspending the physical laws that normally restrict its movement, breaking the social codes that normally regulate its conduct, inverting the usual relations between the body and machinery and generally inscribing the body in relations different from those in which it is caught and held in everyday life' (Bennett, 1983: 147–8). More recently, as I argued in the latter chapters of the book, the new tourism of the body that employs body expanding technologies, involves a highly ritualised world that appears to seek transition and relief from the maddening world of hyperreality and fast time. Thrift (2001) and Hylland Eriksen (2001) argue that the appeal of nature in contemporary times can be understood in these terms and a wide variety of body technologies that resemble prayer, meditation, trance and chant have been employed to expand the experience of the present; cutting liminoid moments of ecstasy from the go-faster world we live in. So for example, activities such as surfing, climbing and skiing take the body to points of concentration and skill where it appears to lose its separation from the natural world and fuses with it in brief moments of ecstasy. These activities, now referred to as high adrenalin activities on *The Times*' travel pages, are joined by slower but equally contemplative tourisms: wilderness retreats, trekking, walking, fly fishing, cross-country skiing and so forth. Through particular physical and technical activities, the body extends itself out into associations with aspects of the natural world, its rhythms and communities.

This brings me to my third criticism, which concerns the way in which the world of *The Tourist Gaze* and most other texts, make a claim for a separable world of tourism from the everyday, a world in which the new and unusual form the focus for depthless experiences of pleasure. Clearly, in the case of the nature-orientated, body-technique tourisms, the practice and mastery of techniques is a world of familiarity and repetition that is based on the continuity and improvement of an individual's body. Tourists cannot escape their own bodies, nor, if their *motives* were as I suggest, would they want to. In Chapter 3, I also spent some time discussing the extent and prevalence of repeat tourism, where people return to the same place, where the familiar is precisely the object of their travel. In some cases, this is to places from which people migrated and where they continue to maintain an association, and to this we can add what is often described as family tourism, where one visits one's family living or working far away – a more typical arrangement now. In other cases, some towns and regions have developed an aesthetic connection to particular areas of forest, mountain or coastline and have established a regularised visitor presence there. These cases undermine our confidence in a theory that places the need for difference and the unusual as the principal motive for tourism. However, one of the main arguments of this book is that increasingly the difference between the everyday and spaces of tourism has become blurred if not collapsed. To be more precise, I have argued that almost everywhere has become mantled with touristic properties, and that our stance to the world we live in whether at home or away, has become increasingly touristic. In a globalised world where old certainties and differences have disappeared and where new mixes and hybrids seem to be an increasing part of our experience, we draw on our experience and skills as a tourist to make sense of it and to consume it. It is impossible now to conceive of contemporary societies as constituted by particular and singular social orders, pursued by clear-thinking, visionary governments of the sort that created stable nation states in the early part of the twentieth century. With the collapse, particularly of the socialist command economies and the western welfare states, and the arrival of fundamentally disordering and globally co-present neo-liberal regimes, we cannot point to a social order anymore, only orderings, cultural configurations that create particular arrangements and consequences such as consumerism itself, environmentalism, feminism, or cosmopolitanism. Tourism has ordered some of the ways in which globalisation has proceeded and been experienced; an interesting ordering that has reproduced itself over and over again, turning more and more surfaces of the everyday into objects of touristic consumption. Indeed, there are now very few places that are not touristic in some sense or another, and those that have escaped touristification themselves are likely to be profoundly influenced by nearby places that have been. I refer you again to the quotations at the beginning of Chapter 2 by way of underlining this point.

This view of tourism in the twenty-first century results, of course, from the very specific conditions of change that have occurred over recent years. Important among these are the ways in which we have all been drawn into a consumerist society. According to Bauman, this means we are no longer looking to satisfy ourselves from consumption but to use the promise of consumption to fuel more dreams, longings and desires. We desire not satisfaction but desire itself and therefore we are in a permanently restless craving for the new. This of course is related to the way tourism has often been conceived but it is now a general and extensive feature of everyday consumerism, not confined to certain magical spaces such as Blackpool in the 1950s. The consumer fantasies and ritual enactments of progress at seasides have to all intents and purposes been realised, and although advanced technologies continue to attract us and Blackpool Pleasure Beach continues to be the single biggest tourist attraction in the UK, technological advances are all around us. Most of us have more things and change in our lives than we can adequately manage, and this is true particularly of our experience of the personal computers that so many of us use. As each year passes personal computers get more and more sophisticated and as each year passes we seem to know less and less about them, or at least, we are less able to keep up with their progress. As the users of the web now swell to include the majority in many places in the west, virtual tourism has brought the sites into our living rooms, and an overload of visual information that seems oppressive rather than pleasurable after a while. As it becomes overabundant and so easily accessible, we begin to tire of it or at least to become blasé. At the very least, it stifles the urgency and desire to visit them in real life, with all the attendant problems and hardships of travel noted in Chapter 1.

In addition, globalisation has brought so much of the world onto our doorsteps. We can access the Mediterranean foods that only tourism provided in the 1960s; we can access Indian spices, foods and condiments that only adventurous tourists sampled in the 1970s; and Japanese sushi, the discovery of the 1980s, is available in every city of the world. These foods and other global commodities flow to our cities for two main reasons. First, as a result of a globalisation of tourism, western taste has been rendered more cosmopolitan. It is no longer good enough merely to eat a national cuisine. One's cultural capital these days is measured by the global reach of one's taste and experience. Once global cosmopolitan taste had run out of significantly different cuisines, in the most travelled culture of the world, Australia, the experimentation with fusions began. Now foods are no longer pegged to ethnic or national cuisines and we can expect fusions to characterise the foods we eat whether we live in Melbourne, London or Los Angeles. In other words, the most exotic and new emerge in the everyday and require little travel.

The second way global things flow to our cities is from migration, diasporas, refugees and labour markets that involve more and more people working away from home, sometimes thousands of miles away. Expatriate communities of a bewildering variety now live in all major cities, and their foods, commodities, clothing, music, dance – indeed their entire culture – are freely available on our doorstep. The exotic other is no longer what we dream of seeing on adventurous holidays; they are our neighbours, our schoolchildren's friends and our colleagues at work.

To compound our sense that the difference between the everyday and tourist spaces have collapsed we have only to look at the reverse experience. Just as we find the exotic other on our doorstep, so we also find *ourselves* and the western 'everyday' increasingly when we travel abroad. Western penetration of the world or what Ritzer (1992) calls 'McDonaldization', means that we find that cities around the world come to look more and more like each other. I was astounded to see so many English pubs in

Oslo and dumbfounded when I found a favourite beer brewed in my home English county on sale in the local Norwegian supermarket. Norway no longer seemed to hold integrity as a singularly different place. More shocking still, I discovered that large numbers of Norwegians left every Thursday or Friday on trips to watch UK premier league football matches. Downtown, there were shops full of Manchester United, Liverpool and Arsenal merchandise. But then there is such a shop in Singapore Airport with exactly the same goods with a TV screen showing premier league matches 24-hours a day and this is repeated all around the world. We could all write our list of similar surprises but underpinning most of these experiences is the characteristic presence of all the global corporations and chains; the Mitsubishi trucks and 'utes'; crates of Coca Cola; Canon photocopiers, McDonald's, Body Shop, Gap, the latest film releases, the current computer games. Increasingly then, when we travel we do not get away from the everyday; like tourism itself, it has come to be more or less everywhere the same.

Finally, the tourist world, where more or less every surface has been rendered consumable in a touristic way, has been completed by the sometimes-desperate search to market almost every conceivable place, past, nature, culture and activity to tourists. This has given tourists a bewildering choice of things to do wherever they go – and the growing size of tourist information leaflet stands in hotels is a register of this growth – but in addition, local people have benefited from the expansion of leisure activities to whom they are almost always very welcome. In places like the UK, which is compact spatially and densely populated with tourist sites, villages, towns and cities are all vying for the tourist pound. The almost universal availability of tourism spaces has changed the pattern of leisure in the UK as a result. With much faster personal and organised transport, afternoon drives, day trips, overnight stays and weekends have added a considerable scope to the tourism industry but also to tourists themselves. I have argued that people are not only tourists more often, but also that the way they relate to the changing world around them has borrowed from their skills as observant, ever-interested and keen-to-experience tourists.

Tourism has given us the ability and desire to track the endless production of the new and the churning nature of modernity, and perhaps also to feel more comfortable with its steady state of change. I have suggested in various places that some forms of tourism actually relate to this potentially alienating feature of modernity, since it allows initiates to come before the new and the unknown in an open, relaxed, enthusiastic and even celebratory manner. The great 'world' exhibitions of the nineteenth and twentieth centuries were set up in just this way; they set out things and technologies at the forefront of progress and fashion in a way that suggested few people knew about them. To visit was to glimpse the future as it unfolded, and this became a much repeated and successful transcendent experience for modern cultures. The advanced technological white-knuckle rides have something of this about them, as do the latest tourist crowd-pullers, the new shrines to modern art, such as the Guggenheim Museum, now with branches at New York, Venice, Bilbao, Berlin and Las Vegas. One can say that understanding modernity itself is one of the projects and appeals of modern art but the intellectual difficulty of this terrain meant it was a relatively minor shrine for intellectual tourism until the late 1990s. This timing is interesting since it coincides with the point where the breathless enthusiasm for the past and heritage, which was established in the 1970s and taken to great heights in the 1980s, began to wane. During the 1990s, much greater interest seemed to gather around the idea of modernity and the future. The Guggenheim opened its Berlin and Bilbao branches in the last years of the 1990s and its Las Vegas Gallery in 2001. London's Tate Modern, which opened in 2000, has been inundated by visitors and the London skyline, once defended by the patrons of heritage against modernism, has been finally ruptured by modern architectural projects. The latest, Renzo Piano's 2002 proposal The Shard of Glass – a tall building in the form a glass spike – looks set to be built. If we stay with the work of Piano, we can make a further comment, that modern architecture and tourism have a longstanding relationship that supports the view that much modern tourism is orientated to the new and the future. Of course, the image chosen for Urry's *The Tourist Gaze* was none other than Delaunay's *La Tour Eiffel* of 1926, which was built to showcase the Paris Exhibition. But less iconic sites have also used modern architecture for touristic effects. This is nowhere clearer than at Blackpool where the leading modernist architect Joseph Emberton redesigned the 'Imperial-looking' Pleasure Beach after the manner of 1930s modernism, providing a wall of clean white buildings with smooth lines; it was state of the art functionalism and in places, cubism. This 'effect' could not last long given the association of pleasure, tourism and progress. In the 1950s the designer of the 1951 Festival of Britain, Jack Radcliffe, was commissioned 'to give it a new look – largely by superimposing an American jazz and glitter on Emberton's clean white facades' (Bennett, 1983: 145). Modernist architects build for all manner of clients but it is notable how many projects fall within spaces of tourism. Twelve of Piano's twenty-two projects of the 1990s were tourist spaces, including the Jean Marie Tjibaou Cultural Center, New Caledonia (1991); the Cy Twombly Gallery, Houston, Texas (1993–5); The Reconstruction of the Potsdamer Platz, Berlin (1996–2000); The Paul Klee Museum, Bern (1999) and the Nasher Sculpture Center, Dallas, Texas (1999-   ).

So tourism is, as Meethan (2001) argues, an expression of consumerism but I would want to say that it is in part a particular form of consumerism, a curiosity endemic to modern cultures born in a constant state of change, novelty, progress and the compelling nature of universal, overarching concerns; those of geography, environment and nature; those of history, the arts and politics; those of peace, trade and communication. However, tourisms of the contemporary period are tempered by the position people occupy in global modernity. First of all globalisation itself keeps many people on the road, in airport lounges, travelling to corporate meetings, conventions and conferences. Globalisation normalises tourism as part of everyday work. The convention trade is enormous and one of the reasons why the biggest tourism centres, those cities of the major airline hubs, compete so aggressively for visitor flows, for sporting competitions such as the World Cup and Olympic Games, for political conventions and conferences, for summit meetings and peace processes, as well as corporate and academic conventions and conferences. Those who travel great distances for work do have days off for tourism and travel but the place of travel in their lives is often viewed as a burden, and a hassle. Being constantly on the move may be as tiring as not moving at all, but certainly it contributes to the sensation that the world is speeding up, and results in demands for activities that slow it all down, of which more below.

It is not just the executive class spending more time on the road and up in the air. The numbers of people working away from home (staying some part of the week or month in another place), for example, is now very significant, over 10 per cent in many places in Europe. Equally, some countries have many of their population working in other countries; in the case of the Philippines, for example, over 6.5 million are currently working overseas. This not only contributes to the numbers on the road or up in the air, it also contributes to the growing sense that more or less everyone is a migrant of one sort or another, so that even the locality in which one works may be experienced with something of the thrill of the tourist. Julian et al. (1997) discovered that refugees resettled in Australia experience profound social and cultural displacement but also the frisson of excitement that goes with living in a new culture, especially Australia where leisure and tourism are part of everyday life. We also saw in Chapter 9 how relatively poor prostitutes travel from the poorer countries to work the convention trade and the major tourist nodes. Moreover, Bauman (1998b) reminds us that although the entire world is now on the move, the affluent travel as tourists, couched in comfort and mantled with pleasurability, while the less affluent travel as *vagabonds*:

> For the inhabitants of the first world – the increasingly cosmopolitan, extraterritorial world of global businessmen, global culture managers or global academics, state borders are levelled down, as they are dismantled for the world's commodities, capital and finances. For the inhabitant of the second world, the walls built of immigration controls, of residence laws and of 'clean streets' and 'zero tolerance' policies, grow taller; the moats separating them from the sites of their desires and of dreamed of redemption grow deeper, while all the bridges, at the first attempt to cross them turn out to be drawbridges. The first travel at will, get much fun from their travel (particularly if travelling first class or using a private jet), are cajoled or bribed to travel and welcomed with smiles and open arms when they do. The second travel surreptitiously, often illegally, sometimes paying more for the crowded steerage of a stinking unseaworthy boat than others pay for business class gilded luxuries – and are frowned upon, and, if unlucky, arrested and promptly deported, when they arrive. (Bauman, 1998b: 89)

Such flows of people are now creating major panics around the world. In 2001, the Tampa affair in Australia and Prime Minister John Howard's firm stand against asylum-seekers is said to have won him the election. In 2002, Italy declared a state of emergency when it was discovered that thousands of asylum-seekers were permeating its less patrolled borders and disappearing into national life, largely thanks to the cultural anonymity and mobility supplied by tourism. Such people are likely to end up, in one way or another, as Bauman's vagabonds, joining the poor echelons of every nation. Bauman describes the poor in the west as tied to space, which becomes 'heavy, resilient, untouchable, which ties them down and keeps it beyond the resident's control'. Unlike the jetting businessmen, such people yearn to be tourists and dream the sorts of dream that the mill workers of Lancashire dreamed in the 1930s of a few days or a week away, exposed to the faster time of modernisation, the new magical rides of modernity and a powerful sense of personal transition and change.

Wanting to get away is still a feature of contemporary tourism, though what people want to escape to or from is an interesting and I suspect contingent question. With the exception of those who are poor or tied in some other way to a restricted space, where nothing ever happens (and time 'is void' Bauman, 1998b: 88), for most people now life is so hectic, and things changing so rapidly that the last thing we want when the wheels are made to stop, is to tie ourselves to hectic itineraries of the sort that characterised earlier cultural tourisms. As I have shown in the later chapters, a new pattern is beginning to emerge, in which, if I can generalise, people caught up in the contemporary fast-time world are seeking in one form or another, respite, shelter, relief, rest or, interestingly, the ritualised space of the present.

So, we can say with some certainty that when most people wish to get away, it is more than ever to escape the stresses and strains of fast-time living. They do not need more stimulation, and the new and the different have become exhaustingly ever-present. Their work may not be boring or uncreative but it might be unremitting and pressured. Rather, in a great many cases people seek quietness, stillness, rest and recreation. Of course it is becoming quite normal for people to escape work *and* tourism in their precious time away, and to state with some triumph that they are staying at home, pottering, doing a spot of gardening, going out to cafés, reading books, trying new restaurants or just vaguely lounging about. It is true too, that there is a residuum of local life – often designed as much for tourists as local people – that somehow manages to escape those caught up in everyday life. In other words, as I have stressed in this book, we can be tourists more or less anywhere we want. However, for those with the energy and the resources to make trips, and to avail themselves of the relatively cheap access to resort destinations, the beach holiday has remained one of the most subscribed-to forms of tourism.

For this very reason rather more time has been dedicated to the beach, the seaside and the resort than in many other texts, and although I leave the economics and marketing of such places to specialist books on the subject, I have concentrated more on what beach tourists are actually doing. This has been done in various places, notably Chapter 6 on seasides itself, the section on surfing in Chapter 8 and Chapter 9 on sex. Critical here, I think, is the ritual space that the beach creates, its liminoid character that enables the rituals of transition to take place in a public space, set to one side, anti-structured, upside-down, and outside normal time, where the moment is suspended and held. Ritual spaces call forth ritual performance and ritual staging: participants dress for it, assemble for it, form a company of the beach and most importantly fall before the need to slow down, rest and devote time to exposing the body to sun, air and sea. Beaches are places where the body lies down for the most part. Swimming is rarely a muscular activity and although the number of beach-related activities seems to proliferate, the essential activity remains to prostrate oneself before the sun, if at all possible.

However, as I outlined in Chapter 8, slowing down the body and stretching the moment can be achieved in other ways, notably through the practice of body techniques where the mind becomes engrossed in contemplative requirements and where such concentrations of effort and skill break down the difference between the body and the natural surface with which it is engaged; where the techniques and tools extend the body outwards onto nature and where temporary moments of ecstasy or 'flow' are experienced. A great many activities seem to me to permit this sort of encounter, and in Chapter 8 I considered surfing and climbing as examples, but many of these focus on water, beach or ocean: sailing, surfboarding, diving, water skiing, white water rafting and canoeing. However, many of them utilise other natures in similar ways.

Nature, generally, has become a major tourism resource (see Franklin, 2002a) and many have seen this growth as evidence of a more embodied apprehension of the world in late modernity. It is interesting that in some of John Urry's more recent works (Macnaghten and Urry, 1998; 2001) sensing nature in touristic ways has been extended to senses other than the visual; however, in all of this discussion, it is the visual that remains dominant. In the fullest expression of this evaluation, in their chapter 'Sensing Nature', Macnaghten and Urry dedicated sixteen pages to the visual sense and just over six to all others. To their credit, their 2001 collection encouraged more elaborate embodied analyses and among them, the essay by Nigel Thrift established a more complex and plausible relationship between the body and nature through what he calls techniques and technologies of the body. These were considered in some depth in Chapter 8 and one can include walking, climbing, survival trekking, birding, fishing, hunting, skiing, running, mountain biking and cycling and many more. Despite their seemingly energetic and muscular nature, these sorts of activity merge the human body into the landscapes, soundscapes, smellscapes, rhythms and times of the natural world, inscribing nature on the body through characteristic effects (calluses and injuries on climbers' hands; muscle configurations for the runners and walkers, eye–body coordination among skiers etc.). Depending upon the activity the effects can be ecstatic, invigorating, energising, aesthetically and spiritually uplifting. Paradoxically, these effects are recreational leaving the tourist body positively changed and refreshed. They are not new effects and their value as an antidote to modern life has a long history (see Simmell, 1997a; 1997b) but their proliferation and extension in recent years *are* new and relate to a more frenzied modern life, more rationalised, more paced and more liquid in its changeability. In the example given of activities offered at Interlaken in the Swiss Alps in the 1960s and 2000s the change is very obvious. In the 1960s foreign tourists were ostensibly there for the intoxicating gazes; by the 2000s 'the alpine' was no longer appealing merely in visual terms, people were clearly going there *to do something* with it. The list of what tourists can now do exceeds what they could possibly have time to do; Thrift's essay strongly suggests that tourists to nature are now specialists, not just tourists but climbers, skiers, snowboarders, hikers, mountain-bikers, rafters and so forth. This of course chimes well with the way tourism has become segmented into specialist active tourisms, with their own companies, resorts, retreats, guides, camps and so forth.

The tourist body of the present is not of course the same as the tourist body of the 1820s, the 1930s, the 1950s or even the 1970s but to chart these bodies, as I have in this book, has enabled a different perspective on tourism to emerge. In the 2000s, the tourist body is attended to very carefully by the tourists themselves; as Lash (1993) argued, their aesthetic reflexivity in this period is new. '[W]ith its emphasis on the body and the physical experience as part of the reflexive self, aesthetic reflexivity enables the sensual and emotional experience to be recognised as inherently worthwhile' (Stranger, 2001). There is of course no limit to the lengths to which this aestheticisation process might go; no longer the tightly bound, regulated world of Victorian or Edwardian sexuality and its after-maths, from the 1970s onwards everyone and perhaps especially tourists were able to pursue sexuality more thoroughly. And as sex became yet another technology of the body, it was routinely included on touristic itineraries.

Postmodern conditions deregulated what came later to be known as 'the sex industry' making it more or less visible, tolerated and unfettered in many parts of the western world. Pornography became more widespread if not normative through the web; censorship was far more liberal and the taboos on non-heterosexual orientations were lifted to a considerable degree and attracted an air of 'fashionability'. For example, The Sydney Gay and Lesbian Mardi Gras and its equivalents elsewhere in San Francisco, Cape Town and Auckland have become major tourist draws for these cities.

However, it was to the pleasure periphery that sexual tourism found its most advanced expression and, in part, Chapter 9 investigated the anthro-pology of this phenomenon: an assorted mix of newly liberated and demanding sexualities of the west and an older sex industry founded initially on servicing wars in the Asian theatre. Sex and sexualities cannot escape the effects of globalisation and although it is possible to view much of this as sad and sordid, and the exercise of unbridled power and uncouth fantasy, it is also possible to see sex as yet another tourist economy in which the world is further transformed; where west meets east more intimately in a manner not completely unreciprocated. The research seems to show not a western sexual free-for-all but rather quite exceptional and unlucky men – from a variety of backgrounds whose paths to sexual fulfilment have been in various ways thwarted.

This book has aimed to rethink not only what tourism means and has meant as a changing form of social behaviour and practice, it has also rethought the place and role of tourism in a globalising world. I have rejected general and universalising theories either because they were theoretically partial or overly embedded in the social thought and anxieties of their day or because they were too anchored in a past that no longer applies. Tourism theory and explanation must always move with the cultural milieux in which they arise and this I have tried to do here. Most important of all, tourism cannot be treated like an industry separable from others and separable from social and cultural contexts. Many texts hide behind preposterous definitions and thereby fail to deliver a firm grasp of tourism, only the business practice that feeds expectantly off it. The tourism industry and the increasing numbers of lives dependent upon it should expect more from tourism studies, and this book is intended as a guide to a better understanding.

As a part of this I have emphasised areas and approaches that are new and very promising. I have emphasised the performative aspects of tourism and these not only give us more open-ended information on what tourists do and how that varies and changes, they also show how tourism can be seen as acts of self-discovery and self-making; that people become tourists and make sense of tourism in the process of performing it as tourists. This is also linked to the cultural conditions of modernity, as Jervis (1998) makes clear:

> Theatricality becomes a key mode of existence for the self in such a world of experience. It is a means whereby one can try on the mask of otherness, experience the world as other, while actively participating in it; and respond to the novelty of situations, in a context of endless flux and change, by drawing on a repertoire of rules and conventions. Through this, the passivity of experience can be fused with the active rehearsal and transformation of images and roles. Thus can the self learn to be multidimensional, adaptable, open to the variety of experiences made possible by modernity. (Jervis, 1998: 9)

There are only a few studies and books where this has been explored ethnographically and exhaustively in tourism locations. One of these is the exemplary *Tourists at the Taj* by Tim Edensor (1998).

Edensor also eschews general theories of tourism in favour of seeing it as *process*:

> The sheer variety of narrative tropes and performative conventions examined here seems to deny that tourism can be typified and classified. Instead, tourism is a set of contesting and ever-changing performances, focusing in this work on narration, walking, gazing, photographing and remembering. This is not intended to be an exhaustive list but designed to stress the ongoing, embodied, active nature of tourism as process. (Edensor, 1998: 200)

I have also emphasised the ritual nature of much tourism and tourism-related activities. In giving tourism this emphasis I am pointing to its more serious side, and particularly its perceived, hoped-for promise of personal growth, positive change and transformation and redemption – though even here such outcomes may be weakly present in tourists' minds and not fully realised until performed. Travel and tourism are hard work, beset with problems, hassles and risks, but the point is, it is worth it because of the multiple benefits it delivers, potentially. At the very least we can say that tourism is very often assumed to deliver some kind of catharsis, a ritual act of purification and deliverance. I do not think tourism is merely (or simply) reducible to pleasure itself, although of course, pleasure is as mixed in with contemporary tourism as it was in medieval pilgrimage. But just as one would not reduce the latter to pleasure-seeking, so one should avoid doing it with the former.

I have also tried to emphasise the fact that tourism belongs to a mobile, liquid modernity in which the older certainties that informed earlier tourism theory have vanished. Such certainties were based on a more differentiated world where one could distinguish leisure from work, home from away, the everyday from the touristic, our culture from their culture, nature from culture, the present from the past. But the collapse of a more differentiated, certain and ordered world does not therefore mean the end of tourism, far from it. This book argues that contemporary modernity is in part ordered by tourism, by a touristic stance to the world, by touristic abilities to make sense of and consume the world of flows, transformations and change wherever and everywhere they occur.

Further Reading

Tourism research will not solve some of the older debates and find a master theory of tourism because tourism, like the cultures that give rise to it, is a moving target. The metaphor of mobility for contemporary societies inspired a recent book by John Urry that overturns the older solid relations between home and away, the workaday and the holiday. *Sociology Beyond Societies – Mobilities for the Twenty-First Century* (London: Routledge, 2000) should inspire fresh evaluations of tourism. Equally, Bauman's *Liquid Modernity* (Cambridge: Polity, 2000) provides an excellent theoretical account of contemporary times and an inspiring framework for thinking about tourism. I have also found Jervis's two books *Exploring the Modern* (Oxford: Blackwell, 1998) and *Transgressing the Modern* (Oxford: Blackwell, 1999) to be full of connections between tourism and contemporary culture.

References

Abram, S. (1997) 'Performing for tourists in Rural France', in S. Abram, J. Waldren and D.V. Macleod (eds), *Tourists and Tourism*. Oxford: Berg.

Adler, J. (1989) 'Origins of Sightseeing', *Annals of Tourism Research* 16: 7–29.

Alexander, J.C. and Smith, P. (1996) 'Social Science and Salvation: Risk Society as Mythical Discourse', *Zeitschrift für Soziologie* 25 (4): 251–62.

Anderson, S.C. and Tabb, B. (eds) (2002) *Water, Leisure and Culture*. Oxford: Berg.

Ansell Pearson, K. (1997) *Viroid Life*. London: Routledge.

Ansell Pearson, K. (1999) *Germinal Life*. London: Routledge.

Anthony, S. (dir) (1998) *Witness*. (TV Documentary about British Naturism). London: Channel 4 Television (broadcast 22 November).

Appadurai, A. (ed.) (1986) *The Social Life of Things: Commodities in Cultural Perspective*. Cambridge: Cambridge University Press.

Ashworth, J.E. and Ashworth, G.J. (1996) *Dissonant Heritage*. New York: J. Wiley.

Augé, M. (1995) *Non-Places: Introduction to an Anthropology of Supermodernity*. London: Verso.

Australian Bureau of Statistics (2000) *Use of the Internet by Householders*. Canberra: ABS.

Baranay, I. (1995) *The Edge of Bali*. London: HarperCollins.

Batchen, G. (1988) 'Desiring Production Itself: Notes on the Invention of Photography' in R. Diprose and R. Ferrell (eds) *Cartographies*. London: Allen and Unwin.

Baudrillard, J. (1983) *Simulations*. New York: Semiotext.

Bauer, I.L. (2001) 'Tourism and the Environment, the Other Side of the Coin', *Tourist Studies* 1 (3): 297–314.

Bauman, Z. (1998a) *Work, Consumerism and the New Poor*. Buckingham: Open University Press.

Bauman, Z. (1998b) *Globalisation – The Human Consequences*. Oxford: Polity.

Bauman, Z. (2000) *Liquid Modernity*. Cambridge: Polity.

Bauman, Z. (2001) *The Individualised Society*. Cambridge: Polity.

Beardsworth, A. and Bryman, A. (2001) 'The Wild Animal in Late Modernity: The Case of the Disneyization of Zoos', *Tourist Studies* 1 (1): 83–104.

Beck, U. (2000) 'The Cosmopolitan Perspective: The Sociology of the Second Age of Modernity', *British Journal of Sociology* 51 (1): 79–105.

Bell, C. and Lyall, J. (2001a) *The Accelerated Sublime*. London: Praeger.

Bell, C. and Lyall, J. (2001b) 'The Accelerated Sublime: Thrill seeking adventure heroes in the commodified landscape' in S. Coleman and M. Crang (eds) *Tourism: Between Place and Performance*. Oxford: Berghahn.

Bell, D. (1978) *The Cultural Contradictions of Capitalism*. London: Heinemann.

Bell, D. and Holliday, R. (2001) 'Naked as Nature Intended' in P. Macnaghten and J. Urry (eds) *Bodies of Nature*. London: Sage.

Bennett, T. (1983) 'A Thousand and One Troubles: Blackpool Pleasure Beach' in *Formations of Pleasure*. London: Routledge and Kegan Paul. pp. 138–55.

Bennett, T., Emmison, M. and Frow, J. (1999) *Accounting for Tastes*. Melbourne: Cambridge University Press.

Berger, J. (1980) *About Looking*. London: Writers and Readers.

Bermingham. A. (1994) 'Resdesigning Nature: John Constable and the Landscape of Enclosure' in R. Friedland and D. Boden (eds) *Nowhere: Space, Time and Modernity*. Berkeley: University of California Press.

Billig, M. (1995) *Banal Nationalism*. London: Sage.

Boissevain, J. (ed.) (1996) *Coping with Tourists*. Providence, R.I.: Berghahn Books.

Boniface, P. and Fowler, P.J. (1993) *Heritage & Tourism in the Global Village*. London: Routledge.

Boorstin, D. (1964) *The Image: A Guide to Pseudo Events in America*. New York: Harper.

Booth, D. (2001) *Australian Beach Culture – The History of Sun, Sand and Surf*. London: Frank Cass.

Bourdieu, P. (1984) *Distinction: A Social Critique of the Judgement of Taste*. Cambridge, MA: Harvard University Press.

Boyer, P. and Nissenbaum, S. (1974) *Salem Possessed: The Social Origins of Witchcraft*. Cambridge, MA: Harvard University Press.

British Tourist Authority (2002) 'Britain's Tourist Industry – Facts and Figures', http://visitbritain.com/corporate/tourism/tourism.factsandfigu) res.htm.

Britton, S. and Clarke, W. (eds) (1987) *Ambiguous Alternative: Tourism in Developing Countries*. Suva: University of the South Pacific.

Brown, T., Rushton, L., Shuker, A., Stevens, J. and Warren, F. (2001) *A Consultation on the Possible Effects on Health, Comfort and Safety of Aircraft Cabin Environments*. Leicester: Medical Research Council Institute for Environment and Health.

Bruner, E.M. (2001) 'The Maasai and the Lion King: Authenticity, Nationalism, and Globalization in African Tourism', *American Ethnologist* 28 (4): 881–908.

Buckart, A.J. and Medlik, S. (1974) *Tourism, Past, Present and Future*. London: Heinemann.

Buckley, P.J. and Witt, S.F. (1985) 'Tourism in Difficult Areas: Case Studies of Bradford, Bristol, Glasgow and Hamm', *Tourism Management* 6 (3): 205–13.

Buckley, P.J. and Witt, S.F. (1989) 'Tourism in Difficult Areas: Case Studies of Calderdale, Leeds, Manchester and Scunthorpe', *Tourism Management* 10 (2): 555–65.

Buckley, R. (1994) 'A Framework for Ecotourism', *Annals of Tourism Research* 21 (3): 661–9.

Budd, M. (1996) 'The Aesthetic Appreciation of Nature', *British Journal of Aesthetics* 36 (3): 207–22.

Butler, T. (1997) *Gentrification and the Middle Classes*. Aldershot: Ashgate.

Campbell, C. (1995) *The Romantic Ethic and the Spirit of Consumerism*. Oxford: Basil Blackwell.

Cantwell R. (1993) *Ethnomimesis: Folklife and the Representation of Culture*. Chapel Hill: University of North Carolina Press.

Cantwell, R. (1992) 'Feasts of Unnaming: Folk Festivals and the Representation of Folklife' in R. Baron and N. Spitzer (eds) *Public Folklore*. Washington, DC: Smithsonian Institute Press. pp. 263–305.

Carlsen J. (1999) 'Tourism Impacts on Small Islands: A Longitudinal Study of Community Attitudes to Tourism on the Cocos (Keeling) Islands', *Pacific Tourism Review* 3: 25–35.

Carroll, P., Donohue, K., McGovern, M. and McMillen, J. (1991) *Tourism in Australia*. Sydney: Harcourt Brace Jovanovich.

Cartmill, M. (1993) *A View to a Death in the Morning*. Cambridge, MA: Harvard University Press.

Cater, E. (1993) 'Ecotourism in the Third World: Problems for Sustainable Tourism Development' *Tourism Management* April, pp. 85–90.

Chambers, I. (1994) *Migrancy, Culture, Identity*. London: Routledge.

Chatwin, B. (1987) *The Songlines*. London: Jonathan Cape.

Cherfas, J. (1984) *Zoo 2000*. London: BBC Publications.

Clarke, J., Critcher, C. and Johnson R. (eds) (1979) *Working Class Culture*. London: Hutchinson.

Clifford, J. (1992) 'Travelling Cultures' in L. Grossberg, C. Nelson and P.A. Treichler (eds) *Cultural Studies*. New York: Routledge.

Cohen, E. (1988) 'Traditions in the Qualitative Sociology of Tourism', *Annals of Tourism Research* 15: 29–46.

Cohen, E. (1993) 'Introduction: Investigating Tourist Arts', *Annals of Tourism Research* 20 (1): 1–8.

Cohen, E. (1995) 'Contemporary Tourism – Trends and Challenges: Sustainable Authenticity or Contrived Post-modernity?' in R. Butler and D. Pearce (eds) *Change in Tourism: People, Places, Processes*. London: Routledge.

Cohen, S. and Taylor, L. (1976) *Escape Attempts*. Harmondsworth: Penguin.

Coleman, S. and Crang, M. (eds) (2002) *Tourism: Between Place and Performance*. Oxford: Berghahn.

Collins, J. (1995) 'Retro-Modernism: Taste Cartographies in the 1990s' in *Architectures of Excess*. London: Routledge.

Collins, J. (1995) *Architectures of Excess*. London: Routledge.

Columbia World of Quotations (2002) 'Johnson, Samuel, English author'. New York: Columbia University Press.

Confraternity of St James (2002) *The Present Day Pilgrimage*. www.csj.org.uk

Connerton, P. (1989) *How Societies Remember*. Cambridge: Cambridge University Press.

Cosgrove, D.E. (1984) *Social Formation and Symbolic Landscape*. London: Croom Helm.

Crang, M. (1994) 'On the Heritage Trail: Maps and Journeys to Olde Englande', *Environment and Planning D: Society and Space* 12 (3): 341–55.

Crang, M. (1997) 'Picturing Practices: Research through the Tourist Gaze', *Progress in Human Geography* 21 (3): 359–74.

Crang, M. (1999) 'Knowing Tourism and Practices of Vision' in D. Crouch (ed.) *Leisure/Tourism Geographies: Practices and Geographical Knowledge*. London: Routledge. pp. 238–56.

Crary, J. (1990) *Techniques of the Observer*. Cambridge, MA: MIT Press.

Crawshaw, C. and Urry, J. (1997) 'Tourism and the Photographic Eye' in C. Rojek and J. Urry (eds) *Touring Cultures*. London: Routledge.

Crichton, M. (1998) *Travels*. New York: Alfred A. Knopf.

Crick, M. (1989) 'Representations of International Tourism in the Social Sciences', *Annual Review of Anthropology* 18: 307–44.

Cross, G. (ed.) (1990) *Worktowners at Blackpool: Mass Observation and Popular Leisure in the 1930s*. London: Routledge.

Crouch, D. (ed.) (1999) *Leisure/Tourism Geographies: Practices and Geographical Knowledge*. London, Routledge. pp. 1–16.

Crouch, D. (1999) 'Encounters in Leisure and Tourism' in D. Crouch (ed.) *Leisure/Tourism Geographies: Practices and Geographical Knowledge*. London: Routledge. pp. 1–16.

Csikszentmihali, M. (1988) 'The Future of Flow' in M. Csikszentmihali and I.S. Csikszentmihali (eds) *Optimal Experience: Psychological Studies of Flow in Consciousness*. Cambridge: Cambridge University Press.

Csikszentmihali, M. and Csikszentmihali, I.S. (eds) (1988) *Optimal Experience: Psychological Studies of Flow in Consciousness*. Cambridge: Cambridge University Press.

Dahles, H. and Bras, K. (1999) 'Entrepreneurs in Romance', *Annals of Tourism Research* 26 (2): 267–93.

Dann, G. (1996) *The Language of Tourism: A Sociolinguistic Interpretation*. CAB International, Wallingford, Oxon.

David, E. (1960) *French Provincial Cooking*. Harmondsworth: Penguin.

Davies, A. (1992) *Leisure, Gender and Poverty*. Milton Keynes: Open University Press.

Davis, J. (1972) 'Gifts and the UK Economy', *Man* 7 (3): 408–29.

De Botton, A. (2002) *The Art of Travel*. London: Hamish Hamilton.

de Certeau, M. (1984) *The Practice of Everyday Life*. Berkeley: University of California Press.

Deleuze, G. (1988) *Bergsonism*. New York: Zone Books.

Desmond, J. (1999) *Staging Tourism: Bodies on Display from Waikiki to Sea World*. Chicago: University of Chicago Press.

Digance, J. and Norris, R.H. (1999) 'Environmental Impacts of Tourism in the Australian Alps: The Thredbo River Valley', *Pacific Tourism Review* 3: 37–48.

Docker, J. (1995) *Postmodernism and Popular Culture*. Cambridge: Cambridge University Press.

Douglas, J., Rasmussen, P. and Flanagan, C. (1977) *The Naked Beach*. Beverly Hills, CA: Sage.

Douglas, M. (1975) *Implicit Meanings*. London: Routledge and Kegan Paul.

Durant, H. (1938) *The Problem of Leisure*. London: George Routledge and Son.

Durkheim, E. (1976) *The Elementary Structures of the Religious Life*. London: George Allen & Unwin.

Eco, U. (1987) *Faith in Fakes*. London: Secker and Warburg.

Edensor, T. (1998) *Tourists at the Taj: Performance and Meaning at a Symbolic Site*. London: Routledge.

Edensor, T. (2001) 'Walking in the British Countryside: Reflexivity, Embodied Practices and Ways to Escape' in P. Macnaghten and J. Urry (eds) *Bodies of Nature*. London: Sage.

Ehrlich, B. and Dreier, P. (1999) 'The New Boston Discovers the Old' in D.R. Judd and S.S. Fainstein (eds) *The Tourist City*. New Haven, CT: Yale University Press.

Evans, W., Ross, C. and Werner, A. (1995) *Whitefriars Glass: James Powell & Sons of London*. London: Museum of London.

Ewins, R. (1999) 'Fijian Social Identity and the Production of Bark Cloth Souvenirs in the Tourism Trade', PhD Thesis, School of Sociology and Social Work, University of Tasmania.

Ewins, R. (2002) *Staying Fijian: Vatulele Island Barkcloth and Social Identity*. Hindmarsh (South Australia): Crawford House.

Fabian, J. (1992) *Time and the Work of Anthropology*. Chur, Switzerland: Harwood.

Fainstein, S.S. and Judd, D.R. (1999) 'Evaluating Urban Tourism' in D.R. Judd and S.S. Fainstein (eds) *The Tourist City*. New Haven, CT: Yale University Press.

Feifer, M. (1986) *Tourism in History*. New York: Stein and Day.

Finnegan, R. (1998) *Tales of the City*. Cambridge: Cambridge University Press.

Fiske, J., Hodge, B. and Turner, G. (1987) *Myths of Oz*. Sydney: Allen and Unwin.

FitzHerbert, C. (2001) 'The Past is a Tartan Picnic Rug', *The Daily Telegraph* 11 August: A5.

Flametree (2002) 'Balancing acts' http://community.flametree.co.uk.

Forty, A. (1986) *Objects of Desire – Design and Society since 1750*. London: Thames and Hudson.

Foucault, M. (1970) *The Order of Things*. London: Tavistock.

France, L. (ed.) (1997) *The Earthscan Reader in Sustainable Tourism*. New York: Earthscan.

Franklin, A.S. (1986) *Owner Occupation, Privatism and Ontological Security*. Working Paper 62, School for Advanced Urban Studies, University of Bristol.

Franklin, A.S. (1995) 'Family Networks, Reciprocity and Housing Wealth' in R. Forrest and A. Murie (eds) *Housing and Family Wealth*. London: Routledge.

Franklin, A.S. (1999) *Animals and Modern Cultures*. London: Sage.

Franklin, A.S. (2002a) *Nature and Social Theory*. London: Sage.

Franklin, A.S. (2002b) 'Consuming Design', in A. Anderson, K. Meethan and S. Miles (eds) *The Changing Consumer*. London: Routledge.

Franklin, A.S. and Crang, M. (2001) 'The Trouble with Tourism and Travel Theory?', *Tourist Studies* 1 (1): 5–22.

Frisby, D. and Featherstone, M. (eds) (1997) *Simmel on Culture*. London: Sage.

Fullagar, S. (2000) 'Desiring Nature: Identity and Becoming in Narratives of Travel', *Cultural Values* 4 (1): 58–76.

Fullagar, S. (2003, forthcoming) 'On Restlessness and Patience: Reading Desire in Bruce Chatwin's Narratives of Travel', *Tourist Studies* 3.

Gaze, J. (1988) *Figures in a Landscape*. London: Barrie & Jenkins.

Geertz, C. (1985) 'Deep Play: Notes on the Balinese Cockfight' in *The Interpretation of Cultures*. New York: Basic Books.

Gellner, E. (1983) *Nations and Nationalism*. Oxford: Basil Blackwell.

Gibson, H.J. (2002) 'How the British will Travel 2005', Review of A. Poon and E. Adams *How the British will Travel 2000*. An der Wolfskuhle 48, 33619 Bielefeld, Germany: Tourism Intelligence International. *Annals of Tourism Research* 29 (1): 279–81.

Giddens, A. (2000) *Runaway World*. London: Routledge.

Gil, J. (1998) *Metamorphoses of the Body*. Minneapolis: University of Minnesota Press.

Gill, A.A. (2001) 'Friends in Tweed', *The Sunday Times (Style)*, 21 October: 7.

Goodwin, A. (1989) 'Nothing Like the Real Thing', *New Statesman and Society*, 12 August.

Gouldner, A. (1975) *For Sociology*. Harmondsworth: Penguin.

Gottdiener, M. (2001) *Life in the Air*. London: Rowman & Littlefield.

Graburn, N. (1976) *Ethnic and Tourist Arts: Cultural Expressions from the Fourth World*. Berkeley: University of California Press.

Graburn, N. (1983) 'The Anthropology of Tourism', *Annals of Tourism Research* 9: 165–87.

Graburn, N. (1989) 'Tourism: The Sacred Journey' in V. Smith (ed.) *Hosts and Guests: The Anthropology of Tourism*. Philadelphia: University of Pennsylvania Press.

Greenwood, D. (1989) 'Culture by the Pound: An Anthropological Perspective on Tourism as Cultural Commoditization' in V. Smith (ed.) *Hosts and Guests: The Anthropology of Tourism*. Philadelphia: University of Pennsylvania Press.

Gregory, D. (1999) 'Scripting Egypt' in J. Duncan and D. Gregory (eds) *Writes of Passage: Reading Travel Writing*. London: Routledge.

Gregson, N. and Crewe, L. (1997a) 'Excluded Spaces of Regulation: Car-boot Sales as an Enterprise Culture out of Control?', *Environment and Planning A* 29: 1717–37.

Gregson, N. and Crewe, L. (1997b) 'Performance and Possession: Rethinking the Act of Purchase in the Light of the Car Boot Sale', Mimeo, from N. Gregson, Department of Geography, Sheffield University.

Gregson, N. and Crewe, L. (1997c) 'The Bargain, the Knowledge, and the Spectacle: Making Sense of Consumption in the Space of the Car-boot Sale', *Environment and Planning D: Society and Space* 15: 87–112.

Hall, C.M., Sharples, L., Cambourne, B. and Macionis, N. (2000) *Wine Tourism around the World*. Oxford: Butterworth-Heinemann.

Hall, M. and Lew, A.A. (1998) *Sustainable Tourism*. London: Prentice Hall.

Halperin, J.L. (1997) *The First Immortal: A Novel of the Future*. London: Ballantine.

Hancocks, D. (1971) *Animals and Architecture*. London: Hugh Evelyn.

Hannigan, J. (1998) *Fantasy City*. London: Routledge.

Harvey, D. (1989) *The Condition of Postmodernity*. Oxford: Blackwell.

Heidegger, M. (1977) *Basic Writings*. New York: Harper & Row.

Herbert, D. (2001) 'Literary Places, Tourism and the Heritage Experience', *Annals of Tourism Research* 28 (2): 312–33.

Herbert, D., Prenctice, R. and Thomas, C. (1989) *Heritage Sites: Strategies for Marketing and Development*. Aldershot: Avebury.

Hewison, R. (1987) *The Heritage Industry*. London: Methuen.

Hinchliffe, S. (2000) 'Performance and Experimental Knowledge: Outdoor Management Training and the End of Epistemology', *Environment and Planning D: Society and Space* 18 (5): 575–95.

Hitchcock, M., Teague, K. and Graburn, N.H.H. (2000) *Souvenirs: The Material Culture of Tourism*. Aldershot: Ashgate.

Holcomb, B. (1999) 'Marketing Cities for Tourism' in D.R. Judd and S.S. Fainstein (eds) *The Tourist City*. New Haven, CT: Yale University Press.

Holloway, J.C. (1989) *The Business of Tourism*. London: Pitman.

Horne, D. (1984) *The Great Museum*. London: Pluto.

Howell, S. (1995) 'Whose Knowledge and Whose Power?: A New Perspective on Cultural Diffusion' in R. Fardon (ed.) *Counterworks: Managing the Diversity of Knowledge*. London: Routledge.

Huggan, G. (1997) 'The Australian Tourist Novel' in M. Dever (ed.) *Australia and Asia – Cultural Transactions*. Honolulu: University of Hawaii Press.

Hume, C. (1997) *Witchcraft and Paganism in Australia*. Melbourne: Melbourne University Press.

Hutnyk, J. (1996) *The Rumour of Calcutta: Tourism, Charity and the Poverty of Representation*. London: Zed Books.

Hylland Eriksen, T. (2001) *Tyranny of the Moment*. London: Pluto.

Inglis, F. (2000) *The Delicious History of the Holiday*. London: Routledge.

Jackson, L. (1997) *Austerity to Affluence: British Art and Design 1945–62*. London: Merrell Holberton.

Jackson, L. (1998) *The Sixties*. London: Phaidon.

James, P. (1996) *Nation Formation*. London: Sage.

Jay, M. (1992) 'Scopic Regimes of Modernity' in S. Lash and J. Friedman (eds) *Modernity and Identity*. Oxford: Blackwell.

Jenkins, S. (1997) *Midwinter Pottery*. London: Richard Dennis.

Jervis, J. (1998) *Exploring the Modern*. Oxford: Blackwell.

Jervis, J. (1999) *Transgressing the Modern*. Oxford: Blackwell.

Johnson, B.R. and Edwards, T. (1994) 'The Commodification of Mountaineering', *Annals of Tourism Research* 21 (3): 459–78.

Johnston, L. (2001) '(Other) Bodies and Tourism Studies', *Annals of Tourism Research* 28 (1): 180–201.

Jokinen, E. and Veijola, S. (1997) 'The Disorientated Tourist: The Figuration of the Tourist in Contemporary Cultural Critique' in C. Rojek and J. Urry (eds) *Touring Cultures*. London: Routledge.

Judd, D.R. (1999) 'Constructing the Tourist Bubble' in D.R. Judd and S.S. Fainstein (eds) *The Tourist City*. New Haven, CT: Yale University Press.

Judd, D.R. and Fainstein, S.S. (eds) (1999) *The Tourist City*. New Haven, CT: Yale University Press.

Julian, R. (1998) '"I love driving!": Alternative Constructions of Hmong Femininity in the West', *Race, Class and Gender* 5 (2): 112–24.

Julian, R., Franklin, A. and Felmingham, B. (1997) *Home from Home – Refugees in Tasmania*. Canberra: Australian Government Printing Service.

Kasson, J.F. (1978) *Amusing the Millions: Coney Island at the Turn of the Century*. New York: Hill and Wang.

Kirshenblatt-Gimblett, B. (1998) *Destination Culture: Tourism, Museums, and Heritage*. Berkeley: University of California Press.

Kruhse-MountBurton, S. (1995) 'Sex Tourism and Traditional Australian Male Identity' in M.E Lanfant, J.B. Allcock and E. M. Bruner (eds) *International Tourism: Identity and Change*. London: Sage.

Lansdell, A. (1990) *Seaside Fashions 1860–1939*. London: Shire Publications.

Larsen, T. (2000) 'Thomas Cook, Holy Land Pilgrims, and the Dawn of the Modern Tourist Industry' in R.N. Swanson (ed.) *The Holy Land, Holy Lands and Christian History*. Woodbridge, Suffolk: Boydell Press.

Lash, S. (1993) 'Reflexive Modernization: The Aesthetic Dimension', *Theory, Culture and Society* 10 (1): 1–23.

Lash, S. and Urry, J. (1994) *Economies of Signs and Space*. London: Sage.

Law, J. (1994) *Organizing Modernity*. Oxford: Blackwell.

Law, J. (2001) 'Machinic Pleasures and Interpellations', Centre for Science Studies and the Department of Sociology, Lancaster University at http://www.comp.lancs.ac.uk/sociology/soc06711.html

Le Roy Ladurie, E. (1978) *Montaillou: Cathars and Catholics in a French Village, 1294–1324*. London: Scolar.

Leach, E. (1961) *Rethinking Anthropology*. London: Athlone Press.

Lee, G. (1990) *Troppo Man*. Brisbane: University of Queensland Press.

Lefebvre, H. (1991) *The Production of Space*. Oxford: Blackwell.

Lencek, L. and Bosker, G. (1999) *The Beach*. London: Pimlico.

Leopold, A. (1949) *A Sand County Almanac*. New York: Oxford University Press.

Leslie, E. (2000) 'Souvenirs and Forgetting: Walter Benjamin's Memory-work' in M. Kwint, C. Breward and J. Aynsley (eds) *Material Memories*. Oxford: Berg. pp. 107–22.

Lett, J. (1983) 'Ludic and Liminoid Aspects of Charter Yacht Tourism in the Caribbean', *Annals of Tourism Research* 10: 35–56.

Lewis, N. (2000) 'The Climbing Body and the Experience of Modernity' in P. Macnaghten and J. Urry (eds) *Bodies of Nature*. London: Sage.

Lingis, A. (1998) *The Imperative*. Bloomington: Indiana University Press.

Lindsay, I. (1983) *Dressing and Undressing for the Seaside*. London: Ian Henry Publications.

Lloyd, D.W. (1998) *Battlefield Tourism*. Oxford: Berg.

Löfgren, O. (1999) *On Holiday: A History of Vacationing*. Berkeley: University of California Press.

Lowe, R. and Shaw, W. (1993) *Travellers - Voices of the New Age Nomads*. London: Fourth Estate.

Lury, C. (1997) 'The Objects of Travel' in C. Rojek and J. Urry (eds) *Touring Cultures*. London: Routledge.

Lyle, M. (2002) *Canterbury*. Stroud, Glos.: Tempus.

Maas, W., de Vries, N. and van Rijs, J. (2000) *MVRDV: Costa Iberica Upbeat to the Leisure City*. Castellano: Actar.

McGregor, C. (1967) *Profile of Australia*. London: Hodder and Stoughton.

MacCannell, D. (1976) *The Tourist: A New Theory of the Leisure Class*. New York: Schocken.

MacCannell, D. (1992) *Empty Meeting Grounds: The Tourist Papers*. London: Routledge.

MacCannell, D. (2001) 'Tourist Agency', *Tourist Studies* 1 (1): 23–38.

MacCarthy, F. (1972) *All Things Bright and Beautiful: Design in Britain 1830–Today*. London: George Allen and Unwin.

MacCarthy, F. (1982) *British Design since 1880*. London: Lund Humphries.

MacDonald, S. (1997) 'A People's Story: Heritage, Identity and Authenticity' in C. Rojek and J. Urry (eds) *Touring Cultures*. London: Routledge. pp. 155–75.

Macnaghten, P. and Urry, J. (1998) *Contested Natures*. London: Sage.

Macnaghten, P. and Urry, J. (eds) (2001) *Bodies of Nature*. London: Sage.

Macnaghten, P. and Urry, J. (2001) 'Bodies in the Wood' in P. Macnaghten and J. Urry (eds) *Bodies of Nature*. London: Sage. pp. 166–82.

Maffesoli, M. (1996) *The Time of the Tribes*. London: Sage.

Margolis, J. (2001) *A Brief History of Tomorrow*. London: Bloomsbury.

Margulis, L. (1998) *The Symbiotic Planet*. London: Weidenfeld and Nicolson.

Markwell, K. (2001) 'An intimate rendezvous with nature?', *Tourist Studies* 1 (1): 39–57.

Marsh, M. (1997) *Collecting the 1950s*. London: Miller's.

Martin, A. (1991) *Walking on Water*. London: John Murray.

Maslow, A. (1970) *Religions, Values and Peak Experiences*. New York: Viking Press.

Mathieson, A. and Wall, G. (1982) *Tourism: Economic, Physical and Social Impacts*. London: Longman Cheshire.

Meethan, K. (2001) *Tourism in Global Society*. Basingstoke: Palgrave.

Meller, H. (1976) *Leisure and the Changing City*. London: Routledge and Kegan Paul.

Mennell, S. (1996) *All Manners of Food*. Chicago: University of Illinois Press.

Merriman, N. (1989) 'Museum Visiting as a Cultural Phenomenon' in P. Vergo (ed.) *The New Museology*. London: Reaktion.

Michael, M. (2000) *Reconnecting Culture, Technology and Nature*. London: Routledge.

Michael, M. (2001) 'These Boots are Made for Walking . . . Mundane Technology, the Body and Human-environment Relations' in P. Macnaghten and J. Urry (eds) *Bodies of Nature*. London: Sage.

Middleton, C. (2001) 'Relocation: Making Visitors Feel at Home', *The Daily Telegraph* 11 August: 6.

Midol, N. and Broyer, G. (1995) 'Towards an Anthropological Analysis of New Sport Cultures: The Case of Whiz Sports in France', *Sociology of Sport Journal* 12: 204–12.

Mieckzkowski, Z. (1990) *World Trends in Tourism and Recreation* (vol. 3). New York: Peter Lang.

Miles, S. (1998) *Consumerism as a Way of Life*. London: Sage.

Miller, D. (1987) *Consumption and Everyday Life: Material Culture and Mass Consumption*. Oxford: Blackwell.

Moeran, B. (1983) 'The Language of Japanese Tourism', *Annals of Tourism Research* 10 (1): 93–108.

Morris, W. (1929) *Hopes and Fears for Art: Five Lectures*. London: Longmans Green.

Mowforth, M. and Munt, I. (1998) *Tourism and Sustainability*. London: Routledge.

Mullan, B. and Marvin, G. (1987) *Zoo Culture*. London: Weidenfeld and Nicolson.

Munt, I. (1994) 'The Other Postmodern Tourist: Culture, Travel and the New Middle Classes', *Theory, Culture & Society* 11: 101–24.

Norton, A. (1996) 'Experiencing Nature: The Reproduction of Environmental Discourse through Safari Tourism in East Africa', *Geoforum* 27 (3): 355–73.

Nye, D.E. (1994) *American Technological Sublime*. Cambridge, MA: MIT Press.

Nye, S. (2000) *The Best of Men Behaving Badly*. London: Headline.

O'Connell Davidson, J. (1995) 'British Sex Tourists in Thailand' in M. Maynard and J. Purvis (eds) *(Hetero)Sexual Politics*. London: Taylor and Francis.

O'Connell, D. (1997) *Jetlag: How To Beat It*. New York: Ascendent Publishing.

O'Reilly, K. (2000) *The British on the Costa Del Sol: Transnational Identities and Local Communities*. London: Routledge.

Oppermann, M. (1999) 'Sex Tourism', *Annals of Tourism Research* 26 (2): 251–66.

Packard, V. (1957) *The Hidden Persuaders*. Harmondsworth: Pelican.

Paul, L. (1938) *The Republic of Children*. London: Allen and Unwin.

Paxman, J. (1999) *The English*. Harmondsworth: Penguin.

Pearce, P. and Moscado, G. (1986) 'The Concept of Authenticity in Tourist Experiences', *Australian and New Zealand Journal of Sociology* 22: 121–32.

Pearce, S. (1995) *On Collecting*. London: Routledge.

Peat, A. (1994) *David Whitehead Ltd: Artistic Designed Textiles 1952–1969*. Oldham: Oldham Leisure Services.

Peck, J.G. and Lepie, A.S. (1989) 'Tourism Development in Three North Carolina Coastal Towns' in V. Smith (ed.) *Hosts and Guests*. Philadelphia: University of Pennsylvania Press.

Peckham, S. (1998) 'Consuming Nations' in S. Griffiths and J. Wallace (eds) *Consuming Passions: Food in the Age of Anxiety*. London: Mandolin.

Peters, G.L. (1997) *American Winescapes: The Cultural Landscapes of America's Wine Country*. New York: Westview Press.

Phillips, J.L. (1999) 'Tourist-orientated Tourism in Barbados: The Case of the Beach Boy and the White Female Tourist' in K. Kempandoo (ed.) *Sun, Sex and Gold – Tourism and Sex Work in the Caribbean*. Lanham, MD: Rowman and Littlefield.

Picard, M. (1996) *Bali: Cultural Tourism and Touristic Culture*. Singapore: Archipelago Press.

Pickering, A. (2000) 'In the Thick of Things and the Politics of Becoming'. Paper given to a conference at the University of Bergen, December 2000.

Pickering, A. (2001) 'In the Thick of Things'. Keynote paper given to the conference *'Taking Nature Seriously'*, University of Oregon, February 2001.

Pickering, J. (1997) 'Agents and Artefacts', *Social Analysis* 41: 46–63.

Pimlott, J. (1947) *The Englishman's Holiday*. London: Faber and Faber.

Porteus, J. (1985) 'Smellscape', *Progress in Human Geography* 9: 356–78.

Prasad, P. (1987) 'The Impact of tourism on Small Developing Countries: An Introductory View from Fiji and the Pacific' in S. Britton and W.C. Clarke (eds) *Ambiguous Alternative: Tourism in Developing Countries*. Suva: University of the South Pacific.

Prentice, R. (1993) *Tourism and Heritage Places*. London: Routledge.

Prentice, R. (1995) 'Heritage as Formal Education' in D.T. Herbert (ed.) *Heritage, Tourism and Society*. London: Mansell. pp. 146–9.

Preston-Whyte (2001) 'Constructed Leisure Space – The Seaside at Durban', *Annals of Tourism Research* 28 (3): 581–96.

Pruitt, S. and LaFont, S. (1995) 'For Love and Money: Romance Tourism in Jamaica', *Annals of Tourism Research* 22: 422–40.

Pugh, S. (1988) *Garden – Nature – Language*. Manchester: Manchester University Press.

Reiko, I. (1991) 'An Army of Japanese Tourists', *AMPO: Japan-Asia Quarterly Review* 22 (4): 3–11.

Ritvo, H. (1997) *The Platypus and the Mermaid and Other Figments of the Classifying Imagination*. Cambridge, MA: Harvard University Press.

Ritzer, G. (1992) *The McDonaldization of Society*. London: Pine Forge.

Ritzer, G. and Liska, A. (1997) '"McDisneyization" and "Post-Tourism": Complimentary Perspectives on Contemporary Tourism' in C. Rojek and J. Urry (eds) *Touring Cultures*. London: Routledge.

Rival, L. (1998) *The Social Life of Trees*. Oxford: Berg.

Roberts, E. (1984) *A Woman's Place*. Oxford: Blackwell.

Rodaway, P. (1994) *Sensuous Geographies*. London: Routledge.

Rojek, C. (1985) *Capitalism and Leisure Theory*. London: Tavistock.

Rojek, C. (1993) *Ways of Escape*. London: Routledge.

Rojek, C. (1995) *Decentring Leisure: Rethinking Leisure Theory*. London, Sage.

Rojek, C. (1997) 'Indexing, Dragging and the Social Construction of Tourist Sites' in C. Rojek and J. Urry (eds) *Touring Cultures*. London: Routledge.

Rojek, C. (2001) *Celebrity*. London: Reaktion Books.

Rojek, C. and Urry, J. (eds) (1997) *Touring Cultures*. London: Routledge.

Roodhouse, S. (2001) 'Creating Sustainable Cultures'. Joint State Conference of Regional Arts, University of Sydney, 5–6 October 2001.

Rorty, R. (1980) *Philosophy and the Mirror of Nature*. Oxford: Blackwell.

Ryan, C. (1998) 'Sex Tourism: Paradigms of Confusion' in S. Clift and S. Carter (eds) *Tourism, Travel and Sex*. London: Cassell.

Ryan, C. and Hall, M. (2001) *Sex Tourism*. London: Routledge.

Ryan, C. and Robertson, E. (1996) 'New Zealand Student Tourists: Risk Behaviour and Health' in S. Clift and B. Grabowski (eds) *Tourism and Health: Risks, Research and Responses*. London: Pinter.

Ryan, C., Hughes, K. and Chirgwin S. (2000) 'The Gaze, Spectacle and Ecotourism', *Annals of Tourism Research* 27 (1): 148–63.

Saldanha, A. (2002) 'Music Tourism and Factions of Bodies in Goa', *Tourist Studies* 2 (1): 43–63.

Savage, M., Barlow, J., Dickens, P. and Fielding, T. (1992) *Property, Bureaucracy and Culture*. London: Routledge.

Scanorama Magazine (2001) Greenwood Communications AB, Stockholm: SAS Media. December issue.

Seabrooke, J. (1996) *Travels in the Skin Trade: Tourism and the Sex Industry*. London: Pluto Press.

Sears, J. (1989) *Sacred Places: American Tourist Attractions in the Nineteenth Century*. Amherst: Univesity of Massachusetts Press.

Selwyn, T. (ed.) (1996) *The Tourist Image: Myths and Myth Making in Tourism*. Chichester: Wiley.

Shackley, M. (1996) *Wildlife Tourism*. London: International Thomson Business Press.

Shaw, G. and Williams, A. (eds) (1994) *Critical Issues in Tourism: A Geographical Perspective*. Oxford: Blackwell.

Shepherd, R. (2003, forthcoming) 'Outside the Temple: Commodification, Culture and Tourism', *Tourist Studies* 3: 1.

Shields, R. (1990) *Places on the Margin*. London: Routledge.

Shoard, M. (1987) *This Land is Our Land*. London: Paladin.

Short, J.R. (1991) *Imagined Country: Society, Culture and the Environment*. London: Routledge.

Simmel, G. (1997a) 'The Alpine Journey' in D. Frisby and M. Featherstone (eds) *Simmel on Culture*. London: Sage.

Simmel, G. (1997b) 'The Adventure' in D. Frisby and M. Featherstone (eds) *Simmel on Culture*. London: Sage.

Simpson, J. (2001) *A Mad World, My Masters*. London: Pan.

Smith, N. (1996) *The New Urban Frontier: Gentrification and the Revanchist City*. London: Routledge.

Smith, V. (ed.) (1989) *Hosts and Guests*. Philadelphia: University of Pennsylvania Press.

Stephen, A. (1995) 'Familiarising the South Pacific' in A. Stephen (ed.) *Pirating the Pacific: Images of Travel, Trade and Tourism*. Sydney: Powerhouse Publishing.

Stranger, M. (1999) 'The Aesthetics of Risk: A Study of Surfing', *International Review for the Sociology of Sport* 34 (3): 265–76.

Stranger, M. (2001) *Risk Taking and Postmodernity: Commodification and the Ecstatic in Leisure Lifestyles*. PhD thesis, School of Sociology and Social Work, University of Tasmania.

Taylor, C. (1992) *Sources of the Self*. Cambridge: Cambridge University Press.

Taylor, J. (1994) *A Dream of England*. Manchester: Manchester University Press.

Taylor, M.C. and Saarinen, E. (n.d.) *Imagologies: Media Philosophy*. Telerotics 11. London: Routledge.

Teague, K. (1997) 'Representations of Nepal' in S. Abram, J. Waldren and D.V. Macleod (eds) *Tourists and Tourism: Identifying with People and Places*. Oxford: Berg.

Tester, K. (ed.) (1994) *The Flaneur*. London: Routledge.

Thomas, N. (1991) *Entangled Objects: Exchange, Material Culture and Colonialism in the Pacific*. Cambridge, MA: Harvard University Press.

Thomas, K. (1983) *Man and the Natural World*. Harmondsworth: Penguin.

Thompson, P. (1977) *The Work of William Morris*. London: Quartet.

Thoreau, H.D. (1965) *Walden or, Life in the Woods*. New York: Holt, Rinehart & Winston.

Thrift, N. (1995) 'A Hyperactive World' in R.J. Johnston, P.J. Taylor and M. Watts (eds) *Georgraphies of Global Transformation*. Oxford: Blackwell.

Thrift, N. (1996) *Spatial Formations*. London: Sage.

Thrift, N. (1997) 'The Still Point: Resistance, Expressive Embodiment and Dance' in S. Pile and M. Keith (eds) *Geographies of Resistance*. London: Routledge.

Thrift, N. (1999) 'Still Life in Present Time: The Object of Nature'. Conference paper presented to *Sociality/Materialism – The Status of the Object in Social Science*. Brunel University, UK, 9–11 September 1999.

Thrift, N. (2001) 'Still Life in Nearly Present Time: The Object of Nature' in P. Macnaghten and J. Urry (eds) *Bodies of Nature*. London: Sage.

Travel Impact Newswire (2002) 'Boost for Buddhist Circuit', New Edition 4, 23 January 2002.

Travel Industry Association of America (1998) *Fast Facts*. http://www.tia.org/press/fastfacts6.stm.

Trinh, M. (1989) *Woman, Native, Other*. Bloomington: Indiana University Press.

Truong, T.-D. (1990) *Sex, Money and Morality: Prostitution and Tourism in South-East Asia*. London: Zed Books.

Turner, L. and Ash, J. (1975) *The Golden Hordes*. London: Constable.

Turner, V. and Turner, E. (1978) *Image and Pilgrimage in Christian Culture*. New York: Columbia University Press.

Urbain, J.-D. (1994) *Sur La Plage: moeurs et coutumes balnéaires*. Paris: Payot.

Urry, J. (1990) *The Tourist Gaze*. London: Sage.

Urry, J. (1995) *Consuming Places*. London: Routledge.

Urry, J. (1999) 'Automobility, Car Culture and Weightless Travel: A Discussion Paper', Department of Sociology, Lancaster University at: http//www.comp.lancaster.ac.uk/sociology/soc008ju.html.

Urry, J. (2000) *Sociology Beyond Societies – Mobilities for the Twenty-first Century*. London: Routledge.

Urry, J. (2002) *The Tourist Gaze* (Second Edition). London: Sage.

van Gennep, A. (1960) *The Rites of Passage*. Trans. M.B. Vizedom and G.L. Caffee. Chicago: University of Chicago Press.

Veijola, S. and Jokinen, E. (1994) 'The Body in Tourism', *Theory, Culture and Society* 11: 125–51.

Virilio, P. (1999) *Polar Inertia*. London: Sage.

Voase, R. (1995) *Tourism: The Human Perspective*. London: Hodder and Stoughton.

Wall, D. (1999) *Earth First! And the Anti-Roads Movement*. London: Routledge.

Walter, T. (1993) 'War Grave Pilgrimage' in I. Reader and T. Walter (eds) *Pilgrimage in Popular Culture*. London: Macmillan.

Walton, J. (1983) *The English Seaside Resort 1750–1914*. Leicester: Leicester University Press.

Ward, M. and Hardy, D. (1986) *Goodnight Campers! The History of the British Holiday Camp*. London: Mansell.

Warde, A. (2001) 'Setting the Scene: Changing Conceptions of Consumption' in A. Anderson, K. Meethan and S. Miles (eds) *The Changing Consumer*. London: Routledge. pp. 10–24.

Weaver, D. and Oppermann, M. (2000) *Tourism Management*. Brisbane: John Wiley & Sons.

Welsch, W. (1996) 'Phenomena, Distinctions and Prospects', *Theory, Culture and Society* 13 (1): 1–24.

Welsch, W. (1997) *Undoing Aesthetics*. London: Sage.

Wilk, R.R. (1991) *Household Ecology: Economic Change and Domestic Life among the Kekchi Maya of Belize*. DeKalb: University of Northern Illinois University Press.

Williams, R. (1983) *Keywords*. London: Flamingo.

Williams, R. (1992) 'Ideas of Nature' in J. Benthal (ed.) *Ecology: The Shaping Enquiry*. London: Longman.

Wilson, A. (1992) *The Culture of Nature*. Oxford: Blackwell.

Withey, L. (1997) *Grand Tours and Cook's Tours: A History of Leisure Travel, 1750 to 1915*. Berkeley: University of California Press.

Wood, M. (1974) 'Nostalgia or Never: You Can't Go Home Again', *New Society* 7 November: 343–6.

Wood, M. (2000) *In Search of England*. Harmondsworth: Penguin.

Woods, B. (2001) 'Wildlife Tourism and the Visitor Experience: Flinders Chase National Park, Kangaroo Island' in C. Pforr and B. Janeczko (eds) *Capitalising on Research*. Proceedings of the Eleventh Australian Tourism and Hospitality Research Conference, 7–10 February, Canberra. pp. 377–94.

Worpole, K. (2000) *Here comes the Sun*. London: Reaktion Books.

Wright, P. (1985) *On Living in an Old Country*. London: Verso.

Index